Urban Poverty in the Globa

One in seven of the world's population live in poverty in urban areas, and the vast majority of these live in the Global South – mostly in overcrowded informal settlements with inadequate water, sanitation, health care and schools provision. This book explains how and why the scale and depth of urban poverty is so frequently underestimated by governments and international agencies worldwide. The authors also consider whether economic growth does in fact reduce poverty, exploring the paradox of successful economies that show little evidence of decreasing poverty.

Many official figures on urban poverty, including those based on the US$1 per day poverty line, present a very misleading picture of urban poverty's scale. These common errors in definition and measurement by governments and international agencies lead to poor understanding of urban poverty and inadequate policy provision. This is compounded by the lack of voice and influence that low-income groups have in these official spheres. This book explores many different aspects of urban poverty, including the associated health burden, inadequate food intake, inadequate incomes, assets and livelihood security, poor living and working conditions, and the absence of any rule of law.

Urban Poverty in the Global South: Scale and nature fills the gap for a much-needed systematic overview of the historical and contemporary state of urban poverty in the Global South. This comprehensive and detailed book is a unique resource for students and lecturers in development studies, urban development, development geography, social policy, urban planning and design, and poverty reduction.

Diana Mitlin is an economist and social development specialist working at the International Institute for Environment and Development (IIED), and a Professor at the University of Manchester, UK, working at the Global Urban Research Centre, the Institute for Development Policy and Management and the Brooks World Poverty Institute.

David Satterthwaite is a Senior Fellow at IIED and a Visiting Professor at the Development Planning Unit, University College London, UK. He is also editor of the international journal *Environment and Urbanization*.

'This is a very important book. Urban poverty is seriously underestimated by dollar-a-day measures and national poverty estimates; it is neglected in terms of policy and action; and it is often sidelined in academic research and debates about development. This is really foolish – as the future of poverty is urban.

This book lays out in detail the ways in which present measures of poverty underestimate urban poverty and presents the data on urban poverty and inequality, and especially urban health deprivations. It demonstrates that research policy and action to improve the lives of low-income urban dwellers are a global priority. Read this book and your understanding of poverty will be transformed. I cannot recommend it highly enough.'

David Hulme, Brooks World Poverty Institute,
University of Manchester, UK

'With urban poverty growing at least as fast as booming urban populations, this is a challenging and constructive book. It challenges claims of global progress on poverty based on dollar-a-day poverty lines – these ignore the real costs and consequences of urban poverty. It challenges urban governments to meet their responsibilities – urban poverty has a local dimension which can and must be measured and tackled if urban poverty is to be reduced. And it shows how the challenges can be met.'

David Piachaud, London School of Economics, UK

'*Urban Poverty in the Global South: Scale and nature* moves the discussion of the multiple dimensions of poverty out of the realm of theory and academic discourse, where the bulk of the literature has been concentrated, and shows how the recognition of multiple disadvantages can reframe and energize pro-poor policies and programs. Mitlin and Satterthwaite do more than outline the general principles that should guide the next generation of policy: they offer detailed, specific insights grounded in long experience with the urban poor of Africa, Asia, and Latin America. This book moves the field forward.'

Mark Montgomery, Stony Brook University, USA

Urban Poverty in the Global South

Scale and nature

**Diana Mitlin and
David Satterthwaite**

LONDON AND NEW YORK

First published 2013
by Routledge
2 Park Square, Milton Park, Abingdon, Oxon, OX14 4RN

Simultaneously published in the USA and Canada
by Routledge
711 Third Avenue, New York, NY 10017

*Routledge is an imprint of the Taylor & Francis Group,
an informa business*

British Library Cataloguing in Publication Data
A catalogue record for this book is available from the British Library

Library of Congress Cataloging-in-Publication Data
Urban poverty in the global South : scale and nature / Diana Mitlin and
David Satterthwaite.
p. cm.
Includes bibliographical references and index.
1. Urban poor--Developing countries. I. Satterthwaite, David. II. Title.
HV4173.M58 2013
362.5'2091724--dc23
2012019196

ISBN13: 978-0-415-62466-4 (hbk)
ISBN13: 978-0-415-62467-1 (pbk)
ISBN13: 978-0-203-10431-6 (ebk)

Typeset in Times New Roman
by Saxon Graphics Ltd., Derby

Printed and bound in Great Britain by the MPG Books Group

Contents

4   Incomes and livelihoods   151

5   Critical issues in urban inequality   214

6   Broadening the understanding and measurement of
    urban poverty   278

Figures

Tables

Boxes

Acknowledgements

This book draws so much on all our friends within the many slum, shack-dweller and homeless people's federations and networks and the local NGOs with whom we have worked or have visited over the last 20 years. It is also through these NGOs that we have come to meet and learn from many grassroots leaders. We learnt much from the perspectives they brought to rethinking poverty and how to reduce it.

We have drawn greatly on what we have learnt from friends and colleagues within the Human Settlements Group at IIED and at IIED-América Latina in Buenos Aires (especially the team that has worked for over 20 years in informal settlements).

In addition, there are the researchers and practitioners that have contributed working papers to our publication series on urban poverty, and papers on different aspects of urban poverty to the journal that we edit, *Environment and Urbanization*. We still owe a tremendous intellectual debt to Jorge Hardoy, who founded our research group and set new lines on which to consider urban poverty and how it should be reduced, lines which, even nearly two decades after his death, still inspire and inform us.

We are also very grateful to Khanam Virjee and Helena Hurd from Routledge for all their encouragement and support and to Kate Manson whose editing so improved our manuscript.

1   Why this book?

Introduction

We believe that the scale and depth of urban poverty is ignored within most low-income nations, many middle-income nations and globally. We believe that this reflects a considerable misrepresentation and underestimation of urban poverty, and occurs because of the very narrow ways in which poverty is usually conceived, defined and measured. This also reflects a lack of interest from governments and international agencies in seeking to understand urban poverty and the many deprivations that it causes or contributes to. This book presents the evidence for these claims. A companion volume, to be published in early 2013, will focus on what has been learnt about the most effective means to reduce urban poverty.

This book also tries to make sense of why a large and growing evidence base on the multiple deprivations that are part of urban poverty has not helped change the ways that poverty is defined and measured. Part of the explanation is the extent to which the general literature on the definition and measurement of poverty does not draw on available evidence on urban poverty. But part of the explanation is the lack of attention given to urban poverty by development specialists. What began as our interest in why urban poverty was so often underestimated led us to more fundamental questions, including why urban issues are given so little attention.

Of course, poverty statistics are important for assessing the success (or not) of governments and of development assistance agencies (including aid agencies, development banks and international NGOs). The setting up of the Millennium Development Goals, with explicit targets for 2015 that have to be monitored in each nation, was meant to ensure more attention to poverty reduction. But as Chapter 2 shows, the main measure used for these goals (the dollar-a-day poverty line) is completely inappropriate for so many urban contexts. In addition, the direct measures of living conditions in the Millennium Development Goals are flawed. The indicators chosen for assessing provision for water and sanitation do not measure who has adequate provision or, for water, whether it is safe to drink (as discussed in more detail in Chapters 2 and 3). And the MDG target for 'slum dwellers' – a significant improvement in the lives of at least 100 million slum dwellers – is so much less ambitious than the other quantitative targets. While other quantitative targets are reductions by half (for hunger), two thirds (for under-five mortality rates) and three quarters (for maternal mortality), the quantitative target for significantly improving the lives of slum dwellers is the equivalent of 10 per cent of slum dwellers in 2000, with no allowance for the growth in numbers of slum dwellers after 2000. And the date for the achievement of this far less ambitious quantitative target is set for 2020, not 2015. This book assembles the evidence to support its claims about the inadequacy of the indicators used and their measurement. In most nations, the evidence base on the scale, nature and location of urban poverty is remarkably limited. Also explored are some of the reasons for the lack of ambition in addressing the needs of slum dwellers, the immensity of the task, the lack of vision and capacity, and the consequences for those who are (and have long been) marginalized by the experts and agencies of international development assistance.

The strong influence of the World Bank in poverty assessment needs to be recognized. The Bank has helped ensure more attention is given to poverty in development plans and discussions. Most poverty lines are set following methodologies recommended by the World Bank and these are at the centre of why urban poverty is underestimated and misrepresented. The World Bank is also the main source for poverty statistics based on the dollar-a-day poverty line – as Chapter 2 explains – which underestimate the scale of urban poverty and misrepresent the tracking of income poverty for the Millennium Development Goals. World Bank data are available for an enormous number of development-related indicators for nations over time, but few are available for rural and urban areas, and even fewer are available for each district or city. When there are urban statistics, most are averages for national urban populations that generalize about what are so often very diverse experiences.

The measurement of poverty is always based on the construction of national poverty lines with limited, little or no adjustment for local costs and realities. As Chapter 2 describes, there is far more adjustment to local costs when setting the allowance for daily expenses for 'experts' – as there is in the official rates set by the United Nations for these experts' per diems when they work in low- or middle-income nations. Poverty lines are often not adjusted upwards for prosperous and high-cost cities, but allowances for much higher hotel costs certainly are made for foreign experts. This is part of a larger issue: so much official data gathering relies on nationally representative sample surveys that can provide no data about each locality. So the understanding of poverty and its causes is constructed mainly on national sample surveys that have too little detail on key aspects of deprivation and sample sizes too small to be useful in identifying the nature, and spatial and social distribution of poverty. Not surprisingly, these surveys completely miss the particular political economy of poverty creation (or occasionally poverty reduction) in each locality. So it means very little detail of where the health or poverty problems identified in these surveys are actually located. And the data provides no basis for planning and implementing local responses. To learn from some national sample survey (including the Demographic and Health Surveys[1]) that some precise percentage of a national (or a nation's urban) population is lacking provision for water or sanitation or health care, or has a high infant mortality rate does not serve needed policy responses, because it does not tell you where those facing these deprivations actually live. Somehow, the 'data' available to inform development has become lacking in information and detail about the local, in part to serve international agencies' desire for national statistics that are comparable. As discussed in more detail in later chapters, this is true for statistics on poverty, on provision for water and sanitation, and on disasters and their impacts.

This lack of attention from the World Bank on understanding, measuring and acting on urban poverty is surprising because it was among the first of the international development assistance agencies to recognize the scale of deprivation in urban centres and to promote new approaches that sought to work with the inhabitants of slums or informal settlements[2] in upgrading their homes and neighbourhoods (Cohen 1983). The World Bank was also, in the 1970s, among the first international agencies to demand greater focus on 'meeting basic needs', which was in effect a recognition of the need to address the needs of those 'living in poverty'. However, whatever the reason for the lack of attention since then, it has been replicated in many national processes – while these may establish poverty lines that are more precise than the 'dollar a day', they often fail to take into account the costs of living (or more specifically the costs of non-food needs) in urban areas.

This book and its companion volume (Satterthwaite and Mitlin 2013) also highlight the lack of any engagement by governments and international agencies with low-income groups ('the poor'[3]) in the definition of poverty and the setting of poverty lines. It is so often external specialists who set the criteria by which poverty is defined and measured within low- and middle-income nations. One wonders whether they have ever consulted these urban dwellers on the deprivations they face. After 60 years of development assistance, there is still very little dialogue between low-income groups, and development assistance agencies and national governments. Those who are often termed 'the poor' are not consulted about the ways in which poverty is defined and measured. Nor are they consulted about their priorities, or about what they do to avoid deprivation. There is no understanding of the knowledge, capacity and resources they bring to coping with poverty – and could bring to reducing it. Our analysis of poverty is not undertaken as an abstract exercise but in the hope that it will support more effective action. Low-income individuals and households in the towns and cities of the Global South face a constant struggle to make something of their lives despite the acute hardship and disadvantage that they face. The companion volume to this will discuss how governments and some international development assistance agencies have sought to address urban poverty, the underlying concepts behind these interventions and the limitations in their approaches. It will also discuss how the transformation of our understanding of urban poverty and its underlying causes can point to far more effective ways of reducing it. It will describe and analyse the depth and complexity of social movement strategies aimed at challenging adversity and securing justice and inclusion.

It seems to us that most of those who define and set poverty lines do not have much understanding of the informal or illegal settlements in which such a high proportion of low-income urban dwellers live, or of the actual costs they face or of the prices paid for non-food needs (most of which are unlikely to be captured in international price comparisons). For instance, as Chapter 2 shows, there are very large differences in the prices paid for water per litre, with those with the worst access usually paying the most and often paying many times the price of water from the mains. How would this be treated in international price comparisons?

There seems to be an assumption in much of the discussion of poverty that it is really only food costs that count. So if the income of an individual or household is enough to afford food costs, they are not really poor. Extreme poverty lines, usually set at levels that allow for only enough to buy food, are still regarded as valid. But access to water, to toilets and to accommodation are also needed by everyone, and these are commodities that have to be purchased in most urban areas. There is also an assumption that if the proportion of income that a household spends on food is less than 70–80 per cent, it is not poor. But in many urban contexts, some non-food needs are so costly that they push down the proportion of income spent on food. A fall in the proportion of income spent on food may be taken as a sign of less poverty – but it may also be a sign of higher prices having to be paid for non-food needs (rent or water prices going up or new or increased payments required to keep children at school).

In many nations, there is little link between how poverty is defined and measured and actions by government and international agencies to address the deprivations faced by those classified as 'poor'. Piachaud suggests the study of poverty is only justifiable 'if it influences individual and social attitudes and actions' and that this 'must be borne in mind constantly if discussion on the definition of poverty is to avoid becoming an academic debate … *a semantic and statistical squabble that is parasitic, voyeuristic and utterly unconstructive and which treats "the poor" as passive objects for attention'* (Piachaud 1987, page 161, quoted in Lister 2004; italics added). Most definitions of poverty and most measurements treat 'the poor' as passive objects. And many, by so underestimating and misrepresenting urban poverty, help ensure that the urban poor gain little attention.

Chapter 2 will challenge official poverty statistics that suggest that a very small proportion of the world's urban population are poor. According to Ravallion, Chen and Sangraula (2007), using the dollar-a-day poverty line ($1.08 a day at 1993 purchasing power parity), in 2002, less than 1 per cent of the urban populations of China, the Middle East and North Africa, and East Europe and Central Asia were poor. In Latin America and the Caribbean, less than 10 per cent of the urban population was poor. For all low- and middle-income nations, 87 per cent of their urban populations were not poor. If these figures are correct, it represents a triumph for development. Deaton and Dupriez (2011) suggest that the dollar-a-day poverty line used by the World Bank is actually too high; they do not give separate figures for rural and urban populations but their figures suggest that in 2005 in the Middle East and North Africa, only 3 million out of 242 million people are poor (i.e. 1.2 per cent). For Latin America and the Caribbean, only 30 million out of 535 million are poor (i.e. 5.6 per cent).

But get the poverty definitions and hence measurements wrong, and it can provide the basis for so many inappropriate responses – including the conviction that almost all poverty is in rural areas. It can produce nonsense statistics about the extent to which the Millennium Development Goals are being met in many nations. It may underpin inaccurate assessments of the extent to which economic growth reduces poverty.

Although there are lots of statistics about poverty, there is actually very little data collected on low-income groups or those that live in informal settlements, the costs they face (especially for non-food needs) and their living conditions. For instance, in most nations, little or no attempt is made to assess the cost that urban dwellers face in meeting non-food needs – including the cost of renting accommodation, of keeping children at school, of transport, of medicines and health care, of paying for fuel, water and access to toilets … . The scale and nature of urban poverty is not well documented in many nations.

At the core of our criticism is the use of inappropriate frameworks, tools and methods for defining and measuring poverty. Most of the tools and methods used today in low- and middle-income nations are based on those developed in high-income nations many decades ago. As these were first applied, they were usually subject to professional and popular scrutiny, and this changed the ways that poverty was understood and measured. But these tools and methods (many of which are no longer applied in high-income nations) have been transferred without questioning many assumptions that underpinned their use which are not appropriate for low- and middle-income nations. For instance, when poverty lines came to be used in the UK, no provision was made to include the costs to individuals or households of health care and education because there was a national system in place that provided these at no cost. But education and health care are not free and not available to very large sections of the urban population in most low- and middle-income nations, where keeping children at school (or having to pay for private schools as they cannot get their children into government schools) and paying for health care and medicines often takes a significant proportion of total income (see Chapter 2). Or the lack of income means that children are not sent to or are withdrawn from school, and needed health-care treatments and medicines are not used.

Similarly, in the use of poverty lines in the UK the costs of housing were not factored in because accommodation for low-income households was addressed by another government department; the costs of housing in low- and middle-income nations are often not factored into poverty lines, or unrealistically low allowances for this are made, yet there is no other provision to support low-income groups in getting accommodation. In high-income nations, almost all urban dwellers, regardless of income, live in houses that meet official standards, with water piped in, toilets in each unit and regular services to collect solid waste. This is not the case for a high proportion of low-income urban dwellers elsewhere – and this often means high costs, as water has to be purchased from vendors or kiosks and access to toilets paid for.

The debates and discussions about better ways to define and measure poverty in high-income nations over the last three decades have had very little influence on how poverty is defined and measured in low-income and most middle-income nations. There is very little consideration of the limitations of setting absolute poverty lines. Indeed, the discussions around the setting of poverty lines in low- and middle-income nations today seem so anxious not to set these too high that they set them unrealistically low. There was actually more accuracy, detail and generosity in the definition and setting of poverty lines in the last years of the nineteenth and the beginning of the twentieth century in the UK than there is today in many nations. It is perhaps also worth noting that the first study that sought to establish the income needed to avoid poverty (and how this would vary for different family sizes and compositions) was for a particular city (York) and involved careful research into local conditions and prices (Rowntree 1902).

There are also very large differences in context and in data. For instance, how can there be a strong official information base about the quality of housing and quality and extent of basic service provision in urban areas if a third to two thirds of the urban population live in informal or illegal settlements, many of which have never been included in any official survey and lack any public provision for water, sanitation and drainage? And if they are included, this is almost universally only for the more official and longstanding of the informal settlements, leaving out those that are likely to have the worst conditions. How can assumptions be made about the value of government services within poverty lines when large sections of the low-income urban population cannot get their children into government schools and cannot access government health care or other entitlements? *This book will make clear that the proportion of the urban population that 'lives in poverty' is often far higher than the proportion defined as poor by official poverty lines.*

Some of the deficiencies in the definition and measurement of urban poverty have been addressed in the last 10 to 15 years. But there is little evidence of any real engagement with most aspects of urban poverty by those who define and measure poverty. For instance, it is common for the long and complex poverty assessments that are often undertaken in low- and middle-income nations (including poverty assessments and poverty reduction strategy papers[4]) not to mention 'slums', 'squatter settlements' or informal settlements, or to only mention them in passing without any considered analysis (see Chapter 2). This raises the issue of whether their inhabitants' needs are actually covered by surveys. Since it is common for 30–60 per cent of the population of cities to live in illegal or informal settlements, one wonders if those who collect household data cover these. Do the sample frames for national surveys ensure sufficient inclusion of those living in informal settlements – including settlements for which there are no maps or street names, and that do not appear in government statistics? Many case studies have pointed to the high prices that those living in informal settlements pay for water and sanitation (and sometimes for education and health care) and the high prices that many tenants pay for housing, but these are rarely reflected in the provisions for 'non-food needs' in poverty lines.

This book will present numerous examples of poverty statistics applied to urban populations that are inappropriate or inaccurate – including some that are nonsense. But inaccurate statistics (and sometimes nonsense statistics) are being used in ways which greatly overstate success in urban poverty reduction. This includes both national poverty lines and the international US$1 per person per day poverty line that is being used to monitor progress towards the Millennium Development Goals. The book will also question the assumption that cities' key role in economic growth necessarily supports urban poverty reduction; indeed, many of the most successful cities in low-income nations have seen a rapid growth in the proportion of their population suffering poverty-related deprivations.

Finally, this book emphasizes the need to assess the validity of official definitions and measures of poverty in the context of particular cities. In most (possibly all) nations, there are likely to be significant differences in the income needed to 'avoid poverty' between different cities (and even between districts within cities) and these need to be taken into consideration. For large, economically successful cities with ineffective government of land, infrastructure and services, the income needed to 'avoid poverty' may be several times higher than the current poverty line. Certainly in a great many urban contexts the dollar-a-day poverty line (including its latest incarnation as $1.25 a day at 2005 prices), even with adjustments for purchasing power parity, is completely inappropriate.

This book includes examples that come from research that might be considered too far in the past to have a contemporary relevance – for instance reports on poverty in Harare (Zimbabwe) and the direct and indirect health costs low-income groups faced in Khulna (Bangladesh) in the early 1990s. We chose to include these and other such studies in part because of the quality and detail of their insights, in part because of the lack of more recent detailed research into urban poverty, and in part because we believe that they provide historical insight that is still relevant today.

The transition to an increasingly urbanized world

We will not discuss in detail the growth in the urban population in the Global South and its underpinnings. Table 1.1 summarizes the most recent statistics available for urban populations and urban trends for different regions from 1950 to 2010, and projections for 2030 and 2050. A few points are worth noting, however.

1   Today, urban areas in what the UN terms the 'less developed' regions – which we term the 'Global South' – have around 2.7 billion inhabitants. This means that these urban areas have close to two fifths of the world's total population and close to three quarters of its urban population. The Global South also has most of the world's large cities and most of its mega-cities. Of the twenty-three cities whose population was reported to exceed 10 million by 2011, only five were in high-income nations (two in Japan, two in the USA, one in France). Of the remaining eighteen, four were in China, three in India and two in Brazil (United Nations 2012).

Table 1.1 The distribution of the world's urban population by region, 1950–2010, with projections for 2030 and 2050

Major area, region or country	Year projected for					
	1950	*1970*	*1990*	*2010*	*2030*	*2050*
Urban population (millions of inhabitants)						
World	745	1,352	2,281	3,559	4,984	6,252
More developed regions	442	671	827	957	1,064	1,127
Less developed regions	304	682	1,454	2,601	3,920	5,125
Least developed countries	15	41	107	234	477	860
Sub-Saharan Africa	20	56	139	298	596	1,069
Northern Africa	13	31	64	102	149	196
Asia	245	506	1,032	1,848	2,703	3,310
China	65	142	303	660	958	1,002
India	63	109	223	379	606	875
Europe	281	412	503	537	573	591
Latin America and the Caribbean	69	163	312	465	585	650
Northern America	110	171	212	282	344	396
Oceania	8	14	19	26	34	40
Proportion of population in urban areas (%)						
World	29.4	36.6	43.0	51.6	59.9	67.2
More developed regions	54.5	66.6	72.3	77.5	82.1	85.9
Less developed regions	17.6	25.3	34.9	46.0	55.8	64.1
Least developed countries	7.4	13.0	21.0	28.1	38.0	49.8
Sub-Saharan Africa	11.2	19.5	28.2	36.3	45.7	56.5
Northern Africa	25.8	37.2	45.6	51.2	57.5	65.3
Asia	17.5	23.7	32.3	44.4	55.5	64.4
China	11.8	17.4	26.4	49.2	68.7	77.3
India	17.0	19.8	25.5	30.9	39.8	51.7
Europe	51.3	62.8	69.8	72.7	77.4	82.2
Latin America and the Caribbean	41.4	57.1	70.3	78.8	83.4	86.6
Northern America	63.9	73.8	75.4	82.0	85.8	88.6
Oceania	62.4	71.2	70.7	70.7	71.4	73.0
Proportion of urban population (%)						
World	100.0	100.0	100.0	100.0	100.0	100.0
More developed regions	59.3	49.6	36.3	26.9	21.4	18.0
Less developed regions	40.7	50.4	63.7	73.1	78.6	82.0
Least developed countries	2.0	3.0	4.7	6.6	9.6	13.8
Sub-Saharan Africa	2.7	4.1	6.1	8.4	11.9	17.1
Northern Africa	1.7	2.3	2.8	2.9	3.0	3.1

Major area, region or country	Year projected for					
	1950	*1970*	*1990*	*2010*	*2030*	*2050*
Asia	32.9	37.4	45.2	51.9	54.2	52.9
China	8.7	10.5	13.3	18.6	19.2	16.0
India	8.5	8.1	9.8	10.6	12.2	14.0
Europe	37.6	30.5	22.0	15.1	11.5	9.5
Latin America and the Caribbean	9.3	12.1	13.7	13.1	11.7	10.4
Northern America	14.7	12.6	9.3	7.9	6.9	6.3
Oceania	1.1	1.0	0.8	0.7	0.7	0.6

Source: Data from United Nations (2012)

2   This concentration of the world's urban population and its largest cities outside high-income nations represents an important change, in that historically most of the world's urban population and most of its largest cities have been in its most prosperous nations. Table 1.1 shows the very large decrease in the proportion of the world's urban population in high-income countries and regionally in Europe between 1950 and 2010, and the very large increase in the proportion of the world's urban population in low- and middle-income countries (and regionally in Asia, with more than half this increase coming in China). In 1950, the nations that now make up Europe had nearly two fifths of the world's urban population; now they have around 15 per cent and they may have less than 10 per cent by 2050.

It is also worth noting the scale of the growth in urban population in the Global South. If we take 1975 as a time when there was a growing concern that rural poverty was being ignored, between 1975 and 2010, the urban population in the Global South tripled (growing by 1.8 billion) while the rural population grew by 38 per cent (848 million). By 2020, the urban population in the Global South is likely to exceed its rural population. By 2010, among the regions in the Global South with more than half their population in urban areas were Northern and Southern Africa, Eastern and Western Asia and the Caribbean, Central America and South America. In 1970 only Central and South America were in this category (United Nations 2012).

3   However, there is still an economic logic underpinning urbanization (the increase in the proportion of a population living in urban areas) and the growth of most large cities. Most new capital investments and most new employment opportunities are concentrated in urban areas – or, more accurately, in particular urban areas (to which there are also generally the largest new migration flows). The world's largest cities are heavily concentrated in the world's largest economies – even if not all of these are among the economies with the highest per capita incomes. (For instance, China is the world's second largest economy and India is among the world's largest economies, and these two nations have a high concentration of the

world's largest cities). All the world's wealthiest nations are predominantly urban[5] and virtually all the low- and middle-income nations that have urbanized most over the last few decades have experienced long periods of rapid economic growth and large shifts in the structure of their economy and employment, from agriculture, forestry and fishing to industry and services. Most nations (and all relatively urbanized nations) have most of their GDP generated by industry and services and most of their workforce in these sectors. There are nations or regions of nations where there have been rapid migration flows to urban areas (or particular cities) that are not responses to economic growth – including some related to civil strife, rural impoverishment or disasters – but this does not alter the fact that most urbanization is linked to economic growth.[6] However, the validity of international comparisons on the relationship between increasing levels of urbanization and economic growth are limited by the different criteria used by governments to define their urban populations (as discussed in Chapter 2).

Almost all commentaries on urban change globally include a comment that sub-Saharan Africa is urbanizing rapidly (or even that it is doing so at unprecedented rates). But some care is needed on this issue because of the lack of census data for many nations in this region. There are also the careful analyses by Deborah Potts that suggest that much of the region has not been urbanizing rapidly in the last decade or two (see Potts 2009). The latest UN statistics on urban trends also suggest that sub-Saharan Africa has not been urbanizing as rapidly as had been previously stated or expected. These suggest that the rate of increase in the level of urbanization was much more rapid in Asia than in sub-Saharan Africa for the periods 1990 to 2000 and 2000 to 2010. Eastern Asia (and China) had particularly high rates of urbanization between 2000 and 2010 (United Nations 2012).

4   Even if most new investment and employment opportunities are in urban areas, there has still been a rapid growth in the number of low-income urban dwellers. As Chapter 5 will describe, most of the benefits of economic growth go to non-poor groups. Certainly, the scale of urban poverty today is much larger than it was in the mid-1970s – and the proportion of the world's population with inadequate incomes who live and work in urban areas has increased. But (as Chapter 2 explains) we do not know by how much because of the inadequacies in the international measurement of poverty.

5   To have detailed statistics on urban change for any nation over several decades does not mean that we understand its underpinnings – and these statistics are often misinterpreted because the degree to which they are based on estimates and projections, in the absence of census data, is not made explicit. The United Nations data sets on urban populations (the latest of which is United Nations [2012]) have long cautioned against this and they also specify which censuses have been drawn on for each nation – but these details are often overlooked. We can learn about the social, economic and political underpinnings of urbanization from a few detailed, historically rooted analyses of urban change in particular nations, and these remind us

how complicated and varied such change is. They also show how much it can vary within a nation and over time, and the complex mix of local, regional and international economic, social and political influences on it, as well as the effects of demographic changes – see, for example, Hasan and Raza (2002), Martine and McGranahan (2010), UNCHS (1996; this report has sections exploring this point for each of the world's regions), and Manzanal and Vapnarsky (1986; an example of a sub-national region). Reading these studies should also encourage more caution in international comparisons of urbanization, which so often are dogged by inadequate knowledge of the countries being compared and inadequate appreciation of the deficiencies or lack of compatibility in the statistics used for comparison.

6   The projections for urban populations in 2030 and 2050 shown in Table 1.1 are, of course, based on certain assumptions. We have long worried about projections for city populations or for levels of urbanization far into the future because future city populations and levels of urbanization are so much influenced by economic change. They are also sometimes influenced by political change – for instance, if the economic and political changes in China in the late 1970s and early 1980s and its subsequent economic success and integration into the world economy had not taken place, the list of the world's largest cities and the scale of the world's urban population would have been quite different today. The size of the world's urban population in 2030 will be much influenced by the economic performance of the low- and middle-income nations with larger populations. Many of the UN projections for the population in the world's largest cities made in the 1970s and 1980s for 2000 proved to be spectacularly wrong (see Satterthwaite 2007a, 2010). Few economists would dare to predict how well the economy of most nations will perform up to 2050. So we urge caution in using these projections. But what we do want to emphasize is the scale of the urban population in the Global South today and the likelihood that it will continue to house an increasing proportion of the world's population.

How we came to be engaged in this issue

For more than two decades, we have had the chance to visit and collaborate with local NGOs that work with the residents of informal settlements or other low-income groups in urban areas in Africa, Asia and Latin America. We cannot produce empirical evidence documenting the precise scale and nature of the very poor quality and overcrowded conditions, and lack of infrastructure and services that exist in the tenements and informal settlements we have visited. We cannot produce evidence of the health burdens, premature deaths, evictions and other difficulties that their inhabitants talk to us about. But spending time walking through Kibera or other informal settlements in Nairobi (which house around half the city's population) makes it difficult to accept suggestions that a very small proportion of Kenya's urban population is poor. Walking through informal settlements in Dar es Salaam and listening to the inhabitants discuss their difficulties with accessing water and sanitation makes it difficult to take seriously official UN statistics on provision. For instance, the UN global assessment for 2000 suggested that 98 per cent of Tanzania's urban population had 'improved sanitation' (and many other sub-Saharan African nations had similar levels), and these very high levels of coverage were widely cited as evidence of urban populations benefiting from biases in development policies (UNICEF and WHO 2000). But at least some later estimates have greatly cut this (the 2012 UN assessment suggests only 15 per cent of Tanzania's urban population had improved sanitation in 2000, rising to 20 per cent in 2010 – see UNICEF and WHO 2012). Sitting in on the discussions of women pavement and slum dwellers in Mumbai (Bombay) about the difficulties they face getting water (see Bapat and Agarwal 2003) makes it difficult to accept the official statistic that 100 per cent of the city's population has access to piped water. When statistics are being produced on urban poverty where data is lacking, perhaps there is a need to develop ways to test the validity of these statistics, drawing on the knowledge of those with experience of conditions in the urban areas in question.

We also made the mistake of not engaging with how poverty is defined and measured until the early 1990s. We work in a research group that has long sought to document the scale and nature of deprivation in urban areas in low- and middle-income nations with regard to housing, infrastructure, services and tenure (see Hardoy and Satterthwaite 1981, 1989), with regard to health (Hardoy, Cairncross and Satterthwaite 1990) and with regard to environmental risks (Hardoy, Mitlin and Satterthwaite 1992, 2001). We have also sought to cover in some detail the most pressing environmental health issues facing low-income urban dwellers (Hardoy and Satterthwaite 1984; Hardoy, Mitlin and Satterthwaite 1992, 2001; Satterthwaite *et al.* 1996); so too have our colleagues (see, for instance, Bartlett 2002; Bartlett *et al.* 1999; McGranahan *et al.* 2001). The environmental health issues associated with water and sanitation have also been covered in two books prepared by our research team for UN-HABITAT (UN-HABITAT 2003a, 2006). The environmental problems associated with disasters have been covered in detail in the 2010 *World Disasters Report* that we helped prepare for the IFRC (IFRC 2010). Some consideration of the environmental health problems associated with climate change were addressed in Bicknell, Dodman and Satterthwaite 2009. The journal we edit and publish, *Environment and Urbanization*, has also had three special issues on urban health,[7] the most recent in April 2011.

It was only when we began to notice the differences between estimates for the proportion of the urban population defined as poor and the proportion 'living in poverty' that we began to look at how poverty was defined and measured. This difference became more evident from the papers presented at an international seminar we helped organize in 1994 on urban poverty.[8] Since then, we have paid more attention to how urban poverty is defined and measured and this book draws together and updates various working papers and reports we have written over the last 15 years.[9]

For people whose research is based more on qualitative techniques, it is often difficult to understand the reasons for what can be judged to be the inadequacies in the questions asked in large-scale quantitative surveys, and for what appear to be questionable assumptions made when interpreting results to define and measure poverty. In addition, much of the general literature on poverty lines is not very accessible to non-economists, but this book suggests that poverty definitions (including poverty lines) need to be scrutinized and questioned by a broader range of people, including urban poor organizations and the professionals who work with them. And, as covered in the final chapter and developed more fully in the companion volume to this, working with these groups can do much to generate the data needed to support poverty reduction that is so lacking today.

Some notes on terminologies used

We use the term 'Global South' because the terms used by the United Nations – 'developing countries', 'less developed countries' or 'less developed regions' – seem so inappropriate. Countries or regions that are more or less developed by what criteria – and by whose criteria? We acknowledge that the term 'Global South' is not very accurate geographically (a lot of the Global South is actually north of the equator). We used to use the term 'Third World' because its origins were based on the idea of the 'Third Estate' (the people) and it was a term chosen by non-aligned nations during the Cold War, but many interpreted this term as implying inferiority to the First World (high-income market economies) and Second World (what was the Soviet Union and other centrally planned economies). The term 'Third World' also became imprecise with the break-up of the Soviet Union and economic and political changes in many of the formerly centrally planned economies.

The 'Global South' is taken to include all nations classified by the World Bank as low- and middle-income that are in Africa, Asia and Latin America and the Caribbean. It does not include low- and middle-income nations in Eastern Europe, including the Russian Federation, although clearly these have serious problems with urban poverty. There are also some countries in Africa, Asia and the Caribbean that have become high-income countries and yet may still be classified as being within 'less developed regions' – for instance South Korea, Singapore, some small island nations, and some oil-rich nations in the Middle East. All European nations are included in the 'more developed' category by the UN, but many are not high-income nations – notably the Russian Federation and nations that emerged from its break-up or were part of its sphere of influence during the Cold War. Of course, when considering likely urban populations up to 2030, many nations may shift from the middle-income to the high-income classification.

We had intended to avoid using the term 'slum' because of its derogatory connotations. Classify a settlement as a slum and it implies that it is poor quality and needs replacing ('slum clearance'), so helping to legitimate the eviction of its inhabitants and the destruction of their homes. The term 'slum' is often used as a general term for a range of different kinds of housing or settlement, many of which provide valuable accommodation for low-income groups and do not need replacement but rather provision for infrastructure and services. However, it is difficult to avoid the term for at least three reasons. The first is that it is used in studies from which we want to draw. Second, some important urban poor groups have organized themselves as slum-dweller organizations or federations; although it could be argued that, while they may choose to include the term 'slum' in their titles, it is not appropriate for others to use it. It is also notable that in some Asian nations there are advantages for informal settlements in being recognized officially as 'slums' – indeed, residents may even lobby to become a 'notified slum'. The third reason is that the only global estimates for deficiencies in housing collected by the United Nations are for slums. We continue to avoid the term where possible.

We also wish we could have avoided the term 'the poor', as it is so often used by external professionals and institutions to define or classify groups in the population without their approval or even knowledge. And working with those classified as 'poor' reveals how 'unpoor' they are in so many respects, especially in their competence and capacity to live with little income, with poor returns for their hours worked, with many costs and deprivations that should not be there. As noted in the acknowledgements, we have learnt so much from our work with and interactions with people and groups classified as being among 'the poor'. The chance to work with them or simply to visit them, sit in on their discussions or watch them work together – and watch them negotiate with politicians and civil servants – is to be reminded of this competence. Their willingness to talk to us and their generosity when we visit them also reminds us of the perils of classifying them as 'poor'. We also see their capacity to work collectively and their willingness to work in partnership with local governments as one of the critical foundations for poverty reduction – as elaborated in the companion volume to this.

Where possible, we have replaced the use of the term 'poor', with something more precise, for example, 'low-income' or 'resident of an informal settlement'.

2   Measuring poverty

Introduction

How different definitions influence the scale of poverty

Defining and measuring poverty is important to the work of governments, since this should help identify who is in need. It should also help identify the nature of need, which then serves as the basis for identifying the actions required to address need. Appropriate and accurate measurement methodologies need to be at the centre of the policies and interests of any aid agency, development bank or international NGO, whose very existence is justified by their contribution to reducing poverty. In this context, it is important to get the definition and measurement right. This may also be important for governance as those suffering deprivations caused by poverty need to feel that their needs and priorities are represented within the definition and measurement processes (as well as in subsequent policies and actions).

Defining poverty may be considered to be relatively simple: there is not much disagreement that everyone needs sufficient nutritious food, access to services such as health care and schools and a secure home with adequate provision for water and sanitation. It is accepted that 'adequate' income is the primary means by which urban individuals or households can meet these needs, in part because in urban areas there is generally less scope for self-production of food, housing or other needs. So a poverty line set at a particular income level can be used to measure who is poor, with a market value being attributed to self-production where relevant. This means that those who have sufficient income for a set of goods and services considered as 'needs' are non-poor and those who do not are poor. There are needs other than sufficient income such as the rule of law and respect for civil and political rights (and the means to ensure these are realized) – although these are not usually seen as part of poverty (even if inadequate rule of law and breaches of civil and political rights are often associated with poverty and may be major causes or contributors to poverty). There is also recognition that asset bases are important for allowing low-income individuals or households to avoid or better cope with poverty (Moser 1998, 2006a, 2006b, 2007) but very few poverty-line definitions include any consideration of assets – although sometimes assets are assessed separately within poverty assessments.

Despite the apparent simplicity of understanding what poverty is, there is no agreement on how best to define and measure it. Different methodologies, the goods included as needs, price estimation techniques, and proxy value estimates all lead to different results. During the late 1990s, there were at least four figures for the proportion of Kenya's urban population who were poor, ranging from 1 to 49 per cent.[10] In the Philippines, in 2000, the proportion of the national population with below-poverty-line income was 12, 25, 40 or 45–46 per cent, depending on which poverty line is chosen (World Bank Philippines 2002[11]). In Ethiopia, the proportion of the urban population with below-poverty-line incomes in 1995–96 could have been 49, 33 or 18 per cent, depending on the figure used for the average calorific requirement per person (World Bank Ethiopia 1999). In the Dominican Republic in October 2004, different criteria for setting the poverty line meant that the proportion of the urban population below the poverty line varied from 35.4 per cent to 2.1 per cent (World Bank Dominican Republic 2006). As this chapter will discuss in detail, research that examines the actual cost of meeting food and non-food needs in particular cities or within urban populations usually shows much higher proportions in poverty than official statistics.

The very large differences in the proportion of the population considered poor (whether for all low- and middle-income nations or for national or urban populations within particular nations) are the result of different definitions of poverty. These differences usually lie in how to define the income level that individuals or households need to avoid being poor, especially with regard to non-food essentials. However, the example from Ethiopia shows how influential the choice of which figure to use for food requirements can be.

The levels at which poverty lines are set are influenced by how food costs are analysed – for instance whether they are based on 'expert' judgements for the cheapest means of meeting food needs or based on the actual food that low-income groups eat. These differences can also be caused by whether the definition and measurement of poverty includes some consideration of basic service provision or housing quality (or the costs of these), and the quality or appropriateness of the data on which this is based. As discussed in more detail in the section on water and sanitation in Chapter 3, the proportion of a nation's urban population judged to have adequate provision for water or sanitation also varies a lot, depending on what is considered 'adequate'. In some cases, differences in estimates may be caused by the level of aggregation, and whether or not adjustments are made for the differences in price levels between, for example, urban and rural areas or between cities of different sizes.

If the different methods available for defining and measuring poverty produced similar figures for its scale and depth, then this concern over definitional issues would be less relevant. For instance, Kanbur and Squire (2001, page 216) suggest that 'Although different methods of defining and measuring poverty inevitably identify different groups as poor, the evidence suggests that the differences may not be that great'. But this is not so if one definition of poverty suggests that 1 per cent of Kenya's urban population are poor and another suggests 49 per cent. Even with the US-dollar-a-day poverty line, small adjustments and better data can mean large differences in the number of people said to be poor. For instance, Chen and Ravallion (2008) note that the population under the dollar-a-day poverty line had been undercounted by 400 million for 2005 (see also Yifu Lin 2008); this does not inspire much confidence in such estimates.

Clearly, the choice of which definition to use matters if one definition means a very small minority of the urban (or national) population are poor while another means that half are poor. In this context, the choice of definition will influence the response of governments and international agencies: if 1.2 per cent of Kenya's or 2.3 per cent of Zimbabwe's or 0.9 per cent of Senegal's urban populations were poor in the mid- or late 1990s, as suggested by Sahn and Stifel (2003), clearly addressing urban poverty is not a priority, as in each of these nations a high proportion of the rural population suffers from poverty and most of their populations in the mid-1990s were in rural areas. But, if between one third and one half of these nations' urban populations are facing serious deprivations (which we show to be the case), and most of the growth in poverty is taking place in urban areas (which is the case in some countries), the needs of the urban poor deserve far more attention.

With many governments and most international agencies now making more explicit commitments to reducing poverty, through poverty reduction strategies and by focusing on the Millennium Development Goals, the question of how urban poverty is defined and measured has great relevance for whether these organizations see urban poverty as worth addressing. An earlier review of the attention given to urban poverty in the poverty reduction strategy papers prior to 2004 suggested that there is considerable variability among governments with regard to whether urban poverty should get much attention (Mitlin 2004).

Much of the general literature on poverty does not recognize that there are particular 'urban' characteristics that most urban areas share which influence the scale and depth of poverty there (see, for instance, World Bank 2000). Much of the general literature also does not draw on the literature on urban problems. This means that key characteristics of urban areas (or of some urban areas or some districts within urban areas) are not taken into account in the definitions of poverty or in its measurement (see Box 2.1).

Combine a lack of knowledge (or data) about housing and living conditions with little or no allowance for the cost of non-food necessities in urban areas (or particular cities), and it is possible to produce statistics that so understate the scale and depth of urban poverty as to render them invalid, whatever definition is being used. For instance, for the city of Pune in India, official statistics suggest that 2 per cent of the population are 'poor' yet close to 40 per cent live in very poor quality housing (Bapat 2009). In 2005, the Pune Municipal Corporation identified 10,800 families as living below the poverty line although nearly 220,000 households lived in 'slums' in that same year (Bapat 2009). This blindness to living conditions is reinforced by the lack of knowledge among poverty specialists of urban contexts; anyone with any knowledge of urban centres in Kenya, Senegal or Zimbabwe would know that the urban poverty statistics noted above were wrong. This chapter has many other examples of urban poverty statistics that are at odds

Box 2.1 Distinguishing between rural and urban areas

There are obvious economic and physical characteristics, and usually also demographic, social and political characteristics, that distinguish urban areas from rural ones, and that have importance for understanding, then defining and measuring, poverty – for instance, as discussed in this chapter, higher monetary costs for many essential goods and services, more monetized housing and land-for-housing markets, and fewer possibilities for growing crops or accessing or using resources at no monetary cost. A higher proportion of urban dwellers than rural dwellers face harassment, eviction or arrest because their homes or their livelihoods are illegal. However, the wide variations between urban areas should be recognized – for instance, many small urban centres may have many rural characteristics (and have more in common with most large villages than with major cities). Similarly, some rural areas have urban characteristics; in some nations, highly urbanized settlements are still classified as rural even though they have urban non-agricultural employment structures, house types, infra-structure provision and density. There are also many (poor and non-poor) individuals and households that have rural and urban components to their livelihoods, asset bases, incomes and social networks, which also cautions against simplistic 'rural versus urban' comparisons.[12]

There is no agreement as to how urban centres should be defined or distinguished from rural areas so there is considerable variation in how governments choose to define urban areas – and this inevitably influences the proportion of the population said to live in urban areas. Some nations define as urban centres all settlements with populations above a threshold – 1,000 or 2,500 or 5,000 are commonly used. This means that a nation's urban population and the proportion of the national population living in urban centres can vary a lot, depending on the threshold used (or other criteria chosen and applied). For instance, India would become predominantly urban if it used a low population threshold for defining urban centres, say 1,000 inhabitants, as a high proportion of its rural population live in villages with more than 1,000 inhabitants. Although in virtually all nations settlements with 20,000 plus inhabitants are classified as urban, differences emerge in the proportion of settlements with between a few hundred and 20,000 inhabitants classified as rural or urban. This cautions against international comparisons between nations' urban populations, given that a significant proportion of the population in almost all nations live in settlements with between a few hundred and 20,000 inhabitants (see Hardoy and Satterthwaite 1989; Satterthwaite 2006).

with well-documented local realities, and other examples where the statistics appear faulty. It is odd to see references in many documents to those 'living in poverty' with no consideration given to housing and living conditions.

One other reason behind this capacity to produce questionable statistics is the lack of engagement by those who produce and use official (government and international agency) poverty statistics with 'the poor' who are meant to be the object of their concern. Given the likely influence of poverty definitions on the policies and resource allocations of most governments and international agencies and the emphasis of international development agencies on participation, one would expect the definition of poverty and its measurement to be one of the key topics for public discussion and debate within each country (and, since the focus of this book is urban poverty, in each city or town). Such public debate is also important to guard against inappropriate definitions of 'need'. But there is little evidence of such a public debate in most low-income nations.[13] This may in part be because in many nations there is little link between the measurement of poverty and the capacity or willingness of government agencies to reduce it. Low-income groups will have little interest in being defined as 'poor' if this does not imply action will be taken to help them. However, part of the reason is the difficulty non-specialists have in engaging in this discussion and in identifying all the influences and assumptions that are involved in the definition and measurement of poverty.

Rural versus urban

As with the other published work of our Institute (the International Institute for Environment and Development, or IIED) on urban poverty, we are not recommending that funds allocated to rural poverty reduction be redirected to urban poverty reduction; it may be that the scale and depth of rural poverty is also underestimated and misrepresented by conventional poverty statistics. The failure of consumption-based poverty lines to capture the extent and nature of deprivation in rural areas may actually be greater than in urban areas, because so much rural deprivation is related to lack of assets (especially fertile land) and lack of access to services, rather than lack of income. Nor is this book seeking to make judgements about the relative scale or depth of 'urban' poverty compared to 'rural' poverty. Where comparisons are made between the two, or between the ways in which they are understood, it is to highlight how the understanding or measurement of poverty in urban areas (or of poverty in general) has failed to take due note of costs or of forms of deprivation that are evident in some (or most) urban areas.

However, we do take issue with much of the general literature on 'poverty' and the writings of rural specialists who discuss 'urban poverty' yet fail to understand how urban contexts can generate or exacerbate poverty. Much of the general literature on poverty assumes that there is an 'urban bias' in international agencies' priorities – this remains unproven[14] and is certainly at odds with our analyses, which show a very low priority given by most international agencies to urban poverty reduction.[15]

The rest of this chapter discusses the value of giving greater attention to understanding and measuring urban poverty in ways that better capture the scale and nature of deprivation in each location and better serve poverty reduction, including supporting the role of local (governmental and civil society) actors. The case for more attention to urban poverty reduction is also reinforced by the evidence that much can be done to reduce urban poverty drawing only on the resources and powers available to urban governments and increasing the scope of action permitted to low-income groups and their organizations and federations; this is the focus of the companion volume to this. In Chapter 6, we return to the issue of where, when and how urban dwellers may enjoy an advantage over rural dwellers.

Understating urban poverty

The gaps between poverty statistics and data on living conditions[16]

If the term 'poverty' is taken to mean human needs that are not met, then most of the estimates for the scale of urban poverty in low- and middle-income countries appear too low. Statistics produced by international agencies consistently suggest that three quarters or more of the urban population in low- and middle-income countries are not poor. For instance, a publication of the Overseas Development Council in the USA in 1989 reported that only 130 million of the 'poorest poor' within low- and middle-income nations lived in urban areas (Leonard 1989); this estimate would mean that in 1989 more than nine out of ten of their urban populations were not among this group. World Bank estimates for 1988 suggested that there were 330 million 'poor' people living in urban areas in low- and middle-income countries (World Bank 1991), which meant that more than three quarters of their urban population were not 'poor' at that date.[17] The 1999–2000 World Development Report (World Bank 1999) suggested that there were 495 million 'urban poor' by the year 2000, which meant that three quarters of the urban population were 'not poor'. As noted in Chapter 1, according to Ravallion, Chen and Sangraula (2007), only a small minority of the urban population is poor and for many regions there is very little extreme poverty in urban areas. For instance, using the dollar-a-day poverty line ($1.08 per day at 1993 purchasing power parity), in 2002, less than 1 per cent of the urban populations of China, the Middle East and North Africa, and East Europe and Central Asia were poor. In Latin America and the Caribbean, less than 10 per cent of the urban population was poor. For all low- and middle-income nations, 87 per cent of their urban population was not poor. If these figures are correct, it represents a triumph for development. It is also noted in Chapter 1 that Deaton and Dupriez (2011) suggest that the dollar-a-day poverty line used by the World Bank is actually too high.

But this and later chapters show that it is common for 40 to 70 per cent of a nation's urban population or a major city's population to have incomes too low to allow them to meet their needs. The World Bank estimates for the scale of urban poverty for 1988 and 2000 suggest that there was no increase in the proportion of the urban population living in poverty between these years. Yet many studies show increasing proportions of nations' urban populations suffering from poverty during the 1980s or 1990s, reflecting poor economic performance and/or structural adjustment (see, for instance, Kanji 1995; Latapí and de la Rocha 1995; Minujin 1995; Moser, Herbert and Makonnen 1993; Maxwell *et al.* 1998; de la Rocha 2007; Perlman 2010), although the evidence is not there to be able to generalize for all low- and middle-income nations.

In general, the proportion of urban dwellers living in poverty (i.e. in poor quality, overcrowded and often insecure housing lacking adequate provision for water, sanitation, drainage, etc.) and exposed to very high levels of environmental health risk is higher than the proportion defined as poor by poverty lines in sub-Saharan Africa and some other low- and middle-income nations.[18] For instance, considerably more than one quarter of the urban population in most low- and middle-income nations live in poor quality (and often insecure or illegal) homes with inadequate provision for water, sanitation and drainage (Cairncross, Hardoy and Satterthwaite 1990; WHO 1992, 1999; Hardoy, Mitlin and Satterthwaite 2001; UN-HABITAT 2003a; see also Chapter 3). If the estimate for the number of 'poor' urban dwellers was based on the number living in poor quality housing with a lack of basic infrastructure and services, then at least 600 million were poor in 1990, with the numbers likely to have increased significantly during the 1990s (Cairncross, Hardoy and Satterthwaite 1990; WHO 1992, 1999; UN-HABITAT 2003b). For instance, a detailed review of provision for water and sanitation in urban areas suggested that, in 2000, there were at least 650 million urban dwellers lacking adequate provision for water and at least 850 million lacking adequate provision for sanitation in Africa, Asia and Latin America (UN-HABITAT 2003a). UN-HABITAT (2003b) suggests that in 2001 there were 924 million people living in inadequate shelter with associated problems of lack of access to secure tenure, infrastructure and services; if these people are considered poor, then it challenges the World Bank estimate of 495 million 'poor' in 2000 and the validity of the dollar-a-day poverty line which suggests that only 291 million urban dwellers were poor in 2002 (Chen and Ravallion 2007[19]).

It is not only global statistics that seem to underestimate the proportion of poor urban households, but also statistics for nations. For instance, the suggestion that 2.1 per cent of Zimbabwe's urban population was poor in 1994 (Sahn and Stifel 2003) bears no relation to the documentation showing the scale of urban poverty in the early 1990s and the large increase in its scale and depth from large price rises, retrenchments and declines in the amount spent by poorer groups on food (see Kanji 1995) – or the official survey in 1996 showing 46 per cent of urban households as poor, including 25 per cent who could not meet their basic nutritional requirements (official government statistics quoted in Bijlmakers, Bassett and Sanders 1998). There is also a considerable literature on the very poor living conditions that much of Zimbabwe's urban population endure (Chitekwe and Mitlin 2001; Potts and Mutambirwa 1991; Schlyter 1990; Rakodi and Withers 1995).

The suggestion that 1.5 per cent of Kenya's urban population was poor in 1988 and that 1.2 per cent was poor in 1998 (Sahn and Stifel 2003) also bears no relation to figures drawn from other sources – for instance, the official survey in 1997 which found that 49 per cent of the urban population was poor (Kenya, Government of 2000) – or to the very poor conditions in which a large proportion of the population of Kenya's three largest cities live. (For Nairobi, see Lamba 1994; Alder 1995; APHRC 2002; Weru 2004. For Mombasa, see Rakodi, Gatabaki-Kamau and Devas 2000. For Kisumu see Karanja 2010.) Chapter 3 includes many more statistics for the inadequacies in provision for water and sanitation in Kenya's urban population that show the high proportion suffering serious deprivation and very high infant and child mortality rates.

For Senegal, the suggestion that less than 1 per cent of its urban population was poor in 1997 (Sahn and Stifel 2003) hardly fits with the very poor conditions in which a significant proportion of the urban population lives, or with the official figure from 2001 which suggested that 44–59 per cent of the urban population was poor, depending on the zone (Senegal, Republic of 2002). Many other figures presented by Sahn and Stifel 2003 can be questioned – for instance, that only 5.4 per cent of Burkina Faso's urban population was poor in 1999 or only 6.8 per cent of Ghana's urban population in 1998.

Drawing from other sources, it is difficult to take seriously the suggestion that less than 2 per cent of China's urban population was below the poverty line in 1994 (World Bank 1999) or that less than 1 per cent of the urban population was poor in 2002 (Ravallion, Chen and Sangraula 2007, applying the dollar-a-day poverty line). Solinger (2006) points to the very large numbers of urban dwellers who have been laid off and are unemployed and the migrant population of 100 million plus living in urban areas; also how different bases for setting poverty lines produce very different totals. One estimate suggests that 13 per cent of China's urban population are poor, and this does not include the 100 million plus migrants. GHK and IIED (2004) show how much the scale of urban poverty in China depends on whether or not the 100 million 'temporary' migrants who live and work in urban areas are classified as rural or urban.

Sabry (2009) notes how poverty statistics for Greater Cairo suggest that only 5–10 per cent of the city's population are poor, and that the proportion is decreasing and contributing to the decrease in the proportion of the national population considered poor. But she then demonstrates that this is because of the unrealistically low value of the poverty lines for Greater Cairo, especially in relation to the high proportion of Cairo's population living in *ashwa'iyyat* (informal settlements) and the rapid growth in their populations. In Greater Cairo, as in so many cities, the proportion of the population said to be poor bears no relation to those who live in poverty.

The government of Ghana claimed that only 3.8 per cent of Accra's population was poor in 1998–99 (Ghana, Republic of 2000) yet Devas and Korboe (2000) describe a government living standards survey that had suggested that 23 per cent of Accra's population was poor (see also Songsore and McGranahan 1993). An IFPRI study on urban livelihoods and food security in Accra also suggested much higher levels of deprivation, and that, based on the calories available to household members per day (2,640 kilocalories per adult equivalent unit), about 40 per cent of households in the sample were food insecure (Maxwell *et al.* 1998).

Official figures for the proportion of Phnom Penh's population with below-poverty-line incomes in 1999 (9.7 per cent or 14.6 per cent depending on which survey is used; see Cambodia, Kingdom of 2002) bear little relation to the proportion living in illegal or informal settlements or crowded tenements with very inadequate provision for water and sanitation, which is estimated at around 40 per cent of the city's population (Asian Coalition for Housing Rights 2001). Official statistics for Colombo in 2009–10 suggest that only 3.6 per cent of the city's population is poor – yet around half of Colombo's population live in what are termed 'under-served' settlements characterized by poor quality, overcrowded housing lacking adequate provision for infrastructure and services. By 2004, there were 1,614 under-served settlements within the municipal limits of Colombo, housing around half its population (Romeshun and Mayadunne 2011).

In interviews with women living in informal settlements in Buenos Aires,[20] all but one had incomes above the official poverty line and all had incomes above the equivalent of US$1 or US$2 per person per day. Yet all live in informal settlements and most in settlements where their tenure of the house site is insecure. Most had built their houses with second-hand materials and many houses were far from finished. Most had struggled for years to get services – and most had difficulties affording the costs of keeping their children at school. Most talked about the difficulties they face in putting sufficient food on their family's table each day, and report buying food in small quantities locally because they only have enough money once or twice a month to be able to go to large supermarkets and benefit from lower unit costs of bulk purchases (Hardoy with Almansi 2011).

Chapter 3 will discuss in more detail the deficiencies in provision for water and sanitation in urban areas and how most reported indicators greatly underestimate the extent and depth of the inadequacies in provision in urban areas because of inappropriate assumptions and poor data. For instance, the UN's Joint Monitoring Programme (JMP) for Water Supply and Sanitation now has data on the proportion of the urban population with water supply piped to their premises. If this data were used in assessing whether the Millennium Development Goal target of reducing the proportion of people without access to safe drinking water had been achieved in urban areas, it would completely change the picture (see Chapter 3). It is also common for inappropriate judgements to be made about the quality of housing based on the limited data available – for instance, the weight given to data on flooring materials, which is obviously a particularly inappropriate indicator for cities or urban districts with multi-storey housing. Much urban housing does not have a dirt floor but still has very high levels of overcrowding and inadequate or no provision for infrastructure and services. More importantly, the limited statistics on housing conditions tell us very little about the level of health risk for occupants from biological pathogens, chemical pollutants and physical hazards (the main means by which poor housing quality translates into illness, injury and premature death – see Hardoy, Mitlin and Satterthwaite 2001).

The gaps between poverty statistics and data on health

Chapter 3 discusses the health problems faced by those with low incomes and what underpins these – including the inadequacies in provision for water, sanitation, drainage and solid waste collection. For this chapter, it is worth noting that in the data, the proportion of the urban population facing high infant, child and maternal mortality rates is often substantially higher than the proportion defined as 'poor'. Again, the suggestion that only 1.5 per cent of Kenya's urban population is poor is inconsistent with the very high infant and child mortality rates within the informal settlements where half of Nairobi's population lives (APHRC 2002).

In Dar es Salaam, Tanzania's largest city, according to official statistics 17.6 per cent of the population was poor in 2000–01, but the under-five mortality rate in the city in 1999 was 173 per 1,000 live births – at least ten times what could be expected for a city with more than four fifths of its population 'not poor' (Tanzania, United Republic of 2002a). The same document that claimed only 17.6 per cent of Dar es Salaam was poor also noted that 30 per cent of households lived in one room, that 60,000 lived in valleys that exposed them to the risk of floods and diseases, and that 15,000–20,000 lived on the streets (Tanzania, United Republic of 2002a). Documentation of provision for water and sanitation in Dar es Salaam shows that far more than 17.6 per cent face very serious deficiencies (Glockner, Mkanga and Ndezi 2004). In addition, around 70 per cent of the entire city's population lives in informal settlements (Ndezi 2009).

Chapter 3 also describes the many nations with high under-five mortality rates and high levels of stunting in children in their urban populations, and these can suggest levels of deprivation that are not reflected in official poverty statistics. The figures available for infant, child and under-five mortality rates and the proportion of children that are underheight or underweight are mostly averages for countries' total urban populations. These will be much higher for low-income groups. For instance, in Kenya, infant and child mortality rates in the low-income settlements in Nairobi, where around half the city's population live, were nearly twice those of the Kenya-wide urban average (APHRC 2002). In India, under-five mortality rates are much higher among the poorest quartile of the urban population when compared to the rest of the population (Agarwal 2011; see also Chapter 3). The problem of undernutrition among lower-income groups in urban areas may be more serious than is assumed, but hidden in any urban average because of the concentration of better-fed middle- and upper-income groups in urban areas.

Thus, there are many nations where the proportion of urban dwellers who are poor according to official poverty definitions is significantly less than the proportion living in poverty, or significantly less than the proportion with health outcomes or nutritional levels that one would assume are associated with poverty. This also true for particular cities. This may be because poverty lines are set too low in relation to the costs of housing and essential services. This is certainly the best explanation for the high proportion of underheight or underweight children. Or it may be related more to the incapacities of public, private or civil society institutions – good quality provision of water, sanitation and health care can greatly reduce the health burden facing those with limited incomes. These are the issues to which the next few sections are devoted.

The unrealistic criteria used to set poverty lines

The increased attention on poverty

From around 1990, poverty began to get more attention in the literature on development – this is perhaps best exemplified by the World Bank devoting an issue of its annual World Development Report to poverty (World Bank 1990). During the 1970s, poverty had got some attention, especially in relation to development assistance agencies making commitments to increase the priority of addressing 'basic needs' (for more details, see the later section in this chapter on 'Incorporating other dimensions of poverty'). During this decade, many international agencies and some governments put great stress on the need to improve basic service provision, although this was less explicitly linked to the discourse on poverty. Indeed, much of this discussion had elements of what later became the Millennium Development Goals. But the focus on basic needs seemed to get lost during the 1980s – in part as the political changes associated with the governments of Thatcher in the UK and Reagan in the USA swept through discussions of development assistance, with cutbacks in state provision and a focus on the preconditions for economic growth.

The 1990s also brought a discussion of poverty that widened beyond consumption-based definitions, to include discussion of the lack of basic service provision and other deprivations. This greater attention to poverty is apparent both in the published literature and in the 'grey' literature of reports produced by international agencies and national governments. Most international agencies and many governments also became more explicit about their commitment to reducing poverty, especially through the poverty reduction strategy papers that were prepared in most low- and many middle-income nations. An increasing number of governments and international agencies also incorporated a commitment to meeting the Millennium Development Goals in their plans and programmes, including specific goals and targets related to poverty.[21] Most governments and international agencies also came to acknowledge that poverty has many dimensions – i.e. that it is more than hunger or insufficient income to purchase food – and the need to improve 'basic service provision' as part of poverty reduction.

What is also clear from our review of poverty reduction strategy papers and poverty assessments is that some attention is usually given to urban poverty, with this attention increasing over time.[22] We reviewed past and recent poverty reduction strategy papers and associated poverty assessment reports with regard to coverage of urban poverty and rural poverty; this included some of the lowest income countries (Tables 2.1 and 2.2). There is no agreement within these papers as to the significance of urban poverty. In some cases, the primary concern is with rural poverty and the recognition that figures indicate that rural poverty is a more

Table 2.1 Number of times that urban poverty is mentioned in 28 poverty reduction strategy papers

Region	More than 10 times	5–9 times	4 times or less
Africa (21 papers)	2	7	12
Asia (4 papers)	1	1	2
Latin America (3 papers)	1	0	2
Total	4	8	16

Source: Details and sources by country are provided in an annex available at http://www.routledge.com/books/details/9780415624671/

Table 2.2 Comparison of the number of times urban and rural poverty are mentioned in 28 poverty reduction strategy papers

Region	Less than ten mentions				Both mentioned more than ten times
	Urban mentioned more than rural	Rural mentioned more than urban	Neither mentioned	Both mentioned the same number of times	
Africa	8	3	8	2	0
Asia	2	1	1	0	0
Latin America	0	2		0	1
Total	10	6	9	2	1

Source: Details and sources by country are provided in an annex available at http://www.routledge.com/books/details/9780415624671/

significant problem (for example, Malawi and Zambia). In other cases, there is a specific consideration of the urban poverty that may be associated with crime (for example, Tanzania) and/or with specific needs such as housing and access to basic services (for example, Uganda and Vietnam). In the strategy paper for the Democratic Republic of the Congo, for example, the authors report that a participatory assessment resulted in the understanding that 'in rural areas, poverty is perceived as a lack of production factors.… In contrast, in urban areas poverty is perceived as a lack of money, jobs, electricity, easy-to-use means of transportation, decent housing, drinking water, and sanitation' (Congo, Democratic Republic of the 2006, page 20).

The kinds of concerns with the methodology for defining and measuring poverty that we explore in this chapter are evident to some extent within specific discussions in these documents, although many of them do not elaborate on the problems of poverty measurement. In a significant number of reports, it is not possible to work out exactly how the poverty line was established. Some report authors are concerned about the sampling among shifting (and in some cases more stable but informal) urban populations, the adequate representation of price differentials, the high costs of accessing (some) basic services including housing, and the general difficulties of costing such expenditures. However, for others, these are seen as less significant issues. Many do not elaborate the price adjustments made, although some price adjustment is relatively common. In some cases this is a regional adjustment (rather than one made between urban and rural areas). In some cases there is more than one urban poverty line, in others an aggregation is made across all urban areas. In a few cases the ratio of food to non-food costs in the poverty line vary between rural and urban areas, in others the same ratios are maintained. At the same time, some of the poverty assessments discuss problems with price adjustments (for example that for Zambia in World Bank Zambia 2007) that raise issues likely to be of general relevance. Table 2.3 on pages 32–34 summarizes the discrepancies that emerge from diverse approaches, and specific issues are further explored in the discussion below.

The way that poverty is defined and measured in most low-income and many middle-income nations remains rooted in questionable assumptions about what 'poverty' is, and is often locked into nineteenth-century attitudes about the needs and rights of the 'poor'. In most nations, poverty is still defined and measured through consumption-based poverty lines, despite recognition of how inadequately these capture many aspects of deprivation. Many poverty lines are still based primarily on the cost of a 'minimum food basket', with a notional allocation to meet non-food needs, yet much urban poverty is related to the inability of individuals or households to afford essential non-food items.

That poverty lines have limitations is widely accepted. For instance, Kanbur and Squire (2001) note that 'conventional measures of poverty draw heavily on the statistical information contained in household surveys, combined with a more or less arbitrary cut-off separating the poor from the non-poor' (page 204). That there are limitations in the ways in which provision is made for non-food needs is also recognized. As Ravallion (1998) notes: 'Of all the data that goes into measuring poverty, setting the non-food component of the poverty line is probably the most contentious' (page 17). The rest of this section examines the extent to which poverty lines are set in ways that can understate the levels and depth of urban poverty.

Problems of getting representative samples

Questions may be raised about whether the samples used in household surveys really are representative for urban areas, especially for those sections of the urban poor who are most difficult to include in surveys. Do the household surveys from which data are drawn for setting poverty lines or assessing living conditions contain a representative sample from urban areas? There are three specific groups that may not be included: those who lack the required registration in countries where this remains relevant (primarily China), those living in informal settlements and/or having informal rental arrangements in formal settlements that are inadequately documented and hence sampled, and those who are homeless.

The Chinese state has long used a household registration system, *hukou*, which requires that households register where they are living and indicates whether they are an agricultural or non-agricultural household (Wu and Treiman 2004). The hukou system was set up in the 1950s and enforced more rigorously during the 1960s. This restricted migration to urban areas, because it controlled access to workplaces, and was used to manage access to a range of basic services including shelter, education and health care. However, the system broke down in the sense of restricting migration, especially as the Chinese economy began to sustain very high economic growth rates, and by 1990 there were an estimated 80 million people living in urban areas with a rural status (Wu and Treiman 2004), with later estimates (as quoted earlier) suggesting 100 million plus. Gao (2006, page 26) discusses the fact that migrants to urban areas who lack urban registration are not included in urban poverty estimates in China. Given that their status puts them in a particularly disadvantageous position, this is, in his view, a serious omission, which makes the urban poverty figures look lower than is the case. Solinger (2006) describes the very large numbers of urban dwellers who were laid off starting in the mid-1990s and the high proportion of these that failed to find alternative employment. Estimates that suggested that 13 per cent of the urban population was poor still did not include the migrants who lived and worked in urban areas but were still registered as rural.

In some national poverty assessments, weaknesses in the sampling frame are acknowledged. For example, the authors of the Cambodia poverty assessment (World Bank Cambodia 2006, page 47) mention their concerns that informal settlements have grown since the sampling frame was constructed in 1999 and hence that their significance is understated in the poverty figures, and that without more information no adjustment can be made. Sabry (2009) notes that in Egypt the sample frame for the 2004–05 Household Income, Expenditure and Consumption Survey used 1996 census data, and this does not take adequate account of the rapidly growing population in newly formed informal areas. She illustrates the scale of the problem using the example of Ezbet el Haggana, which had a census population of 39,432 in 2006; however, GTZ[23] estimated a population of 212,575 in the same year.

Sabry (2009) also notes that the census data and the master list of 'slums' from the central government's statistical agency 'have inaccurate, severely under-counted and out-of-date figures for slum populations. Under-counting slum populations means that these areas will have a much lower probability of actually being part of the household surveys which provide the data for poverty line studies. Given that slums house the vast majority of Greater Cairo's poor, this means that the poor are under-sampled because these areas have a lower chance of appearing in household surveys' (page 15).

Some large informal areas were found to be missing from this agency's lists, while others had estimates for their population that were a small fraction of their real population. Sabry (2009, page 19) reports the comment of one resident of an informal settlement:

> If the government census collectors come here, they only come to the first few streets which are close to the asphalt. Do you expect an employee who is paid a pitiful government salary to go deep into the pockets where most poor

people live, especially when many of these areas have a bad reputation – do you expect them to hop on our mini-trucks or walk for kilometres in these puddles of sewage?

Given that a high proportion of Greater Cairo's population live in informal settlements, if these are under-sampled in household surveys, the scale and depth of urban poverty will be undercounted. Sabry (2009) also notes other groups not living in informal settlements that were undercounted, including the homeless and those living in their workplace.

Even countries in which sample surveys are generally well constructed may face difficulties in poverty assessments because of a lack of information about the numbers of households in informal settlements. In many cities, a significant proportion of the population live in informal settlements not included in official statistics or maps. In South Africa, the Community Organization Resource Centre (CORC) profiled informal settlements in Cape Town in 2006 (CORC 2006). The profiling team began with official Metro maps which identified 176 informal settlements within the Metropolitan Area. CORC identified over 200 informal settlements and profiled 200. Twenty-one of the settlements identified by the City no longer existed as their residents had been relocated and/or evicted, and a further ten were known to the residents by names that were different from those recorded in the municipality. At the same time, 45 of the informal settlements identified by CORC did not have any recorded identity within the city administration. This suggests that results based on the 176 informal settlements would have been considerably under-sampled.

Sabry (2009, page 16) reports on a similar scale of confusion about the numbers of informal settlements in Egypt, suggesting that the causes of this inaccurate information are as much political as they are technical. Agarwal (2011) suggests that many informal settlements in cities in India are not included on official lists of 'slums', for instance, as 'they do not include unaccounted for and unrecognized informal settlements and people residing in poor quality housing in inner-city areas, on construction sites, in urban fringe areas and on pavements' (page 14). He also notes a study in Indore that showed that there were 438 officially recognized slums but that, by a process of mapping, found an additional 101 slums. Official statistics suggest that 18 per cent of Indore's population lived in 'slums' in 2001 but the true figure is likely to be more than 40 per cent (Taneja and Agarwal 2004). Many other cities have 'slum' populations that according to official figures are far lower than the population living in informal settlements (Agarwal 2011). In Cuttack, a city of around 600,000 inhabitants in Orissa, a survey of 'slums', or informal settlements, undertaken by Mahila Milan (the federation of women's savings groups) found a large number that were not included on government lists (Livengood and Kunte 2012).

A further problem that is not discussed in the assessments is the large number of tenants in some informal settlements, and the extent to which they may or may not be included in the sampling frame. In many instances it is difficult to get data from tenants (see Weru 2004; Makau, Dobson and Samia 2012) and to identify families or individuals living in back rooms of residences that look to surveyors as though they only hold one household (it may be that these other families or individuals are not 'allowed' to live there, so will seek to conceal their existence). It is almost certainly frightening for those undertaking the surveys to go into most illegal settlements or areas with tenements and cheap boarding houses, which often have a reputation for being dangerous places for outsiders to visit. Landlords may organize to oppose any survey in the informal settlements where they rent out houses or rooms (see, for instance, the cases of Nairobi in Weru 2004; Kampala in Makau, Dobson and Samia 2012; and Dar es Salaam in Hooper and Ortolano 2012).

It is always difficult to get an accurate sample frame of urban dwellers, and those who are left out are mostly going to be those who have very low incomes (as well as other disadvantages), those who are homeless (sleeping in public places or open spaces, for instance), those who are temporary (for example construction workers and their families who live on the construction sites – see Patel 1990), those who are 'visitors' in other people's homes, and those who sleep in workplaces. Bhan (2009) notes that many of Delhi's most vulnerable poor live in makeshift shacks or sleep on the street and remain uncounted in any assessment of who lives in 'slums'. The authors of the Cambodia poverty assessment are aware that the street homeless are excluded from their assessment of urban poverty (World Bank Cambodia 2006, page 47). Barbara Harriss-White (2005, page 881) discusses the plight of the destitute in India, noting that the 2001 census did not attempt to include them and that the '2001 count of the capital's homeless is reported as having been severely compromised'.

The inadequate allowance made for non-food needs

Most poverty lines use criteria to set an income level below which individuals or households are defined as 'poor' that pay little attention to non-food needs.[24] Yet in urban areas, especially the larger and/or more prosperous urban centres, the income level required to satisfy non-food needs is likely to be particularly high. One of the defining characteristics of cities is that access to living space, goods and services is highly monetized, with most or all goods and services having to be paid for. This includes access to housing, whether this is rented or self-built (with the housing costs being the cost of the land, the building and the materials used, any payments needed to get connections to utility networks and, where credit is used, the cost of credit). It includes access to safe water (often only available at public places where it has to be paid for and is expensive per litre) and a place to defecate (large sections of the urban poor do not have toilets in their homes and in many locations their only access is through pay toilets; Hardoy, Mitlin and Satterthwaite 2001; UN-HABITAT 2003a). It includes transport costs (income earners getting to and from work, children getting to and from school, all family members getting to and from services such as health care); these can be particularly expensive for the lowest income groups, who live in peripheral locations because this reduces their housing costs or allows them more space and/or possibilities for becoming house owners. It includes the costs of health care and medicines and of schools – both of which can be costly for low-income groups. There are also other costs, such as fuel (and, where it is available, electricity) and clothing which may be required for some jobs, for example by domestic workers. There are often payments that have to be made to community organizations, and costs of meeting social obligations; tragically, the cost of funerals has become particularly onerous for a large proportion of low-income families because of so much premature death (of infants and children; also of adults, with death rates boosted by AIDS).

In some cases rural households also have these costs but the nature of access to some goods and services means that needs and/or prices are related to the scale and concentration of population. For example, housing costs may be low in rural areas if it is easy to obtain land and there are building materials for traditional dwellings available. The availability of surface and ground water is likely to be better in lower-density settlements, and low densities also mean that it is more likely that households will be able to construct and use pit latrines, and perhaps also to guard against them contaminating the water table. Later in this chapter the section 'Defining the income needed for non-food needs' summarizes the findings of studies that have looked at the proportion of household income going to different non-food needs, including housing, transport, education, water, sanitation, health care, energy and childcare.

Poverty lines are generally derived from data on the cost of a 'minimum food basket' based on calorific intake, with some additional amount added for non-food needs. The review of how poverty is defined in Tabatabai with Fouad (1993) is particularly interesting, as it gives figures for the level of poverty for urban and rural populations for a great range of nations. For many, there are also details of how the poverty line was set. This shows that, until 1990, many poverty lines were set based only on the cost of a 'minimum' food basket that was considered to constitute an adequate diet in calorific terms. For those poverty lines that made allowances for non-food items, generally this was either based on an assumption that food expenditure would be 70–85 per cent of total expenditure, or based on what a reference group of 'poor' households spent on non-food items (with this group varying – for instance, sometimes it was the lowest 10 per cent, sometimes the lowest quintile). Thus, if allowance was made for non-food needs, it was assumed that only a small proportion of a poor household's income was required for this. The surveys from which data were drawn did not consider whether this small upward adjustment actually allowed poor people to afford non-food needs. Many studies show low-income urban households spending much more than 30 per cent of their income on non-food items and still living in poverty,[25] suggesting that the income required to pay for non-food needs was higher than that allowed for in setting poverty lines.

In recent years, there is some evidence of slightly more generous allowances being made for non-food items. This can be seen in many of the poverty lines in the most recently available documentation for individual nations on poverty assessments or poverty reduction strategy papers which show a larger upward adjustment for 'absolute poverty lines' relative to food poverty lines (see Table 2.3). Some upward adjustments remain low – for instance, for Ghana for 1998–99,

Table 2.3 Levels of urban poverty according to 'upper poverty lines', where some allowance is made for non-food needs, and the extent of the upward adjustment of 'food poverty' lines to take account of non-food needs. There is considerable variation as to whether adjustments are made for differentials in costs between locations, on what basis the adjustments are made (in many documents this is not clear) and which locational categories are used (for instance 'rural' versus 'urban', or different geographic regions)

Nation	Date	Poverty line as a multiple of 'minimum food basket' cost	Urban population below the poverty line (%)	Source
Sri Lanka	1995/96	1.2	25.0	Sri Lanka, Government of 2002
Madagascar	1999	1.21	52.1	Paternostro, Razafindravonona and Stifel 2001
Democratic Republic of the Congo	2006	1.24	61.5	Congo, Democratic Republic of the 2006
Ghana	1998/99	1.29	22.8 (4.7 in Accra)	Ghana, Republic of 2000
Chad	1995/96	1.33 N'Djamena 1.3 other towns	35.0 N'Djamena 39.3 other towns	Chad, Republic of 2003
Mauritania	1996	1.32*	26.8	Mauritania, Islamic Republic of 2000
Cambodia	2004	1.32 Phnom Penh 1.24 other urban	5 Phnom Penh 21 other urban	World Bank Cambodia 2006
Tanzania	2000/01	1.37	17.6–25.8	Tanzania, United Republic of 2002a, 2002b
Vietnam	1998	1.39	9.0	Vietnam, Socialist Republic of 2002
Mozambique	2003	1.43	51.6	World Bank Mozambique 2008
Zambia	2004	1.43	53.0	Zambia, Republic of 2006
Zambia	1998	1.44	56.0	Zambia, Republic of 2002a, 2002b
Niger	1993	1.5	52.0	Niger, République du 2002
Malawi	1997/98	1.5	54.9	Malawi, Government of 2000
Swaziland	1995	1.51	45.2	Swaziland, Kingdom of 1998
Yemen	1998	1.52	30.8	World Bank Yemen 2002

Nation	Date	Poverty line as a multiple of 'minimum food basket' cost	Urban population below the poverty line (%)	Source
Cameroon	2001	1.54	17.9 (10.9 for Douala; 13.3 for Yaounde)	Cameroon, Republic of 2002
Nepal	2003/4	1.63	9.6	World Bank Nepal 2006
Malawi	2007	1.61	25.4	Malawi, Republic of (undated); World Bank Malawi 2007
Gambia	1998	1.66	13.4 Greater Banjul 32.5 other urban	Gambia, Republic of 2002
China	1998/99	1.66	4.7	GHK and IIED 2004
Mozambique	1996/97	1.66	62.0	Mozambique, Republic of 2001
Nepal	1995/96	1.67	23.0	Prennushi 1999; Lanjouw, Prennushi and Zaidi 1999
Honduras	1999	1.68	57.3	World Bank Honduras 2001
Ivory Coast	1998	1.7		Côte d'Ivoire, République de la 2000
York, UK	1899	1.67–2.33**	9.9	Rowntree 1902
Panama	1997	1.74	15.3	World Bank Panama 1999
Ethiopia	1995/96	1.78	33.0	World Bank Ethiopia 1999
Nicaragua	1998	1.9	30.5	World Bank Nicaragua 2001
Bolivia	1999	1.8 La Paz 1.98 Cochabamba	48.4 La Paz 51.2 Cochabamba	World Bank Bolivia 2002
Ethiopia	2005	1.96	70.0	World Bank Ethiopia 2005
Kenya	2005/06	1.98	34.4	World Bank Kenya 2009
Paraguay	1996	2.0	39.5	Wodon 2000
Bolivia	1996	2.0	64.5	Wodon 2000
Ecuador	1996	2.0	55.2	Wodon 2000
Colombia	1996	2.0	52.2	Wodon 2000

Nation	Date	Poverty line as a multiple of 'minimum food basket' cost	Urban population below the poverty line (%)	Source
Mexico	1996	2.0	20.5	Wodon 2000
Brazil	1996	2.0	29.2	Wodon 2000
El Salvador	2002	2.0	28.5	World Bank El Salvador 2005
Dominican Republic	2004	2.0	34.7	World Bank Dominican Republic 2006
Haiti	2001	2.0	45 Port-au-Prince 76 other urban	International Monetary Fund 2008b
Liberia	2007	2.09	55.0	Liberia, Republic of 2008
Kenya	1997	2.1	49.0	Kenya, Government of 2000
Brazil***	2002/03	2.1	17.5	World Bank Brazil 2007
Costa Rica	2004	2.18	20.8	World Bank Costa Rica 2007
Guatemala	2000	2.26	27.1	World Bank Guatemala 2003
Uruguay	1998	2.75–3.1	24.7	World Bank Uruguay 2001
USA	1960s	3.0		Citro and Michael 1995

Source: Details and sources by country are provided in an annex available at http://www.routledge.com/books/details/9780415624671/

* The poverty line for Mauritania was not based on the cost of food but on a poverty line based on US$1 a day.

** Drawn from B. Seebohm Rowntree's 1899 survey (Rowntree 1902). The Engel coefficient – the proportion of family income spent on food – varied according to the size of the family and the number of children. So different poverty lines were established to allow for this, for instance for families with two adults and five children it was 1.67, for single adults it was 2.33.

*** There was also a poverty line set at 3.6 times the food poverty line – which would have classified half the urban population as below the poverty line.

which may explain why there was apparently so little 'poverty' in Accra, yet, as noted earlier, housing and living conditions and basic service provision for large sections of Accra's population remain very poor.

Part of the explanation for a nation having poverty lines set too low for particular cities is that there is a single urban average, as if low-income groups faced similar non-food costs in all urban areas in a nation. Here, there is no recognition that non-food costs can be particularly high in the largest or most prosperous cities. Some poverty studies set higher poverty lines for specific cities – as did, for instance, the assessment in Cambodia in 2004, or Tanzania in 2000–01. But an accurate assessment of non-food needs may need to be made for each city, not just the largest city (see, for instance, the different cost estimates for non-food needs in Zambia's six largest urban centres in Chibuye 2011). If the line is set too low for the major cities then the numbers in poverty will be underestimated, particularly if most of the urban population lives in these cities.

The methodology used to calculate the non-food expenditure needed to avoid poverty may lie at the centre of the problem. The ways in which non-food requirements have been calculated appear arbitrary. In some instances, the allowance for non-food items is based on some multiple of the cost of a minimum food basket, which is made only on the basis of a recognition that there are non-food items that need to be purchased to avoid poverty, with no attempt to calculate how much non-food needs cost. This may be as little as 20 per cent of the food costs or twice food costs (see Table 2.3). It may be based on the cost of a specified bundle of non-food items, in which case its appropriateness depends on the appropriateness of the bundle and the accuracy of price data. Or the allowance for non-food needs may be based on what some defined set of poor households spend on non-food needs.

If the allowance for non-food needs is based on the cost of specified non-food goods or on what a particular set of households spend on specified non-food goods, there are difficulties in knowing what non-food items are 'needs'; also in identifying who should decide what should be included. It appears that most allowances for non-food needs calculated in this way are ungenerous to the point of being unrealistic for many urban contexts. An assessment of poverty in Kenya by the World Bank defined the absolute poverty line as 'the minimum level of expenditure deemed necessary to satisfy a person's food requirements plus the consumption of a few non-food necessities' (World Bank Kenya 1995, page 8). Many poverty lines make no allowance for housing or transport. Most allowances rule out any expenditure on entertainment, cigarettes or alcohol. Expenditure on social obligations, such as weddings, dowries and funerals, also tends to fall outside the lists.[26]

Expenditure on transport may not be considered a 'need' because this is considered not to meet a basic need directly but rather indirectly, through access to needs such as work, education and health services. Deaton and Zaidi (2002), in a paper providing guidelines for constructing consumption aggregates from household survey data for setting poverty lines, acknowledge the problems faced by individuals who have high costs for 'regrettable necessities' (goods and services that yield no welfare in their own right but that have to be purchased), such as transport-to-work. They note that consumption expenditure for such individuals may overstate their welfare. However, they suggest that for those who have high transport-to-work costs, it is not possible to distinguish between those who cannot avoid these costs and those who can (for instance, those who choose to live in a pleasant suburb with high transport-to-work costs). So they suggest that no allowance should be made, while recognizing the 'occasional injustice' in doing so. In many urban contexts, not allowing for transport costs in poverty lines is much more than an 'occasional injustice'.

The way in which allowances in poverty lines for non-food needs may be based on questionable assumptions is illustrated by Good's (1999) discussion of the setting of the poverty line for Botswana in 1991. This reveals attitudes to 'the poor' that have much in common with how the Victorian middle classes viewed poverty in the United Kingdom during the nineteenth century. All measures were taken to keep poverty lines as low as possible. No allowance was made for children growing out of their clothes before they were worn out. There was no allowance for socks (except for school uniform), stockings, overcoats or waterproofs. There was no allocation for furniture, beds, mattresses, chairs or tables, except a bench so that 'the head of household could discharge [his] social obligation ... towards an important visitor' (Botswana, Republic of 1991, quoted in Good 1999, page 196). Blankets and cooking pots were allowed, but their durability was emphasized, stressing that 'with care some could last a lifetime'. There was no allowance for forks, knives, spoons, candles, cups, etc. A poor person's health could be covered through two visits a year to a government clinic and one consultation 'with the traditional doctor'. No allowance was made for travelling (with a comment that the poor would have to walk if they were to seek work or attend social functions). And expenditure on alcohol or cigarettes was ruled out, as were sweets, soft drinks, snacks, toys, books or writing materials (Good 1999).

This example from Botswana may be an extreme one, but much of the literature on setting poverty lines contains explicit comments about the need to keep any allowance for non-food costs to a minimum, or implicit assumptions about what 'poor' households deserve for food. The poverty reduction strategy paper for Zambia notes that the food basket used to set the poverty line is very modest, and is based on a minimal calorific requirement that excludes meat, chicken and fish, and that the measurement 'has also not fully factored in such basic needs of the people as shelter, education, health care, lighting, clothing, footwear and transport' (Zambia, Republic of 2002a, page 22). As is the case with food poverty lines, there is also an assumption that the money available to a family is spent in the most rational way and only on 'needs' (with nothing spent on entertainment or toys for children, for example), and that there are no economic obligations beyond the basic nuclear family, including debt repayments (see, for instance, Wratten 1995 and Maxwell 1998).

Data problems, such as the lack of a recent household income or expenditure survey, may hamper the setting of any allowance in poverty lines for non-food needs. It is also difficult to define and measure the income needed for housing, unless it is rented (and data on rental levels can be obtained[27]), and for the acquisition of any durable good (Ministry of Planning and Finance, Government of Mozambique *et al.* 1998).

The upward adjustment of poverty lines for non-food needs is now usually based on data on the expenditure by particular sets of 'low-income households' on non-food items. This avoids the difficulties noted above in defining 'the income needed for non-food needs' or collecting data on costs of non-food needs. Ravallion (1998) argues the merits of this approach and emphasizes that the allowance for non-food needs should be anchored in the consumption behaviour of the poor.

The two most common ways of doing this appear to be:

- The 'cost of basic needs' method, with the income that a household needs being based on the cost of a food basket, with allowance for non-food needs based on what households whose total expenditure or food expenditure is equal to the food poverty line spend on non-food items. Many poverty assessments work with a lower and a higher poverty line, with the first being based on the non-food expenditures of a sample whose total income equals the food poverty line and the second being based on the non-food expenditure of a sample whose food expenditure equals the food poverty line.
- The 'food-energy intake' method, based on the lowest income level at which households who appear to eat enough spend (on food and on non-food items). Ravallion (1998) notes the advantage of this method's relatively modest data requirements.

Where poverty lines are adjusted for the cost of non-food items (and some are not), most seem to use the first of these methods. Most also base the allowance for non-food needs on what the poorest households spend on non-food items. For instance, allowance for non-food items is based on:

- what the poor who are right on the food poverty line spend on non-food items in Cameroon, Cambodia, Ghana, Guatemala, Kenya, Mongolia, Mozambique, Panama and Peru; also for the lower poverty line in Bangladesh, Brazil and Ethiopia
- what the poor whose expenditure on food is enough to meet their minimum food requirements (plus or minus 5–10 per cent) spend on non-food items in Democratic Republic of the Congo, Guatemala, Liberia, Malawi, Nepal, Vietnam; also for the upper poverty line in Bangladesh, Brazil and Ethiopia
- what the poorest 72 per cent of rural households spend on non-food items in Haiti
- what the poorest 25 per cent of the population spend on non-food items in Tanzania
- what the average household in the middle quintile of all households nationally spends on non-food items (28 per cent of consumption) in Zambia

- an adjustment using the Engel curve methodology in Bolivia
- what the national population spend on non-food items in the Dominican Republic.

If the allowance for non-food needs is based on what a specified reference group spends on non-food items, the size of this allowance is greatly influenced by which reference group is chosen – for instance, those whose total expenditure is at the food poverty line, the poorest 10 per cent, poorest 20 per cent or poorest half of the total population.[28]

It is perhaps worth noting that when the US government first set an income-based poverty line in the early 1960s, it based the allowance for non-food needs on the proportion of household income spent on non-food items for the whole US population (Citro and Michael 1995). This led to a poverty line set at three times the cost of a 'minimum food basket', which is notably higher than virtually all the poverty lines used in low- and middle-income nations today. The moderate poverty line in the Dominican Republic in 2004 also based its non-food component on this (World Bank Dominican Republic 2006). Even in the first recorded use of an income-based poverty line – by Rowntree in the city of York in Victorian England in an 1899 study – the poverty line was set much higher than for most nations today. Rowntree (1902) also stressed that the poverty line used was set very low and that those below it had insufficient to obtain 'the minimum necessaries for the maintenance of physical efficiency'. The poverty line was set at 2.33 times the cost of a minimum food basket for single adults and between 1.67 and 1.76 the cost of a minimum food basket for households with two adults and one or more child.

There seems to be little questioning of the validity of basing the allowance for 'non-food' needs on the non-food expenditure of the groups likely to have the least adequate provision for non-food needs. What poor groups spend on non-food items is not a measure of the income needed to afford essential non-food items, but simply the expenditure by a particular set of low-income households on non-food items, regardless of whether their needs are met. This is especially the case if the allowance for non-food needs is based on the non-food expenditure of households whose *total* income is just sufficient to afford minimum food requirements. As Mearns (2004) notes, this implies that individuals or households with below-poverty-line incomes will have to remain undernourished if they are to afford non-food needs. So the reference group for defining how much households are allowed for non-food needs within poverty lines are those who are guaranteed not to have enough for non-food needs.

As a result, there are often discrepancies between the methodology used for calculating poverty lines and the detail contained in poverty assessments. There are two aspects to this. The first is the difficulties that low-income households face in securing adequate access to non-food necessities – for instance access to water and to toilets. The second is evidence of particularly high costs that have to be paid for non-food needs, such that these take up a high proportion of total income even when these needs are inadequately addressed – as, again, in the case of access to water and to toilets. Chapter 3 will describe in some detail the appalling living conditions in informal settlements in Nairobi which house around half the city's population, 'with only 3 percent of households living in housing with a permanent wall, access to piped water, and an electricity connection' and the very low percentage with their own latrine, meaning they had to rely on shared or public toilets or 'flying-toilets' – defecation into plastic bags or other waste material that is then thrown away (World Bank Kenya 2009, page 70). In Kangemi and Mukuru, two informal settlements, 'toilet facilities are more expensive than food. Research on poverty eradication in Kibera last year showed that toilet facilities cost KSh5 (8 US cents) per visit per family member, regardless of the nature of the call'[29] (page 58). There are further costs in addition to the monetary expenditures. An Amnesty International (2010) report entitled *Insecurity and Indignity: Women's Experiences in the Slums of Nairobi, Kenya* documents how the lack of proximate sanitation facilities is a major risk to women, most of whom have to walk more than 300 metres to a toilet. The women spoke about how it was risky for them to walk alone in the settlement after seven in the evening, and specifically about the dangers of rape. All this points to housing expenditures being too low to purchase safe and secure housing, with households paying the minimum required to ensure access to shelter. And, as the Kenya poverty assessment (World Bank Kenya 2009) points out, it can cost more for low-income households to secure basic services; slum dwellers in Nairobi pay approximately eight times more for water per litre than their non-slum counterparts.

Other poverty assessments note the difficulties that the lowest income households face in securing adequate access to non-food necessities – for instance the assessment for Zambia, where 32 per cent of urban households in the lowest income quintile secure their water from unprotected sources (World Bank Zambia 2007, page 86):

> Residents of informal urban settlements generally rely on self-made shallow wells for water supply and on pit latrines for disposal of human waste, which poses serious health challenges, because of possible contamination of the water. The situation is worsened by the fact that most residents cannot afford to either boil or chlorinate their drinking water. As a result, they generally drink untreated water and are extremely vulnerable to intestinal illnesses.

For Uganda, 'In some cases, such as travel to work and the collection of water, urban households may face higher financial costs that are not fully reflected in the CPI [Consumer price index]' (Uganda, Republic of 2004, page 254).

Some poverty assessments recognize the very poor housing conditions in which large sections of the urban population live. In the case of Cambodia, for example, the poverty assessment (World Bank Cambodia 2006, page 35) argues that 'critical problems of the urban poor revolve around security of housing rights'. In the case of Pakistan, the poverty assessment recognizes that '[o]ne of the more neglected, yet important, correlates of urban poverty and vulnerability is the lack of secure and adequate housing' (World Bank Pakistan 2002, page xiv). The

Vietnam poverty reduction strategy paper (PRSP; Vietnam, Socialist Republic of 2006, page 40) notes that there are a 'lot of difficulties in the provision of housing for the urban poor, workers in industrial zones and beneficiaries of social welfare'. The Uganda plan also highlights the problems the urban poor face in securing access to housing and sanitation (Uganda, Republic of 2005, page 18).

The particular difficulties in incorporating housing quality and cost in poverty lines

Assessing how to factor housing costs into poverty lines can be particularly problematic. Data can be drawn from tenants on the costs paid for housing but the costs they pay are not the same as those facing owner-occupiers. So how can housing costs be established for non-tenants? Owner-occupiers may be facing significant costs for housing, for instance in building, rebuilding and repairing and in interest, if loans have been taken to help pay for the land (where payments are made) and the building. Then there is the problem that what tenants or owner-occupiers pay for housing is hardly an appropriate basis for setting the cost of adequate housing if they live in poor quality, overcrowded housing.

In a study of India's urban population, Chandrasekhar and Montgomery (2010) drew on two official surveys – one on expenditures, the other on housing conditions – to analyse housing characteristics and estimate the costs of minimally adequate housing. Their analysis allowed them to estimate the cost of a house that is safe from flooding and includes water supplies in the building (but not the dwelling), access to electricity, a shared toilet, non-dirt flooring and adequate ventilation. They note that the all-India urban poverty line makes very inadequate provision for the cost of housing and suggest that allowing for the cost of even very modest quality accommodation would require a significant upward adjustment in the official poverty line.

It is also often difficult to get accurate data from tenants as to how much they pay for accommodation, perhaps especially in informal settlements. In the strategy paper for Pakistan, a significant number of households appear not to report the costs they incur and the authors conclude that housing is one of the most problematic areas, with lack of reporting for many households leading to their rental costs having to be estimated (Pakistan, Government of 2003, page 125).

In most instances, it is likely that the larger and more successful the urban centre, the higher the cost of 'minimally adequate' housing, and thus the higher the adjustment for housing needed in poverty lines. In addition, often the larger and more successful the urban centre, the higher the housing costs paid by low-income households and the higher the share of their income spent on housing. The main exceptions to this will be for those living in very poor conditions in peripheral and/or dangerous sites (which bring down the prices) and those able to access land on which they can build at below its cost (for instance by illegally occupying it). The costs of land for housing may also be lessened by purchasing illegal subdivisions – here the land occupation is not illegal but the land's development for housing is (and standards are usually lower in, for instance, plot sizes and infrastructure provision). All this implies that the allowance for housing in poverty lines needs to be adjusted to actual housing costs in each urban centre – or at least with any 'urban' average adjusted for the more prosperous or larger cities.[30]

Although the data needed to provide city-specific estimates of the cost of 'minimally adequate' housing is not available, some poverty assessments at least acknowledge this issue. The Pakistan poverty strategy reports on a detailed assessment of the expenditures of both urban and rural households. This shows that urban and rural households allocate broadly similar shares of their income to many expenditure categories but that the expenditure shares in the case of housing differ by 9 percentage points: housing is 8.3 per cent of total expenditure in rural areas and 17.4 per cent in the case of urban households (World Bank Pakistan 2002, page 35).

Chibuye (2011) reports similar details drawn from the Zambian government's poverty assessment and concludes that, 'on average, non-food items took up 52% of total household expenditure, with urban households recording a much higher share (62%) than rural households (35%)' (page 18). This paper is also unusual in that it collects data on housing costs for Lusaka and four other urban centres, allowing the cost of a minimum house – a house that meets needs of inhabitants – to be established. It also shows that if poverty lines were adjusted to allow a household to afford such a house, it would mean a very large increase in the poverty line and a much higher proportion of Zambia's urban population categorized as poor (Chibuye 2011).

Sabry (2009) considers what the non-food allowance estimated by the World Bank might actually buy the urban poor in Egypt. The monthly non-food allowance for the lower poverty lines was not enough to cover just the costs of (very inadequate) housing, education and transport for many households.

Defining the income needed for non-food needs

Considerable care is needed in drawing on data on the spending of low-income groups (or food-poor groups) on housing and other non-food items as a basis for defining what is needed for urban households. Their non-food expenditure is often simply an indication of the high cost of inadequate provision. It is not appropriate to base what low-income households need for housing, schooling and health care on what they actually spend on these, when these same households cannot afford to spend enough to get adequate housing, schooling and health care. Setting allowances for housing costs within poverty lines based on what a particular set of 'low-income households' spend on housing often means allocating only enough for low-income households to afford very low quality, inadequate accommodation – for instance, whole households living in small one-room shacks made of temporary materials, that they construct themselves, on land sites that are insecure, dangerous and poorly located with regard to income-earning opportunities, and with very inadequate or no provision for water, sanitation or drainage. A low-income family that is paying 20 per cent of its income to rent a tiny room with no piped water supply and no sanitation facility, and another 10 per cent on water purchased from a vendor (but with the water costs too high to allow them to buy enough to meet household needs) is not avoiding deprivation by spending 30 per cent of its income on these. It may need to spend the equivalent of 60 or more per cent of its income to get adequate quality accommodation with adequate provision for water and sanitation, but it cannot do so because other costs have to be met – food, fuel, keeping children at school, transport fares to and from work and services.... The extent to which large sections of the population in most cities in Africa, Asia and Latin America live in conditions such as these has been documented for many years,[31] but this has been all but ignored by most discussions on how to set poverty lines. In most cities, what poorer groups spend on housing is a very inadequate basis for estimating what income they need in order to get reasonable quality housing. In India, for example, poverty lines can be set so low that a significant proportion of people living on pavements are not classified as 'poor'.[32]

Expenditure data showing low expenditure on food or non-food essentials may be the result of low-income groups going without – for instance, cutting back on essential food expenditures to keep children at school (see Mupedziswa and Gumbo 1998) or not seeking treatment for illness or injury (which, in expenditure data, could be interpreted as not needing to spend much on health care). They may be spending less on education because their children do not go to school, and spending less on housing because they live in the streets or squat; see, for instance, the analysis of expenditures by urban households in Dhaka with below-poverty-line incomes which shows that the poorest groups (with incomes of less than 43 per cent of the poverty line income) spent a lower proportion of their incomes on housing and education than those whose incomes were 43–100 per cent of the poverty line (Islam *et al.* 1997). Low-income groups often spend less on water by using dirty, contaminated water for most of their household needs. Low-income households that have no toilet in their home often spend less on using pay-toilets by defecating in the open. They often spend less on transport because they walk very long distances to and from work or services and shops.

Chibuye (2011) compares the official (government) assessment of non-food needs in Zambia with the costs of non-food needs in Lusaka as estimated by the Jesuit Centre for Theological Reflection (JCTR). This civil society group has been collecting information on the cost of living since the early 1990s (its contribution is discussed in the World Bank's poverty assessment for that country; World Bank Zambia 2007). In 2006, the official figure for the cost of non-food needs used in setting the poverty line was K88,709 a month, but the cost of essential non-food needs in Lusaka as estimated by the Centre was more than ten times this amount – K996,100 – because the official figure made no allowance at all for the costs of adequate housing, and insufficient allowance for fuel, soap, electricity and water. Figure 2.1 shows the dramatic differences between the costs of food and non-food needs given in official figures and those estimated by the JCTR, for Lusaka and five other urban centres. Even these much higher figures for the cost of non-food needs do not include costs for clothing, education, health or transport. About two thirds of this non-food cost was taken up, according to the Centre's estimates, by the cost of adequate housing.

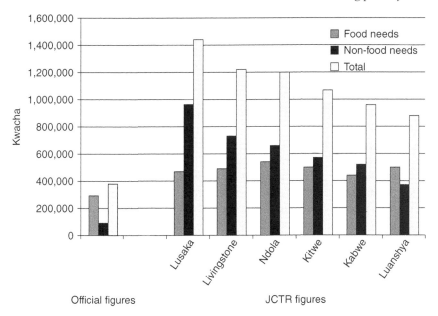

Figure 2.1 Official and JCTR poverty lines in Zambia, 2006

Source: Chibuye (2011)

Many of the studies providing the data from which the Engel coefficient (the proportion of income spent on food) is calculated draw on national or rural expenditure data, not on expenditure data for individual cities. A relatively small change in the Engel coefficient can have a large impact on the poverty line (Mejía and Vos 1997). If the calculation of the income required for non-food needs is based on national data on household expenditure, it will underestimate the income needed in locations where non-food needs are particularly costly, which is likely to be mainly in the larger or more prosperous cities. Low-income groups with livelihoods in high-cost cities may have to spend a high proportion of their income on non-food needs, which means a low Engel coefficient, which is then judged to mean they are not poor. A declining proportion of a household's income spent on food is often taken to mean a decline in poverty, but this might be because of increased costs for non-food needs – for instance for water, transport to and from work, rent or school fees.

Such difficulties have resulted in some nations measuring basic needs in housing separately. Hardoy with Almansi (2011, page 11) explain the criteria used by the government of Argentina to define basic needs poverty: one or more of overcrowding (more than three per room), inadequate housing quality (tenant rooms, vulnerable construction), absence of sanitation or non-water latrines, school-age children not going to school and/or a high number of dependants with low education (four or more dependants to each economically active person or household head with education below third grade). An alternative and more integrated approach to poverty measurement has been designed but not yet implemented which includes absolute costs for food, transport, education, health and rent (Hardoy with Almansi 2011).

Equivalence scales

Another issue to consider in relation to the way consumption-based poverty lines may understate (or overstate) the scale and depth of poverty is whether equivalence scales are used to adjust household data to produce statistics for the proportion of people who are poor, and how these scales are used. Often, the unit for expenditure or income data is the household, but most statistics on poverty refer to individual status. In these cases, the household data must be scaled down to represent an individual. When the literature does not ignore the problem of accounting for the effect of household size on expenditure (and it has become more common for equivalence scales to be used), it is not always apparent how particular authors have adjusted their data to handle this problem (Grewe and Becker 2001).

Many governments ignore differences in household size and in the number of dependants, although there is some evidence suggesting that adjustments for household size can make a significant difference to poverty estimates (Grewe and Becker 2001). The differences in the income needed to avoid poverty between households of different sizes and compositions (infants, young children, adults of working age, non-working adults including those unable to work or who have retired, etc.) are often taken into account using 'equivalence scales', which may either be imposed externally or constructed from survey data. Equivalence scales adjust for demographic differences in the household. There have also been attempts to recognize the existence of economies of scale in the household – for instance, feeding, housing and providing consumer durables for six people is not six times the cost for one person (see, for instance, Deaton and Zaidi 2002).

Setting accurate equivalence scales is difficult, even in high-income nations with much richer and more detailed data available. A review on measuring poverty in the USA noted the lack of agreement on how equivalence scales should be calculated, and that many different scales are found which have 'very different implications for the total number of people in poverty as well as the distribution of poverty among families of different types' (Citro and Michael 1995, page 160). Where equivalence scales are used, it may be that only food items are considered (Deaton and Paxson 1995) and if this is the case they may give inadequate attention to non-food costs.

This can be seen in how equivalence scales are used with respect to children. Equivalence scales assume that children under 18 consume less than adults (and so need less income to ensure their consumption needs are met), so poverty lines for households with children are adjusted downwards. The recommended scale of this downward adjustment can be large. Deaton and Zaidi (2002), for instance, note that 'Most of the literature – as well as common sense – suggests that children are relatively more expensive in industrialized countries (school fees, entertainment, clothes, etc.) and relatively cheap in poorer agricultural economies' (page 52). They suggest that the cost of each child is close to the cost of each adult in the USA and Western Europe and perhaps as low as 0.25 or 0.3 times the cost of each adult in the poorest economies. But whether or not costs for children are lower than for adults (and by how much) depends on many factors, such as the cost of keeping children at school, whether day care has to be paid for to allow one or more adult to increase their income-earning possibilities, the cost of getting children treatment and medicines when they are sick (and how often they are in need of treatment and medicines), the cost of keeping them clothed and with shoes that fit as they grow.... Also, small children are unable to consume the quantities of low-nutrient foods necessary to meet their growth needs – is their need for more nutritious (and generally more expensive) food considered when setting equivalence scales?

Perhaps equivalence scales developed in nations where children have free access to schools (and where associated items such as stationery, text books, exam fees, school lunches and transport to and from school are also provided free) and health services (including free or subsidized medicines) are being applied in nations where none of these are available to low-income households. For those living in poor quality homes with inadequate provision for water, sanitation, drainage and garbage removal, infants and children are likely to need more frequent visits to health services and more medicines, and this can be expensive. There is also the loss of income when working adults have to stay at home to nurse sick children. And, as discussed in the section on costs for non-food essentials, households living in informal settlements may have to pay fees to private schools because they cannot get their children into government schools. This may make children who go to school and who visit health services and get medicines when they are sick as costly as adults, or at least more costly than the equivalence scales assume.

Extreme poverty lines

Most governments set lower poverty lines that claim to measure 'extreme poverty' and that are based only on the cost of a minimum food basket. These are sometimes called food poverty lines. Among the 59 nations whose methods for defining poverty were assessed, virtually all use an extreme poverty line, while some set this as the only poverty line (implying that it is valid to measure poverty based on income levels that make no allowance for non-food needs). It is still common for documents on poverty to stress that the proportion of the population in 'extreme poverty' is much higher in rural areas than in urban areas. This is often stated with no explicit recognition of the higher income needed to avoid poverty (including the income needed to pay for many non-food needs) in many urban areas.

If we were to take high infant and child mortality rates as an indicator with some validity in indicating extreme poverty, in many sub-Saharan African nations the differences in such mortality rates between rural and urban areas appear to be much less than the discourse on poverty – which emphasizes that rates of extreme poverty are much higher in rural than in urban areas – would imply. As Chapter 3 describes, there are several nations in which recent Demographic and Health Surveys have shown that under-five mortality rates are higher in urban areas than in rural areas and many more in which there is little difference between urban and rural rates.

In most urban contexts, where access to virtually all needs is monetized, a poverty line based only on the cost of food should be recognized as having no validity, unless it is used to ensure that those facing 'extreme poverty' get the necessary support. So those identified as being in extreme poverty get support to allow them to meet their nutritional requirements and non-food needs – for instance, accommodation that has adequate provision for water and sanitation, and also access to health care and schools. The lower poverty line measuring extreme poverty based only on the income needed to afford an adequate food basket had more validity in European high-income countries at a time when access to health care, education (and often childcare or nursery schools) was free, where virtually all housing had adequate provision for water, sanitation and drainage, and where there were additional welfare measures aimed at finding accommodation for those with below-poverty-line incomes or covering their housing costs. But, as Beck (1994) notes, this concept has been transferred uncritically to nations where few if any of these conditions are present.

A further issue that should be taken into account when assessing extreme poverty or food poverty is the actual cost of food that is incurred by low-income households through their normal purchasing habits. Chibuye (2011) presents a detailed assessment of urban poverty levels in Zambia using both the government's methodology for required 'food baskets' and that of the Jesuit Centre for Theological Reflection. The Centre's research shows that both of these assessments of the minimum income required to avoid poverty may be misleading because the costs of the required quantities are based on relatively large purchases – for example, in the case of maize meal, the purchase of 25-kg bags. In practice, low-income households do not purchase in these quantities but buy smaller units of repackaged goods. In part this reflects the nature of incomes in the informal sector, where money may be secured daily, or every few days in the case of trading. However, it may also reflect the need to manage consumption within the family. The cost implications are significant. Chibuye (2011, page 16) elaborates:

> According to the Satellite Homes Survey … a 400g packet of mealie meal costs on average K1500, resulting in household expenditure of K93,750 for 25kg. The average nominal price for a 25kg bag of mealie meal for May 2010 in Lusaka was K64,300, making the sub-optimal packages more expensive by 31%. Middle-income households would purchase mealie meal in 25kg bags. This pattern extends to sugar, salt, and soap, among other goods. It generally costs significantly more to buy these goods in sub-optimal packets but neither 'basket' takes this into account.

Sabry (2009, page 23) makes a very similar point in relation to Egypt, suggesting that the urban poor may be paying 20 per cent more for oil because they purchase in smaller units. In this case, she suggests it is because men typically give women enough money to purchase food for the day. As noted earlier in this chapter, interviews with women living in informal settlements in Buenos Aires highlighted that they bought much of the food for their families in small quantities and locally because they only have enough money once or twice a month to be able to go to supermarkets (Hardoy with Almansi 2011).

How ineffective local governance increases non-food costs

Where local government institutions are too weak or ineffective to ensure provision of basic infrastructure and services or choose not to ensure provision for those in informal settlements, the gap between official poverty lines and the income needed to avoid living in poverty can be particularly high.

The term 'governance' is used in the title of this section because it encompasses both the performance of government institutions (political, bureaucratic and legislative) and the nature and quality of their relationships with civil society actors (including citizens, community organizations and NGOs). Local government responsibilities for infrastructure and service provision may be realized through support for private and community provision – and provision in partnership with urban poor organizations often allows under-resourced local authorities to considerably increase the scale and effectiveness of their infrastructure and service provision (a point to which we return in the companion volume to this).

As discussed in more detail later (see the section 'Costs for non-food essentials'), studies of the expenditures of low-income urban households show that many face particularly high costs for many non-food essentials – typically for water from vendors or kiosks, sanitation from pay-as-you-use facilities, health care and medicines (especially where there are no government or non-profit services), housing rent or the cost of land and self-build, schools (especially where government provision is poor or unavailable) and public transport (especially where low-income groups choose peripheral or distant locations because the land is cheaper or households have more chance of developing their own homes without fear of eviction). More effective local governance can reduce these costs or provide better living conditions, so reducing poverty without increasing incomes. Most urban settings also provide agglomeration economies for infrastructure and services, which means greater possibilities for providing water piped into homes, toilets linked to sewers, accessible health care and good quality public transport, which in turn should reduce the gap between good quality provision and what poor households can afford to pay.

Thus, in most urban contexts, whether or not a household has an income that is above or below a consumption-based poverty line may have little bearing on their access to many essential goods or services. In most urban contexts, this access is influenced by many other factors, including the quality of local governance and individual or household factors such as whether the household has a legal address, educational level, the information available, legal rights (and whether there are provisions to ensure these are respected), gender (including, in many locations, constraints on women's opportunities for obtaining land, credit, house ownership, etc.) and political affiliations.

Little or no adjustment for variations in costs and prices within nations

Where a poverty line is used, whether based on price or consumption data, it has little validity unless it accurately reflects the income level that an individual or household needs to avoid poverty in their particular neighbourhood (whether it is a village, small town, city or large metropolis).

The income level needed to avoid poverty is likely to vary considerably between different locations within nations. It is likely to be particularly high in larger or more prosperous urban centres. It may be that price differences between locations for some essential goods and services are unusually high in some low- and middle-income countries because of the large differences between locations in the extent to which access is monetized and the local economy is incorporated into wider regional, national or global economies. For instance, in India there are likely to be very large differences in the price of the cheapest reasonable quality, secure, legal shelter between, say, Mumbai and most small urban centres, which serve primarily as administrative centres within poor farming regions where much production is still subsistence level. In sub-Saharan Africa, one would expect large differences in the price of reasonable quality, secure, legal shelters between national capitals and most small urban centres in low-income regions. It is likely that the more inadequate the quality of local governance with regard to provision for infrastructure and services, and land-use planning and management (especially as this influences the supply and price of legal land available for housing), the higher the price of the cheapest reasonable quality accommodation relative to local incomes will be. Obviously, the price of all housing with infrastructure and services is influenced by the quality and extent of infrastructure and service provision; where provision lags far behind need and demand, the price of housing with adequate provision becomes inflated. The price of the cheapest legal house can be much increased by expensive and slow official regulatory frameworks for approval of land subdivisions and by unnecessarily large minimum plot sizes – and decreased if more realistic standards are applied and land approval measures streamlined (Mitlin and Muller 2004).

The need for poverty lines to be adjusted so that they reflect the real costs of food and non-food essentials in each location is widely acknowledged in the poverty literature (see, for instance, Montgomery *et al.* 2003), yet governments and international agencies still appear to struggle with appropriate adjustments when setting poverty lines. In an analysis of how 53 countries approach poverty assessments and poverty lines, it appears that 12 use poverty lines with no allowance made for spatial differences, 9 use a simple differentiation between urban and rural and 25 follow a more complex differentiation. There were seven countries for which the approach to taking account of cost of living differences could not be ascertained.

The nations that apply the same poverty line throughout their national territory are basing their approach on an assumption that the income needed to avoid poverty is the same in all locations, from the largest and most prosperous cities to small rural settlements. Over the last 10 to 15 years, examples of this approach have become fewer – so it seems that increasing numbers of national governments are making some adjustment, typically an upward adjustment of the poverty line for 'urban areas'. If the poverty definitions used in recent poverty assessments or poverty reduction strategy papers are compared to the definitions listed in Tabatabai with Fouad (1993), it appears that many more nations are making adjustments for regional variations than in the 1980s or early 1990s. A poverty assessment for Togo notes that,

> When applied to a country with considerable regional variation, overall poverty lines can become meaningless. In Togo, setting a single national poverty line that is applied to the population as a whole results in significant over-estimates of the number of poor households in rural communities compared to urban communities, particularly in the north.
>
> (World Bank Togo 1996, page 5).

But a general adjustment for 'urban areas' still misses the fact that in most nations there are likely to be large differences between urban centres, so income poverty may still be understated for the urban locations where prices are particularly high.[33] It might overstate income poverty in some of the poorer (and generally smaller) urban centres. In addition, it may be that the adjustments for spatial variations in the cost of living are based on food prices when the spatial variation in the cost of non-food items is greater (Hentschel and Lanjouw 1996).

For those nations in which provision is made for spatial variations in the income needed to avoid poverty, this can be in the form of adjustments by geographic region, province or state, adjustments between urban and rural, or a combination of the two.[34] In some nations there is simply an adjustment for all urban areas (for instance in Kenya); in others, adjustment is made for multiple areas (for instance, for the capital or largest city, 'other urban centres' and rural areas, as in Gambia and Tanzania). In Yemen's 1998 assessment (Yemen, Republic of 2002), poverty lines were adjusted both regionally (by governorate) and between rural and urban areas, although unusually rural poverty lines were set slightly higher than urban poverty lines).

Of course, the appropriateness of the allowances made for spatial variations in poverty lines depends on whether these actually measure spatial differences in the income levels needed to avoid poverty. For instance, there may be little data available on prices for non-food items, or all the data that are available for non-food items are for prices in shops or markets, and so no account is taken of the spatial variations in spending on items such as transport, health care, water bills, housing and keeping children in school.

Perhaps the most astonishing gap revealed by the review of literature on which this chapter draws is the lack of research examining how much income would be needed in particular locations to allow an individual or household to avoid poverty. It would be revealing to see for different urban and rural locations (and different locations within cities) the income levels at which households would typically be able to afford sufficient food, a legal, reasonable quality house with adequate provision for water, sanitation and electricity (and the utility bills these entail), schooling for their children, and health care and treatment for those who are sick. It is likely that the income needed would be far above official poverty lines in many urban locations in most nations.

In discussing the adjustments to poverty lines needed to allow for differences between locations, there may be an assumption that urban poverty is over- rather than understated. For instance, Ravallion (1998), discussing the food-energy intake method, suggests that it is likely to overstate urban poverty because urban dwellers may spend more on food since non-food items are cheaper, have lower activity levels and so need less food, have different tastes and spend more per calorie (so it is choice rather than need that makes them spend more on food), pay lower prices for other goods and services and consume a diet that is nutritionally better balanced because of better access to health care and schooling. But it can also be suggested that urban households spend more on food (or pay more per calorie) because of constraints on time for preparing food or the high cost of fuel; due to the practice of buying in small quantities, reflecting the pattern of income and the control of consumption; because of the very high activity levels that many groups within the urban labour force have (which Ravallion acknowledges); and because significant sections of the urban population face higher costs for many non-food necessities (as discussed in more detail later). Deaton and Tarozzi (2000) suggest that urban poverty is overstated in India because the urban poverty line is set too high – but, as the authors admit, the rural and urban poverty lines omit the costs of housing and transport.[35] For many urban poor households (especially those living in larger or more prosperous cities), these are major costs – or, if they are not, it is because there is inadequate provision (as is the case, for example, of living on pavements). This issue is discussed in more detail in the section on costs for non-food essentials.

The findings of Chibuye (2011) in Zambia with regard to how the cost of a food basket can change when it is based on the foods people eat rather than some 'expert' opinion have already been noted. Maintaining the same calorific intake as the government's food basket, but allowing the contents to reflect what people actually buy (using official surveys) means a considerable increase in the monthly costs. In the case of non-food costs, the study suggests that price differentials between urban and rural areas are less important than what is included in the calculation. The comparability questions cannot be answered simply. Chibuye (2011) explains that, while rural households are more likely to live in traditional dwellings with mud walls and grass or straw roofs, they may benefit from more space and lower population densities. A further relevant point is that, at high densities, dwellings built from wood, straw and grass are a greater hazard. Despite these complexities, the official response is to use a uniform

30 per cent adjustment to allow for non-food costs. In the six towns studied, the monthly non-food costs (based on a basket of necessities including housing, fuel, soap and other personal goods, water and sanitation) vary between K966,100 and K378,580. The significance of food in the total (food and non-food) poverty line varies from 33 per cent for Lusaka's poverty line to 57 per cent for Luanshya.

In the case of Zambia, the World Bank's poverty assessment acknowledges some of these difficulties when it concludes that,

> Due to weaknesses in the price data, it was not possible to satisfactorily adjust the consumption data for urban-rural price differences. As a result comparisons in poverty figures across the urban-rural divide do not reflect differences in the cost of living between urban and rural areas. Poverty comparisons between rural and urban areas should therefore be treated with caution.
>
> (World Bank Zambia 2007, page 57)

The authors suggest that these problems are not unique to Zambia and are symptomatic of inadequate data collection: 'like much price data from developing countries, [the data] is extremely noisy, with implausibly large variation in prices across time and space' (page 61).

The significance of price differentials in poverty estimates is also apparent in an overview of studies of urban poverty in Ethiopia (Kedir 2005). Kedir and McKay (2005) consider a three-wave panel data set (1994, 1995 and 1997) for urban households in Addis Ababa and six regional towns and find an increase in urban poverty. Using the same data set, Bigsten *et al.* (2003) report a decline in poverty. Kedir (2005) suggests that one of the explanatory factors is differences in the way in which spatial price deflators are used to adjust prices in the different urban centres.

The World Bank's own poverty assessment in Ethiopia is interesting because of the depth of analysis offered (World Bank Ethiopia 2005). The authors explain adjustments to the government poverty lines: the Ethiopian government sets a common basket across all households, based on national average expenditure and adjusted for regional prices, while Bank staff use a more complex approach, with three amendments to produce two different estimates. For the first adjustment, in terms of expenditures, they impute rents rather than use those estimated by the enumerators, to improve accuracy and exclude energy because the data was unconvincing. This gives them new estimates of the costs of household consumption which are then used to calculate two different poverty lines, as elaborated in the second and third amendments. For the second, they develop a more complex adjustment for the different regions and allow for region- and time-specific poverty lines that include changes in household consumption due to changes in relative prices. This recognizes that if, for example, prices rise for one good, households will adjust by purchasing less of it and replacing it with something else. It also recognizes that the staple food may vary in different regions, and allows for consideration of regionally specific non-food costs. After estimating the food poverty line, the non-food component of the poverty line is estimated at this regional level to develop a set of specific regional poverty lines for each of the two time periods studied (1995 and 1999). For the third adjustment, as an alternative methodology to that in the second adjustment, they calculate regional price indices based on changes in the costs of food to adjust the poverty line for changes in regional prices.

The results suggest that rural poverty is lower than the government estimates but urban poverty may be significantly higher. The government estimates urban poverty at 33 per cent in 1995 and 37 per cent in 1999. In respect of the first and third amendments, the report concludes that the percentage of the urban population below the lower poverty line was 31 per cent in 1995 and 37 per cent in 1999 (broadly similar to the government). The figures for a higher poverty line are 46 per cent and 53 per cent for the two periods. However, taking into account the first and second amendments (i.e. locally specific poverty lines) increases the level of urban poverty more significantly. Urban poverty estimates for the lower poverty line are 32 and 46 per cent for 1995 and 1999, and for the upper poverty line are 47 and 70 per cent respectively. The authors conclude, 'When we allow households to substitute their food consumption bundles in response to price changes, rural poverty substantially declines and urban poverty starkly increases' (page 15). These results suggest that the more detailed analysis of the food and non-food costs of living in urban and rural areas significantly increases the numbers of urban residents estimated as having consumption below the poverty line.

International agencies may not acknowledge the need for adjustments in poverty lines within nations to reflect spatial variations in the income needed to avoid poverty, but they do acknowledge very large differences in the cost of living within these same nations for their own staff, as the daily 'per diems' they receive to cover their living costs are adjusted by location. Within most low- and middle-income nations, the daily rate that international agency staff receive to pay for hotels and 'other costs' varies by a factor of 2–5, depending on whether they stay in capitals or other high-price cities, lower-price urban centres or rural areas (see Table 2.4). In some nations, the variation is much higher than this (as in, for instance, Bangladesh and Zambia), although the most expensive options are sometimes particular hotels rather than rates for specific cities.

Table 2.4 also includes the figures for the daily allowance independent of the hotel bill, and these vary by a factor of 2–3 within most nations and 4 or more for some. Thus relatively sophisticated measures are taken to guarantee that international agency staff and international consultants have their 'daily cost of living' adjusted to meet the differences in costs between locations within nations – but little or no such recognition is accorded 'the poor' in setting poverty lines.

Table 2.4 Intra-national variations in the per diems paid to international staff to cover living costs (note that, for some nations, the highest daily costs are not for a city but for a specified hotel)

	Variation between locations in daily subsistence allowance (US$)	
Nation	*Including hotel*	*Not including hotel*
Angola	130–530	59–205
Argentina	176–394	117–186
Bangladesh	38–270	17–98
Benin	57–250	33–121
Bolivia	87–164	38–72
Brazil	137–363	55–82
Burundi	41–209	19–72
Cambodia	49–232	24–84
Chad	107–345	47–104
China	144–393	58–152
Colombia	105–266	35–85
Congo, DR	86–361	14–128
Côte d'Ivoire	93–363	51–148
Ethiopia	52–398	21–135
Ghana	80–323	25–139
India	167–367	45–114
Kenya	108–420	14–119
Malaysia	98–199	37–80
Mexico	143–309	55–123
Mozambique	88–176	41–86
Namibia	82–378	23–111
Nigeria	102–550	41–247
Uganda	100–293	26–93
Venezuela	142–467	29–182
Zambia	103–660	18–147
Zimbabwe	105–219	41–59

Source: Data from UN ICSC website (see http://icsc.un.org/resources/csd/icscdata.asp#dsa), based on April 2010 rates

Little adjustment for variations in costs between nations

The price of most essential goods and services is also likely to vary a lot between countries; in general, the monetary income required for most non-food essentials in urban areas is likely to be higher in more urbanized middle-income nations than in less urbanized low-income nations.[36] As noted earlier, the dollar-a-day poverty line was based on a selection of national poverty lines (for 2005 poverty estimates, it was the mean of the national poverty lines for the poorest 15 nations, with the $2-a-day poverty line based on the median of poverty lines for low- and middle-income nations; see Chen and Ravallion 2008). The adjustment to dollars with purchasing power parity may improve the accuracy of comparisons between nations, but if the national poverty lines on which the dollar-a-day poverty line is based are faulty, underestimating the costs faced by low-income groups for non-food needs in most urban contexts, then it too is faulty. And it is unlikely that data collected on prices within each nation actually look to the often much higher costs paid by low-income groups.

Although the poverty reduction strategy papers that many nations have developed in collaboration with external donors (including the World Bank) do not use the US$1-a-day poverty line or, if they do, consideration is also given to nationally set poverty lines, the World Bank still uses the US$1-a-day and $2-a-day poverty lines in much of its general literature. This implies that the income needed to avoid poverty does not vary within nations. It assumes that the income needed to avoid poverty is the same in large and successful cities – where access to all goods and services is highly monetized and where access for many poorer groups is particularly expensive – as it is in small urban centres and rural areas in much less prosperous parts of the nation. It also suggests that the poverty lines on which it is based made appropriate allowance for the cost of non-food needs – which is unlikely. Does a dollar per person per day, even when adjusted for purchasing power parity, really allow an individual or a household to avoid poverty in São Paulo or Mexico City – or in major cities in nations with much lower per capita incomes than Brazil or Mexico, such as Delhi and Mumbai in India or Nairobi in Kenya? Does it also make allowance for the much higher prices that urban poor groups often have to pay for non-food needs?[37] We noted earlier that the proportion of the urban population in the Dominican Republic said to be 'poor' in 2004 varied from 2.1 to 35.4 per cent, depending on the criteria used to define poverty. The 2.1 per cent figure is based on the dollar-a-day poverty line (World Bank Dominican Republic 2006).

But for international agencies the attraction of using a single measure to capture and compare situations between different national and regional settings remains. Ravallion and Bidani (1994) highlight the pros and cons of using a consistent poverty line that reflects 'local' (by which they mean national) perceptions of what constitutes poverty (referred to as *specificity*). Using national perceptions would mean that two households deemed to have the same standard of living could not both be said to be either above or below the poverty line. Ravallion and Bidani (1994) note that the use of nationally set poverty lines can have 'absurd' policy implications, illustrating this by comparing the incidence of poverty between Indonesia and the USA: estimates for poverty incidence in 1990 were at about the same level in both countries, at 14–15 per cent of the population, but there are clearly more people in Indonesia than in the United States who would be deemed poor. One wonders, however, what the absurd policy implications of this actually are – official discussions in Indonesia about setting the poverty line are hardly likely to be influenced by poverty levels in the USA. It is likely that the policy implications of using the US$1-a-day poverty line are more absurd, especially for the poor who live in the worst governed and most expensive cities. We noted earlier that if the dollar-a-day measure is used (as in Ravallion, Chen and Sangraula 2007), only a small minority of the urban population is poor – and there is very little poverty in urban areas for many regions. Using this poverty line means that only 13 per cent of the urban population of low- and middle-income nations are poor. Sadly, this does not reflect a triumph for development but simply the inappropriateness of the measure used.

The next section illustrates the high costs paid by so many low-income urban dwellers for non-food essentials. Just the cost of renting (poor quality) accommodation in a city or just the cost of getting to and from work or services in a peripheral settlement, may be more than a dollar a day, even when adjusted for purchasing power parity. Chibuye (2011) shows that even in Zambia, a low-income nation, a realistic poverty line for its cities is far above the dollar-a-day poverty line level. Hardoy with Almansi (2011) show the deprivations faced by households in informal settlements who have incomes well above the dollar-a-day poverty line. Sabry (2009) similarly shows that avoiding deprivation in Cairo needs an income well above the dollar-a-day poverty line.

Costs for non-food essentials

The high proportion of income spent by low-income urban groups on non-food essentials

Many empirical studies show the high costs paid by particular urban groups (or those living in particular settlements within urban centres) for non-food essentials, or the high proportion of their income that goes on these. Given the importance of assessing these costs and how they relate to what can be afforded, these studies do not appear so numerous. They do raise questions about the validity of poverty lines that make no allowance for non-food items, or poverty lines that are set on the assumption that non-food items require only a small proportion of income. The studies showing high non-food costs should also serve as a caution for poverty lines that draw on price or expenditure data, in that they highlight how particular (urban) groups are often paying or spending well above any 'average'. They highlight the high prices paid by many low-income urban households for housing and for transport, expenditure items that may not be included in the setting of poverty lines. In addition, data on household consumption or expenditure may be from surveys that under-represent those living in informal settlements or who are homeless – as noted already in the cases of sample frames based on government data that under-represent or don't include these groups, or where those carrying out surveys are afraid to go into informal settlements.

Thus, two key issues are, first, what basis is used for incorporating the cost of non-food needs into poverty lines and, second, how differences in these costs by location are factored in. Most household expenditure surveys show urban populations or particular groups within the urban population spending an above-average proportion of their incomes on housing and transport.[38] It would be surprising if costs such as housing and transport to and from work were not generally more expensive in urban than in rural areas (and higher in larger and more prosperous cities). In most urban contexts, access to housing (to rent), land for housing (to rent or own) and building materials (for building, extending, upgrading or repairing a house) are all monetized, whereas in many rural contexts they are not. Getting permission and official approval to build a house is also generally monetized in urban areas (or in the more important urban centres), and this can be costly (in professional time and fees, for instance, or because of informal payments that have to be made). Similarly, it is likely that large sections of the low-income urban population face higher costs for transport than most of the rural population because they live in locations at some distance from where they earn incomes or where services are available. The best locations in urban areas are relatively costly, including those with good access to employment and services, so many low-income households choose peripheral locations because accommodation is cheaper (or the possibilities for owner-occupation and self-build are greater). It is also likely that the larger and more prosperous the urban centre, the larger the rural–urban differences in the prices paid by poorer groups for housing and land and in daily expenditures on transport.

There are few empirical studies of poverty in small urban centres, even though a substantial proportion of the urban population in virtually all nations lives in small urban centres (see Satterthwaite 2006). These include many centres with a few thousand inhabitants. In many small urban centres and in some larger urban centres (or urban districts within larger urban centres) in low-income regions, access to land for housing and materials for building may be less monetized, and there may be few or no administrative controls to limit supplies or increase costs. There are also likely to be many rural areas where markets for housing and for the components of housing (also permission to build) are monetized, including rural areas that become desired locations for higher-income groups (for instance for tourism, second homes or homes from which to commute to urban areas) or non-agricultural enterprises.

Housing or transport costs are not always higher in urban areas than in rural areas; agricultural labourers or temporary farm workers may be paying significant proportions of their income to rent (usually very poor quality) accommodation, and may face particularly high costs for many essential commodities. A comparison of how much rural and urban dwellers spend on transport does not take into account what (rural and urban) households forgo because transport is too costly or time consuming or unavailable – and obviously rural disadvantages in this regard are generally much greater than urban disadvantages. Urban dwellers will generally benefit from cheaper manufactured goods than rural dwellers, and the larger and better located the urban area, the larger this benefit is likely to be. The same is true for many services.

However, with these reservations in mind, it is worth noting the empirical studies that show the particularly high cost of non-food essentials for urban populations or for particular urban groups, or the high proportion of incomes spent on these.

(a) Public transport

Earlier sections noted the high transport costs that low-income households often face, for instance in getting to and from work, accessing shops, markets and services, and for children going to and from school. They also noted that many poverty lines make little or no allowance for transport – and even that expenditure on transport may not be considered a 'need.'

As with housing, it is difficult to know how to make allowance for transport when setting poverty lines when the transport costs faced by individuals or households vary so much depending on their location, livelihood and the quality of public transport. In many cities, a proportion of low-income groups have very low or no transport costs because they live very close to their work and to services – for instance pavement dwellers in Mumbai, or those renting rooms (or simply renting beds) in Dharavi, or construction workers that live on their construction sites (see Patel 1990; Lantz and Engqvist 2008; SPARC and KRVIA 2010). Here, they are putting up with very poor and overcrowded housing conditions to get this access and save time and money on transport. But it is also common in cities for a high proportion of low-income groups to experience high costs for transport, in terms of both time and money, as they choose to live in peripheral locations in order to get more space and/or lower costs (and often this represents their only chance of getting their own home, even if on land illegally occupied or subdivided). The trade-offs that individuals or households make in regard to housing quality, location and access to services are discussed in more detail in section (c) on housing. An individual who rents a bed in a small room packed with beds for rent for particular hours in Dharavi (the 'hot-bed' system) can be seen to have very inadequate accommodation – but it has great advantages for them with regard to access to work and services.

For at least two decades, there have been studies showing the high proportion of household expenditure going to transport among urban populations – or the high costs facing urban poor communities. These include studies showing public transport costs representing a significant part of total household expenditure. In Karachi, interviews with 108 transport users who lived in one central and four peripheral neighbourhoods found that half were spending 10 per cent or more of their income on transport (Urban Resource Centre 2001). In Buenos Aires, a 2002 survey found that the poorest quintile spent over 30 per cent of family income on public transport (Carruthers *et al*. 2005). In São Paulo, a 2003 survey showed low-income groups spending 18–30 per cent of their incomes on travel; by comparison, wealthy residents spent 7 per cent of their incomes and were able to travel far more frequently (Carruthers *et al*. 2005). In Salvador (Brazil), many low-income residents live in the urban periphery, and a household survey in two low-income neighbourhoods found that transport costs averaged 25 per cent of monthly expenditures (Winrock International 2005). In informal settlements in Nairobi, residents spend 8 per cent of their income on transport (World Bank Kenya 2006), although given the variety of locations for informal settlements in Nairobi with regard to how close they are to income-earning opportunities, there is likely to be considerable variation in this.

In South Africa, one legacy of apartheid is the large informal settlements that grew up around cities but at some distance from them, and living in these means high transport costs for those who work in the city. For instance, in two of Cape

Town's poorest suburbs, Khayelitsha and Nyanga, a 2002 livelihoods survey found that some 40 per cent of main breadwinners take more than an hour to reach their workplace, and 60 per cent pay more than R20 a day for transport – equivalent to more than US$3 a day (De Swardt *et al.* 2005; see also CORC 2006). In many cities there are also many low-income people who have been evicted from informal settlements in central locations. Often they are rehoused in poor quality housing in peripheral locations, meaning they face high transport costs.

Some studies show average household expenditures across urban populations – for instance a study in Zambia found that 12 per cent was spent on transport (Central Statistical Office, Zambia 1998);[39] in Malawi, an analysis of household expenditure in four cities found that transport costs represented 12.5–14 per cent of total expenditure (Malawi, Government of 1994).

But what these studies do not show are the consequences of high public transport costs. These include the time and energy burden of having to walk more. Some studies have shown how many low-income groups walk long distances to keep their transport expenditures down (see, for instance, Huq *et al.* 1996 for various cities in Bangladesh; Barter 1999 for central Mumbai and Jakarta). In a survey of Wuhan, China, the bottom quintile reported walking for almost half of their journeys; so too did the bottom quintile in Buenos Aires (Carruthers *et al.* 2005). A survey in Nairobi showed the high proportion of trips made by walking for those living in 'slums'; women were more affected – 67 per cent of low-income women walked, significantly higher than the 53 per cent of their male counterparts (Salon and Gulyani 2010). High transport costs may also result in employment opportunities forgone because the time and monetary costs of getting to work are too high. A 2003 survey in Wuhan, China showed how prohibitively high transit costs resulted in low-income groups rejecting jobs far from their homes (Carruthers *et al.* 2005). Sabry (2009) in her study of eight informal settlements in Cairo noted that high travel costs were one reason why few children went to secondary school. A neighbourhood in Montevideo actually called itself barrio *Nicole*, meaning *ni-colectivo* – 'no bus'.

(b) Education (including school fees and associated costs, school uniforms, books and getting to and from school)

Sabry (2009, 2010) discusses in some detail the high costs of keeping children at school among households in informal settlements in Greater Cairo, including the costs of transport to and from school (especially for secondary schooling), uniforms, bags, shoes, books, and the pressure from poorly paid teachers for informal payments. In the settlements studied, the monthly cost of primary education was 30–80 LE and secondary education 95–135 LE. To this was added the monthly cost of transport from low-income settlements to areas of employment (50–200 LE) and housing costs (70–100 LE for one room with shared bathroom facilities). How could even these minimum costs be afforded, along with food and other non-food items, by families with incomes close to the lower poverty line of 179 LE a month for a household of five persons? For many households, the allowance for non-food items is not enough to cover only the costs of (inadequate) housing, education and transport (Sabry 2009, 2010).

Devas and Korboe (2000) note the difficulties that poor urban households in Kumasi face in affording the fees and additional costs for primary schools. Even where entry to schools is free, there may be other costs – for transport, unofficial fees, uniforms, school meals, textbooks and exam fees, for instance – which make it expensive for poor urban households to keep their children at school (as an example, see Kanji 1995, who discusses a settlement in Harare).[40]

Some of the evidence for the high cost of keeping children at school comes from national averages. A poverty profile for Cameroon notes how much households spend on keeping their children at school, including expenditure on materials and supplies (books, notebooks, uniforms, etc.), fees (for tuition, parent–teacher associations, room and board, rehearsals, exams, registration) and other costs such as home instruction, school lunches and transport (Cameroon, Republic of 2002). Various other studies point to the high proportion of income spent by many low-income households on education – for instance in South Korea (Kwon 1998; Lee 1998) and Kenya (Kenya, Government of 2000). In other instances, the evidence is from urban areas. In a survey of four Indian cities (Baroda, Bhilwara, Sambalpur and Siliguri), Ghosh *et al.* (1994) found that the expenditure of low-income households on education (including on fees, books and uniforms) ranged from 4.8 to 15.6 per cent of household income in the four cities. Bigsten and Kayizzi-Mugerwa (1992) found that a high proportion of the income of the poorest quintile in Kampala was spent on educational services. A study in Côte d'Ivoire (Côte d'Ivoire, République de la 2000) showed a sharp increase in the proportion of urban household expenditure going on education between 1993 and 1998 (from 1.8 to 5.8 per cent[41]), and comparable increases may have been common in many other nations as charges in education were introduced or increased during the 1990s. The study in Kenya noted above also emphasized how high the expenditure on education was among the urban poor, especially for secondary education. It also provided further support for the point made earlier – that even if primary schools are free, there are still many expenses that have to be met to keep children there, for uniforms, payment for watchmen and contributions to school supplies (Kenya, Government of 2000).

As noted earlier, low-income groups may also have to bear the cost of sending their children to 'private' schools because they cannot get places at government schools. Private schools might be assumed to be used only by wealthier households but studies in informal settlements show many large, poor quality but cheap private schools. For instance, the Pakistan NGO the Orangi Pilot Project found that in Orangi, Karachi's largest informal settlement (with around a million inhabitants), a high proportion of the population sent their children to private schools because there were so few government schools (Orangi Pilot Project 1995; Hasan 2006). Sabry (2009) notes that there are private schools in informal settlements in Cairo with tuition fees of a few hundred Egyptian pounds a year. In Kibera, one of Nairobi's largest informal settlements, there are cheap and overcrowded private schools that cater for those unable to get their children into government schools. We suspect that the use by low-income households living in informal settlements of private schools and private tuition, because they cannot get places for their children in government schools or they need additional tuition to advance, is more widespread than just a few examples – with obvious consequences for expenditure on education.

(c) Housing

Most low-income households in urban areas spend a significant proportion of their income on housing and on the services associated with it (such as water, sanitation, solid waste collection and, where available, electricity). But it is difficult to ascertain what proportion of income is spent on this because of the many different ways in which these costs manifest themselves. For instance, for tenants or lodgers these costs may take the form of regular rent payments, but getting rental accommodation may also require a one-off payment or a large deposit. Households gaining connection to a piped water supply, sewers or electricity usually have to pay connection fees.

We noted earlier that in most urban contexts, access to housing (to rent), land for housing (to rent, lease or own) and building materials are all monetized; also that getting permission to build a house is generally monetized in urban areas (or in the more important urban centres), and this can be costly (for instance, in professional time and fees or because of informal payments that have to be made). Much of the low-income population in urban areas in low- and middle-income nations live in houses or shacks whose construction was organized by their occupiers.[42] For those living in a self-built house, payments may arise from getting the land site for the house. It may be assumed that those who live in illegal settlements as *de facto* owner-occupiers obtained the land free – but many illegal settlements are illegal subdivisions rather than illegal occupations, so the sites had to be purchased even if their development for housing was not approved by the relevant government authority. Illegal subdivisions are often too expensive for low-income households, unless they are poorly located and/or on dangerous sites. In addition, even in squatter settlements where the land occupation is illegal, many households may have 'purchased' the site from the original occupier or had to make informal payments to local politicians, civil servants or leaders (see, for instance, Hasan 1999 for Karachi; Yapi-Diahou 1995 for Abidjan). Even where land sites for housing are allocated by government rather than by market mechanisms, it cannot be assumed that the poor benefit or that they get the land free (see, for instance, Kironde 1995 for Dar es Salaam).

For those who build their own homes, there are also the costs of building, extending and maintaining the house, including the cost of building materials and fixtures, and, where needed, payment to those employed to undertake this work. Maintaining poor quality housing is often expensive and requires expenditure each year, but this would not be considered part of 'non-food needs' in most poverty line calculations. There are also the often high costs of rebuilding or repairing housing after storms and floods; we know that a high proportion of informal settlements are on land sites that flood regularly and much of their housing stock is not of a quality to resist floods or high winds. The scale of these costs is only now becoming apparent, as more detailed local databases on disasters and their impacts are being built (see United Nations 2011a; also the section in Chapter 3 on disasters). There is also the cost of rebuilding after being evicted or having the house demolished. In a large, centrally located 'slum' in Mumbai called Kaula Bandar, a small group who recently built homes on remaining open grounds had their homes demolished with no warning, and their possessions taken. One of those who lost their home told of having spent 35,000 rupees on flooring and proper walls, which were now lost (Subbaraman *et al.* 2012). Many low-income households take out loans to help acquire, build, repair or rebuild their homes, or to pay for the sites, and they may also be spending a significant proportion of their incomes on loan repayments.

Owner-occupiers may face other costs that are expensive – for instance connection fees for piped water, sewers or electricity, or land registration costs. Households seeking land for housing from local authorities may have to pay each year to remain on the housing list. Many sources acknowledge the difficulty of getting appropriate data on housing costs (especially for owner-occupiers). Deaton and Zaidi (2002) note that 'Of all the components of the household consumption aggregate, the housing sub-aggregate is often one of the most problematic' (page 37). It is likely that most poverty lines make inadequate allowance for the income needed for housing in cities or city locations (where, particularly in the larger and more prosperous cities, housing is expensive), because of:

- inappropriate assumptions – for instance the assumption that 'owner-occupiers' face no housing costs or that what low-income households spend on housing is what they need to meet their housing needs
- the application of an average figure for the income needed for housing for all locations, when there are large variations in housing costs within the nation.

In Dhaka in 1995, 11 per cent of expenditure in households with below-poverty-line incomes went on housing (Islam *et al.* 1997). In Maputo (Mozambique) in 1996–97, 17.7 per cent of average household expenditure was housing-related (official government statistics, quoted in Jenkins 2000). But such averages can hide a higher proportion of income spent by many low-income tenants. Expenditure surveys in Honduras and Kenya highlighted the high proportion of expenditure going on rents in urban areas (World Bank Honduras 2001; Kenya, Government of 2000); in Kenya, among the urban poor, it was the largest single expenditure on non-food items. World Bank Kenya (2006) finds that in informal settlements in Nairobi rent (excluding water and electricity) accounts for 17 per cent of expenditure and 12 per cent of income. In four low-income settlements in Dhaka, on average residents spent between 17 and 22 per cent of their income on rents (including water and electricity); in three of the four settlements, over 60 per cent of residents were tenants (Banks 2010).

Other studies show that many tenant households spend more than one quarter of their income on rent.[43] In a study of eight informal settlements in Cairo, Sabry (2009) notes how renters in informal areas are at the mercy of the market and landlords, especially those without rental contracts. Most have no contract. The cost of renting a two-room flat in which the children sleep in the living room would take up most or all of the allowance for non-food needs in the lower poverty line. In South Korea, at least in the 1980s and 1990s, it was common for low-income households to pay one quarter of their monthly income on rent (Asian Coalition for Housing Rights 1989; Lee 1998). Rakodi and Withers (1995) show how the lowest income group of lodgers in the high-density areas in Harare and Gweru spent a much higher proportion of their income on housing (39 per cent in Harare, 46 per cent in Gweru) than other groups. It is also worth noting that land invasions by low-income households have often been driven by households seeking to escape high rental costs. In the large-scale land invasions that took place in Buenos Aires in 1982, many of the households were moving from rental accommodation that they were having great difficulty affording.[44]

There are also the costs faced by particular low-income groups as they get 'legal' housing. For instance, the 20,000 households in Mumbai who were resettled from land beside the railway tracks to better quality and more secure accommodation had to learn how to manage the payment of regular utility bills (Patel *et al.* 2002). Interviews with the occupants of Santa Maria, an informal settlement in Greater Buenos Aires formed by a land invasion, reported that the cost of services took a high proportion of their household income. These households also had to make regular payments towards the cost of the land (their occupation had been legalized, but the condition was that they had to pay fixed instalments towards the cost of the land and public works). And the cost of services, especially those that had been privatized, had risen to the point where this jeopardized their ability to keep up the payments under the land tenure regularization scheme (Herzer *et al.* 2000).

(d) *Access to water and sanitation*

In many urban settings, low-income groups are paying particularly high prices for water and also often for sanitation (pay-to-use toilets). For instance, a review of data on what urban households pay for water per litre found that this varied by a factor of more than 1,000 (see Table 2.5). In this section, the focus is on the costs facing low-income groups in getting water and access to toilets, but it should be noted that they are usually receiving very inadequate provision. These inadequacies as they relate to health are discussed in detail in Chapter 3.

As Chapter 3 will describe in more detail, those who live in informal settlements generally lack water piped into their home and so have to rely on provision outside their home. Most water sources have to be paid for – for instance from water kiosks, water vendors, water tankers or households that have wells (or connections) and sell the water to neighbours. The high costs that have to be paid are shown in Table 2.5. The table also shows the cost that would have to be paid for 150 litres,

Table 2.5 Differentials in the prices paid for water

	Price paid per litre (US$)	Price of 150 litres per day (US$)
Water tariff in Cairo	0.00004	0.006
Co-operative in Santa Cruz	0.00025–0.00055	0.0375–0.0825
Public tap in Bandung	0.00026	0.039
Utility in Lima	0.00028	0.042
Independent water provider in Asuncion	0.00035	0.0525
House connection in Bandung	0.00038	0.057
Price of water from a standpipe in Ouagadougou	0.00048	0.072
Water tariff in Amman	0.00061	0.0915
Water vendor in Dhaka (1995)	0.00084	0.126
Price paid for water to standpipe operators in Nairobi	0.001–0.0025	0.15–0.375
Average paid by urban households in East Africa with piped water connection (1997)	0.001	0.15
Water tariff in Ramallah	0.00111	0.1665
Water from water point in Huruma, Nairobi	0.0013	0.195
Kiosks in Kampala	0.0015–0.007	0.225–1.05
Standpipes in Dar es Salaam drawing water from mains	0.0015	0.225
Average paid by urban households in East Africa that lack piped water	0.002	0.3
Average price paid to vendors by low-income groups living in salinated areas in Jakarta (1991)	0.002	0.3
Water trucker in Lima	0.0024	0.36
Handcarts delivering to homes in Dar es Salaam	0.0035–0.0075	0.525–1.125
Water vendor in Bandung (1995)	0.0036	0.54
Price of water from tankers in Luanda in 1998	0.004–0.02	0.6–3.0
Price of water from a handcart in Conakry	0.004	0.6
Average price paid to vendors in East African urban areas (1997)	0.0045	0.675
Bicycle water vendor in Kampala, delivering to non-serviced area	0.0054–0.0108	0.81–1.62
Water from public tap in Lae, Papua New Guinea	0.00596	0.894
Water from vendor in Kibera, Nairobi	0.0065	0.975
55-gallon barrels of water from vendors in Tegucigalpa (US$1.75 per barrel)	0.0072	1.08
Vendor in Male (1995)	0.011	1.65
Vendor in Kibera, Nairobi during local water shortages	0.013	1.95
Water from a tanker in Luanda for those in areas distant from water sources	0.02	3.0

Sources: Data for Cairo, Amman and Ramallah – Saghir *et al.* (2000); Santa Cruz, Lima, Tegucigalpa and Asuncion – Solo (2000); Bandung, Male, Dhaka and Lae – McIntosh and Yñiguez (1997); Ouagadougou and Conakry – Water and Sanitation Program (2000); Nairobi – Champetier and Farid (2000); East Africa – Thompson *et al.* (2000); Huruma, Nairobi – Pamoja Trust (2001); Kampala – Champetier and Wandera (2000); Jakarta – McGranahan *et al.* (2001); Dar es Salaam – Champetier *et al.* (2000); Luanda – Cain *et al.* (2002); Kibera, Nairobi – Katui-Katua and McGranahan (2002)

taking this volume as an approximation for the minimum standard that a household needs each day. Of course, low-income households that are purchasing water that is expensive would not purchase anything approaching 150 litres a day from these sources, as they could not afford to do so. They either make do with the inadequate supply or draw most of the water they use from cheaper but poorer quality sources.

In some instances, they may have access to public standpipes where no charge is made, although this seems increasingly rare and, where provided, may require lengthy queuing. Low-income households often keep down their expenditures on water by drawing from local water bodies (rivers, lakes) or using these water bodies directly (for instance for washing or laundry).

Households who rent rooms or who live in illegal settlements often pay particularly high prices for water. Table 2.5 shows the very large variations in water prices, both between cities and between different sources in the same city. Those who rely on water vendors or water kiosks (typically those living in illegal settlements) generally pay much more per litre than those who have piped water connections. For instance, in a study covering urban areas in Kenya, Uganda and Tanzania in 1997, the average price paid for water per litre by households with piped water connections was less than one quarter the average price paid by those with no household connection (Thompson *et al.* 2000). Those living in settlements with no piped provision generally pay most. For instance water from kiosks in Kampala was generally much cheaper than water from bicycle vendors who delivered to non-serviced areas (Champetier and Wandera 2000). Those living in peripheral locations generally pay the most; the prices of water from tankers in Luanda varied considerably depending on the settlement's distance from water sources from which the tankers could draw (Cain *et al.* 2002).

For many low-income urban households, the payments made to water vendors represent a major item of household expenditure – often 10 per cent and sometimes 20 per cent of household income, with particular case studies showing even higher proportions.[45] For instance. the 10,000 or so residents of Kaula Bandar, a long-established informal settlement in Mumbai that is not recognized by the government, spend between 6 and 17 per cent of their income on water, most of it from vendors who illegally tap a fire brigade water line, and this still means most managing with far less water than they actually need (Subbaraman *et al.* 2012). There is also the issue of water utilities charging rising block tariffs for water, which is meant to benefit poorer households (low-volume users) through a cross-subsidy, with funds drawn from charging more to high-volume users (presumed to be the higher-income groups). But in many instances low-income households, when able to access the piped system, only have water connections that they share with other households, meaning that the water for these shared connections is charged at higher rates (see Devas and Korboe 2000 for a discussion of this in relation to Kumasi).

Many urban households also have to pay for access to toilets. There is a growing literature[46] showing the extent to which large sections of the population in many cities have no sanitation facility at all in their home, and public or communal provision is so poor or so expensive that they resort to defecation outside, or what is termed 'wrap and throw' in the Philippines or 'flying toilets' elsewhere. Where pay-to-use public toilets have developed, these can take up a significant proportion of poor households' incomes. For instance, in Kumasi, the cost of using a pay-to-use toilet for a family of five, each using it only once a day, would be equivalent to at least 10 per cent of a basic wage (Devas and Korboe 2000). In India, pay-to-use toilets can cost as much as 2 rupees per use (and more for using washing facilities) which is far too expensive to allow all members of a low-income household to use it regularly – although there are also community toilets designed, built and managed by grassroots organizations where charges fund maintenance but are much lower, for instance family passes costing 30 rupees a month (Burra, Patel and Kerr 2003). The high costs of using toilet facilities in Kangemi, Kibera and Mukuru, informal settlements in Nairobi, were noted previously (World Bank Kenya 2009, page 58).

(e) Health care

Some studies show that the costs of health care and medicines represent a significant share of expenditure for urban poor households. A survey in Kampala in 1990 highlighted the high proportion of total household income spent on education and health care (Bigsten and Kayizzi-Mugerwa 1992). Ghosh, Ahmad and Maitra (1994) found that 10 per cent or more of the income of 'slum' households in two of the four cities they looked at went on health care. Dinye (1995) noted that 15 per cent of household expenditure among a sample of households in a low-income settlement in Kumasi was going on health. A study of poverty in Honduras found that 9 per cent of expenditure in urban areas was on health care (World Bank Honduras 2001).

But there are also the costs related to the inadequacies in health care that do not appear in expenditure surveys. For instance, a study in a 'slum' area in Khulna, Bangladesh highlighted the very large economic burden caused by poor health associated with poor quality housing and lack of basic services – and that the economic cost in terms of income lost from days off work and from medical expenses was greater than the cost of improving the infrastructure to eliminate the health problems (Pryer 1993). A comparable study in Dhaka showed that ill-health was the most important cause of deterioration in financial status among Dhaka slum households (Pryer 2003). In Karachi, the low-cost sanitation system supported by the Orangi Pilot Project brought the cost of good quality sewers down to the point where the cost of installation per household is likely to be less than the savings made in one year because of improved health, from reduced time off work and treatment costs (Orangi Pilot Project 1995; Hasan 2006). In settlements where there are high risks of malaria, low-income households can spend a significant proportion of their income on mosquito coils or sprays (see, for instance, Thomas *et al.* 1999). As noted earlier, expenditure on health care by low-income groups is often not an indicator of the income they need for health care, as they cannot afford to seek treatment or purchase the most appropriate medicines. Devas and Korboe (2000) note that, with the introduction of charges for health care in Ghana, many people in Kumasi no longer used the health care services when sick or injured, or they sought cheaper alternatives.

(f) Energy (including fuel for cooking and heating water and, where needed, space heating and electricity)

As Chapter 3 discusses in more detail, the two most common implications of poverty for energy use among urban populations in low- and most middle-income nations are, first, use of the cheapest fuels and energy-using equipment (including stoves), implying high levels of indoor air pollution and risk of fire and, second, no access to electricity. So the problem is not the high cost of energy or the high proportion of household income spent on energy but the health risks from energy use. However, even here, costs may be significant.

In other circumstances, energy costs can take a high proportion of household income. A survey of 300 homes in Rio de Janeiro's informal settlements found that energy problems did not lie with the fuels used – LPG was the main cooking fuel, while electricity was used for lighting and appliances – but the fact that households were spending 15 to 25 per cent of their incomes on energy (World Energy Council 2006). In Thailand, a study of 'slum' households found that they spent about 16 per cent of their monthly income on energy (cooking, electricity, transport) in Bangkok and about 26 per cent in Khon Kaen. Households in these slums with incomes below the poverty line spent 29 per cent of total household income on energy in Khon Kaen and 18.5 per cent in Bangkok – mainly because of the high cost of electricity (Shrestha *et al.* 2008). In Ethiopia, fuel and power took 11 per cent of expenditure among low-income urban dwellers (Kebede, Bekele and Kedir 2002). In Kibera, one of Nairobi's largest informal settlements, for over 100 households surveyed energy expenditures reached 20–40 per cent of monthly incomes (Karekezi, Kimani and Onguru 2008). In Cairo, households with incomes at the lower poverty line spent 8–20 per cent of their income on electricity (Sabry 2009). For the bottom three urban deciles in Guatemala in 2000, cooking and lighting took up about 10 per cent of household expenditures (ESMAP and UNDP 2003).

Even if households have access to electricity through illegal connections, this can still mean significant costs. If connection is through a neighbour, connection and/or usage fees are paid to them (see Fall *et al.* 2008 for Dakar; Shrestha *et al.* 2008 for Bangkok; Cowan 2008 for an informal settlement in the Cape Peninsula). Studies in Ahmedabad and Manila have shown that households served by illegal connections may pay their landlords more for electricity than if they were legally connected (USAID 2004; ESMAP 2007). Where low-income households obtain electricity through shared electricity meters, this can result in their being charged higher rates because of rising block tariffs.[47]

(g) Other costs

Many low-income urban households have other costs that go unrecognized by those who set poverty lines, including payments to community-based organizations and the payment of fines (for illegal street-vending, for instance) or bribes to be allowed to work. For instance, a study of street children in Dhaka (Conticini 2005), which examined their perspectives on poverty and their ingenuity, including sophisticated coping strategies, pointed to the range of costs they had to pay which depleted their incomes, including taxes/bribes to *mastaans* (mafia members), *matabbars* (community leaders), police, guards, and station and passenger launch staff.

> Girls said they were subjected to higher taxes than boys, even when performing the same work. In a number of cases, the taxes paid by girls reached 50 to 60 per cent of their income. The boys' taxes were between 30 and 50 per cent, varying according to the nature of work, the connections of the child and the workplace.
>
> (pages 75–6)

Tova Solo (2008) identified the high costs facing those who lacked bank accounts in various Latin American cities – for example in terms of additional time and transaction fees when paying bills. While those with bank accounts can often pay local utility bills and taxes through electronic transfers and direct debits, those without bank accounts have to go to particular offices (and often queue) to pay monthly bills for water, electricity, sanitation, telephone, health insurance, schools, etc. Getting paid by cheque for the unbanked usually means paying fees to those who cash the cheque, such as commercial stores or money changers.

Childcare can be costly for low-income households where all adult members have to find income-earning opportunities, but there may be no low-cost or no-cost solutions – though often this difficulty is solved through reciprocity at community level or by leaving older siblings in charge. It is also a difficulty often 'solved' by leaving young children unattended at home or young siblings in charge of the very young, with all the attendant risks.

It is common for urban dwellers to be transferring a significant proportion of their income to family members living elsewhere, including in rural areas. For instance, in a study of livelihoods in Accra, 7 per cent of households were sending large sums of money out of the city or to other households within the city and sacrificing food (Maxwell *et al.* 1998). Seventy-one per cent of households in Nairobi's informal settlements send remittances to relatives or friends, with a significant proportion being sent to other urban centres rather than rural areas (World Bank Kenya 2006).

Various studies have also shown how many urban poor groups are paying a significant proportion of their income on debt repayments (see, for instance, CARE/ Bangladesh 1998; Amis and Kumar 2000; Kwon 1998). The cost of funerals can be particularly onerous in areas where there is high child mortality or high adult mortality (for instance, in areas where the incidence of AIDS is particularly high and where the availability of drugs is inadequate). Many urban households also have to face costs from evictions, when they are forcibly evicted from a settlement and lose their home and many household possessions. Many of those who are evicted also lose the investments they made in building and improving their homes. There are also other costs brought by evictions, such as disruption to livelihoods and to social networks, which are often of great importance in helping people avoid deprivation.[48] Those living in informal settlements may be paying for solid waste collection; an evaluation of provision for water and sanitation in informal settlements in Dhaka found that in several locations residents were paying small amounts monthly for garbage collection services (Hanchett, Akhter and Khan 2003). This was also found to be the case in Nairobi (World Bank Kenya 2006).

Finally, the way that poverty lines are defined does not usually make any allowance for households to save, as all resources would be required to satisfy basic needs (Mejía and Vos 1997). But it is increasingly recognized that savings can have particular importance for low-income urban households because of the emergency credit that community-based savings groups can provide to help cope with shocks and stresses. Many urban poor federations have at their base community or group savings schemes from which members can draw funding to cope with emergencies (see, for instance, Patel and d'Cruz 1993; Boonyabancha 2003; Patel and Mitlin 2004; Mitlin, Satterthwaite and Bartlett 2011). As described in detail in the companion volume to this, community-based savings schemes are also often the basis on which schemes to support community members to acquire and develop their own homes are developed.

One wonders as to the basis on which the dollar-a-day poverty line ever factored in non-food costs. The original dollar-a-day poverty line was set after research done for the 1990 *World Development Report* (World Bank 1990) and it drew on a review of national poverty lines across 33 countries (Chen and Ravallion 2008). The later poverty estimates presented in Chen and Ravallion (2008) used a poverty line based on 'the mean of the national poverty lines for the poorest 15 countries in terms of consumption per capita' (page 4). We suspect that most of these national poverty lines made very little allowance for non-food needs and so these too set the poverty lines too low.

The variations in what poor urban households spend on different non-food items

Clearly, low-income households cannot be spending high proportions of their incomes on all the items discussed (i.e. 15–30 per cent on housing, 10 per cent on fuel, 10–20 per cent on water and toilets, 10–15 per cent on transport, 5–10 per cent on health care, 5–10 per cent on keeping children at school...) because this would leave little or no money for food. Data on average non-food expenditures among urban populations or for particular groups (for instance the poorest 20 per cent) are easily misinterpreted if there is no recognition of the variation between low-income households in any city with regard to which of the items discussed are the main non-food expenditures.

The earlier section on the costs low-income groups face for transport noted the trade-offs that they have to make between location and housing quality, for instance putting up with very overcrowded, poor quality accommodation (even renting a bed by the hour or sleeping in public places) because it is close to income-earning opportunities. To keep total expenditure on housing, infrastructure and services at levels they can afford, each individual or household makes the trade-offs that best suit them with regard to location for access to income-earning opportunities, housing size and quality, degree of security of tenure, and quality of infrastructure and service provision. Of course, the lower the amount they can afford or want to pay, the fewer options they have from which to choose. Most low-income groups in urban areas will prioritize locations with good access to income-earning opportunities above housing quality because without income they cannot survive. For instance, young single people will often rent space in very overcrowded central tenements or boarding houses because these provide easy access to places where income can be earned (for example in casual labour markets or jobs with very long hours) and because this keeps down accommodation costs. Cheap boarding houses may be particularly useful for individuals who come to cities for short periods (such as circular or temporary migrants). Housing costs may be minimized and central locations ensured by sleeping in public places, parks, graveyards or streets. In Mumbai, one of the key reasons why so many people live in tiny shacks constructed on pavements is that this allows them to walk to the places where they earn their income (SPARC 1985). The many poor households in Mumbai that live or used to live in tiny shacks next to railway tracks also did so because of the access this provided to income-earning opportunities (Patel, d'Cruz and Burra 2002). In most cities, there are central districts with high levels of overcrowding (in tenements or cheap boarding houses, for example) which arise because their inhabitants have incomes that are too low to allow them to afford the transport costs if they lived further away in less overcrowded dwellings (Hardoy and Satterthwaite 1989).

Other low-income groups will prioritize more space. Low-income households with children will be more likely to seek more room, but to find this they generally need to live in less central locations – building or purchasing their own home in a less central informal or illegal settlement, for instance. Here they may also have the (eventual) possibility of gaining legal tenure of the land and so becoming owner-occupiers, which in turn means that their house becomes a valuable capital asset. But for low-income households finding such land usually means a peripheral location, with high costs for transport to and from work and services. It often also means a site at high risk from floods or landslides. The priority an individual or household gives to access to infrastructure and services often increases when they have or plan to have children.

Thus, to understand housing needs and costs for low-income households requires some understanding of the different housing sub-markets, each representing different trade-offs in terms of price, quality, tenure, location and access to services. There is often considerable diversity within a city's 'informal settlements' in quality, price, tenure (and the future possibilities for tenure), location and availability of rooms for rent. Our work has long stressed the need to better understand legal and illegal housing and land markets in each city in order to understand how housing need and cost can be incorporated into discussions of poverty (see, for instance, Hardoy and Satterthwaite 1989; *Environment and Urbanization* 1989). Obviously, the choices made by each individual or household between the different rental or owner-occupier housing sub-markets are much influenced by their income – but they are also influenced by household composition, source of income, plans, etc. The options available to those with limited incomes also depend on (among other things) the nature of the city economy, the distribution of income, the land market (and land-owning structure), the measures taken by governments to help or hinder people and companies acquiring and developing land for housing, and the quality and efficiency of companies and utilities responsible for provision for water, sanitation, drainage, schools, public transport, etc.

Thus, to be an accurate reflection of the income needed to avoid poverty, a poverty line needs to be set within each local context, or adjusted to each local context. It has to be set at an income that allows the individual or household not only to have an adequate diet but also to afford safe accommodation with adequate basic infrastructure and services (water, sanitation, drainage, garbage removal, fuel and electricity, health care, etc.), as well as the costs of transport (to and from work and essential services, for instance), clothing and, for households with children, keeping children at school. As a report on urban demography noted, without knowledge of the full range of circumstances in each neighbourhood or district, it is difficult to specify the level of income required to avoid poverty. A lack of local data means that governments establish simple, administratively feasible poverty lines, resulting in the misclassification of many households (Montgomery *et al.* 2003).

Other limitations of poverty lines

There is a considerable literature on the inappropriateness or limitations of poverty lines – both in general and specifically for urban areas – that raises issues other than those discussed in the previous sections in this chapter. One set of concerns relate to the extent to which poverty lines divide the urban population into the 'poor' and the 'non-poor', with little idea of the diversity within 'the poor' and the 'nearly poor' with regard to their deprivations, vulnerabilities and needs. Table 2.6 is a reminder of the diversity that is likely to occur in any urban area with regard to the degrees of poverty. Of course, any poverty analysis should seek a greater disaggregation than this in, for instance, income source and employment base, household composition, gender, age or social groups that may face discrimination. Within all urban areas, there is considerable differentiation among those with inadequate income levels in (among other factors) the stability of their income source, the access their accommodation provides to income-earning opportunities, household size and composition, gender, educational attainment and access to services, and all these influence the level and intensity of poverty. Official statistics on poverty and urban poverty are very often drawn from national sample surveys that have sample sizes too small to show differences in poverty between different urban centres (including differences related to urban centres'

Table 2.6 Degrees of poverty in urban areas

Aspect of poverty	Degree of poverty			
	Destitution	Extreme poverty	Poverty	At risk
Income	Income below the cost of a minimum food basket	Income just above the cost of minimum food basket but far too low to allow other needs to be met adequately	Income below a realistic poverty line* but enough to allow significant expenditure on non-food essentials	Income just above a realistic poverty line*
Housing and access to infrastructure and services	Homeless or no-cost or close to no-cost shelter	Very little to spend on housing – often a household renting a room in a tenement or illegal or informal settlement or a single person sharing a room	More accommodation options, e.g. slightly more spacious, better quality rental housing or capacity to self-build a house if cheap or free land is available; extent and quality of affordable options much influenced by government land, infrastructure and services policies	
Assets	Typically no or very few assets (although community-based savings groups may provide access to credit for emergencies)		Often some capacity to save, especially within well-managed savings and credit schemes	
Vulnerability	Extreme vulnerability to food price rises, loss of income or illness or injury; often also to discrimination and unfair practices (from employers, landlords, civil servants, politicians, the law …)		Similar kinds of vulnerability to those faced by people experiencing destitution or extreme poverty, although usually less severe; often vulnerable to running up serious debt burdens	

* A realistic poverty line would be one calculated based on real prices and costs in each city and which took into account the cost of non-food essentials (safe, secure housing; transport; water; sanitation; health care; keeping children at school, etc.) as well as the cost of an adequate diet.

population, prosperity and economic base) or within them (for instance between inner cities, the areas around inner cities and urban peripheries).

Another set of concerns about poverty lines is that they may be manipulated by whoever sets or uses them, meaning they are not based on data. But this is simply additional to the concern over where inappropriate poverty lines that are based on data are set, when either the data or their interpretation are inadequate (for instance they are not accurate as regards non-food needs). Because governments and international agencies often want to highlight their achievements in poverty reduction, they can choose inappropriate poverty lines (such as the dollar-a-day poverty line or poverty lines making inadequate provision for non-food needs). They can also choose not to adjust poverty lines for inflation, since inflation can make them obsolete very quickly, especially where no provision is made to adjust them in relation to rising costs. Or the problem may be adjustments that systematically set poverty lines below the real rise in costs or that fail to allow sufficiently for real changes in prices for low-income groups. The failure to adequately adjust poverty lines or poverty-reducing measures for inflation can be one of the ways in which higher-income groups allow an erosion of total expenditures on poverty reduction (Kanbur and Squire 2001).

A further set of concerns is the lack of attention given to intra-household differentials. Poverty lines are set based on household data, yet differences often exist in levels of consumption and in the allocation and use of household income and control of assets across household members. Consideration needs to be given to whether these are disadvantaging particular people within households, for instance by age (the elderly or young), gender (women or girls) or social status (see Moser 1993; Wratten 1995). The fact that all members of a household do not have equal command over resources can mean that those with the least control may be facing deprivation within households with above-poverty-line incomes or consumption patterns. For some time researchers have attempted to study how resources are allocated within households, and why it matters from a policy perspective. This is also an important issue in the discussion of 'household' expenditure (see, for instance, Haddad, Hoddinott and Alderman 1997).

There is also the issue of vulnerability, raised in Table 2.6 above. Poverty lines can be criticized for ultimately being a static measure that gives little idea of the processes that cause or help avoid poverty. Inadequate income or consumption levels are symptoms of poverty but do little to explain underlying causes, including discrimination and exploitation. They give little indication of any particular circumstances that need particular responses (for instance, the erosion in the real value of state pensions that has put many older people at risk in various Latin American nations). They do not capture poorer households' responses and how their capacity to cope can be enhanced. They also fail to capture the vulnerability of individuals or households to falling below the poverty line, instead identifying only the proportion who at the time of the survey were below it. So no distinction is drawn between transient poverty and long-lasting (often termed 'chronic') poverty, yet individuals or households facing a temporary fall in income generally need a very different policy response to those who have long had or always had below-poverty-line incomes (Kanbur and Squire 2001).

Clearly, in all urban contexts, individuals and households move between destitution, extreme poverty, poverty and being at risk of poverty – as well as, for some, moving out of poverty. These movements result from a range of factors, and obviously from changes in food prices or prices of non-food needs or changes in real income. There is surprisingly little research on the extent to which economic growth supports a shift of people out of destitution or extreme poverty (or out of poverty and being at risk of poverty) and who benefits from these shifts. There is some research on the movement the other way – from being at risk to poverty to extreme poverty and destitution – for instance on how this shift can originate in serious illness, injury or premature death, or in loss of employment, loss of income, depletion of assets or rising debt burdens, or in eviction.

A growing body of research over the last ten years has sought to better understand how levels of poverty (or the deprivations that are part of poverty) vary within the population and change over time. This includes an interest in extreme poverty and, within this, chronic poverty – those that experience extreme poverty for long periods (even all their life, carrying through to their children). The Chronic Poverty Research Centre[49] has suggested that poverty is chronic if it lasts for five years, although other time periods can be used, such as the time between surveys. The proportion of a population facing chronic poverty is usually assessed based on income or consumption, and looking at the characteristics of households that remain poor across several years can help better identify causes. It could also be revealing to assess the persistence of extreme poverty with regard to living conditions, i.e. among those individuals or households that cannot buy, rent or build better quality accommodation; however, this would require the household surveys used to measure poverty to collect detailed data on living conditions.

Although analyses drawn from successive national surveys can show the proportion of households that suffer from chronic poverty, insights into chronic poverty are more likely to come from studies that look at specific groups within cities, particularly those that track households over time. These may include studies of particular occupational groups, such as the rickshaw pullers in Dhaka (Begum and Sen 2005) or informal traders in Kinshasa (Iyenda 2005), or particular age groups, for instance street children in Dhaka (Conticini 2005) or those living in particular settlements (see Moser 2009). However, there are few panel data sets that exist for the urban context. All but one of the studies mentioned are snapshots taken at a particular point in time rather than longitudinal studies that follow families over time.

The longitudinal studies that exist point to significant numbers in chronic poverty, but also suggest that some mobility takes place. The problems of poverty assessment notwithstanding, this indicates that some upward progression is possible and that attention should be given to what enables households to build on such movement. An analysis of urban poverty in Ethiopia draws on three surveys

(1994, 1995 and 1997) to analyse the scale of chronic poverty over a four-year period (Kedir and McKay 2005). The study found that 57.4 per cent of urban households were poor for at least one of these years and 21.5 per cent were poor in all three surveys. Herrera and Roubaud (2005) found that a three-year panel (1997–99) for two countries identified 13 per cent of the urban population as chronically poor (poor in each year) in Peru and 65 per cent in Madagascar, with 48 per cent in Peru being poor in at least one round and 91 per cent in Madagascar. Moser (2009) considered a longer trajectory, with data from 1978, 1992 and 2004 for 51 households in a low-income settlement in Guayaquil. She found that 51 per cent of the sample were poor (below the poverty line) in both 1978 and 1992, and that the number of poor households was the same in 1992 and 2004. From 1978 to 2004, 45 per cent of households experienced some upward mobility and 22 per cent some downward mobility. Only four households experienced upward mobility in both periods. Over time, more households did better than not – but this reflects the large numbers below the poverty line in the initial research period (Moser 2009, pages 33–4).

The literature on livelihoods and on the importance for low-income groups of asset bases for avoiding or better coping with poverty has tended to focus on rural areas, although there is an urban literature (see, for instance, Moser 1998; Maxwell *et al.* 1998; Rakodi with Lloyd Jones 2002; Begum and Sen 2005; Kedir 2005; Iyenda 2005; De Swardt *et al.* 2005). It may be that large sections of the urban population are particularly vulnerable to falling incomes or loss of income because of changes in urban labour markets, including the contraction in the number of secure jobs (in part from government retrenchments), the increasing use by employers of sub-contracting, a greater reliance on casual labour and a greater use of home workers (Wratten 1995; Latapí and de la Rocha 1995; UNCHS 1996). Chronic poverty is often associated with casual work (see Kedir 2005; De Swardt *et al.* 2005) or work in the informal economy (Iyenda 2005; Begum and Sen 2005). Most urban dwellers have fewer possibilities than do rural dwellers to fall back on self-production or foraging as a way of coping with loss of income or employment. Moser (1998) also notes that focusing only on income overlooks future implications of current choices. Households that take children out of school to work because they cannot meet their needs, for example, may be more 'income rich', but will also be more vulnerable in the near future and the children will lose out on the education that is important for their future earning capacity (see Latapí and de la Rocha 1995). Household expenditure data can also miss various other measures households take to cope with impoverishment – including households doubling up and household members taking on more onerous and dangerous work – which then mean they appear to be better off.

One important characteristic of poverty is the limited capacity to cope with crises, which is often combined with higher risk of crises because of dangerous living and working conditions. Chapter 3 will give many examples of the impacts on poverty of ill-health or injury and of the costs of health care and medicines. In the case of rickshaw pullers in Dhaka,

An extraordinarily high proportion (75 per cent) ... reported having encountered at least one crisis in the last five years, with an average incidence of two major crises per household. Of these, two-thirds of the crises and almost half of the crisis-related expenses relate to health shocks.

(Begum and Sen 2005, page 23)

HIV/AIDS is an example of an illness putting tremendous strain on the resources of low-income households, both in terms of reducing adult capacity to work (including the loss of income earners through premature death) and in terms of expenditure on treatment and sufficient food (which is important to minimizing vulnerability to infection; Kedir 2005; De Swardt *et al*. 2005; van Donk 2006; Mabala 2006).

One additional aspect of poverty that conventional poverty definitions and poverty lines miss is the large amount of time (and often effort) needed for daily living among those with limited incomes. This includes the time and effort needed to fetch and carry water from standpipes, kiosks, tankers or other water sources, which may also involve queuing. Accessing public toilets and washing facilities (or simply to places to defecate) involves longer journeys and takes more time than it does for those who have these facilities within their homes; this may also involve long queues. Washing, doing laundry or washing household utensils is often far more time consuming for low-income households who lack water piped into their home, and may involve journeys to and from water bodies. For large sections of the low-income population, getting to and from livelihoods and services is time consuming, involving walking and public transport, and for those living in peripheral settlements that work in central areas in large cities this can take two hours or more a day. Accessing health care may involve long queues and/ or time spent getting to a hospital or health care facility. Using cheaper fuels often takes time – for instance the time needed to fetch and carry fuels (solid fuels, kerosene, or LPG canisters if these can be afforded) – whereas those with gas and electricity in their homes spend no time on accessing these. As noted earlier, for those without bank accounts, the procedures that have to be followed for paying bills are often time consuming (Solo 2008). Add up the time needed to fulfil these and other tasks and it is often seriously diminishes time available for income earning and, of course, for rest and social activities.

There are also the trade-offs between time and monetary costs that low-income groups often make to reduce expenditures – for instance walking long distances to keep down transport expenditures. Hanchett, Akhter and Khan (2003) note that the very poor in Dhaka often turn to public standposts provided free by the water and sanitation agency but these are usually on the edge of the informal settlement where they live so they have to walk long distances and wait in long queues.

Many of the activities mentioned are taken on by women and so the extra time and effort falls on them. Women may get pushed out of queues for public toilets by men (see Chapter 3). One of the features introduced into the community toilets designed and managed by women's savings groups in India was separate queues for men and women (Burra, Patel and Kerr 2003). So even where some goods and services may be provided 'free' for the poor, the amount of time needed to access them is equivalent to a high monetary cost. It may also be that low-income households turn to services that have to be paid for because this represents better value than 'free' services that are time consuming to access.

Most high-income nations have moved away from setting absolute poverty lines to setting relative poverty lines (set at 40 or 50 per cent of the mean income, for instance), in recognition that this provides a better indication of the income needed to avoid poverty in that particular society. Within discussion on how to define and set poverty lines in low- and middle-income nations there is little mention of this, although some studies of poverty have used relative poverty lines. Perhaps this is because of the limitations of relative poverty lines in tracking how absolute poverty levels change and in providing international comparisons, both of which are of particular interest to international agencies.

Incorporating other dimensions of poverty

The section on 'The reformulation of "basic needs" within contemporary development policy' reviews how attention to living conditions came to be incorporated into discussions of poverty but was less of a factor in its measurement. For at least four decades, there has been some discussion of the need for governments and international agencies to give more attention to 'meeting basic needs' even if the lack of 'basic needs' was not incorporated into definitions and measurement of poverty. Much of the early literature explicitly recommending a higher priority for basic needs comes from the 1970s and early 1980s, and covers the inadequacies in provision for water, sanitation, education and sometimes housing and health care. Although this concern for meeting basic needs almost disappeared during the 1980s, it came back in the 1990s within discussions of human development and appears in the 'basic needs' of the International Development Targets, now included in the Millennium Development Goals.

The early concern for 'basic needs'

A concern for basic needs within international development is of course older than this and can be seen in the early development of the United Nations, especially in the UN Universal Declaration of Human Rights adopted in 1948, which is explicit about each person having

> [T]he right to a standard of living adequate for the health and well-being of himself and his family, including food, clothing, housing and medical care and necessary social services, and the right to security in the event of unemployment, sickness, disability, widowhood, old age or lack of livelihood in circumstances beyond his control.
>
> Article 25(1), quoted in Wisner (1988, page 25)

This can be seen to reflect the thinking at the time about the role of governments in welfare provision and poverty reduction within high-income nations. Another indication of the importance attached to basic needs can be seen in the request of the General Assembly in 1949 to the Economic and Social Council to consider preparing a general report on the world's social and cultural situation – from this came the first *Report on the World Social Situation* in 1952 (United Nations 1964).

But it was not until the 1970s that a commitment to meeting basic needs became a key development goal in its own right. Many influential books published in the late 1960s make little or no reference to the failure of aid to meet 'basic needs' (see, for instance, Pincus 1967; Currie 1967). Higgins's influential book on economic development (published in its revised edition in 1968) manifests a major concern for poverty and includes a long discussion on planning for education and other aspects of social development, but it does not question the prime role of foreign aid as being to promote sustained economic growth. Some aid agencies increased their commitments to education during the 1960s but the justification was not meeting people's need for education (i.e. improved education as an end in itself), rather it was the use of education as a means to improve the 'human capital' needed for economic growth. A new priority was given to higher education as part of the conventional economic growth model, because it was seen as relieving a bottleneck that inhibited domestic growth and development.

The recommendation that more attention be paid to social issues as an end in itself appears in the report of a United Nations expert group meeting held in 1969 (United Nations 1971). A critique of conventional aid policies and the demand for greater focus on the needs of poorer groups is also evident in the work of Myrdal (1968, 1970). The Pearson Commission, set up to review the successes and failures of aid, included in its recommendations a greater emphasis on 'social' projects, although this was not one of its central concerns (Mason and Asher 1973).

The World Bank was among the first of the official development assistance agencies to make explicit its support for giving a higher priority to 'basic needs'. For instance, in a speech in 1972, the Bank's President Robert McNamara called for nations 'to give greater priority to establishing growth targets in terms of essential human needs: in terms of nutrition, housing, health, literacy and employment – even if it be at the cost of some reduction in the pace of advance in certain narrow and highly privileged sectors whose benefits accrue to the few' (Clark 1981). An analysis of World Bank lending priorities shows a clear increase in the late 1970s to the priority given to meeting basic needs (Satterthwaite 1997b, 2001). Various books recommended giving to basic needs greater priority, including ul Huq (1976), Ward and Dubos (1972) and Ward (1976). Indeed, Ward (1976) has a chapter entitled 'the cost of justice' that includes some costings for meeting a range of basic needs. Between 1972 and 1978, many development assistance agencies and multilateral banks made explicit their support for increased allocations to basic needs. The influential book *Redistribution with Growth* (Chenery *et al*. 1974) was also supportive of giving more attention to basic needs, though this was in the context of giving strong priority to economic growth, with basic services seen as a means of improving human capital.

The justification for a greater concentration on 'basic needs' came from what were judged to be failures or inadequacies in the conventional development strategies implemented during the 1950s, 1960s and early 1970s by most governments of low- and middle-income countries, usually with the advice of Western experts and often with funding from Western aid agencies and multilateral development banks. The demand that basic needs receive a higher priority can also be seen as part of the concern during the 1970s that development assistance distance itself from the commercial self-interests and foreign policy priorities of aid-giving governments.

But the issues that became the centres of debate were the nature of 'basic needs' and how they would be fulfilled. There is agreement that basic needs include some minimum quantity of goods and services which meet physiological requirements, including adequate food, water and sanitation, education, shelter and health care. For instance, Streeten (1981) lists five basic needs sectors – nutrition, education, health, shelter, water and sanitation; Stewart (1985) suggests that meeting basic needs includes the fulfilment of certain standards of nutrition (food and water), health and education services, and sometimes shelter and clothing; and McHale and McHale (1981) describe 'deficiency needs', which are those (mainly biophysical) needs which must be met to maintain survival. But the debates were around which other 'needs' are 'basic' and the preconditions for their fulfilment (see Sandbrook 1982; Wood 1986; Wisner 1988). For instance, the International Labour Organization (ILO) stated that a basic needs-oriented policy 'implies the participation of the people in making decisions which affect them' (ILO 1976, page 32) and that the satisfaction of an absolute level of basic needs should be placed within a broader framework – the fulfilment of basic human rights. The ILO also indicated that a basic needs orientation requires redistribution of income and assets, even if this was carefully worded so as not to be too explicit (see ILO 1976). Some proponents of basic needs stress the extent to which their fulfilment supports economic growth and how this can be done within conventional development models, while others stress the importance of political change for the fulfilment of basic needs, especially changes that allow what came to be termed the 'bottom up' approach (Stohr and Taylor 1981; Lee 1981). Much of the early discussion and debate on basic needs took place during the presidency of Jimmy Carter, a period in which there were moves to realign the US government's aid agency, USAID, towards a greater commitment to poverty alleviation and a diminished role in national security.

But this commitment to basic needs fell away during the 1980s, when so much of development policy focused on 'creating the conditions for economic growth' and the structural adjustments thought necessary to achieve this (Mosley, Harrigan and Toye 1991). This was also a time in which most governments in high-income nations sought to 'roll back the state', and this too implied reducing the attention given to basic services generally considered to be the responsibility of government

(Toye 1993). The fact that support for basic needs had been justified on such a moral basis helps to explain why the approach lost influence during the 1980s, when a move to the right occurred in most governments elected to office in the countries that were the largest sources of development assistance, through bilateral aid programmes and contributions to multilateral agencies. Support for basic needs projects is always likely to be reduced if donors' economic and political self-interests come to have a greater influence on their aid programmes. In addition, support for basic needs within aid programmes could be seen by these governments as exactly the kind of social welfare expenditures that they were seeking to cut in their own domestic spheres.

The shift to the right in the governments of most donor countries during the 1980s often meant increased pressure on aid programmes to support domestic economic and political ends. This, combined with the burgeoning debt crisis and the economic recession that affected much of the Global South, changed the discourse about development assistance. It ended the focus on basic needs, and with the priority given to economic growth renewed, it also questioned whether public provision should expand. This was the era when ambitions from the 1970s within development assistance agencies – to provide everyone with basic needs including primary health care and good provision for water and sanitation – were scaled back, and the focus shifted to cheaper, more limited but more easily implemented measures.

New proponents of basic needs emerged in reaction to the increases in the scale and severity of poverty that became apparent in many countries during the 1980s and to the social impacts of the debt crisis and structural adjustment. Perhaps the most influential early criticism of the social impact of structural adjustment, a 1987 UNICEF-sponsored study (Cornia, Jolly and Stewart 1987), suggested that 'adjustment with a human face' might be thought of as the basic needs approach to adjustment. During the 1990s, a new body of literature that recommended giving a higher priority to basic needs used a different vocabulary, most commonly advocating 'human development', 'social development' or basic service provision within a greater commitment to poverty alleviation or reduction. There was often also a commitment to 'good governance', with international funding usually coming with attached governance and social policy conditions (Toye 1993). By the late 1980s and early 1990s, there was also an increasing volume of literature on the scale and nature of poverty and within this the issue of basic needs not being met was raised once again (see, for instance, Chambers 1995; Wratten 1995). The sudden increase in the priority that the World Bank gave to basic needs in its loans in the first half of the 1990s (Satterthwaite 1998) was also linked to explicit policy statements about the central role of basic services in the alleviation or reduction of poverty.

Giving priority to basic needs was also reinvented as the International Development Targets in 1996, then as the Millennium Development Goals – although within the MDGs the targets often reflected the outcomes of basic service provision (for example the proportion of children completing primary school, or a reduction in under-five and maternal mortality).

The reformulation of 'basic needs' within contemporary development policy

During the 1990s, five factors helped to raise again the issues that the basic needs debate had highlighted during the 1970s. The first was the economic stagnation or decline that most nations in Africa and Latin America and many in Asia experienced during the 1980s and early 1990s, and its impact on the scale and intensity of poverty (see, for instance, World Bank 1990; UNDP 1990; UNCHS 1996; Minujin 1995). The debate about the social impacts of structural adjustment was woven into this, as most countries in the Global South underwent some structural adjustment. In a large number of countries there was either a deterioration in the provision of basic services such as education and health care or a slowdown in the expansion and improvement of provision (Cornia 1987a, 1987b; Woodward 1992a, 1992b; Moser, Herbert and Makonnen 1993). Moser, Herbert and Makonnen (1993) noted that, in the early years of the adjustment process, economists believed that structural adjustment would be a temporary phenomenon and assumed that economic growth would resume, and in so doing would reduce poverty and temper some of the adverse effects.

The second factor was the widening of discussions about the nature of poverty which gave more emphasis to the extent to which inadequate or no provision of basic services causes or contributes to poverty (see, for instance, Chambers 1995; Satterthwaite 1995; Wratten 1995; Moser 1995; Satterthwaite 1997a; see also Pryer 1993; Kanji 1995; Latapí and de la Rocha 1995 for specific case studies). One theme of this work is that people's access to the basic services essential for a healthy life had not been considered in most measurements of poverty (see Tabatabai with Fouad 1993). As Chambers (1995) notes, poverty had come to mean what was measured and measurable, and it missed many aspects of deprivation that were not directly or indirectly associated with income.

The third factor was increased understanding of the health burden and much greater work burden placed on households that lack access to basic services such as piped water, sanitation and health care. The recognition of the health burden imposed on individuals, households and communities who lacked basic services was considerably enhanced by work by the World Bank and the World Health Organization on the Global Burden of Disease and its regional differences, work published in the 1993 *World Development Report* (World Bank 1993). There were also some empirical studies that revealed the very large health burden faced by low-income groups in terms of work days lost to illness and injury and the dire economic consequences this brought, in terms of increased debt and undernutrition for all family members. Most of these health costs could have been prevented or greatly reduced at low cost through the provision of basic services (Pryer 1993). In the absence of health care, not only are adults and children in low-income households sick more often, the chances of making a rapid recovery are much poorer. In addition, low-income households often face the most serious constraints in allowing one adult to take time off work to nurse sick or injured family members (WHO 1992).

The fourth factor explaining the greater attention paid to basic needs was research that concentrated on the needs and priorities of women, or more broadly on the gendered division of tasks and responsibilities within households. This highlighted how a lack of basic services such as accessible water supplies, health care and, in urban areas, provision for the removal of household and human wastes greatly increases the work burden of the person responsible for household maintenance – which is usually women (and girl children). The large volume of theoretical and empirical work published over the last two decades on women's needs and priorities, and on reducing discrimination against women with respect to access to employment, housing and basic services also helped to highlight the scale of unmet basic needs. It also showed that lack of provision of basic services generally impacts most on women (or girl children) as they are generally the person(s) responsible for household tasks and child-rearing. Various studies on the impact of structural adjustment showed the negative impact on women of declining provision of basic services or of increased service or living costs for which women were forced to take primary responsibility (see, for example, Moser, Herbert and Makonnen 1993; Kanji 1995).

The fifth factor was the interest in 'human development'. Although many of the proponents of human development sought to distance themselves from the proponents of basic needs, there is considerable common ground between the two. The first *Human Development Report* in 1990 defined human development as a process of enlarging people's choice, the most critical choices being to lead a long and healthy life, to be educated and to enjoy a decent standard of living. It also stressed the importance of political freedom, guaranteed human rights and self-respect within the context of human development (UNDP 1990). The human development approach sought to distance itself from the basic needs approach by characterizing a concentration on basic needs as the provision of goods and services to 'beneficiaries', while a focus on 'human development' involved an emphasis on human choice and people as 'participants' rather than 'beneficiaries'(UNDP 1990, 1993) – although, as noted earlier, these had also been concerns in discussions of basic needs during the 1970s.

Another way in which the proponents of human development sought to distance themselves from the basic needs approach was by claiming that human development was rooted in the theory of entitlements and the notion of capabilities drawn from the work of Amartya Sen (Desai 1991). Anand and Ravallion (1993) suggest that the basic needs approach was different because it centred on the provision of commodities rather than on the support of people's capacity for living a healthy life, avoiding premature death and hunger, avoiding illiteracy and enjoying personal liberty and freedom. Important elements of Sen's recommendations that more attention be paid to whether development enhances poor people's functioning and capabilities (Sen 1992) can also be found in some of the work of earlier basic needs proponents. Both basic needs and human development proponents recommend giving greater priority within development assistance to health care, education and other interventions which directly improve health. When the 1994 *Human Development Report* (UNDP 1994) sought to assess the extent of aid agencies' commitment to human development, it simply measured the priority they gave to basic needs.

The proponents of human development probably felt it important to distance themselves from the basic needs literature to increase the impact of their recommendations. At the time, development policies were much more neo-liberal than they had been during the 1970s and recommendations for greater government provision would not have found much support among governments of high-income nations and their bilateral aid agencies. The stress on the distinction between the constituents of well-being, such as health and freedom of choice, and the determinants of well-being, such as health care, education, access to legal aid and income (see Dasgupta and Weale 1992), was a reminder that the provision of basic needs is a means rather than an end in itself, but this is also implicit in much of the 1970s literature on basic needs. The means of measurement recommended by the proponents of human development also had precedents from the 1970s, which had been aimed at reorienting the expenditures of governments and international agencies towards giving greater priority to basic needs. What perhaps separates the basic needs from the human development literature is the former's assumption that it will generally be government agencies that ensure basic services are met whereas the latter, in line with the debate about governance and civil society, allows for a greater diversity of service providers. This includes support for privatization of basic service provision, including the many initiatives to support private sector provision for water and sanitation – although in other instances it included provision by community organizations and NGOs.

The Millennium Development Goals and beyond

The Millennium Development Goals have particular importance for any consideration of poverty reduction because they include goals and targets linked to reducing both income poverty and some of the other deprivations linked to poverty. We noted previously that the Millennium Development Goals and associated targets are based less on service provision and more on its outcomes. But the 8 goals and 18 targets (summarized in Table 2.7) do include better performance in outcomes that go far beyond income and are important for low-income groups – for instance addressing hunger and inadequacies in provision for water and sanitation, achieving universal primary education and achieving a 'significant' improvement in the lives of at least 100 million slum dwellers. There are also commitments to eliminating gender disparities in primary and secondary schools, reducing under-five mortality rates by two thirds and reducing maternal mortality rates by three quarters. Over half of the targets have specified years by which they have to be achieved – most between 1990 and 2015 – with much attention paid to monitoring whether these targets are being met in low- and middle-income nations. The official aid agencies and development banks have in effect set themselves up to be judged by whether they can ensure that these targets are met.

There are a range of concerns about the MDGs and about the accuracy of the indicators to be used for measuring whether they meet their quantitative targets.

Table 2.7 Summary of the Millennium Development Goals and their associated targets[1]

Millennium Development Goals	*Millennium development targets*
1 Eradicate extreme poverty and hunger	1 and 2 Between 1990 and 2015, halve the proportion of people: • whose income is less than US$1 a day • who suffer from hunger
2 Achieve universal primary education	3 By 2015 all boys and girls able to complete the full course of primary school
3 Promote gender equality and empower women	4 Eliminate gender disparity in primary and secondary education preferably by 2005 and to all levels of education no later than 2015
4 Reduce child mortality	5 1990–2015: Reduce by two thirds the under-five mortality rate
5 Improve maternal health	6 1990–2015: Reduce by three quarters the maternal mortality ratio
6 Combat HIV/AIDS, malaria and other diseases	7 and 8 By 2015 to have halted and begun to reverse: • the spread of AIDS • the incidence of malaria and other major diseases
7 Ensure environmental sustainability	9–11 • Integrate principles of sustainable development into country policies and reverse the loss of environmental resources • 1990–2015: Halve the proportion of the population without sustainable access to safe drinking water and basic sanitation • Significant improvements in the lives of at least 100 million slum dwellers by 2020
8 Develop a global partnership for development	12–18 • Fairer trading and financial system, including a commitment to good governance, development and poverty reduction – both nationally and internationally (also targets that include aid flows equivalent to at least 0.7% of high-income nations' gross national income) • Address special needs of least developed and landlocked countries and small island states • Deal with debt problems • Strategies for 'decent and productive' work for youth • Provide access to affordable essential drugs • Make available benefits of new technologies, especially information communications technology

[1] For the complete text and also details of the indicators to be used to monitor progress, see website of the UN Millennium Development Goals Indicators at: http:unstats.un.org/unsd/mi/mi_goals.asp.

There is the worry that little attention has been given to changing the means by which they are to be achieved: if the period up to 2000 had been so unsuccessful in addressing the goals and targets within the MDGs, it suggests a need for change within international development assistance towards being more effective on the ground – for instance in achieving the needed improvements in health care provision or provision for water and sanitation.

The setting of time-bound targets is not new. In the 1970s, a UN supported and sanctioned target for the provision of safe drinking water and basic sanitation – an aim now included in the MDGs – was set and agreed by most of the world's governments. In the late 1970s, governments committed themselves to achieving universal provision by 1990 or as soon afterwards as possible. There was even a special UN-designated Drinking Water Supply and Sanitation Decade for the 1980s and a special unit within the World Health Organization to monitor progress (including the scale and nature of relevant international development assistance). But of course this target was not met – in part because of the previously mentioned political changes in high-income nations during the 1980s. And the MDG targets for this are much less ambitious: there is only a commitment to reduce by half the proportion of people without access to safe drinking water. Sanitation was even left out of the Millennium Declaration and so the list of MDGs; this omission was only noticed and the sanitation target inserted later.

Another example of the limited ambition in the MDGs is the target of achieving significant improvements in the lives of at least 100 million slum dwellers. First, it is much less ambitious than all the other quantitative goals: it does not seek to reduce the slum population by half or two thirds or three quarters (in contrast to most of the other quantified targets) or even to halt and begin to reverse the number living in slums (in contrast to the targets aimed at reducing the incidence of major diseases); rather it seeks to achieve significant improvements in the lives of at least 100 million slum dwellers by 2020. This means reaching about 10 per cent of those living in 'slums' in 2000 by 2020. Given the rapid growth in the population living in 'slums' in so many nations, it will represent a much smaller proportion of the likely 'slum' population by 2020. Also, why is its target set to be met in 2020 when all the other time-bound targets are for 2015?

The MDGs have become much the most widely used framework for assessing and reporting on the reduction of different aspects of poverty. There are three concerns regarding the measurement of achievements. The first is that the baseline for most of the quantitative targets is 1990 rather than 2000 (when the commitments to the goals were made). This is presumably because this allows more progress to be shown than if the base year was 2000 (assuming some progress was made between 1990 and 2000). The second concern is that reporting on achievements will be aggregated with too little attention paid to what has been achieved in each nation. One of the main motivations for setting up the MDGs was that the development assistance agencies could show that development assistance was delivering real benefits – and so generate more public support. International agencies who have publicly committed themselves to the MDGs will want to highlight results that imply success. The easiest way to do so is to aggregate results so that good performances in some of the more populous nations hides the very poor performances in many of the less populous nations. So if China does particularly well in meeting some of the targets, the size of its population can make statistics for Asia or even global statistics look good, even if development assistance agencies had very little to do with the achievements. Within Latin America, what Brazil has achieved, mostly through its own policies and investments, will help make figures for South America look good. The achievement of the very modest target of significant improvements in the lives of 100 million slum dwellers by 2020 will probably be achieved by middle-income nations in which national and city governments have made a commitment to 'slum' upgrading – again, development assistance has had little to do with this.

But the third concern – and our main concern with the MDGs – is the use of indicators that are very inadequate measures of the actual goals and their associated targets in urban areas. Earlier sections in this chapter discussed how the dollar-a-day poverty line (even when adjusted for purchasing power parity and given the adjustments made since it was set) is unrealistically low for large sections of the urban population. The dollar-a-day poverty line is being used as one of the two measures for progress on the MDG of eradicating extreme poverty and hunger. There are so many urban areas or districts within larger cities where a dollar per person per day (adjusted for purchasing power parity) is far too little to ensure non-food needs are met.

The indicators used to monitor provision for water and sanitation are also very inadequate. Chapter 3 will discuss in more detail why. But here, it should be noted that what is actually measured is not who has 'sustainable access to safe drinking water' or who has access to sanitation of a standard that greatly reduces health risks. For water, households will be classified within the MDG reporting as having 'sustainable access to safe drinking water' if they have piped water into dwelling, yard or plot, public tap or standpipe, tubewell or borehole, protected dug well, protected spring or rainwater collection (this is termed 'improved' provision by the Joint Monitoring Programme (JMP) for Water Supply and Sanitation, the agency responsible for providing the statistics; UNICEF and WHO 2012). But water available from such sources is not water of drinking quality (or safe), nor is it 'sustainable' in the sense of being a regular supply (see Chapter 3 for many examples). For sanitation, a household will be reported as meeting the target of 'basic sanitation' if they use flush or pour-flush toilets to piped sewer system, septic tank or pit latrine, ventilated improved pit latrine, pit latrine with slab or composting toilet (also termed 'improved' provision by the JMP).

Our research group has been highlighting the (often very large) inaccuracies in the official UN statistics on provision for water and sanitation for over 30 years. In our review of housing, land and settlement policies in 17 nations (Hardoy and Satterthwaite 1981), we noted the exaggerations – for instance, the proportion of the urban population said to have adequate excreta disposal facilities in 1980 was 93 per cent for Tanzania, 100 per cent for Bolivia and 80 per cent for the Sudan. Amazingly, 100 per cent of Kenya's and Bolivia's urban population was said to have reasonable access to water; for Nigeria it was 92 per cent, for Tanzania

82 per cent, for India 82 per cent. The official statistics for 2000 (UNICEF and WHO 2000) contained as many nonsense statistics. By 2000, the proportion of the urban population said to have 'improved sanitation' was 96 per cent for Uganda, 98 per cent for Tanzania and 99 per cent for Zambia. For Nigeria it was 85 per cent, for Mali 93 per cent, for Malawi 96 per cent.

A 2007 report noted that 'Today, it is becoming more and more evident that, in many Sub-Saharan African countries, official data on MDG progress in the area of water and sanitation do not reflect the real situation on the ground. In urban and presumably also in rural areas, coverage is overestimated, which, as a result, means that the gaps to be bridged are underestimated' (Schäfer, Werchota and Dölle 2007, page 4). The report noted that a 2004 nationwide assessment in Zambia found that the proportion of the urban population with sustainable access to safe water was far lower than the official statistics.

However, for many nations, the figures for water and sanitation provision in urban areas in the 2012 assessment (UNICEF and WHO 2012) bear no resemblance at all to those in the 2000 assessment. Both the 2000 and the 2012 assessments claim to be measuring who has access to 'improved sanitation' and the criteria used are almost exactly the same. So if the criteria have not changed, then the heavily revised figures must come from surveys or censuses that were not available in 2000. In Uganda, according to the 2000 assessment, 96 per cent of the urban population had 'improved sanitation' in 2000; suddenly in the 2012 assessment the figure for 2000 was 33 per cent. For Tanzania, the proportion of the urban population with 'improved sanitation' in 2000 was no longer 98 per cent but 15 per cent. The 2000 assessment reported that in Tanzania, Guinea, Kenya, Zimbabwe, Zambia and Uganda, 93 to 99 per cent of the urban population had improved sanitation. In contrast, the 2012 assessment puts the percentage of their urban populations with improved sanitation at between 20 and 35 per cent. *These are statistics for the same year.* There are also very large differences between these two sources in the statistics for 2000 for many other nations; also very large differences in the statistics for 1990. For almost all nations, the 2012 assessment shows a much smaller proportion of the urban population with improved sanitation – although not for Angola, Congo, Sierra Leone and Rwanda.

These later assessments indicating much lower proportions of the urban population with 'improved' provision are likely to be more accurate than those in the 2000 assessment. But they also mean that the previous figures were completely wrong for many nations – and these have been much used and quoted in the literature on poverty as evidence that urban areas are favoured over rural areas in the provision of services. One of the reasons for the inaccuracy of some of the composite indicators used to assess urban and rural poverty is that they assume that the figures for improved provision for sanitation in urban areas in the 2000 assessment were correct. For instance, we noted the very large undercounting of urban poverty in various African nations in the figures given in Sahn and Stifel (2003), but this may in part be because the authors used the inaccurate figures for provision for sanitation from the 2000 assessment in their composite index. Perhaps the inadequate attention given by many governments and international agencies to urban sanitation was to some extent the result of seeing the official UN figures suggesting that coverage was much better than it actually was.

During the 1980s and 1990s, the reason for inaccurate statistics on water and sanitation was in large part misreporting by national governments. The Joint Monitoring Programme for Water Supply and Sanitation has had to shift from using official government statistics to using data from Demographic and Health Surveys or other surveys or censuses because of the inaccuracies in government-provided statistics. This Programme also makes clear that it is not providing statistics on who has 'sustainable access to safe water'. Its 2012 report notes that 'It does not take into account other important parameters such as drinking water quality, the availability of adequate quantities of water for domestic use, the number of service hours available, the distance to a water source or sanitation facility or the time household members spend on access and use of sources and facilities' (UNICEF and WHO 2012, page 25). But other UN agencies use the statistics as if they measure progress towards the MDG of sustainable access to safe water.

To date, the JMP has not recognized that the criteria for improved water and sanitation should not be the same in rural and urban contexts: the large, high-density populations common in urban contexts present particular problems both for water provision if there is no piped supply and for sanitation provision if there are no sewers or septic tanks. However, the 2012 report noted the Programme's intention to examine the adequacy of particular sanitation options in high-density urban areas and to explore different standards for rural and urban areas (UNICEF and WHO 2012).

Of course, the new statistics enormously reducing the proportion of the urban population with improved sanitation in 1990 and 2000 also mean a much lower baseline from which to assess progress. So nations such as Tanzania, Guinea, Kenya, Zimbabwe, Zambia and Uganda, which were reported in 2000 as providing improved sanitation for more than 90 per cent of their urban populations, now have much lower figures – but figures which enable greater progress on meeting the MDGs to be reported for the period 1990 to 2015.

The Multidimensional Poverty Index

One final initiative to consider in this chapter is the Multidimensional Poverty Index (Alkire and Santos 2010) developed by the Oxford Policy Development Institute, as this appears to support this book's contention that far more attention needs to be given to aspects of deprivation other than income. The index is constructed on the basis of two health-related indicators (whether any child in the family has died and whether any adult or child is malnourished), two education-related indicators (no household member having completed five years of school and any school-aged child out of school in years 1–8) and six standard of living indicators (no electricity; no 'improved' provision for water and sanitation; a floor made of dirt, sand or dung; use of wood, charcoal or dung for fuel; and ownership of one or fewer of the items on a list of household assets, such as a telephone, radio or refrigerator). The standard of living indicators each have a weighting of one eighteenth in the index (as there are six of them), while the four health- and education-related indicators each have a one-sixth weighting. A household is identified as multidimensionally poor if the sum of the indicators is 30 per cent or more of the score of a household with all of these deprivations.

However, the index will understate the scale of multidimensional poverty in urban areas as it uses the same data on provision for water and sanitation used for the MDGs (and produced by the UN's Joint Monitoring Programme). The index claims that using the MDG indicators (which are actually the JMP indicators) means including information on who has access to clean drinking water – but, as noted above, these indicators do not say who has access to clean drinking water. The index will also understate the scale of urban poverty because of the method by which it assesses housing conditions. The only indicator for housing conditions – a floor of dirt, sand or dung – is not a good indicator for most urban contexts. It is obviously particularly inappropriate for cities or for urban districts with multi-storey housing, since above the ground floor the flooring will not be dirt; however levels of overcrowding and inadequacies in infrastructure and services and in the building conditions can be very serious in tenements and cheap boarding houses in multi-storey housing. Imagine if this indicator based on what the floor is made of was replaced by indicators such as spending more than 20 per cent of household income on rent, water and use of public toilets or more than 10 per cent on fuel and electricity, or having less than a square metre of open space per person within 100 metres of the house, or living in a dense settlement with illegal electricity. Or imagine if the indicators for sanitation took into account the size and density of the population where there is reliance on pit latrines.

We also return again to the huge inadequacies in the data of relevance to understanding and measuring poverty, as they are collected in low- and middle-income nations. One of the problems with the water and sanitation statistics produced by the JMP is that the Programme does not collect new data, it simply analyses data from Demographic and Health Surveys or other national sample surveys, and so has to live with all their limitations, in terms of the questions that were not included and of the accuracy and specificity of the data. This is why the statistics cannot show who has 'adequate' or 'safe' drinking water. The same is true of the Multidimensional Poverty Index, which is also based on existing data sets. This means that it shares the limitations of these data sets – especially the limitations in data about provision for water and sanitation, which can greatly overstate the extent to which needs in urban areas are actually met.

We also have reservations, similar to those expressed by Ravallion (2011), as to the usefulness of aggregating different aspects of deprivation into a single index, as well as worries about the validity of the weightings given to different indicators. Will this or other aggregated indexes gain poverty more attention, and will they improve the understanding of how best to address it?

A framework for considering multiple deprivations

Broadening the definition and measurement of poverty beyond absolute poverty lines which reflect only income or consumption helps to change fundamentally the basis of understanding and action. Box 2.2 shows eight additional aspects of poverty (or of the deprivations associated with poverty), beyond inadequate income. Further, if poverty is defined and measured based only on income or consumption, it may also bias poverty reduction measures towards those that increase incomes or consumption, obscuring the many poverty-reducing measures that can be taken by addressing other aspects of poverty. Such measures, by reducing the expenditures required to secure basic needs, also increase the income available for other purchases that are essential for household well-being.

Box 2.2   Different aspects of poverty[50]

1   *Inadequate and often unstable income* Associated with: inadequate consumption of necessities, including food and, often, safe and sufficient water; inability to afford high or rising prices for necessities (food, water, rent, fuel, transport, access to toilets, school fees, etc.); and problems of indebtedness, with debt repayments significantly reducing income available for necessities.

2   *Inadequate, unstable or risky asset base* This is both non-material and material, and includes educational attainment and housing. It applies to individuals, households or communities, and includes those assets that help low-income groups cope with fluctuating prices or incomes.

3   *Poor quality and often insecure, hazardous and overcrowded housing* Associated with often very large burdens of ill-health, injury and premature death, all of which reduce household income.

4   *Inadequate provision of 'public' infrastructure* This covers piped water, sanitation, drainage, roads, footpaths, etc. It increases the costs households face, the likely health burden and often the work and time burden.

5   *Inadequate provision of basic services* This includes day care, schools, vocational training, health care, emergency services, public transport, communications, and law enforcement; it also applies to inadequate or no access to banks or other formal financial services.

6   *High prices paid for many necessities* This is often because of inadequate or no public provision, which means that, for example, water has to be purchased from vendors or kiosks, access to toilets has to be paid for and fees must be paid in order for children to go to school. Similarly, higher prices are often paid by low-income groups for privately provided transport and health care. They can also pay higher prices for necessities because they are only able to afford small quantities, and cannot benefit from lower unit costs for larger quantities.

7   *Limited or no safety net* Such a safety net ensures basic consumption can be maintained when income falls or income sources are lost. A lack of such provision means no security of access to housing, health care and other necessities when these can no longer be paid for.

8   *Inadequate protection of rights through the operation of the law* Includes laws, regulations and procedures related to civil and political rights, occupational health and safety, pollution control, environmental health, protection from violence and other crimes, and protection from discrimination and exploitation.

9   *Voicelessness and powerlessness within political systems and bureaucratic structures* Leads to little or no possibility of: receiving entitlements to goods and services; organizing, making demands and getting a fair response; or receiving support in developing initiatives. Also leads to having no means of ensuring accountability from aid agencies, NGOs, public agencies and private utilities, and no means of participating in the definition and implementation of poverty reduction programmes.

This broadening of the consideration of poverty to include these eight other aspects is now considered in Chapters 3, 4 and 5, in relation to health, livelihoods and inequality

3   Why is health so poor among low-income urban dwellers?

Introduction

Low-income urban dwellers in the Global South generally have much worse health than middle- and high-income groups. A high proportion die at an early age, mostly from diseases or injuries that can and should be easily prevented. This can be seen in the large differences in, for instance, life expectancy at birth, or in infant (0 to 1 year old), child (1 to 4), under-five and maternal mortality rates between income groups. This is illustrated in Figure 3.1, which shows the far higher under-five mortality rates among the poorest urban quartile for India and for different states in India compared to the rest of their urban populations. Many of those who have inadequate incomes also face much larger risks of debilitating injury or illness.

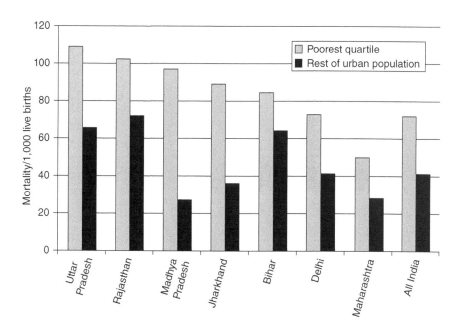

Figure 3.1 Under-five mortality rates within the poorest quartile and the rest of the urban population for different states in India, 2005/06. A wealth index incorporating assets and housing conditions was used to classify households

Source: Agarwal (2011)

Such differentials are partly shaped by low quality housing, unhealthy living conditions and limited access to health care services, and it is also common for these to be measured. For instance, the paper from which Figure 3.1 is drawn (Agarwal 2011) also presents differentials between the least wealthy urban quartile and the rest of the urban population for nutrition (the percentage of children under five who were stunted), health care services (the percentage of children completely immunized, percentage of mothers with at least three antenatal care visits and percentage of births assisted by health personnel) and living conditions (the percentage of households with access to a piped water supply at home, using a flush or pit toilet for disposal of excreta, living in houses built with poor quality materials, and without a toilet facility).

In most cities, there are large differences in mortality rates and the prevalence of many life- and health-threatening diseases between neighbourhoods or districts with concentrations of low-income groups and those areas with a predominance of middle- and high-income groups. Figures 3.2 and 3.3 illustrate this for Nairobi, showing differentials in under-five mortality rates and the prevalence of serious cases of diarrhoea.

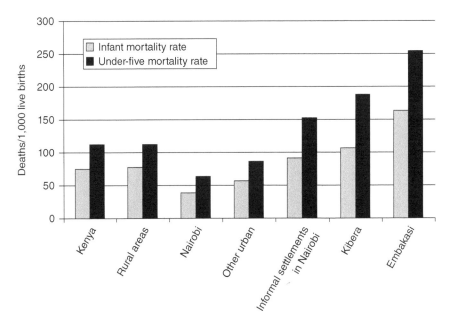

Figure 3.2 Infant and under-five mortality rates for Kenya overall, rural areas in Kenya, Nairobi, other urban areas in Kenya, informal settlements in Nairobi overall, and the informal settlements of Kibera and Embakasi

Source: Data from APHRC (2002). The data for Kenya, rural areas, Nairobi and other urban are from the 1998 Demographic and Health Survey. The survey of informal settlements was made in 2000

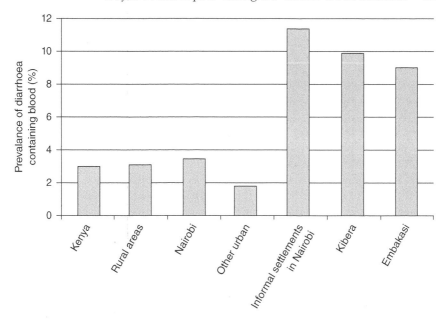

Figure 3.3 Prevalence of diarrhoea containing blood in children under three years in two
weeks prior to interview for Kenya overall, rural areas in Kenya, Nairobi,
other urban areas in Kenya, informal settlements in Nairobi overall, and the
informal settlements of Kibera and Embakasi

Source: Data from APHRC (2002)

Figures 3.2 and 3.3 show *spatial* differentials: they compare data drawn from
particular areas (in this instance Nairobi's informal settlements) with those for
Nairobi as a whole, for other urban centres, for rural areas, and Kenya as a whole.
Figure 3.1 on page 91, by comparison, shows *social* differentials, using data from
a sample survey that covered all of India's urban population and the urban
populations of particular states, with the differentials examined between the
quartile with the lowest wealth (asset) ranking and the rest of the population.
These figures illustrate the two ways in which differentials in health or in factors
that influence health – often called 'health determinants' – are measured and
presented. Health determinants are the economic, social and environmental factors
that affect the health of individuals or groups, such as housing conditions and
access to services.

Spatial differentials are generally more useful for policy because they provide
data for particular units of area and can guide priorities for addressing health
problems – but their usefulness depends on obtaining data for each small area unit.
For instance, health-related data may be available for different municipalities
within a large city, but these can hide large differentials within each municipality.
Getting to the level of disaggregation for health or health determinants that is most
useful for policy responses – small area units or even street by street – needs a

much larger sample than conventional household surveys and thus involves greater expense. Figures 3.2 and 3.3 come from a survey that focused on Nairobi's informal settlements, with a large enough sample to be able to provide data for each settlement. It was also designed to ensure that the data collected were comparable to data drawn from the national Demographic and Health Survey, which had too small a sample to provide data on differentials within Nairobi (APHRC 2002).

Census data should solve this problem, as data should be collected from each household, but censuses usually have a rather limited range of questions about health status or key health determinants. Census authorities often do not provide the data in a form that allows its analysis by street or small areas (see, for instance, Vlahov *et al.* 2011; Navarro 2001). It is important to note that spatial differentials are not the same as social differentials. For instance, there will be a range of income groups in many of Nairobi's informal settlements and a proportion of Nairobi's low-income population will not live in informal settlements. But the smaller the area unit for which health-related data are available, the closer the correspondence between these units is likely to be: the spatial differentials will increasingly reflect social differentials.

Comparisons of health-related indicators, including housing conditions, between income groups or between districts have long been common in high-income nations. These often helped influence government policies and resource allocation. For instance, the production of very detailed maps of London supported and directed by Charles Booth in the late nineteenth century showed both the scale and location of extreme poverty (Whitfield 2006). Ironically, Booth initially embarked on (and funded) the survey and map preparation because he believed that statistics on the extent of poverty in London were overstated; his research proved they were actually understated. Today, data on differentials in death rates (usually for infants, children or mothers) or on the prevalence of particular diseases or risks faced (for instance in regard to exposure to air pollution, road traffic accidents or extreme weather) between different income groups or between districts are increasingly common.

Differentials are usually larger (and often much larger) in urban areas in low- and middle-income nations. Higher-income groups in urban areas in these nations may enjoy life expectancies and levels of health comparable to those enjoyed by well-off groups in high-income nations, but low-income groups generally have much worse health than their counterparts in high-income nations. This reflects universal infrastructure and service provision in high-income and some upper-middle income nations – for instance water piped into homes, toilet facilities in the home, regular collection of household wastes and health care services.

These comparisons, between those with poor or good health, and those with poor or good housing and living conditions, can also be made between nations or between subsets of their populations – for instance comparing health indicators for different nations for their urban populations or for particular urban centres or for particular urban districts. This can be illustrated using under-five mortality rates since this is among the most commonly measured aspects of premature mortality. The nations with the highest rates among their urban population have twenty times the under-five mortality of nations with the lowest rates. International comparisons between cities can also show a twenty-fold difference in under-five mortality rates, although there is less availability of data for cities. Of course, the differentials would be even larger if the comparison was between the districts in cities in high-income nations with the lowest under-five morality rates and the districts in cities in low-income nations with the highest under-five mortality rates. Here, under-five mortality rates can be as low as two or three per 1,000 live births in the best-performing city districts and 250 plus in the worst performing.

The scale of the differentials in health or in living and working conditions is always influenced by the choice of groups to be compared. For instance, the differentials in comparing the wealthiest and the poorest 2 per cent of the population will generally be much larger than if comparing the wealthiest and poorest quartiles. Similarly, the differentials between spatial units will generally be larger the more disaggregated the data, unless there is universal provision in these areas.

Focusing on differentials means that health and provision for its determinants are usually discussed in relative terms; however, ill-health, like poverty, can also be discussed in absolute terms. So there is a literature that focuses on the scale and nature of ill-health, injury and premature death among low-income urban dwellers and on the quality of provision for key determinants of health (such as quality of diet, housing, provision for water and sanitation and health care services) presented in absolute terms, not as comparisons to other groups. Of course, how the 'urban poor' are defined influences whose health is considered (and whose is not). Here, we are faced with the inadequacies in how poverty is defined and measured discussed in Chapter 2. For instance, if the US$1-a-day poverty line is considered valid, then there is so little urban poverty in many regions that not much attention needs to be paid to it. Poverty lines should provide the basis for identifying who lacks the income to meet their needs, allowing a review of the health issues they face. We can also look at the health issues for a subset of those classified as poor (for instance those in extreme poverty, the urban poor, particular age groups, the homeless), or compare the health of those defined as poor (or a subset of them) with the health of non-poor groups. But, as discussed in Chapter 2, most poverty lines do not accurately distinguish between who can afford sufficient food and non-food needs and who cannot.

The health burden associated with poverty becomes much larger if having an inadequate income also means facing other deprivations, including an inadequate asset base, poor quality housing, lack of infrastructure and services and safety nets, lack of the rule of law and lack of voice. Here, there are very large overlaps between the determinants of ill-health or premature death and the determinants of poverty. Once again, we see the huge limitations of using only an income-based poverty line. For a proportion of those with low incomes, they will not experience most or any of these other deprivations. They are much less disadvantaged than those with similar incomes who suffer most or all the other deprivations. As the next section discusses, much of the ill-health associated with low income in urban areas in low- and middle-income nations can be reduced by addressing these other deprivations.

In this chapter, we discuss the determinants of good health and why urban health conditions can be so bad. We then review what is known about urban poverty and premature mortality (for infants, children, adolescents and adults), morbidity and nutrition, and consider what is known about the environmental health burdens associated with urban poverty, including those related to water, sanitation, fuel, physical hazards, disasters and climate change.

The determinants of health for urban populations

If we consider what underpins health in urban centres, it includes a bewildering range of what can be termed the economic, social and environmental determinants of health (Cairncross, Hardoy and Satterthwaite 1990; Vlahov *et al.* 2007; Kjellstrom and Mercado 2008). An analysis of what contributes to these will highlight what could be termed the political determinants of health – this includes whether there are local governments able and willing to act on improving or helping improve the key determinants of health for their lower-income population. But it is difficult to get comprehensive data on many of the very large range of factors that influence health. Table 3.1 lists examples of differentials in health and in health determinants for which there may be data for the worst- and best-performing settlements within the urban population in low- and middle-income nations. This is not a complete list, but illustrates the range of health disadvantages that the low-income population may face. Many of the items can be further disaggregated, for instance just measuring the quality of provision for water requires many different indicators: not only the availability of piped water taps, for example, but also whether the water is available, drinkable, affordable and how much time needs to be spent in getting it. Data may also be available to allow analysis of health disadvantage by income group.[51]

Table 3.1 Examples of differentials in health and in health determinants between the worst- and best-performing settlements within the urban population in low- and middle-income nations

	Worst-performing urban settlements	*Best-performing urban settlements*
Health outcomes		
Infant mortality rates	> 120 per 1,000 live births	< 3 per 1,000 live births
Under-five mortality rates	> 250 per 1,000 live births	< 5 per 1,000 live births
Maternal mortality rates	> 1,500 per 100,000 live births?	< 10 per 100,000 live births?
Life expectancy at birth	< 20 years[*]	> 85 years

	Worst-performing urban settlements	Best-performing urban settlements
Prevalence of diarrhoea containing blood among children	> 13%	0?
Children under five who are underweight or underheight for their age	> 50%	0?

Home and neighbourhood environment

Quality of house	Poor quality, often made of flammable and waste materials; dirt floors; poor ventilation; often damp	Good quality, safe home meeting official regulations for health and structural safety
Size of house	Very small; often one small room per household; can be less than 1 m² per person	20–50 m² per person; no need for children to have shared bedrooms
Water	No safe water supply within easy access; often high prices paid for water from vendors, kiosks or tankers; also time burden of queuing, fetching and carrying	Water of drinking quality piped to kitchens, bathrooms and toilets 24 hours a day
Sanitation	No toilet in the home (or limited access for tenants) and often no public or community toilet that is accessible and clean	At least one high quality easily cleaned toilet per household with provision for hand washing
Solid waste collection	No collection	Regular collection
Drainage	Not served by storm drainage system	Protected from floods by comprehensive storm drainage system
Clean energy	No electricity and reliance on dirty fuels (including wastes); often means high levels of indoor air pollution, to which women and young children often have much greater exposure	Electricity available 24 hours a day; clean fuels for cooking and, where needed, heating
Children's play and recreation	No provision	Good range of safe provision within walking distance
Loans to support buying or building better quality housing	None available	Loans available

	Worst-performing urban settlements	*Best-performing urban settlements*
Tenure	Insecure tenure of home (usually as tenant) or land on which it is built; constant threat of eviction	Secure home; protection from forced eviction
Location of housing or settlement	Precarious sites often at high risk of landslides or located on floodplains or other areas at risk from flooding; high risk of fire in very dense settlements constructed with flammable materials	Safe houses on safe sites

Service provision (key health determinants)

Schools	No or very inadequate public provision. For the rule of law, this includes not only civil and political rights and their protection and application, but also policing services that are present, effective and accountable to residents and that provide protection from violence and other crimes; in some contexts policing also requires an understanding of how to blend statutory and customary laws	Full public provision for all these services (and sufficient income to purchase private provision if needed)
Health care		
Specialist health care services and outreach for infants, children, the elderly and those with disabilities, and for sexual and reproductive health		
Emergency services (fire protection, ambulances, etc.)		
Safety nets, including measures to protect individuals and households from poverty such as cash transfer and insurance		
Rule of law		
Public transport	No public provision	Good quality provision
Disaster preparedness	None	Effective early warning systems that reach all those at risk and provisions to support actions that need to be taken (e.g. temporary evacuation)
Protection of asset base	No insurance available or affordable for housing or personal possessions	Homes and possessions fully covered by insurance

	Worst-performing urban settlements	Best-performing urban settlements
Provision for voice, including procedures by which to make demands on and hold to account government and service providers; measures to ensure individual and collective influence in government and service provision; and the willingness of government to hold meaningful consultations	Where there are elections, unable to get onto register of voters; no means of holding politicians, civil servants or public service provision agencies to account	On voters' register; political influence; access to channels for complaints or redress if needed (local or national politicians, courts, ombudsmen, etc.)
Work environment	Very low quality and dangerous; no support for treatment if ill or injured, or for lost income	High quality environment; health and safety regulations enforced; health care services available; income support or compensation available for occupational injuries

* Life expectancy at birth is reported to be below 40 years for some cities in sub-Saharan Africa; it is likely that among low-income groups in these cities, it may be 20 years or less.

Figure 3.4 provides a summary of the key determinants of health. It underscores how each person's health is simultaneously linked to the physical environment (the home, workplace, neighbourhood and everywhere she or he travels), socio-economic factors such as income level, type of work, diet, asset base, level of education and time available (for caring for children, for instance, and other tasks important for health) and the availability of health care and other social services (including health care that covers needs of women and men at all ages, preventive measures and emergency services). It is also a reminder of how health determinants range from the broad based (the prosperity of the nation and the competence and capacity of its national government) to the very specific (including household behaviours and actions and local provision of infrastructure and services). There are also multiple connections between them.

Urban dwellers fortunate enough to live in good quality housing in urban centres with effective local governments generally enjoy very good health. Wealthy, well-governed urban centres have among the world's highest life expectancies at birth. But the links between good health and the different characteristics of the home, workplace, neighbourhood and wider city may have become obscured or forgotten. Over time, many serious health risks that these urban residents would have faced in the past have been eliminated (there are no cholera, typhoid or measles epidemics any more) or enormously reduced (for instance the dramatic reductions in fatalities from waterborne and food-borne

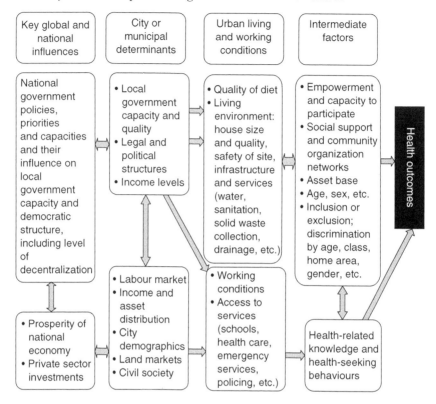

Figure 3.4 The many economic, social and environmental determinants of health in urban areas

Source: An early version of this figure is presented and discussed in Cairncross, Hardoy and Satterthwaite (1990); it has been improved and added to since then – see, for instance, Kjellstrom and Mercado (2008). See also Vlahov *et al.* (2007)

diseases, acute respiratory infections, tuberculosis, accidental fires or extreme weather). This has happened gradually, over a period of 150 years, as particular health risks were identified and acted on, although generating the political momentum for action often took time and concerted pressure. Sometimes, it took a focused civil society-driven campaign to help get the measures needed – for instance for lead additives (which contributed to lead pollution) to be removed from gasoline. Table 3.1 is a reminder of just how many kinds of health risks low-income groups can face.

Action was also needed on new health risks created in part by affluence – for instance fatalities and injuries from accidents involving motor vehicles, and these vehicles' contribution to air pollution. It is also now accepted that the quality of provision for sport, recreation and exercise (including encouraging walking and cycling) has importance for health, as do a range of measures to reduce health burdens from non-communicable as well as communicable diseases. The exact contribution of each health-related initiative to addressing the determinants of health is not known, although clearly more adequate diets and large improvements in environmental health (in the home, workplace and wider city) and in health care and emergency services have made important contributions. Similarly, the precise contribution to such improvements of different drivers is not clear but certainly these achievements were supported by good science (which helped identify particular health problems and their causes), increasing literacy (which allowed more knowledgeable individual and household responses), more precise and more disaggregated data (so the scale, extent and location of problems were understood), more accountable local and national governments (in part through shifts to universal franchise), better-resourced local governments, wealthier economies, and scrutiny, demands and action from civil society organizations. A list of all the innovations that helped contribute to better urban health would be very long and would include innovations in almost all sectors and institutions. Many of these advances have been incremental and have taken place in different sectors and institutions, including many outside of the sphere of public health or health care. They include changes to or more effective implementation of building regulations, land-use management, and infrastructure and service standards.

The number and range of the advances, and the fact that they did not happen in the context of any coordinated vision of 'health', means that we forget that the health of urban dwellers is influenced by many factors, and that health improvements may be facilitated by complex and often unpredictable or unquantifiable interactions.[52] A high proportion of younger age groups within the population directed attention to their particular needs and the needs of mothers. Greater focus on gender issues resulted in more notice being paid to the health impacts of the discrimination faced by women and girls, and beyond this to the differing needs of women and men. Meanwhile, nations with a large increase in the proportion of older people within their populations made greater provision for their particular needs. Better records of violence or other crimes and accidents (such as accidental fires) helped inform policies to address these. Or a disastrous fire, flood or other event catalysed initiatives to reduce health risks, for instance measures to reduce air pollution were introduced in the UK after the 'great smog' in London in 1952 had elevated mortality rates, and measures to better respond to heat waves were taken in many European nations after the massive premature mortality caused by high temperatures in 2003. In other instances, the influences are not so easily measured, for example the importance to the health of low-income groups of growing real incomes that reduce undernutrition and help support a range of choices contributing to better health. Here, social protection measures including cash transfers have been important in many nations.

The quality of the living environment is obviously central to health (see Figure 3.4 and Table 3.1). Housing characteristics that influence health include the amount of space per person, the quality of the house and the materials used, site characteristics (for example, risk from flooding, landslide or other disasters) and the quality of provision for water and sanitation. For the wider neighbourhood, factors include the level of provision for all-weather roads, paths and electricity, the quality of schools, the proximity and quality of health care services and policing, provision for solid waste collection, and storm and surface drainage. In urban areas, health is also influenced by house location – which determines the time needed and monetary cost for accessing income-earning opportunities and services – and working conditions, including the quality of the indoor environment, the hours worked and the degree of protection from injury by machines, toxic chemicals or physical exertion.

All these factors are in turn influenced by city or municipal determinants, for instance the quality and capacity of local government with regard to ensuring or supporting provision. Obviously, what city and municipal authorities do (or do not do) that has relevance for health is influenced by laws, codes, norms and practices, especially those that influence the quality of the living environment, the quality of the workplace and income. Health in any urban centre or district is also influenced by the actions and activities of civil society organizations, including those formed by the urban poor. Other health influences include demographic structures, labour markets and the distribution of incomes and assets.

As Figure 3.4 illustrates, these city or municipal health determinants are in turn impacted by the wider national and global context, including the prosperity of the national economy and the nature of private sector investments in or around the city or municipality. The capacity of local governments to act on health determinants within their jurisdiction is obviously influenced by the roles, responsibilities, powers and resources they get from higher levels of government, and of course the investment and services provided to each local government area by higher levels of government.

Figure 3.4 can serve as a reminder of determinants that have been acted on in high-income countries. For low- and middle-income nations, it is more a list of areas where action is needed, and it could be expanded to reflect the availability of funding from aid agencies and development banks to address key determinants of health. But this is mediated by national governments and most funding agencies have given a very low priority to supporting initiatives in urban areas that address health problems. There are also the international influences that affect prices, in particular food prices, which can have serious impacts on health for low-income urban dwellers. One of the most important indicators for effective social protection policies is a rise in food prices which is not matched by increased under-nutrition.

There is also a range of 'on the ground' factors that influence health outcomes. These include what low-income urban households do individually or collectively to address health problems they face and the nature of the discrimination they face. Also relevant here is the knowledge of health-enhancing behaviour held by individuals, households and organizations that act at neighbourhood and district level, including community organizations.

Factors leading to poor health

Figure 3.4 can be seen as a checklist of health determinants for any city or city district. The fact that health is so poor in so many urban centres or settlements is explained by poor performance in providing for most or all of these health determinants. Of course, there are multiple linkages between the different determinants; for instance, in many nations, local governments have little power or capacity, and this helps explain why a large proportion of the population does not have the housing or working conditions, infrastructure or services essential for good health.

In many cities, the lack of action on improving health or the determinants of health among individuals, households and governments can in part be explained by weak economies, which mean low incomes for most of the population and a low revenue base for governments. But there are also many cities with strong and successful economies in which the health of a high proportion of inhabitants is very poor. Why has this happened? What has stopped or inhibited the drivers of better urban health, i.e. improvement in provision for key determinants? For many cities, this can be explained by unrepresentative political structures, but in many nations and cities with elected governments a large proportion of their populations still suffer heavy and easily prevented health burdens. For instance, in India, why, more than 60 years after independence, is health so poor among much of the urban population?[53] For all low-income and many middle-income nations, why has 60 years of development assistance, meant to be oriented towards meeting the needs of 'the poor', achieved so little in improving health among low-income urban dwellers?

Perhaps the fact that international agencies have little, if any, accountability to 'the poor' helps explain this (see Satterthwaite 2001 for a discussion of the absence of such channels of accountability). In high-income nations, low-income urban dwellers have votes and channels through which to demand provision for their health (and other) needs and hold politicians to account; in 'recipient countries' there are no such channels for holding to account aid agencies in high-income nations or the politicians that oversee them – a point to which we will return in Chapter 6.

Another reason that might be advanced is the absence of relevant data on the health of low-income groups or of those living in informal settlements. Many reforms in high-income nations were underpinned by detailed health or poverty data, for instance the data carefully collected by John Snow to show how cases of cholera in London's 1854 Broad Street outbreak were clustered around a water pump, or the Charles Booth poverty maps mentioned previously. Over time, detailed health-related data became available from hospitals and health care services, from disease surveillance systems and records of causes of mortality and morbidity. But in most low- and middle-income nations, there are serious limitations in the data available on health and the determinants of health. In many cities, large sections of the low-income population have no access to official health care services and their health problems are not recorded. Disease surveillance systems, records on causes of mortality and morbidity and records from emergency services may be very inadequate (Vlahov *et al.* 2011). Most health data comes from national sample surveys, but these often lack the detail needed, and because they rely on nationally representative samples they provide no data for individual cities (except perhaps the largest) and obscure the scale and nature of differentials within urban populations. However, a lack of data cannot explain the lack of attention paid to health, as the scale and depth of poor health linked to poverty is obvious – rather the lack of attention paid to health can in part explain the choice of governments and international agencies not to address the lack of data.

The lack of data on health can be partly overcome by looking at data on key determinants of health. It is possible to classify urban populations according to quality of housing and then to look at key determinants of health, such as space per person, quality of house, quality of site, fuels used, provision for water and sanitation, and protection against extreme weather events. As discussed in this chapter, there is a rich and growing literature on the health of those who live in poor quality housing, especially those who live in what are generally termed 'informal settlements' or classified by governments as 'slums'. Chapter 5 includes a discussion of inequalities in health and health determinants within cities.

This chapter therefore discusses the health implications of living in poor quality housing, rather than the health implications of having an inadequate income – although it does discuss the housing conditions faced by those with inadequate incomes. There will be very considerable overlap, however – a high proportion of those who live in poor quality housing (however defined) will be those with inadequate incomes; and a high proportion of those living in reasonable or good quality housing (however defined) will have adequate incomes. But the overlap is not complete. For instance, surveys in informal settlements or overcrowded inner city tenements find a proportion of individuals or households with adequate incomes that choose to live there. In urban centres where there are significant constraints on getting legal housing or legal land sites on which to build, a considerable proportion of the population in 'informal settlements' may have incomes higher than that considered enough to afford basic needs; these may be the people renting rooms to others, for example. They will generally be living in better quality informal settlements where the occupation of the land is not illegal (it is the subdivision rather the occupation which is illegal), with reduced risk of eviction and greater provision of public infrastructure and services. At the same time, a proportion of those with inadequate incomes will not live in poor quality housing, for instance domestic servants who receive very low wages but live in the homes of those they serve. In many cities, a proportion of individuals or households with inadequate incomes live in 'formal' housing in 'formal' settlements, although these are often poorly maintained, and have high levels of overcrowding and shared facilities, since 'formal' houses or apartments are subdivided, often with a whole household living in a single small room.

However, much of our understanding of the health implications of urban poverty is based upon studies of particular informal settlements where most or all the population have inadequate income. If they had better incomes, most would move to better quality housing. The sections that follow include discussion of health issues in relation to those with inadequate incomes where data are available and discussion of health issues for those living in poor quality housing – that is, in a real sense living in poverty – and experiencing multiple deprivations.

Urban poverty and mortality

Given how obvious the multiple threats to health in informal settlements are, and even though they house a large and probably growing proportion of the world's population, there are surprisingly few studies of illness, injury and premature death in these settlements. Some of the reasons for this have been discussed already – the lack of interest in urban poverty (and in urban issues more broadly) among national governments and international agencies, and the difficulty of collecting data in settlements for which there are no maps or addresses, and where the population may be reluctant to be interviewed or even hostile to external interviewers.

One of the exceptions to this lack of research is the work of the African Population and Health Research Center, as shown by the data presented in Figures 3.2 and 3.3. This centre's work has included a study of two large informal settlements in Nairobi aimed at quantifying the burden of mortality and showing how its causes change by age group (Kyobutungi *et al.* 2008). Data were collected for Korogocho and Viwandani between January 2003 and December 2004 on core demographic events, including deaths and causes of death. Years of life lost due to premature mortality were calculated by multiplying deaths in each subcategory – sex, age group and cause of death – by the Global Burden of Disease standard life expectancy at that age. The overall mortality burden was 205 years of life lost due to premature mortality per 1,000 person years. Among the leading causes of death were communicable, perinatal, maternal and nutritional causes, which accounted for 77 per cent of the mortality burden. Injuries accounted for another 13 per cent and non-communicable diseases accounted for 10 per cent. Children under the age of five years had more than four times the mortality burden of the rest of the population, mostly due to pneumonia and diarrhoeal diseases. Among the rest of the population, AIDS and tuberculosis were the leading causes (contributing about 50 per cent of the mortality burden). Interpersonal violence (homicide) was the second most common contributor, followed by road traffic accidents. It is worth noting that these contributors to mortality, except perhaps road traffic accidents, would have almost no presence in middle- or upper-income residential areas in Nairobi.

Life expectancy at birth and inter-urban comparisons

There is a thirty-year difference between the reported life expectancies at birth of the best- and worst-performing cities in low- and middle-income nations. Cities such as Lima, Bangkok, Pôrto Alegre and Tunis have life expectancies at birth of between 72 and 78 years; cities such as Conakry and Lilongwe have life expectancies at birth of less than 45 years. No recent reliable data were found on differentials within city populations, but it would be expected that high-income groups in the cities in Table 3.2 would have life expectancies at birth which are 15

Table 3.2 Life expectancy at birth for cities in sub-Saharan Africa

Life expectancy at birth (years)	Cities
< 50	Lilongwe, Conakry, Banjul, N'Djamena, Kigali
50–55	Brazzaville, Libreville, Bujumbura, Nouakchott, Monrovia, Maseru, Kinshasa
55–60	Nairobi, Abidjan, Porto-Novo, Lomé, Bamako, Dakar

Source: UN-HABITAT (2008)

to 25 years above the city average and 20 to 30 years above the average for the low-income population (UN-HABITAT 2008). High under-five mortality rates are the primary reason for these very low life expectancies at birth, although mortality rates for older age groups far above average are also common.

Urban poverty and infant and child survival

More than 8 million deaths in 2008 were of children under five years of age,[54] and 99 per cent of them were in low- and middle-income countries (WHO 2011a). As noted earlier, in most low-income and many middle-income nations, infant, child or under-five mortality rates in urban areas are five to twenty times what they would be if the urban populations had adequate nutrition, good environmental health and a competent health care service. In some low-income nations, these mortality rates increased during the 1990s (Montgomery *et al.* 2003). However, there are nations with relatively low urban infant, child and under-five mortality rates – for instance Colombia, Moldova, Jamaica, El Salvador and Vietnam have under-five mortality rates of 16 to 21 per 1,000 live births – while there are also particular cities that have achieved low rates – for instance Pôrto Alegre in Brazil.[55] However, under-five mortality rates should be under 10 per 1,000 live births.[56]

Table 3.3 gives examples of nations with high average under-five mortality rates within their urban populations. These are all the more astonishing because, in all these nations, most middle- and high-income groups live in urban areas and will generally experience much lower under-five mortality rates (often fewer than 10 per 1,000 live births), meaning these averages can hide the extent of the problem faced by low-income urban dwellers; for many of the nations listed, it is likely that under-five mortality rates in 'slums' and informal settlements will be two to three times the average, and commonly one child in four living in such settlements will die before their fifth birthday.

For Nairobi in 2000, as shown in Figure 3.2 on page 92, under-five mortality rates were 150 per 1,000 live births in its informal settlements (where over half the population live) and 61.5 per 1,000 live births for Nairobi as a whole (APHRC 2002). In Bangladesh, the under-five mortality rate in 'urban slums' in 2009 was 95 per 1,000 live births compared to 53 in urban areas overall (Westhof with de

Table 3.3 Examples of high under-five mortality rates among national urban populations. For each nation listed, data is from the last available survey; note that for some nations, data is from over 20 years ago

Urban under-five mortality rate (per 1,000 live births)	Nation and year of survey
> 150	Chad 2004, Sierra Leone 2008, Burundi 1987, Mali 2006
100–150	Mozambique 2003, Niger 2006, Liberia 2009, Burkina Faso 2003, Guinea 2005, Zambia 2007, Central African Republic 1994/95, Côte d'Ivoire 1998/99, Democratic Republic of the Congo 2007, Nigeria 2008, Cameroon 2004, Sudan 1989/90, Benin 2006, Uganda 2006, Malawi 2010, Mauritania 2000/01, Congo/Brazzaville 2005, Swaziland 2006/07, Togo 1998
50–99	Ethiopia 2005, Yemen 1997, Tanzania 2010, Gabon 2000, Rwanda 2007/8 (interim), Lesotho 2004, Eritrea 2002, Comoros 1996, Pakistan 2006/07, Haiti 2005, Ghana 2008, Kenya 2008/09, São Tomé and Principe 2008/09, Turkmenistan 2000, Senegal 2008/09, Zimbabwe 2005/06, Madagascar 2008/09, Bangladesh 2007, Tunisia 1998, Timor-Leste 2009/10, India 2005/06, Namibia 2006/07, Kyrgyz Republic 1997, Botswana 1988, Bolivia 2008, Azerbaijan 2006, Uzbekistan 1996, Turkey 1998, Kazakhstan 1999

Source: Data from Demographic and Health Surveys, using STATcompiler (http://www.statcompiler.com)

Rooy, Wang and Musa 2010). Figure 3.1 on page 91 shows the large differences in under-five mortality rates between the poorest quartile and the rest of the urban population within several states in India; although not the same as a comparison between 'slums' and non-slums, this is further evidence of the health disadvantages of low-income groups. For Kisumu, Kenya's third largest city, the under-five mortality rate average for the whole city was reported as 220 per 1,000 live births in 2008 (Maoulidi 2011), which puts it at more than twice the average for Kenya's urban population (also its rural population).

In virtually all cities in low-income nations for which data are available, and for most in middle-income nations, there are dramatic contrasts between different city areas (districts, wards, municipalities) in infant, child or under-five mortality rates, as well as in living conditions and other health outcomes (Stephens 1996; Hardoy, Mitlin and Satterthwaite 2001). For informal settlements in one part of Nairobi, Embakasi, the under-five mortality rate in 2000 was 254 per 1,000 live births – in other words, a quarter of all children were dying before the age of five (APHRC 2002). The under-five mortality rate in the wealthier parts of Nairobi is likely to be much lower – perhaps 10 or fewer per 1,000 live births. The study from which this example is drawn (APHRC 2002) is unusual in that it shows the differentials in infant and under-five mortality rates between particular informal settlements and the average for the city (and the nation's urban population); but the scale of the differential is probably not unusual.

As Table 3.3 shows, twenty-three nations had urban under-five mortality rates of over 100 per 1,000 live births in their last survey; all are in sub-Saharan Africa. Four have rates of over 150 per 1,000 live births. Under-five mortality rates are likely to be significantly higher among the lowest income groups, and may be two or more times higher (the scale of the differential being influenced by how the lowest income group is defined, e.g. poorest quartile, quintile or decile). Antai and Moradi (2010) show that in the most disadvantaged urban quintile in Nigeria under-five mortality rates were more than twice those of the least disadvantaged quintile, and that most of the difference was explained by poor quality living conditions. Gupta, Arnold and Lhungdim (2009) show that, in a range of cities in India, infant and under-five mortality rates for the poorest quartile of the population were consistently higher than the average, and often much higher, as in Hyderabad, where they were more than twice the average. The differences would be more dramatic if data for the poorest quartile could be compared to data for the wealthiest quartile.

In most of the countries listed in Table 3.3 for which more than one survey exists, under-five mortality rates have fallen. In earlier surveys, under-five mortality rates exceeded 200 for the urban populations of Niger (in 1992), Malawi (in 1992) and Liberia (in 1986). However, there are many nations in which urban under-five mortality rates rose between surveys. Some of the largest rises include Kenya (75 in 1993, 94 in 2003), Namibia (50 in 2000, 60 in 2006–07), Nigeria (108 in 1999, 153 in 2003), Tanzania (120 in 1996, 142 in 1999) and Zimbabwe (53 in 1988, 69 in 1999 and 64 in 2005–06). Antai and Moradi (2010) show that the under-five mortality rate among the urban population in Nigeria was much higher in 2003 than it had been in 1998, 1993, 1988 or 1983; indeed it was nearly three times the rate in 1984–88.

There are surprisingly few studies of the role of particular diseases in high infant or child mortality among urban populations. For instance, little is known about the contributions of malaria, dengue fever, diarrhoeal diseases or respiratory infections to infant and child mortality in low-income urban populations. A survey on malaria for children of between 6 and 60 months in Kumasi and Accra (the two largest cities in Ghana) found that prevalence varied by location, from 6 to 22 per cent in Accra and from 2 to 33 per cent in Kumasi (Klinkenberg *et al.* 2006). Here, high prevalence may be linked to more children travelling to rural areas (so the infection did not take place in the city). This is a reminder of health burdens migrants may bring with them, for instance schistosomiasis or, in some regions of Latin America, Chagas' disease. The study of two of Nairobi's informal settlements mentioned earlier showed that pneumonia was the single leading cause of premature mortality in young children, comprising 22 per cent of deaths among under-fives for 2003–05; diarrhoea accounted for 19.5 per cent (Kyobutungi *et al.* 2008).[57] Contributing factors for pneumonia were inadequate, overcrowded shelter and indoor air pollution.

One review of malaria suggested that there has been a large underestimation of the risks that urban poor groups face from malaria in many cities and smaller urban centres in sub-Saharan Africa. Studies from a range of cities in this region showed that malaria is a considerable urban health problem (Donnelly *et al.* 2005). A study of malaria transmission in a range of sub-Saharan African nations based on the number of infective bites per person per year showed high levels of transmission in many cities, although within cities transmission rates were generally much higher in peri-urban areas (and were higher still in rural areas), except where dwellings in central areas were close to marshlands or lakes. Between cities, rates were much higher in wet savannas and forest zones than in dry savannas. The study identified many factors that influence transmission rates, including different urban characteristics. It suggested that, in general, low-income groups were at greater risk of infection in part because of higher physical proximity to water sources, in part to less access to health care services and preventive measures. It also noted that malarial control should be much easier in well-governed urban areas as larval sites are few, easily located and accessible (Robert *et al.* 2003).

As any parent or child carer knows, health risks for children change as they get older, more mobile and more adventurous (see Bartlett *et al.* 1999; Bartlett 2002). Here too, there is remarkably little data on the contribution of falls, burns, scalds, cuts, road traffic accidents and accidental poisonings to infant and child injuries or deaths in informal settlements. Yet the quantity and range of physical hazards are usually much higher in informal settlements.

Within this general picture of poor health and avoidable health burdens for large sections of the urban population, there are important exceptions. For instance, many Latin American nations that now have predominantly urbanized populations have managed to sustain long-term trends of falling infant and child mortality rates and increasing average life expectancy. This has in part to be linked to city and municipal governments acting to improve many health determinants; this in turn is related to political changes – in many nations, the return to democracy, decentralization and elected mayors and city governments (Campbell 2003; Cabannes 2004; Satterthwaite 2009). There are also examples of improved health in some Asian and African nations, although the scale of improvement in urban areas is not clear, as the data are for nations or sub-national (state or provincial) units rather than for urban populations or particular urban areas.

Urban poverty and mortality among adolescents and adults

The health risks impacting on infants and young children also impact on children above five. For the period through adolescence to adulthood, to these risks are added risks associated with sex and with work, and in some cities also risks associated with violence. In informal settlements, older children and adolescents often face many serious health risks that they should not. Patton *et al.* (2009) note that few studies have examined health risks for adolescents, in part because adolescence is considered 'a healthy time of life' (page 881). Much of the mortality among older children, adolescents and young adults is preventable, as shown by the dramatic differences in the mortality rates in such groups both within cities, when informal settlements are compared to other areas, and between cities. This is often hidden, however, as the very basic data needed on mortality by age group, by income and by city district to inform health policy is absent.

An analysis of causes of death among youths aged 10–24 years based on 2004 Global Burden of Disease data (Patton *et al*. 2009) showed that, in low- and middle-income countries, all-cause mortality was 2.4 times higher in youths aged 20–24 than in adolescents aged 15–19 and this was associated with a rise in reproductive health problems, road traffic accidents and mental illness. In some regions, the health risks affecting younger children continue to threaten adolescents, for instance, for youths in sub-Saharan Africa and South-east Asia, tuberculosis and lower respiratory tract infections (Patton *et al*. 2009).

The study mentioned earlier of the causes of premature mortality in young children in two informal settlements in Nairobi (Kyobutungi *et al*. 2008) also showed that health risks shift over time, with injuries and HIV becoming more important. Leading causes of mortality for those over the age of five were HIV, tuberculosis, violent injuries and road traffic injuries, representing more than two thirds of this age group's years of life lost to premature mortality. Sinha and Lipton and colleagues (1999) suggest that violence is a particular problem associated with youth in some larger cities (although evidence is reported in Chapter 5 that at the international level this association is not statistically valid):

> Violence (mostly murders) in São Paulo, Brazil, in 1992 accounted for 86 per cent of all deaths in males aged 15–19 years, and the death rate from murders for adolescent males from deprived areas was 11 times that of males from wealthier areas.
>
> (Sinha and Lipton with others 1999, page 22)

The very low life expectancy at birth for many cities in sub-Saharan Africa, as shown in Table 3.2, is known to relate in large part to high mortality rates among adolescents and adults from HIV/AIDS and to the lack of treatment available to those who are HIV positive, as well as to other diseases to which populations with HIV are vulnerable, especially tuberculosis.

HIV/AIDS and its associated health problems is one of the leading causes of adult mortality in many cities, especially in many sub-Saharan African nations – although this is due not so much to the infection as to the lack of access to the drugs and associated treatments that do so much to prolong life and limit its health impacts. There is a lack of consistent and reliable data on the geography of HIV/AIDS infection in sub-Saharan Africa, but it is accepted that in most nations levels of HIV infection are *usually* higher in urban areas than in rural areas, with large urban areas having the highest prevalence of HIV (van Donk 2006; Dyson 2003). The HIV epidemic impacts most on the poorest, youngest and least powerful sections of the population, who are unable to avoid, mitigate the effects of or leave unsafe relationships (Bruce and Joyce 2006). They are also more susceptible to infection, as their health and immune system have been undermined by undernutrition and other health problems such as tuberculosis.

The World Health Organization states that tuberculosis (TB) is second only to HIV/AIDS as the greatest killer due to a single infectious agent worldwide, and that over 95 per cent of deaths from tuberculosis occur in low- and middle-income countries; tuberculosis is also among the top three causes of death for women aged 15 to 44. In 2009, there were about 10 million orphan children as a result of TB deaths among parents and TB is a leading killer of people living with HIV, causing one quarter of all deaths (WHO 2012a). Among low-income urban dwellers, adolescent girls and young women are disproportionately affected because they are least able to avoid the risks and protect themselves (Mabala 2006).

A number of overlapping social groups can be identified as having disproportionate levels of risk to HIV infection, although the reasons for this and the urban contexts in which these happen are likely to differ (van Donk 2006; Mabala 2006). These groups include women and girls subject to sexual coercion; in urban areas in some nations it is common for girls from the age of 10 upwards to be household or domestic workers living in homes without parents (Mabala 2006). These young people are particularly vulnerable and there are, or are thought to be, high levels of rape in some nations and cities.

The reasons for premature mortality and morbidity are thus a complex mix of factors linked to disease burdens, undernutrition and lack of appropriate health care services (all associated with poverty), inadequate incomes and the absence of safety nets when incomes fall or livelihoods are lost (when sex becomes a commodity needed for survival), and inadequate or no provision for the rule of law.

The UN 2010 revision of *World Population Prospects* 'confirms yet again the devastating toll AIDS has in terms of increased morbidity, mortality and population loss' (United Nations 2011b, page 19). Although the statistics provided are for national populations and are not available for urban and rural populations:

Life expectancy in the most affected countries already shows dramatic declines. In Botswana, where HIV prevalence is estimated at 24.8 per cent in 2009 among the population aged 15–49 years, life expectancy has fallen from 64 years in 1985–1990 to 49 years in 2000–2005. By 2005–2010, life expectancy is expected to increase again to 53 years as a result of declining HIV prevalence and increased access to anti-retroviral therapy. In Southern Africa as a whole, where most of the worst affected countries are, life expectancy has fallen from 61 to 51 years over the last 20 years. While the impact in Southern Africa is particularly stark, the majority of highly affected countries in Africa have experienced declines in life expectancy in recent years because of the epidemic.

(United Nations 2011b, page 55)

The report also notes the toll that HIV/AIDS is taking in retarding progress in reducing child mortality because of the high proportion of children infected through mother-to-child transmission.

It is likely that the differentials in maternal health and mortality would be as dramatic as the differentials in infant and child health and mortality if data were available to compare urban populations in high- and low-income nations and high- and low-income groups within cities. However, there is a lack of data.

The World Health Organization reports that 99 per cent of all maternal deaths are in low- and middle-income countries; more than half occur in sub-Saharan Africa and a third in South Asia (WHO 2012b). Maternal mortality rates in high-income nations are around 14 per 100,000 live births, with the average for low- and middle-income countries being 290 and some nations having rates of 1,000 or more. WHO notes that there are also large disparities within countries between people with high and low income and between people living in rural and urban areas, although we suspect that if there were data on maternal mortality rates in informal settlements, in many cities these would be particularly high. For instance, the maternal mortality rates for two Nairobi informal settlements for the period January 2003 to December 2005 was 706 deaths per 100,000 live births (Ziraba *et al.* 2009). A study of the contribution of HIV/AIDS to maternal mortality in Benin City, Nigeria suggested that the maternal mortality rate for the hospital studied was an astonishing 1,875 per 100,000 live births (Onakewhor *et al.* 2011). A maternal mortality rate of 645 deaths per 100,000 live births was estimated from a study in Dakshinpuri, a 'slum' in New Delhi (Mayank *et al.* 2001). In the early 1990s, the maternal mortality rate in Dar es Salaam was reported as being 572 per 100,000 live births (Nyamtema *et al.* 2008) and this is likely to have been higher in the city's many informal settlements. Agarwal (2011) examines the quality of care available to mothers in urban areas in India, comparing the poorest quartile with the rest of the urban population. Within the poorest quartile, a little over half of mothers have at least three antenatal care visits and only half have births assisted by health personnel; for the rest of the urban population, over 80 per cent have at least three visits and births assisted by health personnel.

Urban poverty and nutrition

More than one third of urban children in low-income nations may be stunted (see Table 3.4; stunting is associated with chronic malnutrition). A study of ten nations in sub-Saharan Africa showed that the proportion of the urban population with energy deficiencies was above 40 per cent in all but one nation and above 60 per cent in three – Ethiopia, Malawi and Zambia (Ruel and Garrett 2004).

As with infant and child mortality rates, in most cities there are large differentials in the prevalence of severe malnutrition between wealthy and poorer areas. For instance, the prevalence of severe malnutrition – measured as the percentage of children aged 12–59 months with a mid-upper arm circumference of less than 12.5 cm – among boys in the informal settlements of Bangladesh's two largest cities was nearly 2.5 times that in the 'non-slums' (UNICEF 2000). In a survey of children from 252 households in a 'slum' in Dhaka, 39 per cent were malnourished and 32 per cent stunted; children who were malnourished and stunted had elevated rates of diarrhoea, as expected, averaging more than two episodes per year as

Table 3.4 Percentage of urban children stunted

Urban children stunted	Nation and year of survey
> 35%	Timor-Leste 2009–10, Malawi 2010
30–34.9%	Zambia 2007, Benin 2006, India 2005–06
25–29.9%	São Tomé and Principe 2008–09, Nigeria 2008, Guatemala 2008, Niger 2006, Bangladesh 2007, Tanzania 2010
20–24.9%	Democratic Republic of the Congo 2007, Sierra Leone 2008, Kenya 2008–09, Mali 2006, Egypt 2008, Liberia 2007, Uganda 2006, Nepal 2006, Cambodia 2010, Namibia 2006–07, Albania 2008–09,
15–19.9%	Swaziland 2006/07, Maldives 2009, Ghana 2008, Haiti 2005–06
10–14.9%	Bolivia 2008, Jordan 2007, Azerbaijan 2006, Guyana 2009, Nicaragua 2006

Source: Data from Demographic and Health Surveys, using STATcompiler
(http://www.statcompiler.com)

against 1.6 episodes in better-nourished children (Haque *et al.* 2003). A 1997 study found that over half of Dhaka informal settlement residents over the age of 16 years suffered from malnutrition, while 73 per cent of children under five suffered from undernutrition, with 69 per cent stunted and 31 per cent wasted (Bangladesh Bureau of Statistics 1997).

A study across five cities in Indonesia surveying almost 140,000 low-income households between 1999 and 2003 examined differences in diarrhoea prevalence in the seven days before the survey between groups that purchased cheap drinking water, groups that purchased more expensive water and groups that accessed water from a well, lake or spring. Children in households buying cheap water had a higher diarrhoea prevalence and were more likely to be undernourished, but nutritional deficiencies were common in all three groups: rates were 24–29 per cent underweight, 30–35 per cent stunted and 11–12 per cent wasted (Semba *et al.* 2009)

For India's urban population in 2005, over half of the children in the poorest quartile were stunted and 47 per cent underweight; what is perhaps as astonishing is that a third of children in the rest of the urban population were also stunted. In addition, in Delhi and Maharashtra, two of the wealthiest states, the proportion of children in the poorest quartile who were stunted was higher than the average for India (Agarwal 2011). A study of informal settlements in Delhi found that 51 per cent of households were food insecure (Agarwal *et al.* 2009).

A household survey in two low-income settlements in Cape Town in 2002 found that more than 80 per cent of households had insufficient food, and more than 70 per cent reported hunger; the responses to questions about the types of food eaten also showed diets lacking in meat, eggs, fruit and vegetables (De Swardt *et al.* 2005).

Urban poverty and morbidity

Apart from studies on undernutrition, studies of morbidity (illness and injury) among low-income groups or within settlements where most residents have inadequate incomes are even rarer than those on mortality – although there are some studies on the physical hazards that contribute to injuries among children (Bartlett *et al.* 1999; Bartlett 2002). There are also various studies showing the high proportion of children (and sometimes adults) with serious intestinal parasite infections (Bartlett *et al.* 1999; Hardoy, Mitlin and Satterthwaite 2001).

Most of the documentation of illness and injury among low-income groups or those living in informal settlements is related to the health risks from homes and to the lack of supporting infrastructure and services. There is much less documentation on health problems faced by low-income groups in the workplace (i.e. occupational health and safety), especially for those working in informal enterprises or home workers, although the occasional case study highlights how serious these problems can be – see, for instance, the health issues in small enterprises in Kolkata involved in lead battery breaking and lead smelting documented by Dasgupta (1997). Some studies have documented the occupational health problems faced by working children and how and why they are at much higher risk of death or permanent disablement than adults (Bartlett *et al.* 1999).

There is an evident link between manual labour and poor health. In a study of informal settlements in Dhaka, Kabir *et al.* (2000) note:

> Fear of employment loss often pushes sick individuals to resume work before complete recovery. Unskilled workers, engaged in hard physical labour, are particularly vulnerable in this regard. Employment insecurity forces these workers into a cycle of repeated illness, poor nutritional status and low work productivity resulting in the continuous degradation of their human and material capital.
>
> (page 712)

Amis and Kumar (2000) report similar findings in a study of Visakhapatham (India); noting, moreover, that 'the problem is not one of direct ill-health but of overall nutritional level, poor diet, physical fitness and the severity of the physical labour' (page 192).

Some occupations have particular vulnerabilities. Begum and Sen (2005) document the health problems of rickshaw pullers in Dhaka, noting that only 42 per cent of long-term pullers feel good about their health compared to nearly 70 per cent of those that recently began the work.

In 2006 there were an estimated 676,000 people working as manual scavengers in India (WaterAid India 2009). Remuneration is low and the health risks are considerable, a situation exacerbated by a poor information base:

> Common health ailments reported are parasitic infections, gastrointestinal disorders, skin ailments, diminished vision and hearing due to the toxic fumes

inhaled during cleaning of septic tanks and manholes. Respiratory diseases like breathlessness and consistent cough were also experienced by some. Communicable diseases such as dysentery, typhoid, malaria and mainly tuberculosis (TB) were found to be prevalent among scavengers. The cases of TB are rarely revealed, primarily because of the attached social stigma. Heavy menstruation, miscarriage, severe anemia, irregularity in heart beat are some of the health problems which women face.

(WaterAid India 2009, page 9)

The research into informal settlements in Dhaka mentioned previously (Kabir *et al*. 2000; also Pryer 2003) assesses the contribution of illness to poverty and highlights the extent to which ill-health causes a deterioration in households' financial status. In this study of 850 households, ill-health was the single most important cause of such a deterioration, explaining 22 per cent of cases reported. In any month, 30 to 40 per cent of households reported days lost due to illness. On average about four days per month were lost in casual unskilled households and eight days in female-headed households. Illness led to reductions in income and increased expenditures; often more loans taken out and assets sold, with some adults resorting to begging (Pryer 2003). Kabir *et al*. (2000) report that the most significant shocks included the death of income earners, income earners becoming ill or disabled and (to a lesser extent) the sickness of non-working members of the household. Reporting on the incidence and consequences of illness, 52.2 per cent of men and 66.2 per cent of women said they had been ill in the previous fourteen days. The responses highlight the vulnerability of these households: 'During my child's illness I did not go to work for one day but they deducted my salary for two days' (garment factory worker quoted in Kabir *et al*. 2000, page 711).

Aliber (2003) quotes a study of urban areas in Côte d'Ivoire showing that the average decline in household income when a household member becomes ill with AIDS is 52 to 67 per cent, and that '[m]eanwhile household health expenditure quadruples and food consumption declines by 41 per cent' (pages 18–19). The implications of HIV/AIDS for chronic urban poverty are rarely considered, although the broader impacts are assessed. For example, a recent analysis for Namibia suggests that growth in national GDP will be 2 per cent by 2015 rather than the 3.5 per cent that might have been achieved without HIV/AIDS (World Bank Namibia 2001).

The link between illness, increasing indebtedness (to cope with the drop in income) and increase in health care expenditure and poverty is also described in a study of Visakhapatnam, India (Amis and Kumar 2000). Although it is dangerous to draw general conclusions, the living conditions described in this study and the two studies of informal settlements in Dhaka (Kabir *et al*. 2000 and Pryer 2003) are similar to those in informal settlements or tenements in many other urban centres in low- and middle-income nations. Comparable relationships between high health burdens and impoverishment would be expected.

The significance of ill-health as a trigger for income loss is illustrated by the study of rickshaw pullers in Dhaka, all of whom lived in slum settlements (Begum and Sen 2005). Much the most common cause of crisis was ill-health. Two fifths of the rickshaw pullers interviewed had been ill in the month prior to the interview. Each episode of illness on average cost the rickshaw puller six days' income (combining cost of treatment and work days lost). More than half of the pullers had no savings and no assets, one fifth were unable to secure three meals a day, half could not generate any surplus income and a similar proportion had outstanding debt.

For Accra, Maxwell *et al.* (2000, page 40) reported on focus groups' identification of significant livelihood shocks, the most frequent being the loss of income from primary earnings though death, abandonment, illness or accident.

Of course, the impacts of illness and injury are much increased by the lack of good quality health care and, where needed, emergency services (including ambulances and access to emergency responses in hospitals).

Alice Sverdlik's (2011) review of health problems in informal settlements notes that mental health issues in informal settlements or associated with inadequate incomes in urban areas in low-income nations had received too little attention, even though their importance has been highlighted for a number of years (Ekblad 1993; Harpham and Blue 1995; Hardoy, Mitlin and Satterthwaite 2001; Montgomery *et al.* 2003). Figure 3.4 and Table 3.1 show the very large list of potential psycho-social stressors linked to poor living and working conditions, to the deprivations associated with inadequate incomes and to factors such as lack or disruption of social support networks, disempowerment and exclusion or discrimination. The health interventions needed to address these are only beginning to be studied in low-income settings (Montgomery 2009).

Beard (2000, page 376) describes the analysis of one elderly widow living in an informal settlement in Yogyakarta with her widowed daughter and a granddaughter and grandson. The widow described how a lack of food and proper clothing causes self-esteem and mental health to deteriorate, so that, for her, 'the physical and psychological manifestations of poverty are interdependent. Blue (1996) discusses a study of three sub-districts of São Paulo:

> The data revealed a highly significant ($p < 0.001$) variation in the prevalence of probable cases of mental disorder across the three sub-districts: 21 per cent in Brasilândia (the lowest socio-economic sub-district); 16 per cent in Vila Guilherme (the middle socio-economic sub-district); and 12 per cent in Aclimação (the highest socio-economic sub-district).
>
> (page 95)

Focus groups in such areas help illustrate the causes of mental health problems, with major factors being poor physical infrastructure (and related family ill-health) and violence. Moser (1997) discusses the problem of depression in Cisne Dos, Guayaquil, Ecuador, with 79 per cent of women saying that they thought other women in the immediate area suffered from this problem and 76 per cent acknowledging that they themselves had been depressed.

Urban poverty and environment

Having considered the studies that inform us of the nature, extent and causes of health problems in low-income settlements, we move on to review the literature on the quality of the urban environment and discuss a range of anticipated and observed health-related issues.

Environmental health burdens

Any consideration of environmental health issues associated with urban poverty needs to include biological pathogens (disease-causing agents), chemical pollutants and physical hazards in the home, workplace and wider city environment (Satterthwaite 1993; Hardoy, Mitlin and Satterthwaite 1992, 2001). One of the most striking differences between urban areas in high-income nations and those in low- and most middle-income nations is the scale of the health burden from infectious and parasitic diseases (these are 'environmental' in that they are transmitted in the environment – they are airborne or spread through contaminated food or water, contact, insects or other disease vectors).

The documentation is incomplete, but it is clear that infectious and parasitic diseases have a very large impact in terms of serious illness and premature death among large sections of children and youth in most urban centres in low- and middle-income nations, and very little impact among these groups in high-income nations (WHO 1992; Satterthwaite *et al.* 1996). There is also some evidence of much larger health burdens for adults (Bradley *et al.* 1991; also WHO 1992; Pryer 2003). Thus, for most urban centres in the Global South, the most pressing environmental issue is reducing the burden of 'environmental' diseases, including diarrhoeal diseases, typhoid, acute respiratory infections, malaria, tuberculosis and many parasitic infections.

Despite the inadequate documentation of the scale and depth of environmental health burdens, there is plenty of evidence that large sections of the urban population live in very poor quality environments (or what can be termed life- and health-threatening environments). Table 3.1 on pages 96–9 lists the many factors that contribute to this, including poor quality, overcrowded housing with inadequate or no basic infrastructure (piped water, sewers, drains, paved roads and footpaths, electricity) or services (health care, emergency services, schools, provision for children's play and for pre-school children; Hardoy, Mitlin and Satterthwaite 2001; WHO 1992; UNCHS 1996). Although the proportion of an urban centre's population suffering serious deficiencies in most or all of these areas will vary, as will the extent of the deficiencies, only a very small proportion of urban centres in low- or middle-income nations get close to the coverage and quality of provision expected by urban populations in high-income nations for, for instance, water, sanitation, drainage and solid waste collection. No family in urban areas in high-income nations, however poor, has to walk several hundred yards to collect water from a communal standpipe shared with hundreds of others, or is without a toilet in their home or services for household waste collection.

Given the size of the urban population in low- and middle-income countries and the scale of the environmental health problems, surprisingly little attention has been given to documenting and addressing these problems. Interest in this issue developed in the late 1980s and early 1990s, supported by WHO and UNICEF,[58] but this generated little answering interest among governments or large international funders and subsequently waned in both agencies. More recent attempts to reinvigorate this area include the work of Montgomery *et al.* (2003), GRNUHE (2010) and Vlahov *et al.* (2011).

Perhaps the key issue in regard to environment and health in urban areas is that the clustering of people, enterprises, transport systems and their wastes provides many potential advantages for a healthy environment because of returns on agglomeration (including economies of scale and proximity) in the infrastructure, services and regulations needed for a healthy environment. But this same clustering has many potential health disadvantages in the absence of such infrastructure, services and regulations (and in the absence of a government structure able to ensure their provision). Concentrations of people mean most infectious and parasitic diseases are more easily spread. Concentration of people and production also concentrates solid, liquid and gaseous wastes – including, obviously, human excreta. If these consequences are not well managed, they create severe health problems. Cities concentrate motor vehicles too; again there is much potential to reduce air pollution and numbers of accidents, but very large adverse health impacts if this potential is not acted upon. Many cities concentrate industries, with a proportion that may produce hazardous wastes, although these need not create health disadvantages if appropriate regulations for occupational health and safety, pollution and solid waste management are in place and enforced. As discussed, there is plenty of evidence for how unhealthy and dangerous city environments can be, but there are also examples of cities with very healthy environments and much better than average health indicators.

Perhaps the key issue in regard to poverty and health is that cities can be healthy places for those with low incomes too, if the key health determinants (social, economic, environmental and political) are in place for those with low incomes. In Figure 3.4, many of the most influential determinants are environmental, acting in the home and its surrounds, the workplace and the wider city (Hardoy, Mitlin and Satterthwaite 2001). There are vast disparities in urban environmental conditions and health outcomes, with low-income communities usually facing much greater burdens than wealthier areas. Drawing on available studies, the generalizations that follow seem valid for urban populations in the Global South:[59]

1   *It is common for between one and two thirds of an urban centre's population to live in housing of poor quality.* Much of the housing in which lower-income groups live is made partly or wholly from non-permanent, often flammable materials. There are often high levels of overcrowding in terms of indoor space per person and number of persons per room.

2   *A perhaps surprisingly large proportion of urban dwellers in most low-income and many middle-income nations still use dirty fuels.* These fuels are

used for cooking and, where needed, heating. This creates risks from high levels of indoor air pollution, which can have severe health impacts (Smith and Akbar 2003; see also WHO 2011c). In 2005, 700 million urban dwellers still lacked access to clean fuels and 279 million lacked electricity (Legros *et al.* 2009).

3 *Much of the urban population lacks safe, regular, convenient supplies of water and provision for sanitation.* The extent is far greater than the official statistics suggest; this is discussed in more detail later.

4 *Much of the urban population lack regular (or even irregular) services for the collection of household waste.* Many live in settlements that lack the paved roads needed to allow conventional garbage collection trucks to provide a door-to-door service. In low-income nations, it is common for large sections of middle- or even upper-income groups to have inadequate or no provision. Again, it is likely that the extent of the problem in smaller urban centres is underestimated, as most existing documentation focuses on larger urban centres. The environmental health implications of a lack of garbage collection services in urban areas are obvious – most households dispose of their wastes on any available empty site, into nearby ditches or lakes, or simply along streets. The problems associated with this include the smells, the disease vectors and pests encouraged by rubbish, and drainage channels blocked with waste. Where provision for sanitation is also inadequate (as it usually is), many households dispose of their toilet waste into drains or dispose of faecal matter within their garbage. Uncollected waste is obviously a serious hazard, especially for children playing in and around the home and playing with items drawn from uncollected rubbish, as well as for those who sort through rubbish looking for items that can be reused or recycled (Hardoy, Mitlin and Satterthwaite 2001; Hunt 1996).

5 *There are very large health burdens relating primarily to infectious and parasitic diseases and accidents.* Even if there are relatively few detailed studies of the health problems of populations in urban centres, this is what available studies suggest (McGranahan 1991; Bradley *et al.* 1991; Hardoy, Mitlin and Satterthwaite 2001; WHO 1992; Pryer 2003). It is almost certain that there are large health burdens arising from unsafe working conditions for low-income urban dwellers, with exposure to diseases, chemical pollutants and physical hazards in the workplace being a significant contributor to premature death, injury and illness (and their obvious economic consequences). Although some sense of these working conditions is given in Chapter 4, there is no general assessment of the scale of the health impacts. A considerable part of these impacts occurs within the residential environment, since this is where a significant proportion of low-income people work.

6 *In many urban locations, there are also large and often growing health burdens from non-communicable diseases.* For instance, cancer, diabetes and strokes often create a 'double burden', as low-income urban dwellers face both communicable and non-communicable diseases (see Sverdlik 2011 for a review; see Moser 2011 for a powerful example of the economic impact of

cancer on a low-income household; see also Montgomery *et al.* 2003). But much more work is needed on understanding the health problems that impact on urban populations (and especially low-income urban populations) disaggregated by age, sex and occupation, including the relative roles of non-communicable diseases, and importantly which non-communicable diseases (Reardon 2011). As Sara Reardon (2011) commented, diabetes that comes from starvation is not the same as diabetes linked to obesity, and the kinds of cancers and heart diseases that affect low-income groups are often not the same as those that affect high-income groups.

7   *Physical hazards evident in the home and its surroundings are likely to be among the most common causes of serious injury and premature death in informal settlements and other housing types used by low-income urban dwellers.* These include, burns, scalds and accidental fires, cuts and injuries from falls (Goldstein 1990; WHO 1999). The health burdens these cause are particularly heavy where housing is made of flammable materials, there are high levels of overcrowding and a reliance on open fires or unstable stoves for cooking and heating, and candles or kerosene lamps for lighting. Large health burdens and high levels of accidental death from physical hazards are also related to the lack of provision for rapid and appropriate treatment, both in health care and from emergency services.

8   *Road traffic accidents are among the most serious physical hazards in urban areas.* However, there are no data that separate rural from urban. The World Health Organization reports that about 1.3 million people die each year as a result of road traffic accidents and over 90 per cent of these fatalities occur in low- and middle-income countries, even though these have less than half of the world's vehicles. Nearly half (46 per cent) of those dying are pedestrians, cyclists and motorcyclists, and these represent up to 80 per cent of all deaths in some low- and middle-income countries. Between 20 and 50 million more people suffer non-fatal injuries, with many incurring a disability as a result (WHO 2011b). Road traffic accidents did not figure in the top ten causes of death for low-income nations in 2008, but was seventh in middle-income nations (WHO 2011a). Children and young people under the age of 25 years account for over 30 per cent of those killed and injured in road traffic crashes. Given that low-income groups will be disproportionately represented among those who walk or cycle, they are also likely to be more at risk from road traffic accidents. The WHO (2011b) notes that '[e]ven within high-income countries, people from lower socioeconomic backgrounds are more likely to be involved in ... road traffic crashes than their more affluent counterparts'.

9   *There are also many cities and smaller urban centres or particular settlements within cities where levels of outdoor air pollution considerably exceed WHO guidelines.* These include centres of heavy industry, mining or quarrying, and cities with high concentrations of motor vehicles with elevated levels of polluting emissions. The World Health Organization has data on suspended particulate matter (annual mean PM_{10})[60] for over 1,000 cities. The WHO has estimated that for 2008 the number of premature deaths attributable to urban

outdoor air pollution was 1.34 million worldwide; of these, 1.09 million deaths could have been avoided if the WHO Air Quality Guideline values were implemented (WHO 2011e). All the cities with the highest levels of air pollution by this measure are in low- and middle-income nations. Of the 11 cities with annual mean PM_{10} above 200 (more than ten times the WHO guideline), four were in Iran, three were in Pakistan, two in India and one each in Mongolia and Botswana. Of the 75 cities with annual mean PM_{10} above 100, 16 were in China, 15 were in India, 14 were in Iran, 6 in Pakistan, 6 in Saudi Arabia and 4 in Turkey.[61]

The range and quality of data available on air pollution, traffic accidents and their health impacts have improved considerably over the last 15 years, but none of the global or national data, or, for air pollution, city data, has any information on where and when these have a disproportionate impact on low-income groups or on residents of informal settlements. If more detailed, spatial data were available it is obvious that certain informal settlements would be likely to show up as having particularly high levels of road traffic accidents, for instance the informal settlements that develop beside major roads or highways which their inhabitants have to cross without traffic lights or bridges. It is also likely that the areas in cities with much higher than average air pollution levels will generally be predominantly low-income areas.

10 *Within this general picture of very limited achievement in reducing the health impacts of environmental hazards in urban areas there are important exceptions, where environmental health is substantially better.* There are examples of urban areas in both low- and middle-income nations that show that it is possible to greatly improve environmental health, even in informal settlements or among low-income populations. Many of the examples of success have been achieved by a combination of grassroots organizations and local NGOs; some of the largest-scale successes were achieved by innovative city governments (Hardoy, Mitlin and Satterthwaite 2001; Campbell 2003; Cabannes 2004; Satterthwaite 2009; Almansi 2009).

11 *There are also urban centres where environmental health conditions are even worse than the generalizations noted above.* Hundreds of millions of people live in urban centres where, at least in terms of public and environmental health, there is no functioning government for them – there is no provision or management of piped water, sewers (or other excreta disposal systems that meet health standards), drains or solid waste collection; and no provision for the land-use management needed to encourage and support good quality housing. Nor is there pollution control. There is often no or limited public provision for schools and for health care for large sections of the urban population. In many ways they resemble the cities in Europe and North America in the mid-nineteenth century, before public and environmental health issues were addressed by government. Life expectancies and infant and child mortality rates among these groups may today be comparable to those in mid-nineteenth century cities. We know little about some of the most

deficient urban centres, as there is little or no documentation. Take, for instance, India: the 2011 census recorded over 8,000 urban centres – for most of these, there is no documentation of environmental health problems. A website from the International Water Association profiling water and sanitation for many sub-Saharan African cities provides examples of major cities where there is, in effect, no government provision for public or environmental health for most of their populations (IWA, undated). Among the cities covered, the following have no sewers or sewers that reach a very small proportion of the population: Addis Ababa, Bamako, Benin, Brazzaville, Dar es Salaam, Douala, Freetown, Ibadan, Kaduna, Kinshasa, Kumasi, Lagos, Lubumbashi, Maiduguri, Mbuji-Mayi, Port Harcourt, Yaoundé and Zaria. These are all major cities: all have populations of more than a million and many are much larger. Several other cities are reported to have sewers serving a small proportion of their population, often in poor repair or no longer functioning. Of course, it is possible to have good quality sanitation in some urban contexts without sewers, but most of the cities named also have large proportions of their population living in dense informal settlements that do not have provision for (for instance) septic tanks or good quality, easily serviced pit latrines. A high proportion of households have no toilet in their home.

12 *In the absence of data for each city or smaller urban centre on the most serious environmental health problems and who is most at risk, it is obviously difficult to set priorities for either action or research.* When this lack of data is combined with research and action agendas strongly influenced by external funding and the preferences and choices of external professionals, it can lead to inappropriate decisions. In part, this is the result of assumptions that topics which are important in urban areas in high-income nations are also important for urban centres in low-income nations. But it is also because research is funded externally and supports professionals from high-income nations who have no experience in the fields of most relevance to poverty and health – for instance no training in or knowledge of the infectious and parasitic diseases that represent such significant health risks for low-income urban dwellers in most low- and many middle-income nations.

A consideration of city environments and poverty requires a focus on two factors: environmental health in the home, workplace and outdoors, and factors relating to overuse or degradation of resources, including sinks for waste. The two are not the same, although they are often confused, especially in the environmental literature. Cities can have good environmental health while at the same time contributing to the overuse or degradation of resources and global warming – generally a characteristic of relatively wealthy cities. Cities can have very poor environmental health yet contribute relatively little to overuse or degradation of resources and have very low levels of greenhouse gas emissions per person – a characteristic of most urban centres in low-income nations. Poverty is often assumed to be associated with environmental degradation but this is not actually true, in that

poverty is associated with very low levels of resourc
(Satterthwaite 2003). However, poverty is strongly
environmental health because of poor quality housin
water, sanitation, drainage and solid waste managemen
of all cities.

Urban poverty and water and sanitation

As with most urban infrastructure, concentrations of pec
it easier and cheaper per person served to provide good qi
safe to drink, and sanitation and drainage for each bu ....ng. There are many
examples showing that this is possible even in informal or illegal settlements with
a predominance of low-income households, especially in Latin America but also
in some middle-income nations (see Boonyabancha 2005). These include
examples of good quality provision for water and sanitation at low unit costs and
with close to full cost recovery from the inhabitants (UN-HABITAT 2003a, 2006;
Hasan 2006). But in most of Africa and Asia this is still the exception – and in the
absence of good provision, concentrations of people and their wastes greatly
increase health risks from a great range of waterborne, water-washed or water-
related diseases. At any one time, half the world's population is suffering from a
disease associated with inadequacies in provision for water, sanitation and
hygiene; virtually all are in low- and middle-income nations (WHO 1999).
Inadequate provision for water and sanitation contributes to many of the health
problems and the high levels of infant and child death described in earlier sections.
Good quality provision for water and sanitation is also known to dramatically
lower morbidity from a wide range of diseases including cholera, typhoid,
leptospirosis, scabies, trachoma, schistosomiasis and many diarrhoeal diseases
(WHO 1986).

For most nations in the Global South, the proportion of the urban population
with provision for water and sanitation to a standard that is healthy, affordable and
convenient is unknown. Estimates for 2000 suggested that around half the urban
population in Africa and Asia lacked such provision; for Latin America and the
Caribbean, more than a quarter lacked such provision (UN-HABITAT 2003a,
2006; see Table 3.5). It is likely that the numbers of urban dwellers without
adequate provision has risen significantly since then, except perhaps in Latin
America where there is evidence of an increased proportion of the urban population
being well-served.

The official UN statistics produced by the Joint Monitoring Programme (JMP)
for Water Supply and Sanitation for urban areas suggest that the situation is less
serious than shown in Table 3.5. The JMP's figures show that the proportion of
the urban population lacking 'improved' provision for water and sanitation is
much lower – for instance, in 2000, 94 per cent of the urban population in low-
and middle-income nations was said to have 'improved' provision for water,
which suggests only around 118 million urban dwellers lacked such improved
provision. In this same year, around 700 million urban dwellers lacked 'improved'

nates of the number and proportion of people without adequate provision
r water and sanitation in urban areas in 2000

Region	Urban dwellers without adequate provision (number and approximate percentage)	
	Water	*Sanitation*
Africa	100–150 million (35–50%)	150–180 million (50–60%)
Asia	500–700 million (35–50%)	600–800 million (45–60%)
Latin America and the Caribbean	80–120 million (20–30%)	100–150 million (25–40%)

Source: UN-HABITAT (2003a)

sanitation (UNICEF and WHO 2012). These figures might be taken to suggest that Table 3.5 exaggerates the problem, but as the JMP states there are for most nations no data available on the proportion of urban (or rural) dwellers with provision of water and sanitation to a standard adequate for health. The JMP statistics reflecting 'improved' provision do not equate to adequate provision. For water, 'improved' provision includes piped water into dwelling, yard or plot, public tap or standpipe, tubewell or borehole, protected dug well, protected spring or rainwater collection. For sanitation, 'improved' provision includes use of flush or pour-flush toilets to piped sewer system, septic tank or pit latrine, ventilated improved pit latrine, pit latrine with slab or composting toilet (UNICEF and WHO 2012).

However, as noted in Chapter 2, the UN statistics for 'improved' sanitation have been dramatically lowered in sub-Saharan Africa. In the JMP's 2000 assessment, 85 per cent of Africa's urban population was said to have improved sanitation, but in the 2012 assessment the figure is 55 per cent. The 2000 assessment had reported that many sub-Saharan African nations provided almost the whole of their urban populations with improved sanitation by 2000, but the 2012 assessment presents much lower figures.

The only recent data on water and sanitation for most nations comes from responses to a few questions from nationally representative samples of households within surveys aimed at collecting demographic and health data. It is not possible to ascertain whether a household has adequate provision for water or sanitation from a few such questions, especially when it relies on a range of water sources. Asking a household whether it has access to piped supplies close by, for example, does not establish whether the water is of adequate quality, the supply is regular or access is easy (there may be a tap close by but if it is shared with hundreds of others long queues will be common). Similarly, asking a household whether it has access to an 'improved' toilet will provide no indication of whether the toilet is adequate, available or used by all household members (toilets may be on the premises but some inhabitants, such as tenants, may have limited access). It is also likely that most household surveys under-represent the population living in illegal settlements in cities because those administering the surveys are frightened to undertake interviews there. This is why the JMP is careful to state that the UN statistics (which draw heavily on these household surveys) do not reveal who does and does not have 'adequate' provision or safe drinking water. However, as noted in Chapter 2, the UN agencies reporting on water and sanitation provision for the Millennium Development Goals use these statistics and often label them as figures for provision of safe or clean water. For instance, *The Millennium Development Goals Report 2011* uses JMP statistics in a section that discusses 'progress to improve access to clean drinking water' (United Nations 2011a, page 54). It also claims that the MDGs' drinking water target is likely to be surpassed; however, the MDGs' target is for 'safe' water, not 'improved' provision.

However, the JMP has recently provided statistics on the proportion of the urban population for each nation with water piped into the home. For urban populations this is a much better indicator of 'adequate' provision; reliance on any public source (standpipe, kiosk, vendor, tanker) rarely provides adequate supplies for good health and usually involves heavy time and cost burdens. This statistic is still not a measure of adequate provision – this would need data on the regularity of supply, quality of water and cost – but it does highlight two key issues. First, both for many nations and globally, the proportion of the urban population with water piped into their premises is much lower than the proportion said to have 'improved' provision (see Figure 3.5). In 2010, 700 million urban dwellers in the Global South were reported as being without water piped into their premises, compared to 130 million without 'improved' provision (UNICEF and WHO 2012). Second, the findings indicate the very large number of nations where half or more of their urban population lack such piped water (see Figure 3.5).

For the 173 nations for which 2010 data were available, less than a quarter of the urban population had water piped into their premises in 18; most of these nations are in sub-Saharan Africa but they also include Bangladesh, Myanmar, Afghanistan and Haiti (UNICEF and WHO 2012). This probably understates the scale of the problem because data were not available for some low-income nations. Among the nations for which data are available, 35 showed *decreases* in the proportion of the urban population with water piped into their premises between 1990 and 2010. Some nations showed dramatic falls. Democratic Republic of the Congo was reported to have 51 per cent of its urban population with water piped to the premises in 1990 and 21 per cent in 2010. Figures for the Sudan fell from 76 to 47 per cent. Other nations for which coverage dropped more than 20 percentage points were Rwanda, Nigeria, Vanuatu and Mongolia. Zimbabwe, Dominican Republic, Malawi, Yemen, Zambia, Tanzania, Haiti, Kenya, Namibia and Madagascar all had falls of 10–20 per cent. Coverage in India dropped by 1 percentage point. Declines are likely to have taken place in other nations, but these are not recorded as no data were available for 1990 (UNICEF and WHO 2012). There were also many nations with low levels of coverage that increased little if at all. These included Sierra Leone (no increase) and Myanmar and Pakistan (2 per cent increases). A study in the late 1990s in Kenya, Uganda and Tanzania showed that in many cities provision for water and sanitation was worse

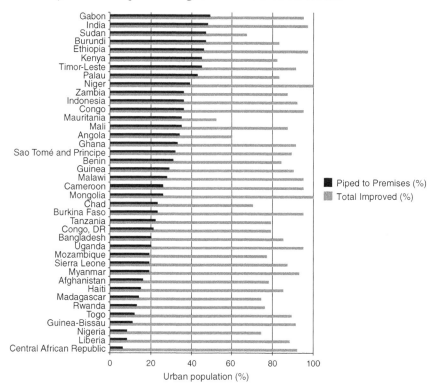

Figure 3.5 Proportion of urban populations said to have 'improved provision' for water and water piped to their premises

Source: Data from UNICEF and WHO (2012)

than it had been in the early 1970s, with a lower proportion of the population adequately served and with a lower quality of provision (Thompson *et al.* 2000).

Seventy-eight nations managed to increase the proportion of their urban population with water piped to their premises during these two decades, although in many cases not by much, or the increase reflected very low provision in 1990. However, there was obviously considerable progress in a proportion of nations. Latin American nations showed some of the largest increases in the proportion of their urban populations with piped water and reached high levels of coverage – with many over 90 per cent by 2010.

There is also the issue of quality of provision for those with piped connections. Egypt is said to have universal coverage for piped water for its urban population (UNICEF and WHO 2012) but according to the government's National Research Centre, 40 per cent of those living in Cairo do not get water for more than three hours per day (UN-HABITAT 2011). Additionally, some districts do not receive any piped water at all, and those in low-income districts face more than twice as many water cut-offs lasting more than 24 hours and nearly twice as many lasting up to 24 hours than those in high-income districts (UN-HABITAT 2011).

Figure 3.6 shows the percentage of urban populations with water piped to their premises plotted against per capita gross national income. The result shows that, in general, the proportion of the urban population with piped water is higher, the higher the country's per capita income. But Figure 3.6 also shows the remarkably low proportion of the urban population so served in all low- and most lower-middle income nations. For instance, the UN JMP statistics for Nigeria suggest that in 2010 only 8 per cent of its urban population (the largest urban population in Africa) had water piped to their premises. In 2010, for nations with per capita incomes below $2,000, it was still common for 60–85 per cent of the urban population in low-income nations *not* to have piped water in their homes; this was also the case for some nations with per capita incomes above $2,000, including Nigeria, Indonesia and Angola. Above a per capita income of $5,500, in almost all nations, 80–100 per cent of the urban population had piped water; above a per capita income of $30,000, 99–100 per cent coverage was the norm (not shown in the figure).

There is also a remarkable spread in the proportion of the urban population with piped water for nations with per capita incomes between $2,000 and $5,500, suggesting a role for political determinants and not just income levels. Many of the Latin American nations with per capita incomes in this range show 90 per cent or more of their urban population having water piped to their premises, including Guatemala, Bolivia and Honduras, with Nicaragua on 89 per cent. Sadly, but not surprisingly, Haiti had much the lowest score in this region. Among the nations with per capita incomes of between $2,000 and $5,500 in which half or less of the urban population has piped water in the home are India, Sudan, Mongolia and Angola and, as mentioned above, Nigeria and Indonesia. Among the middle-income nations reporting 99–100 per cent coverage are Egypt, Costa Rica, Mauritius, Turkey, Malaysia and Chile.

One good example of the extent to which statistics on water and sanitation can vary depending on what is considered 'adequate' provision comes from a citizen report card initiative in Kenya's three largest cities, as part of which households were interviewed in 2006. In Kisumu, 58 per cent of households had mains water if water kiosks were included in the definition, but the figure was only 13 per cent if they were not. For Mombasa, the figures were 84 and 13 per cent respectively (*Maji na ufanisi? Njooni tujadiliane* 2007).

The UN Joint Monitoring Programme does not provide statistics on the proportion of urban populations with toilets in the home connected to functioning sewers, or other types of toilet that can be judged to be adequate for good health in urban contexts (for instance those linked to functioning septic tanks). In some urban contexts, good quality pit latrines might be included in this list of adequate provision but it is very difficult to ascertain when and where pit latrines are in fact adequate – in many urban contexts they are not, for instance where they serve multi-storey buildings, where there are small plot sizes, in places where it is difficult or impossible to get them emptied hygienically, and in places where it is difficult to prevent groundwater contamination. Even where pit latrines may be adequate, sewers or covered drains are still needed to dispose of waste water, so the proportion of an urban population with connections to functioning sewers is an

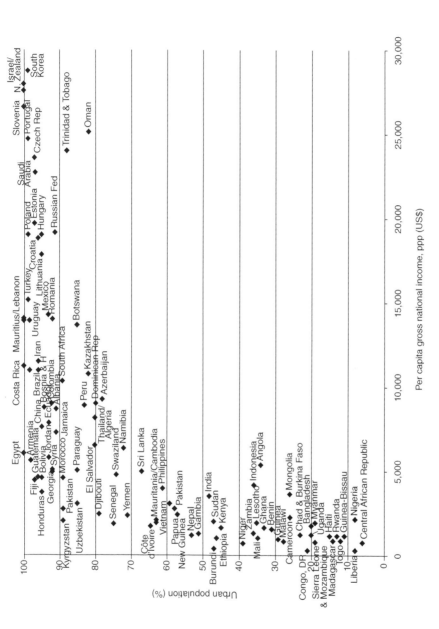

Figure 3.6 Percentage of the urban population with water piped into their premises compared to per capita gross national income (ppp), 2010

Source: Data on percentage of urban population with water piped into their premises from UNICEF and WHO (2012); data on per capita gross national income from World Bank (2012)

important indicator of whether sanitation and waste-water removal needs are met. We noted earlier the many major cities in sub-Saharan Africa with no sewers, or sewers that serve less than 10 per cent of the population.

Even within the broad definition of 'improved' sanitation, in many nations only a small proportion of the urban population have such sanitation. In eight nations in 2010 a quarter or less of the urban population had 'improved' sanitation; in another 22 the proportion was less than half. Provision has actually declined in many nations: for 21 nations the proportion of the urban population with 'improved' sanitation is lower in 2010 than in 1990; cutting out those countries with high levels of coverage and small decreases, this still leaves Haiti, with a decrease from 44 to 24 per cent, Rwanda, with 69 to 52 per cent, Djibouti, with 73 to 63 per cent, and Sudan, with 51 to 44 per cent. Other nations without high levels of coverage showing a decrease were Namibia, Cameroon, Nigeria, Zambia, Côte d'Ivoire and Zimbabwe.

Thus, hundreds of millions of urban dwellers currently live in homes that have no regular, safe piped water supplies and no safe, convenient provision for sanitation. Lack of provision for sanitation means that large sections of the population in many urban centres defecate in the open or into waste materials ('wrap and throw').

It is difficult to comprehensively estimate the impacts of inadequate provision of water, sanitation and drainage, but these will include impacts on health, on incomes available for food and non-food needs, and on time and energy. Health problems such as diarrhoeal diseases and intestinal parasites certainly contribute to malnutrition, but it is difficult to separate the contribution to this health burden of inadequacies in provision of water and sanitation from the contributions of other factors. These inadequacies are also implicated in a wide range of other diseases, although, again, it is difficult to separate their contribution from those of other factors. The water and sanitation-related health burden also generates costs in the form of treatment costs and working time lost through illness or due to caring for others that are ill.

The high price that hundreds of millions of urban dwellers pay for water from kiosks, vendors and tankers, and the significant proportion of their income that goes to pay for water (as described in Chapter 2), often directly reduces their expenditure on much-needed food.

In many urban areas, household members have to fetch and carry all the water they use from distant communal or public taps or water tankers, with long queues being common. A family of five needs at least 150 litres of water a day to meet all their needs; this is equivalent to six heavy suitcases. Interviews with a range of households in 16 sites in nine urban areas in Kenya, Uganda and Tanzania in 1997 found that those without piped supplies spent an average of 92 minutes every day collecting water, compared to an average of 28 minutes a day in the late 1960s (Thompson *et al.* 2000).

Provision for water and sanitation: drawing on local studies

It is difficult to reconcile the suggestion that only 4 per cent of the urban population in the Global South lack 'improved' provision for water with the many local studies that describe in detail the deficiencies in the quality and extent of provision.

Of course, these studies may all be from within the 4 per cent – but this is unlikely. Box 3.1 presents extracts from interviews with women living in informal settlements in Mumbai and Pune from Bapat and Agarwal (2003) describing the difficulties they face with regard to water and sanitation. Based on the criteria used to define 'improved' provision, most of the women quoted do have access to a public tap, standpipe, tubewell or borehole; but they certainly do not have adequate provision.

Box 3.1 Women inhabitants' assessments of provision for water and sanitation in informal settlements in Mumbai and Pune, India

Source: Bapat and Agarwal (2003)

When we came here, we did not have water taps at all. We used to get water from Dhake Colony or Gandhi Nagar. We had to stand in a queue and wait for the water tanker day and night. There used to be so many fights. Even sisters used to fight for water .... Then a bore well was drilled. The water was saline, but even so we had to wait in a long queue and pay ten rupees every day. We had no choice. *We may not eat once in a while, but we can't do without water.* Then, about ten years ago, we paid the BMC for water connections and got water taps. There was enough water then. But six months ago, they reduced the water supply. Now, there is very little water and very low pressure. We get just a couple of handaas [10–12 litre urns used for collecting water] of water for drinking and a few buckets for washing. We have to manage somehow. On some days, we do not wash clothes and on some days we do not bathe the children. Look at the way we have to fill the water. We have to put the bucket in a pit so that it is low enough for the water to flow from the tap. The water is very dirty. We have to strain it through cloth. Look here, you can see white larvae on the cloth.

(Residents of Mahatma Phule Nagar living on land owned by the Brihanmumbai Municipal Council (BMC); italics added)

I have been here for the past 18 years .... Eighteen years ago we had to go the Ganesh temple for water. We used to go at four in the morning and stand in a line until six and get two handaas of water. We had to leave the children at home. Five years ago, we got a water connection. But when they drilled a bore well, they broke the pipe. Now, the water that we get is dirty and we can only use it for washing. We have to go looking for water. The toilets are near the road crossing. Every time we use the toilet, we have to pay one rupee. It is a problem. In the morning, I have to send the children to school and husband to the office. I have to cook. There is very little time and there is a long queue at the toilet. Even if you go at five thirty in the morning, there are at least four people ahead of you. Once you get in, the people in the queue start shouting at you to hurry up.

(Bhagwati, a resident of Dharavi, a large informal settlement in Mumbai)

I have been here for 39 years .... There was no water, no toilets or drains. We had to beg for water .... We used to manage to get only four to six handaas of water, and we couldn't bathe because there was not enough water. Now we have a water tap. But the water is so dirty that we cannot drink it. We have to fill up drinking water in one of the buildings around here. This we must do stealthily. If anyone allows us to fill the water, the others shout at that person.

(Kalyani, also living in Dharavi)

We have to pay 200 rupees per month for water. This is a fire brigade water line that serves the BPT, not a municipal line. So there is water supply the whole time. But it is controlled by the local thugs who have fitted motors on the pipe. If we challenge them, they stop the water supply. Then there is no water. We have to cooperate with them. If we complain to the councillor of the area, he says that he is unable to do anything since we are living illegally on the land belonging to the BPT. There is only one toilet here built by the BPT .... We have to stand in a queue for an hour at least. There is another toilet on the other side, but it has been closed for some time because it is choked up .... Many people go near the sea to defecate. Women go at night.

(Jyotimani and Arogya Das,
residents of a settlement on Bombay Port Trust (BPT) land)

Getting water is a big problem here. We pay 200 or 300 rupees every month, but we get water only once every few days. This hosepipe is connected to a tap near the road, and people have fitted a motor on the pipeline. Our turn for filling up the water can come at any time of day or night. If a woman has to go out to work, her neighbour may help by filling the water for her. The day before yesterday, my turn came at four in the morning. I was able to fill only a small quantity of water because I had to leave to go to work. We use the water very sparingly since we are not sure how many days it will be before we get water again. Even those families that survive by begging have to buy water. There is no choice. There is nowhere around here where we can get water free. This whole area is a slum. *People may not have food in the house but they have to buy water.* Most of the people who live here are daily wage labourers. They are paid around 100 rupees a day. Out of this, they have to spend 20 to 50 rupees just for water. Often the water is dirty. It stinks. Even after paying for it we have to throw that water away.

(Uma, resident of a settlement on Bombay Port Trust land;
italics added)

Our houses are precariously perched on the bank of the river. The rainy season is an anxious time for us because, if the water level in the river rises high, our tin sheds can get washed away. The last time this happened was in 1997. About two weeks after that flood, Mahila Milan [a federation of women's informal savings groups] members came to meet us and we started working with them. After that, we succeeded in getting a water connection and street lights. Now we have a water tap for 28 families. We take turns to fill the water. We go down to the river to wash clothes. Until we got the water tap, I used to pay 50 rupees a month to a family living nearby, and would fill 10 to 15 handaas of water from their tap every day. The tap was just outside their house ....
I filled water there for three years.

(Padma Gore, resident of a small informal settlement in Pune)

Until 1977, we had no water taps. Now we have one tap used by 35 families. Water is available from two in the afternoon until six in the evening. Each of us fills four handaas first and, if the water has not stopped by then, we take turns to get more. Since the water runs only a few hours each day, some people get it every other day. If a woman got no water one day, she is given first turn the next day. We are all members of Mahila Milan, but in spite of our efforts to share fairly, there are so many quarrels. We do not have toilets. We have to use the open ground as a toilet. We do not even have drains in the settlement.

(Shobha Adhav and Manda Hadavale,
residents of an informal settlement in Pune,
on land that belongs to the government mental hospital)

There are 280 families in our settlement. Many of them have been there for more than 20 years. The slum has occupied land that belongs to the Ministry of Defence. And because of that, the municipality has not been able to provide us any facilities. Every day, we get water brought to us in tankers. The delivery timings are not regular. We start queuing for water in the morning by putting our water containers in a line. If we have to go out, we can leave the house only after we have filled the water. I have to go to work. My children are very young and cannot fill the water. So my sister stays at home and waits for the tanker. In order to be at home when the tanker comes, she has stopped going to school .... Occasionally, if the tanker does not come, we are really short of water. We cannot wash the cooking utensils or bathe. We have to get water from Nagpur Chawl [a slum settlement] which is more than a kilometre away. When the tanker comes there is a scramble for water. There is always a big commotion. We had an awful accident two years ago. A young girl got crushed under the wheel of the tanker as she hurried to get her turn to fill the water before the tanker came to a halt.

(Chhaya Waghmare, resident of an informal settlement
near the airport in Pune)

We have been in this settlement ... for more than 12 years, since we worked as labourers on the construction of these apartment blocks that you see all around here. Nearly 700 families live here now. When the construction work was in progress, we got water at our work sites. But now we face acute shortage of water. We have public standposts in the settlement, but the water is available for only two to three hours a day. In such a short period of time, it is not possible for all of us to fill water. There is always a long queue and frequent fights. Women come to blows because some try to fill many handaas or jump the queue. Those who do not get their turn before the water is turned off have to walk 20 to 30 minutes to fetch water. Some pay up to five rupees for one handaa of water. Some collect the water that keeps percolating in a small ditch by the side of the path near the water taps. As you can see the water is turbid. We cannot drink it, but we can use it for washing.

(Women from Laxminagarm in Pune)

To give another illustration of the contrast between general statistics and local realities, Box 3.2 draws on three studies covering Nairobi (much the largest and wealthiest urban centre in Kenya) or Nairobi and Kenya's two other largest cities, Mombasa and Kisumu. Data from a study of one informal settlement are also used. It must be remembered that the official UN statistics for Kenya in 2000 suggested that 87 per cent of its urban population had improved provision for water and 96 per cent had improved provision for sanitation (UNICEF and WHO 2000); although the most recent assessment shows coverage for water falling to 82 per cent in 2010, while figures for improved sanitation were lowered enormously, indicating only 30 per cent with improved sanitation in 2000 and 32 per cent in 2010 (UNICEF and WHO 2012).

Box 3.2 Provision for water and sanitation in Kenya's largest urban centres

APHRC (2002) reported on provision for water and sanitation in the half of Nairobi's population that live in informal or illegal settlements. The findings of surveys in 1998 (for Nairobi) and 2000 (for informal settlements) are shown in Table 3.6.

Another sample survey of informal settlements in Nairobi in 2004 showed that only 4 per cent of households had their own piped water supply and only a quarter had their own toilet (World Bank Kenya 2006). Kiosks were the primary source of water for 64 per cent of the population. Sixty-eight per cent relied on shared or public toilets, most of which were pit latrines. Twelve per cent had an official connection to a public sewer with 12 per cent with informal connections; almost all the rest were pit latrines. These poor conditions were confirmed again in a 2009 poverty assessment for Kenya (World Bank Kenya 2009).

Table 3.6 Provision for water and sanitation in Kenya's largest urban centres (for 1998 in Nairobi and 2000 in informal settlements)

Provision for water and sanitation	Households served in Nairobi (%)	Households served in informal settlements (%)
Water piped into residence	78	22
Water purchased from kiosks or vendors	No data	75
Public taps	15	3
Flush toilet	56	7
Pit latrine (household and shared)	43	84
No facility/open defecation	1	9

Source: Data from APHRC (2002)

Huruma is an informal settlement in Nairobi now in the middle of an upgrading and house-building programme undertaken by the Kenyan Homeless People's Federation. Before the upgrading work started, Weru (2004) found that:

- *Sanitation* Almost all the 6,569 inhabitants used the few public or community toilets or defecated into plastic bags and threw these away ('flying toilets'). There were 500 persons per toilet. Very few households had toilets within their homes.
- *Water* Water was only available from 45 commercially run water points or the river (which was very polluted). Water from the water points was too expensive for the inhabitants to be able to afford adequate quantities for health.

A study of provision for water, sanitation and solid waste collection in Kenya's three largest cities in 2007 (*Maji na ufanisi? Njooni tujadiliane* 2007) interviewed 2,905 households. Only in Nairobi did the majority of the population have mains water around the home (including a shared source within a compound). The findings for water services used by those in informal settlements include some astonishing statistics, especially for the time needed to fetch water and how much this increased during times of scarcity, and the incidence of problems encountered when fetching water, such as heckling, quarrelling and queue jumping (Table 3.7). For sanitation, only a minority in each city has a private flush toilet at home. In Kisumu and Mombasa, only a minority have their household wastes collected, with a large proportion of households throwing rubbish into open areas or drains or burning it (Table 3.8).

Table 3.7 Time needed for and incidence of problems in getting water in informal settlements in Kenyan cities, 2006

City	Mean daily time spent fetching water from outside the home (minutes)		Respondents reporting problems encountered when fetching water in normal times (%)		
	In normal times	In times of scarcity	Heckling and quarrelling	Long queues	Queue jumping
Nairobi	54	126	17	34	20
Kisumu	112	200	28	74	31
Mombasa	40	34	17	47	24

Source: Data from *Maji na ufanisi? Njooni tujadiliane* (2007)

Table 3.8 Household waste disposal in Kenyan cities, 2006

Rubbish disposal method	Households (%)		
	Nairobi	Kisumu	Mombasa
Collection by private company	61	14	32
Collection by council from doorstep	1	1	4
Council bins or official sites in area	3	3	9
Thrown into open areas or drains	32	48	44
Burnt	12	51	33
Buried	3	3	5

Source: *Maji na ufanisi? Njooni tujadiliane* (2007)

The 2000 JMP assessment suggested that 95 per cent of Malawi's urban population had improved provison for water and 96 per cent had improved provision for sanitation (UNICEF and WHO 2000). The 2012 assessment similarly suggested that 93 per cent had improved provision for water in 2000, rising to 95 per cent in 2010, while the proportion with improved provision for sanitation had been revised downwards to 49 per cent in 2000, remaining at the same figure in 2010 (UNICEF and WHO 2012). Malawi's three largest urban centres, Blantyre, Lilongwe and Mzuzu, have a combined population of over 1.5 million. Over half live in informal settlements and most rely on water kiosks for water and pit latrines (often shared with other households) for sanitation. A 2008 study (Manda 2009) looked at provision in three low-income settlements in each city: a planned area that had become a 'slum', a squatter settlement, and a settlement developed through a community initiative from the Malawi Homeless People's Federation. Of the 1,178 households interviewed in the nine settlements:

- 26 per cent had individual water connections
- 53 per cent purchased water from kiosks
- 13 per cent bought water from another house plot
- 23 per cent reported that it took 15 or more minutes to obtain water (for travelling to and from the water point and queuing).

The JMP statistics must include those who use kiosks as having improved provision. Kiosk water in Malawi is expensive so most households use this only for drinking and cooking. Some families purchased just one bucket of water a week, getting the rest of their water from other (unprotected) sources such as shallow wells and rivers. Kiosks did not provide a 24-hour service; most were open for only 3 hours in the morning and 3 hours in the afternoon, and remained closed overnight. Interruptions to supply were common (Manda 2009).

In respect of sanitation, 90 per cent of Blantyre's population and 92 per cent of Lilongwe's population did not live in homes connected to sewers; in Mzuzu, there were no sewers. Most in all three cities relied on pit latrines; in Lilongwe, 71 per cent of the population used pit latrines, with 20 per cent using toilets linked to septic tanks. Of the households in the nine low-income settlements studied:

- none had sewers
- 27 per cent had their own pit latrines
- 67 per cent used shared pit latrines (with many pit latrines shared between several households)
- 4 per cent used toilets with septic tanks (Manda 2009).

There is a growing number of case studies of smaller urban centres which suggest that provision in such centres is usually much worse than it is in large cities (UN-HABITAT 2003a, 2006). For instance, a study in 2000 in Kumi in Uganda, with 17,000 inhabitants, showed that almost everyone relied on public kiosks from which water was only available for two hours a day, or on water vendors who drew their water from these kiosks. There were no sewers or septic tanks. Around 60 per cent of households had pit latrines and there were two public latrines (Colin and Morgan 2000).

There is also a growing number of studies of smaller urban centres in Asia that show that provision for water and sanitation is very inadequate. For instance, in Chertala, India, which had 43,000 inhabitants in 2000, most of the population relied on 437 standpipes (about one per 100 users) but the water was not considered safe to drink. There were no sewers and most inhabitants had pit latrines (Colin and Morgan 2000). In Bhatatpur, with 200,000 inhabitants in 2000, 39 per cent of households relied on standpipes or non-piped water sources. Water in the piped system was intermittent. There were no sewers; half the population had toilets connected to septic tanks, with 15 per cent using pour-flush latrines and 33 per cent having no latrine or using a latrine cleared each day by a 'sweeper' (Water and Sanitation Program – South Asia 2000).

Asia has more than 1.5 billion urban inhabitants. Estimates for 2000 suggested that 35 to 50 per cent of the urban population lacked adequate provision for water. In the mid-1990s (the last time there was a careful survey) more than half the population in many large cities lacked house connections, including Bandung, Kolkata, Cebu, Dhaka, Jakarta and Manila. For sanitation, estimates for 2000 suggested that 45 to 60 per cent of the urban population lacked adequate provision (UN-HABITAT 2003a).

Very poor provision for water and sanitation is evident even in successful cities, which may have highly inequitable provision. For instance, in Bangalore, one of the most economically successful cities in India (with 5.6 million inhabitants by 2001), a 2000 survey (Sinclair Knight Merz *et al.* 2002) showed that, for the whole city, only 36 per cent of households had individual connections to the official water network; 66 per cent had toilets in the home, 4 per cent used public toilets and 1 per cent defecated in the open. In Dhaka there are over 3.4 million slum dwellers, representing over 37 per cent of the population. While 81.7 per cent of slum dwellers have access to shared municipal taps, only 26 to 35 per cent use hygienic latrines (CUS, NIPORT and Measure Evaluation 2006; World Bank Bangladesh 2007).

Urban poverty and energy

Discussions of energy poverty often focus on the difficulties that low-income households face in paying for energy, but the 2012 *Global Energy Assessment* suggested that for urban dwellers in low- and middle- income nations, a consideration of 'energy poverty' should also include the time and effort needed to obtain energy, the health implications of energy use, and the quality and convenience of the fuels used for meeting daily needs (Johansson *et al.* 2012).

The two most common implications of poverty for energy use among urban populations in low- and most middle-income nations are, first, use of the cheapest fuels and energy-using equipment (including stoves), which often cause high levels of indoor air pollution and fire risk, and, second, lack of access to electricity. Low income may also mean households limit fuel use, for instance by cutting down on cooked food (in extreme circumstances to one meal a day) or switching to faster-cooking but less nutritious food (see Adelekan and Jerome 2006 for a discussion of this for Ibadan).

Access to electricity at prices that low-income households can afford obviously brings multiple advantages. These include cheaper, more reliable and safer lighting (compared to candles and kerosene lamps) and the ability to use appliances (including fridges and, where needed, fans). It also creates advantages for household enterprises such as better lighting at night and the use of equipment such as sewing machines or fridges. A study of small-scale entrepreneurs in Kibera, one of Nairobi's largest informal settlements, found that electricity use was limited in home-based enterprises due to the large upfront connection costs (Karekezi, Kimani and Onguru 2008).

Households with electricity and gas connections also save time and effort, as fuels do not have to be fetched and carried and they require no storage space.

Moving out of poverty is associated with shifts away from dirtier and less convenient fuels and gaining access to electricity, as well as limiting total monetary expenditures on energy. 'Cleaner' fuels – in the sense of minimizing pollution and health impacts for the users[62] – include electricity and gas or energy derived from renewable energy sources. Coal and biomass are 'dirty' (how dirty depends in part on the technology used in the home). Kerosene and charcoal fall between these two extremes (Satterthwaite and Sverdlik 2012).

In many middle-income and some low-income nations, a high proportion of low-income urban households use cleaner fuels and have access to electricity (Legros *et al.* 2009) – although, as discussed in Chapter 2, fuel and electricity costs can take a sizeable proportion of their income. Here, the discussion of 'energy poverty' in high-income nations has relevance, as this focuses on the cost to low-income households of energy, for instance defining energy poverty as a household's expenditure on fuels and electricity exceeding 10 per cent of income. This may also in part be related to poor quality housing, for instance inadequate insulation in climates requiring space heating, or inefficient or expensive-to-use heating equipment.

Unsafe fires or stoves and the absence of electricity for lighting, meaning that candles or kerosene lights are usually used, contribute to much higher risks of burns and scalds for household members, especially children, and accidental fires; other factors contribute to these risks, including extreme overcrowding, housing built using flammable materials, high-density settlements, a lack of firebreaks, a lack of emergency services including fire services, and a lack of piped water supply to help fight fires (Hardoy, Mitlin and Satterthwaite 2001; Pharoah 2008). All these factors are also associated with informal settlements, and fires figure prominently among the disasters that affect these settlements – although they may not be recorded, because there is no emergency fire service or, if there is, it will not serve or cannot get to the settlements. Within the history of cities, the same factors meant devastating fires were once commonplace in Europe and North America, but this is no longer the case.

Cape Town is unusual in having a detailed record of fire incidents that covers most informal settlements. There were 18,504 fire incidents reported between January 1995 and the end of 2004, and 8,554 of these occurred in informal settlements. Most were localized, small or medium-sized events, but cumulatively they affected over 40,000 people (Pharoah 2008). Box 3.3 describes an informal settlement close to Cape Town where serious fire disasters have been commonplace.

Although the proportion of the urban populations of low- and middle-income nations using clean fuels and having access to electricity has increased, data from the 2000s indicates that several hundred million urban dwellers are still unable to afford this, or lack such access (Legros *et al.* 2009).[63] Some 700 million lacked access to modern fuels and 279 million lacked access to electricity. For all low- and middle-income nations, around 10 per cent of the urban population lacked access to electricity; for the least developed nations and sub-Saharan Africa the proportion rose to about half. More than two thirds of the urban population in the

---

Box 3.3 Fires and fire risks in Imizamo Yethu, South Africa

A fire in February 2004 in Imizamo Yethu, an informal settlement in Hout Bay, destroyed 1,200 homes and left some 5,000 people homeless. The settlement had been created in 1990 when forestry land was converted into an 18-hectare, 429-plot site and service scheme; the name 'Imizamo Yethu' means 'through our collective struggle'. The settlement is a mix of brick houses and shacks. It has provision for piped water, mostly through public taps, but the supply is irregular and at the time of the fire there had been no water in the system for the previous 24 hours. The fire brigade was called, but half an hour after the fire started (few people knew the right telephone number to call), and the fire engines were unable to get to some areas because of the lack of roads or because people had moved their possessions out into the roads to try to save them.

The settlement has had other serious fires. Before the February 2004 fire, there had been fires destroying between 40 and 90 buildings in 1995, 1997, 2001 and 2003 (MacGregor *et al.* 2005). During 2008, about 23 houses burnt down in February, a further 60 in August, 200 in late November and 200 in early December (Cowan 2008).

The initial causes of these fires is often unclear, but the widespread use of candles for lighting and open fires or dangerous paraffin stoves for cooking and heating is clearly part of the reason. The close physical proximity of buildings and the many that are made of flammable materials helps explain why fires spread from house to house – although many of the more severe fires here and in other informal settlements in Cape Town are also associated with high winds (MacGregor *et al.* 2005; Pharoah 2008).

---

least developed countries and more than half the urban population in sub-Saharan Africa were using wood, charcoal, dung or coal for cooking (Legros *et al.* 2009).

The proportion of the urban population using wood or charcoal for cooking falls with a nation's per capita GDP. In most nations with per capita GDPs of less than US$1,100, 85 per cent or more of the urban population use wood and charcoal for cooking; all these nations are in sub-Saharan Africa, with the exception of Haiti. In nations with per capita GDPs above US$14,000, virtually no urban households use wood or charcoal (Satterthwaite and Sverdlik 2012).

In China and India, the nations with the world's largest urban populations, since the 1980s there has been a rapid increase in the proportion of the urban population using cleaner fuels and with access to electricity (Pachauri and Jiang 2008). But in India in 2005–06, 23 per cent were still using firewood or straw for cooking fuel.

In almost all nations with per capita GDPs of US$6,000 or more, 95 to 100 per cent of the urban population have access to electricity. In many middle-income nations, a high proportion of low-income households in urban areas have electricity connections, although a significant proportion of these connections may be illegal or accessed through neighbours (Satterthwaite and Sverdlik 2012; see also Fall *et al.* 2008 on Dakar). Electricity companies may refuse to connect those in informal settlements or those lacking official addresses, or it may be that upfront connection charges are too high; in Kibera, Nairobi, the upfront cost for electricity connections represented three to five months' income for residents (Karekezi, Kimani and Onguru 2008). For nations with per capita GDPs below US$3,000, there is a fairly consistent picture of rising proportions of urban households with electricity, with some variation.

It is clear, therefore, that in lower-income nations a higher proportion of the urban population tend to use dirty fuels. Within nations or particular cities, the use of dirty fuels is much more common among lower-income populations. For instance, a survey of 950 women and children in Accra showed that low-income households were far more likely to use solid fuels (usually charcoal or wood) and report respiratory infections (Boadi and Kuitunen 2006). Of the 29 per cent of children with respiratory infections, over 85 per cent were from low-income households. Nearly 30 per cent of women from low-income households had respiratory problems in the two weeks preceding the survey, more than twice the rate reported by women of medium wealth and 10 times that of wealthy women (who mostly use LPG or electricity). Respiratory infections were common in households using firewood (67.5 per cent) and charcoal (31.6 per cent), compared to cooking with kerosene (12.9 per cent), LPG (4.8 per cent) and electricity (1.7 per cent). However, a study of 230 households in Dhaka and Narayanganj showed that there were very large variations in indoor air pollution levels for low-income respondents using 'dirty' fuels, which are explained by factors such as differences in cooking location, ventilation and housing materials (Dasgupta *et al.* 2006). In China, coal is a key heating fuel for low-income groups, particularly in cold northern cities (Pachauri and Jiang 2008), and coal-using urban residents are exposed to extremely high levels of indoor air pollution (Mestl *et al.* 2007). The shift to cleaner cooking fuels among India's urban population was noted earlier, but among the lowest-income groups, this shift was much less pronounced (Viswanathan and Kumar 2005; Gangopadhyay, Ramaswami and Wadhawa 2005).

The data collected on energy use in most nations has similar limitations to the data collected on living conditions or health determinants – it is collected by surveys with sample sizes too small to provide data for individual cities or to see how energy use varies across income groups.[64] The exception is the very considerable documentation on the health impacts of pollution from the use of 'dirty' fuels (and related factors, including poor ventilation and inefficient stoves), although much of this literature focuses on rural households and perhaps underestimates the extent of the problem among low-income urban households (WHO 2006).

Urban poverty and disasters

The impact of disasters on urban poverty, in the sense of both hitting low-income groups hardest and creating poverty among those who previously had not been poor, has been greatly underestimated. In part this is because most disasters go unrecorded in national and international disaster databases. In part it is because the metrics used to assess the impact of disasters exclude many of the impacts most relevant to low-income groups, for instance damage to housing, injury, disruption to livelihoods and loss of assets. This has been revealed by new, more detailed analyses of disasters (United Nations 2009, 2011a), but as yet, these analyses are available for only a limited range of nations and urban populations, and their implications need more attention.

This and other chapters discuss in some detail the high proportion of the population in most cities in low- and middle-income nations living in informal settlements, which includes most of the low-income population. Many informal settlements are on dangerous sites at high risk of disaster – for instance large concentrations of informal settlements can be seen on hills prone to landslides in Rio de Janeiro (Brazil), La Paz (Bolivia), Caracas (Venezuela) and Chittagong (Bangladesh); or in deep ravines, as in Guatemala City; or in sandy desert, as in Lima (Peru) and Khartoum (Sudan); or on land prone to flooding or tidal inundation, or underwater, as in Guayaquil (Ecuador), Recife (Brazil), Monrovia (Liberia), Lagos and Port Harcourt (Nigeria), Port Moresby (Papua New Guinea), Delhi and Mumbai (India), Bangkok (Thailand), Jakarta (Indonesia), Buenos Aires and Resistencia (Argentina), Accra (Ghana), Dhaka (Bangladesh) and elsewhere.[65] Low-income settlements develop on such sites because the land is unsuited to residential or commercial development, meaning those who settle and build their homes there have more chance of avoiding eviction, and the location is often good for income-earning opportunities.

Cities figure heavily in the lists of places that have experienced the most serious disasters (IFRC 2010). Cities can be seen as inherently risky because of their concentration of people, economic activities and assets. However, no-one has compiled a list of cities where few, if any, disasters have occurred in the past decade or more because the buildings and infrastructure can cope with, for instance, storms and floods, and because urban expansion has avoided dangerous sites. What is now being recognized is the extent to which disasters in urban areas caused by extreme weather are concentrated in low- and middle-income nations and intimately linked to the inadequacies of local governance there (United Nations 2009, 2011a). This might suggest that economic growth reduces disaster risk for cities – but it will only do so if it is accompanied by better local governance. There are many cities with successful economies where the number (and probably the proportion) of the population living in informal settlements is still growing. Many are on risky sites and most lack risk-reducing infrastructure and services. For instance, Dhaka is a very large and successful city with a rapidly growing economy and population. But city and national government agencies have proved unable to address the processes that are creating or increasing risk over time. The city has had many devastating floods in recent years, and many areas are flood prone during the rainy season. These floods are made worse by the many drainage canals and other water bodies that have been built over (Alam and Rabbani 2007; Haque, Grafakos and Huijsman 2012). Much new development is on floodplains where soil can liquefy from an earthquake. Despite guidelines for earthquake resistance, many modern buildings are vulnerable, reflecting faulty design and poor construction (United Nations 2011a).

For cities for which careful records of disasters are compiled and mapped, the records show that many or most disasters happen in informal settlements. They also give some sense of the disruption to the lives of those living in such settlements, for instance of the number of houses damaged and destroyed, also the damage or destruction of schools, health centres and roads. But most cities and smaller urban centres have no such records. As with almost all aspects of poverty, the data available on the scale and nature of disasters and their impacts are very inadequate, meaning there is very little basis on which to undertake an analysis of the extent to which disasters are concentrated among low-income populations and identify where risks and vulnerabilities are concentrated.

In part this is because of very inadequate national and international recording. A very large number of disasters are not included in international disaster databases. For a disaster to be included in the most widely used database, EM-DAT, at least one of four criteria must be fulfilled: ten or more people reported killed, one hundred or more people reported affected, declaration of a state of emergency, or a call for international assistance. Detailed analyses of disasters in particular cities and localities have shown how much impact results from disasters which do not meet any of these criteria, or which do but are still not included in this database. There is also no attempt to separate out urban from rural data, and the limitation of focusing only on deaths and recorded economic losses. These are hardly appropriate metrics with regard to damage or destruction of housing in informal settlements or loss of livelihoods, possessions or assets among low-income populations, all of which may be ignored in estimates of economic losses or assigned very little value (United Nations 2009). But deficiencies in local data are as problematic. Often there are no city maps that include informal settlements and little or no data are collected on their populations.

However, it is clear that deaths from disasters which are included in international data sets are very heavily concentrated in low-income nations. Mortality risk from tropical cyclones is 225 times greater in low-income countries compared to OECD countries, when the severity of the storm and numbers of people exposed are similar (Peduzzi *et al.* 2012). Or, to put it another way, high-income nations have 39 per cent of the exposure to tropical cyclones but only 1 per cent of the mortality risk; low-income nations have 13 per cent of the exposure but 81 per cent of the mortality risk (United Nations 2009).

There are less global data on urban populations or, within this, on the extent to which low incomes are associated with higher levels of disaster risk, though, as noted above, there are many case studies of cities in low- and middle-income countries showing the concentrations of informal settlements on dangerous sites.

Recent reviews of disasters in urban areas (IFRC 2010; United Nations 2009, 2011a) suggest a rapid growth in the number of disasters, with most associated with extreme weather, including heavy winds and rains, floods, landslides and fires. These reviews also suggest that the number of locations where such disasters are happening is expanding geographically. Although the factors that underpin these disasters vary, as do their relative importance, in most instances they are linked to increases in the urban population in informal settlements, increases in run-off due to urban growth and poor land-use and watershed management, and chronic underinvestment in drainage. Here, urban expansion and development are actually generating new patterns of hazard, exposure and vulnerability.

The extent to which countries manage (or fail to manage) urban development and ensure provision of infrastructure has a very strong influence on the number and scale of disasters. Thus urban disaster risk is configured in most low- and middle-income nations by the lack of infrastructure and public services and the inadequacies of urban governance. Extreme weather events and climate change are not responsible for the growth of informal settlements in flood-prone areas or the lack of investment in drainage, nor for the lack of social safety nets (United Nations 2009). Low-income households are hit hardest by extreme weather because of greater exposure to the hazards of high-risk sites, poor quality housing, lack of hazard-removing infrastructure, less capacity to cope with the impacts, less adaptive capacity (to reduce risks from future events), less state provision and less legal protection or insurance.

Key local opportunities for disaster risk reduction are unrealized because many national disaster risk reduction initiatives do not have mechanisms for engaging effectively with local stakeholders, particularly the rural and urban poor. Most are also unaware of or do not consider small disasters, even though their aggregate impacts contribute greatly to overall disaster impacts. Most give priority to protecting strategic economic sectors and wealthier areas rather than vulnerable rural and urban households.

If disaster reporting systems for nations or cities move to include smaller disasters and assess a broader set of impacts, moving beyond mortality and economic losses to include damage or destruction of housing, schools and health centres, other risk patterns emerge, based on thousands of frequently occurring small-scale disasters. These are associated with specific local concentrations of exposed vulnerable populations and assets spread over wide areas. The UN International Strategy for Disaster Reduction has sought to better understand the significance of smaller disasters and their causes, drivers and impacts. It supported the development of national disaster data sets in 19 countries and two states in India – for a total population of 850 million – spanning 40 years. This allowed analysis of nearly 200,000 local-level disaster reports. Disasters are divided into 'intensive' disasters, those with at least 25 deaths or 600 houses destroyed, and 'extensive' disasters, those with fewer deaths or houses destroyed. The analysis found that extensive disasters accounted for a small proportion of disaster mortality but for a much larger share of damage to housing, livelihoods and local infrastructure and of impacts on low-income (urban and rural) households and communities, for instance damage or destruction of schools, health facilities, municipal water and sewer systems and power stations. Almost all extensive risk disasters were weather-related, and these accounted for 54 per cent of houses damaged, 80 per cent of people affected, 83 per cent of people injured, 46 per cent of damage to schools and 54 per cent of damage to health facilities (United Nations 2011a). To give one example of the impact of an extensive disaster: in February 2009, four municipalities on the Pacific coast of Colombia were flooded. This attracted little attention, with two people killed and twenty reported missing, but 1,125 houses as well as schools, health centres and roads were destroyed. More than 25,000 people were displaced and 1,400 houses damaged (United Nations 2011a).

Most extensive disaster risk is associated with informal urban settlements and vulnerable rural livelihoods. A study of the average annual occurrence of extensive hydro-meteorological disasters in 12 nations showed that these had multiplied five-fold between 1980 and 2006; across the sample, associated mortality doubled, meaning the average number of deaths per disaster had fallen, perhaps due to better disaster risk reduction and management. However, housing damage increased at least ten-fold, meaning the average number of damaged houses per disaster had at least doubled. This can only be explained by an increase in the number of vulnerable houses or an increase in the intensity of hazards. It is likely that much of this increase in damage to housing was the result of the rapid growth of exposed and vulnerable population through urban development (United Nations 2009).

Intensive disaster risk is concentrated in particular locations, for instance along fault lines, around active volcanoes, on cyclone paths, or on tsunami-exposed coastlines. Concentrations of intensive risk may change, due to increases in vulnerable populations or of assets in particular locations, for example. Extensive risk is far more dynamic and geographically mobile, and much of it is associated with expanding urban areas. Extensive disasters include a large number of disasters in small urban centres, often those in the expanding agricultural frontier where local governments are particularly weak and ineffective, and disasters in major cities, often caused by flooding associated with increased run-off due to new urban development, chronic underinvestment in citywide drainage and the concentration of informal settlements on low-lying land.

Urban poverty and climate change

This chapter has considered in some detail the much higher environmental health risks facing large sections of the low-income urban population in low- and middle-income nations. It also reviewed briefly the often very high disaster risks that large sections of the low-income urban population face. Climate change is increasing risk levels for some environmental health and disaster hazards – and usually the number of people exposed to these hazards – as well as adding new risks. Reviewing Figure 3.4 on page 100, the direct and indirect impacts of climate change are likely to impact negatively on many of the social, economic and environmental determinants of health listed.

There are four further particular worries associated with climate change. First, the risks it brings are increasing and will continue to increase over the next few decades. Because of time lags in global systems, this is the case even if national governments reach agreement on the very serious need to cut greenhouse gas emissions and implement measures that rapidly reduce total greenhouse gas emissions. However, the sooner such an agreement can be reached and implemented, the greater the likelihood of avoiding or limiting the most dangerous aspects of climate change. This has importance for poverty because low-income groups are usually among those most at risk.

The second worry is that most of those who are and will be most at risk are those that have contributed the least to climate change. High levels of consumption and the production and use of goods and services by those with high consumption levels underpin most human-induced greenhouse gas emissions. But most of the groups facing the highest risks from climate change to their homes, assets and livelihoods are low-income urban and rural dwellers with low levels of consumption. Similarly, many of the cities most at risk from climate change have relatively low greenhouse gas emissions per person, whether these are measured as emissions within geographical boundaries or as emissions arising from the consumption of the population (Dodman 2009; Hoornweg, Sugar and Gomez 2011). What will happen to international relations as disasters caused or exacerbated by climate change become more frequent and larger in scale in countries and cities with low adaptive capacity and low historic and current contributions to climate change, especially if countries which have made the largest contributions have not acted urgently?

Third, there is often no way for those living or working in a particular city to remove or reduce many of the hazards to which climate change contributes. This is not the case for many of the local environmental hazards facing low-income urban dwellers, where local actions can be effective, for instance extending piped water supplies to all homes and treating water to remove pathogens. Many climate change impacts are different – a city government cannot reduce the intensity of a cyclone or stop sea-level rise, even if it can reduce their impacts.

Fourth, as described in this chapter, most urban centres in low- and middle-income nations have very large deficits in the infrastructure and services needed to limit the direct and indirect impacts of climate change, and local governance structures that lack the capacity and funding – and often the willingness – to address this. They also lack the capacity or willingness to manage changes in land use to limit extreme weather risks.

In the next few decades, much of the likely direct impact of climate change will be an exacerbation of extreme weather events, such as more intense or more frequent storms, rainfall or heat waves, but these are events from which many low-income urban dwellers are already greatly at risk. In part this is because they are concentrated on sites at high risk: floodplains, steep slopes, river banks or coastal locations. In part it is because they live in poor quality houses that may not withstand high winds or floods, or that are part of heat islands. In part it is because their settlements lack risk-reducing infrastructure – drains that can cope with storm water and surface run-off, or all-weather roads and paths.

In addition, most of the urban centres most at risk from extreme weather are in low- and middle-income nations, for instance populations in low-elevation coastal zones (see McGranahan, Balk and Anderson 2007); regions hit by cyclones, hurricanes or typhoons; regions which already have extreme rainfall; or locations that experience heat waves, which gain greater impact due to heat islands within larger or more concentrated urban centres (see Bicknell, Dodman and Satterthwaite 2009). So climate change will have disproportionate impacts on these populations, for whom the burden of climate-sensitive disease is already high (Kovats and Akhtar 2008); who often live in urban centres with economies linked to climate-sensitive resources including agriculture and tourism (Wilbanks *et al.* 2007); and who often face significant water constraints, which are predicted to become more severe as a result of climate change.

It is likely that, among the world population, low-income urban dwellers in low- and middle-income nations will face among the largest increases in risk and exposure due to climate change, with these increases concentrated in particular urban centres, and within urban centres in particular districts or settlements. As with most risks among low-income urban populations, this will have a disproportionate impact on the most vulnerable groups – vulnerable because they are more exposed, more impacted when exposed, less able to cope with impacts and less able to adapt to reduce risk in the future. Table 3.9 gives examples of the likely impacts of climate change on urban populations.

Table 3.9 makes clear that low-income groups often face much higher levels of risk from the impacts listed, and these usually have particularly serious implications for vulnerable populations. These typically include infants and very young children, and sometimes their carers (see Bartlett 2008), older age groups and those who are disabled or are affected by chronic diseases. Low-income groups are also more vulnerable because they generally have the least adaptive capacity, for example they cannot afford to move to safer locations, build more resilient homes or get local governments to make the needed investments in risk-reducing infrastructure and services in their settlements. There are case studies that show the coping mechanisms that low-income individuals or households use to reduce impacts, for instance adding ventilation, building low walls around doorways, setting shelving as high as possible, altering arrangements for food preparation and storage and moving temporarily to safer sites (Stephens, Patnaik and Lewin 1996; Jabeen, Allen and Johnson 2010; Adelekan 2010), but these rarely create the resilience necessary to cope with increased risk levels or new risks. Residents of informal settlements may have developed sensible, effective, pragmatic measures that work well as responses to the extreme weather events experienced in the past, but these are unlikely to meet the challenges posed by changes in extremes or in timing brought about by climate change. Lack of capacity to adapt in low-income communities and local governments will mean that even relatively small changes – for instance in the intensity of heat waves, wind speeds or rainfall – can cause disaster.

Once again, what is notable is how much the deprivations associated with urban poverty reduce adaptive capacity. The ability of low-income groups to cope with and adapt to climate change impacts will depend on these other deprivations being addressed. In most urban contexts there are serious limitations on what

Table 3.9 Examples of likely impacts of climate change on urban populations

Projected changes	Examples of likely impacts	Reasons for disproportionate effects on low-income groups
Changes in simple extremes		
Higher (and increasing) maximum temperatures: more hot days and heat waves over nearly all land areas	Rise in mortality and illness from heat stress in many urban locations, with greatest impacts among particularly vulnerable groups – infants and young children, the elderly, expectant mothers, those with certain chronic diseases	Often concentrations of low-income populations in heat islands with very high densities, lack of open space and little ventilation; vulnerable groups within low-income populations less able to take measures to avoid or reduce impacts
Higher (and increasing) minimum temperatures: fewer cold days, frost days and cold waves over nearly all land areas	Decreased cold-related human morbidity and mortality. Extended range and activity of some disease vectors, including mosquito- and tick-borne diseases, with infants and young children often at greatest risk	Many settlements with concentrations of low-income groups are without public health measures to control or remove disease vectors and without health care systems to provide needed responses
More intense precipitation events and riverine floods	Increased flood, landslide, avalanche and mudslide damage resulting in injury and loss of life, loss of property and damage to infrastructure. Increased flood run-off often brings contamination to water supplies and outbreaks of water borne diseases	Low-income groups usually concentrated on sites most at risk of flooding, in poor quality housing less able to withstand flooding and in settlements lacking risk-reducing infrastructure, with homes and possessions not covered by insurance
Wind storms with higher wind speeds	Structural damage to buildings, power and telephone lines, communication masts and other urban infrastructure	Adelekan (2012) shows that a relatively small increase in wind speeds for wind storms in Ibadan caused extensive damage to many buildings
Changes in complex extremes		
Increased summer drying over mid-latitude continental interiors and associated risk of drought	Decreased water resource quantity and quality, increased risk of forest/bush fire, decreased crop yields and higher food prices	Low-income groups often face greater water constraints and are more vulnerable to food price rises

Projected changes	Examples of likely impacts	Reasons for disproportionate effects on low-income groups
Increased tropical cyclone peak wind intensities and mean and peak precipitation intensities	Increased risk to human life and damage to property and infrastructure, risk of infectious disease epidemics, increased coastal erosion and damage to coastal ecosystems and coral reefs	Informal settlements are on sites most at risk, having poor quality housing and lacking risk-reducing infrastructure
Intensified droughts and floods associated with El Niño events in many different regions	Decreased agriculture and range-land productivity in drought-prone and flood-prone regions	Impact on food availability and prices
Increased Asian summer monsoon precipitation variability	Increased flood and drought magnitude and damage in temperate and tropical Asia	In many cities in Asia, most of those most at risk of flooding are low-income groups
Changes in the mean		
Water availability	Reduced water availability in many locations – with obvious impact on agriculture and on cities where fresh water availability declines significantly	In cities facing constraints or shortages of fresh water supplies, it is likely that low-income areas will be the most affected
Sea-level rise	Coastal erosion, land loss, more floods from storm surges, potentially affecting hundreds of millions of urban dwellers living in low-elevation coastal zones	Many low-income settlements with poor quality housing and lacking drainage infrastructure are in areas most at risk
Higher average temperature	Disease vector range spreading, worsening air quality, higher water demand and water loss, often more heatwaves	Low-income groups are often concentrated in areas that lack the infrastructure and the environmental health and health care measures needed to control disease vectors and reduce their health impacts

Source: Based on McCarthy *et al.* (2001), Table SPM-1, supplemented with material from Parry *et al.* (2007)

low-income groups can achieve collectively to build adaptive capacity without support from government. For example, community action cannot create 'trunk' infrastructure – water mains, sewers, drains, all-weather roads – or build water treatment plants.

In sum, what best explains the very large differentials between urban centres in low- and high-income nations in deaths, serious injuries and impoverishment due to extreme weather events is the quality and comprehensiveness of risk reduction integrated into urban life.

In high-income nations, urban populations have become so accustomed to a network of institutions, infrastructure, services and regulations which protects them from extreme weather events that it is taken for granted. Many of the measures – such as health care services and surface drainage – also serve everyday needs. Early warning of approaching storms is expected, as is a rapid emergency response from the police, armed services, health care and fire service, whenever it is needed. In high-income nations, it is rare for extreme weather events to cause a large loss of life or to seriously injure many people – although there are important exceptions. It is more common for such events to cause serious damage to property, although the economic cost to those impacted is much reduced by insurance. All this is also underpinned by almost all buildings conforming to health and safety regulations and being served by piped water, sewers, all-weather roads, electricity and drains 24 hours a day. The costs of such infrastructure and services represent a small proportion of income for most citizens, whether paid direct as service charges or as part of taxes.[66]

Local government plays an important role in most or all of these actions – although systems vary greatly in terms of the role taken by local government in planning, provision and finance, and in terms of the nature of local government relationships with government at higher levels. Private companies or non-profit institutions may provide some of the key services, but the framework for provision and quality control is provided by local, provincial or national government. For the most part citizens engage very little in the management of these systems, assuming that government will ensure provision, although there are channels for complaint, in the form of local politicians or lawyers, ombudsmen, consumer groups and watchdogs. While coverage for some services may be substandard and some groups ill served or excluded, a high proportion of the urban population is well served and well protected.

In addition, city planning and land-use regulation can adjust to the new or heightened risks that climate change may bring, and this is likely to be supported by changes in private sector investments, shifting over time from high-risk areas, and changes in insurance premiums and coverage. For at least the next few decades, this 'adaptive capacity' in most urban centres in high-income nations will be able to deal with most of the likely impacts of climate change. Obviously, the continued ability to adapt to risks after this depends on effective mitigation.

But the institutional capacity for urban adaptation is much weaker in low- and most middle-income nations. Large sections of the urban population and workforce are not served by a network of institutions, infrastructure, services and protective regulations comparable to those in high-income nations. This can be seen in the inadequacies in provision for infrastructure and services, and in the extent to which the homes, neighbourhoods and livelihoods of the population fall outside the regulatory framework. Earlier sections have described how most urban centres in low-income nations in Africa and Asia have no sewers and very limited drainage systems, and how much of their populations are without water piped into the home or an official solid waste collection service. These inadequacies often reflect local governments that are unrepresentative, unaccountable and anti-poor, as they regard the population living in informal settlements and working within the informal economy as 'the problem'. There are also cities and smaller urban centres with some deficiencies in provision for infrastructure, but which affect a much smaller proportion of the population. This often reflects city and municipal governments which are more accountable to the citizens in their jurisdictions and which operate within national structures that have strengthened this level of government, resulting in many instances in stronger local democracies. However, even in middle-income nations where considerable progress has been made in creating more effective local government, much needs to be done to develop adaptive capacities.

In conclusion to this chapter, we have enough evidence to show that urban health is often very poor in the Global South, as illustrated by the indicators of infant, child and maternal mortality, malnutrition and provision for key health determinants, and that health problems are usually far more serious for low-income groups. But to get real insights into the linkages between health and urban poverty, we have to rely on relatively few studies. Most data on health or key health determinants, including provision for water, sanitation, drainage and health care, are limited in what they measure and are based on national surveys with sample sizes too small to give the detail needed. We know from the African Population and Health Research Center of the very large differentials in a range of health-related indicators between informal settlements in Nairobi and other parts of the city, and of the very large health burdens facing those living in these informal settlements (APHRC 2002). It is likely that there are comparable differentials within most cities in sub-Saharan Africa and within many cities in Asia, North Africa and Latin America – but where are the studies to show this? We know of the devastating impacts of illness, injury and disasters on low-income households and their implications for income, nutritional status and poverty – but only a small handful of studies have had the depth, detail and level of engagement with low-income households to produce these insights. It is difficult to know why this is so. In part, it must be the reluctance of many international agencies to engage in urban issues, perhaps also the blindness of many environmental specialists to the health burden generated by infectious and parasitic diseases and physical hazards, and the lack of focus among urban researchers on health issues.

4   Incomes and livelihoods

Introduction

The urban poor have to find work that provides cash income to survive. Unlike in many rural areas, it is not possible to exist on subsistence agriculture or by foraging in towns and cities.[67] Urban residents have to enter the labour market, make and sell goods or sell services through a lack of alternatives. Even if the required natural resources for agricultural production (such as land and water) are available, in most instances access to them has been commoditized. A cash income is essential not only because most or all food and fuel has to be purchased but also because urban dwellers face costs that may be avoidable in rural areas, for example payments to access housing, water and toilets, and transport costs to and from work.[68] But available opportunities for earning a cash income frequently have very low returns, very long work hours and dangerous working conditions. In this chapter we consider how low-income urban households engage with this challenge, focusing on their livelihoods and the labour markets in which they seek income-earning opportunities.

The literature on the livelihoods of low-income groups and the markets in which they operate reflects the different backgrounds and disciplines of researchers interested in this topic. Some accounts focus on the individual worker (singly, within their family and sometimes in the context of wider social networks) and the ways in which she or he has found employment, while others focus on particular trades, such as waste pickers, street food vendors or rickshaw pullers; another, smaller group of studies focuses on particular localities. In some cases, there is a rich elaboration of the ways in which the product or service market functions; in others, the emphasis is much more on individuals' experiences of working life. But given the importance for poverty reduction of understanding and acting on what constrains incomes and working conditions for the urban poor, there is far too little study of this area.

This is perhaps because official data collected on employment and livelihoods has never been able to capture the variety, complexity and diversity of income-earning sources and their implications for income levels and health. A study of poverty within urban centres in Zambia noted that the broad employment and income categories in household surveys do not adequately capture the diversity of urban employment (Chibuye 2011). Official data often fail to capture the different contributions to household income of various family members, including those working in other locations and those who are unpaid. Official data from employer or employee surveys have limited value if most of the workforce is in informal sector enterprises or informal employment for which no data are collected. Unlike surveys of housing and infrastructure, there is much less that can be recorded from observation or drawn from regular surveys and censuses. For obvious reasons, low-income individuals and households are reluctant to answer questions on their incomes. Even if they do seek to answer truthfully, it is often difficult for those in the informal economy or casual work to answer questions about incomes, as these fluctuate and questions are often constructed around conceptions of formal work. This explains why governments and international agencies usually use expenditure rather than income data.

The standard questions used in employment and livelihood surveys tell us little or nothing about working conditions, working hours, work-related illnesses and injuries, and whether there are work-linked benefits such as access to subsidized health care, paid holidays and sick pay. For instance, simply classifying someone as working in the formal sector says nothing about income level (some formally employed professions have very low pay) or job security (whether employment is permanent, temporary or casual). Surveys that cover employment or livelihood issues rarely give a sense of where and when there are expanding opportunities or who benefits from them. Then there are the many surveys that do not cover employment or income issues. The data collected by the Demographic and Health Surveys are heavily used in discussions or analyses of poverty, but collect no data on income or livelihoods.

What we have are just enough detailed studies of livelihoods in particular households, settlements or trades to show the variety, complexity and diversity of income-earning sources and their implications for income levels, income security and health. This chapter summarizes what we learn from these studies.

The studies also show how incomes and their sources are shaped by the specifics of local contexts, and so represent a caution against generalization. For instance, are there societal constraints that limit or prevent women working outside the home? Are there government schools and are they considered safe and good quality for both boys and girls (which influences whether children participate in the labour market and the form any participation takes)? Are average earnings higher in the formal private sector, formal public sector or informal economy (it is common for all three to include groups with very low incomes)? A review in 2003 notes that the evidence on wage differences between the formal and informal sectors revealed 'much country-to-country variation' and offers few general lessons (Montgomery *et al.* 2003, page 337). However, many studies do not examine the specifically urban components of local livelihood strategies. There is little information on the significance of densification and concentration, and often little on the specificities of the production process and how livelihood activities within low-income neighbourhoods are linked into systems of production and consumption beyond the boundaries of the settlement.

What does emerge from descriptions of the micro-level strategies of households is the scale of their agency. Individuals make considerable (often extraordinary) efforts to earn incomes, seek to improve the size and reliability of their incomes and ensure household needs are met. Households and their members may make an income from employment within the formal or informal sectors of the economy. If the latter, they may be self-employed (own-account[69] workers making goods for sale or selling services) or be employed in an informal sector enterprise. In terms of location, they may work from home, on the street or in other public spaces, or in the building of their employer. If they are employees of the formal or informal sector, they may be permanent, temporary or casual. If self-employed, they may be making goods or providing services under contract to companies, or may have a greater degree of autonomy.

Households may be dependent on one source of income with just one income earner, or may have a diversity of income streams as multiple members contribute to the household economy, and of course within most households this changes over time. Children may work full- or part-time, or may be involved in seasonal labour. Children's work may be integrated with schooling or they may have dropped out from school or be unable to get into a school. Older children (especially girls) may have household and childcare responsibilities that allow adult members to work or to work longer hours. Older age groups may continue to work and find ways to contribute to household incomes well beyond what in high-income nations is regarded as retirement age. For a proportion of low-income urban households, incomes from renting part of their house or house plot may be critical to household income, but overlooked in studies due to a focus on income earning and enterprise. Individual or household income may be affected by remittances – either money coming in from household members working elsewhere or money going out to support others. It may also be affected by debt repayments. In addition, agency is necessarily constrained by structural conditions and there are indications that changes in the labour market have reduced the potential for low-income households to secure their livelihoods.

Cities concentrate very large and diverse demands for goods and services from households, enterprises and government institutions, and it is important, though difficult, to understand how these shape income levels, employment patterns and livelihood opportunities. Of course, this demand for goods and services is also constantly changing and in so doing impacting on people's incomes and livelihoods. Cities with growing economies usually have new employment or income-earning opportunities. These often include a larger and more diverse demand for goods and services from middle- and upper-income groups whose incomes are rising (Montgomery *et al.* 2003), but there may be constraints on the possibilities for low-income groups (or particular sub-groups) to take advantage of this demand. It is difficult to unpick the extent to which a rising demand for goods and services from middle- and upper-income groups benefits low-income groups; also to identify which low-income groups benefit and the nature of these benefits. As discussed in Chapter 5, economic success in cities may also bring impoverishment to some groups.

An alternative approach to studying individuals or households is to consider the totality of markets with a focus on particular trades – for instance waste pickers, construction workers, domestic workers, home workers – or particular areas of the economy. The range of possible contexts includes markets in which an advanced formal sector has long been established to those where informality dominates – in some cases integrated within the formal sector and in others not.

Whatever the level of consideration, economic prosperity or its absence is a critical determinant of labour market opportunities. Contexts vary: there are cities that have experienced sustained medium to high economic growth for long periods, those in which growth has been minimal at least during some periods over the last three decades, and those with economies that have been contracting. There are examples of these extremes in each continent, although cities with sustained rapid economic growth are more common in the successful Asian economies and less common (until very recently) in sub-Saharan Africa. Some urban centres have benefited from new opportunities in global or local markets while others have suffered from competition from other cities or changing trends in global markets. In some cases, external markets have relatively little influence, and many small town economies may primarily serve local markets, for instance to meet the demands for producer and consumer goods and services from farming enterprises and agricultural populations.

Understanding labour markets and livelihood opportunities is made all the more complicated where governments neither provide nor ensure provision of basic infrastructure and services such as piped water, sewers, drains, household waste collection, schools, health care services and policing or rule of law. As a result of such neglect, enterprises emerge in response to demand. These have particular importance for low-income groups, both as providers of services and often as income sources. They may be meeting demand mainly from low-income groups, as do for instance water vendors, pit latrine emptiers, solid waste collectors, or low-paid staff in cheap 'private' schools and informal health care services. Or they may provide services to higher-income groups, for instance improving provision for water, sanitation, solid waste collection and security guards.

This chapter reviews the ways in which low-income individuals and households manage to find a living, and considers the diversity of strategies they use and the multiple problems that they face. It also considers the significance of particular employment and income generation options and the reasons for particular labour market outcomes. It explains what we know, examines details and attempts to draw conclusions. The next section begins by considering the nature of urban livelihoods and definitions of informality (and formality), and the almost infinite gradations within these broad categories. Understanding urban livelihoods requires us to both engage with the complexity of the subject and with the partial nature of the information that is available. The third section explores the problems that the urban poor face in employment and business, looking at issues of remuneration, regularity of income, working conditions, and labour market opportunities. The fourth section explores reasons for the particular disadvantages experienced by some, with a focus on gender and generation. It analyses forms of social stratification that define and restrict opportunities in both the labour markets and entrepreneurship. In the fifth section the discussion moves beyond the specifics of individuals and households and their social characteristics to consider the ways in which economies influence opportunity through their structural composition. This provides insight into both the nature of the struggles households face in securing incomes, and the opportunities for state influence and interventions.

Understanding the informal economy

One of the characteristics of the economies of most urban areas in the Global South is a high degree of informality. The complexities of the informal sector are considerable and understanding it is made more difficult because of the paucity of information and, related to this, a deeper reticence about examining the role of informal economic activities within a 'modern' society. Despite the frequent presence (and sometimes dominance) of informality in many aspects of livelihoods in the Global South (and to a lesser extent also elsewhere), there is a strong sense in many discourses that formal is better. This has several consequences, one of which is simply to confuse research into employment and enterprise. In some cases, the informal is simply ignored. This may be because it is seen as criminal; a common mistake among those being introduced to the concept for the first time is to equate the informal sector with criminality. As shown by WaterAid India (2009, page 5) for the case of manual scavenging of human waste in Indian cities, it may simply be because of the sense of collective shame in some occupations, or because aspects of it are illegal, such as the use of child labour. In other cases, the term 'informal' is used to bring together a diverse set of activities with little awareness of the clumsiness of the aggregation. What are termed informal livelihoods may include small-scale entrepreneurs, personal servants such as domestic workers, those working for informal businesses, casual staff in formal businesses and those working for free in family businesses. They may include long-term full-time employment or very temporary employment for just a few hours a day. Much previous research has implied a relatively precise distinction between formal and informal work, but it is increasingly recognized that the boundaries are blurred and that each person's income-earning activities have a range of characteristics on a formal–informal continuum. In part this reflects the awareness that trends in the labour market, particularly growing casualization, have increased the level of insecurity and reduced the degree of supervision and employer accountability within formal employment.

Chen, Vanek and Heintz (2006) identify three alternative 'schools of thought' regarding the informal sector. The first is the dualist school, in which the informal economy is both distinct from and marginal to the formal sector. The second is the structuralist school, in which there is a recognized interdependency between the two sectors, with the informal economy enhancing profitability within the formal (often corporate) sector. The third is the legalistic school, in which the informal economy is seen as a result of state bureaucracy, with regulations resulting in many businesses of different kinds and scales avoiding formality. Chen, Vanek and Heintz (2006) also suggest that, notwithstanding these approaches to the sector, over time there has been a recategorization of the informal sector to include all types of informal employment including those outside of informal enterprises, and the term is now recognized as covering:

- *Informal self-employment* This includes employers in informal enterprises, own-account workers in informal enterprises, unpaid family workers (in informal and formal enterprises) and members of informal producers' co-operatives.
- *Informal wage employment* This describes employment without formal contracts, worker benefits or social protection in formal or informal enterprises or by households. Certain types of wage work are more likely than others to be informal, for instance employees of informal enterprises, casual or day labourers, temporary or part-time workers, paid domestic workers, unregistered or undeclared workers and industrial outworkers (also called home workers).

The scale of informal employment depends on how it is defined. The UN's International Labour Organization now reports on informal employment as including both those employed in informal sector enterprises and those in informal employment outside informal sector enterprises (ILO 2011), and in most nations for which data are available, persons in informal employment outside the informal sector make up a significant proportion of those in informal employment (although usually a smaller proportion than do those employed in informal sector enterprises).

Tables 4.1 and 4.2 summarize the major types of work and employment that span the informal and formal sectors. Adequate remuneration may be the most important aspect in relation to avoiding poverty, although it is wrong to assume that informal sector remuneration is necessarily less than that in the formal sector. However, there are also other aspects important for avoiding poverty or reducing vulnerability including a level of income security and other (work-related) benefits. Services outside the workplace can also contribute to this, for instance access to high-quality health care. For those informally employed, the insecurity of income may be as significant as the level of income. As the tables suggest, most of these employment and entrepreneurship strategies do not provide secure incomes. While the tables make clear that much work in informal employment is not within informal sector enterprises, there is a remaining ambiguity as to whether 'own-account' workers making goods or providing services from their home and not regularly employing others are included as informal sector enterprises, or whether there are circumstances in which this type of employment can be considered formal.

Table 4.1 Insecurity and vulnerability: a typology of employment and enterprise categories for the self-employed, both in enterprises and as own-account workers

Type of employment	*Security of remuneration*	*Legal protection related to work*	*State benefits such as pension, national insurance*	*Examples*
Informal non-compliant and criminal	No	No	No	Prostitution, involvement in illegal drugs or alcohol production or sale, 'protection' services
Informal non-compliant but not criminal (although in contravention of regulations)	No	No	No	Traders without licences or not paying municipal fees, some traders and/or services in contravention of regulations such as waste collection
Informal for tax and employment purposes but recognized as traders	No	Yes (limited)	No	Traders with licences or paying municipal fees
Sub-contracted to formal enterprise	Limited to contract	Perhaps	No	Outsourced clothing manufacturers, bidi (cigarette) makers, some waste pickers and recycling enterprises, construction
Seller of services to households	No	Very limited	No	Domestic workers for multiple houses, electricians, semi-skilled or skilled builders

Table 4.2 Insecurity and vulnerability: a typology of employment and enterprise categories for the employed

Type of employment	Income security	Job security	Benefits (private or state)	Examples
Informal and casual in informal or formal enterprise	No	No	No	Daily construction labourers, serving customers on informal market stalls
Informal and regular in informal or formal enterprise	No	No	No	Shop staff in informal settlements, cleaners, workers in small-scale enterprises
Casual in formal enterprise	No	No	No (or very limited)	Temporary staff, casual staff
Formal in formal enterprise	Yes	Of some kind	Yes	Office staff, teachers, nurses, managers
Informal in domestic service	No	No	No	Cooks, maids, gardeners, security guards
Formal in domestic service	Yes	Yes	Yes	Cooks, maids, gardeners, security staff

While the crude distinction between formal and informal activities continues to be made, it is evident from many studies that this is not an accurate representation of many urban centres and that attention has to be paid to the complexity of different outcomes. Brown (2006a) exemplifies this in discussing the case of street traders working in Dar es Salaam, Kumasi, Maseru and Kathmandu. Here, there has been a shift in the attitude of governments, from hostility and repression towards some form of acceptance and tolerance, even a degree of recognition. In the case of Dar es Salaam, Nnkya (2006, page 88) highlights the opportunities for informal traders to gain a degree of formality:

> According to Ilala Municipal Council Trade Office, traders are considered to be informal if they have a capital below TSh300,000 … and do not have a permanent trading structure. The three municipal councils classify informal traders into two categories: *recognized* and *unrecognized*. To become recognized they had to pay a fee of TSh26,400 for *nguvu kazi* licence, an application fee of TSh2,000 and TSh1,000 for an education fund …. However, most traders are unrecognized and are charged a daily fee by the sub-ward office of TSh100 a day for the space and TSh100 for street cleaning, an annual cost of almost three times as much as a registered trader. Municipal revenue from unregistered traders is considerably more than from registered traders.

Such complexities reflect the reality that, for this city at least, the authorities recognize that the informal sector is a legitimate component of the economy. A companion study in the same volume discusses Kumasi and provides further examples of the overlap in categorizations (King 2006). It is evident that the simple distinction between formal and informal activities is meaningless in contexts such as these. Drawing on this, Table 4.3 presents a categorization of enterprises with their associated implications for poverty.

Table 4.3 Subcategories of formal and informal work and their implications for poverty

Legal status	Level of compliance and legality	Relation to poverty
Formal	Processes comply with regulations and activities are legal	Formal sector, waged employees. The relationship between these enterprises and poverty depends on the regulatory framework and capacities of the state. Does a minimum wage exist and is it sufficient for survival? Are there enforced standards for safe working conditions?
	Deviations from processes and/or illegal activities (e.g. illegal dumping of waste, tax evasion, illegal employment)	As previous, plus potential dangers for the general public and consumers (who may lack the resources they need to protect themselves). The relationship between these enterprises and poverty depends on compliance with regulations, including governmental capacity to enforce them and workers' and citizens' organizations' ability to monitor and report.
Informal	Registered informal	These companies are likely to have low capital investment and relatively low earnings for the entrepreneur. Any workforce is likely to be paid very little and minimum wages may not be enforced.
	Non-registered but paying daily charges for trading or other activities	As above, plus the additional charges; however, these charges may be less than those informally imposed by rent-seeking individuals able to exert control over the business owner. These enterprises are unlikely to have substantial capital investments.
	Non-compliant in processes but activities legal	Vulnerable due to illegality. Likely to be unregistered due to inability to pay. May have to make payments to others able to extract resources due to lack of formal status.
	Non-compliant in processes and activities illegal	Vulnerable both to illegality and exclusion from some social processes. May also exacerbate the poverty of others.

A further perspective on relations between informal and formal economic activities is that the significance of formal status may be overstated due to the scale and depth of informal politics. In this context, the legal framework is modified in practice by alternative attitudes and informal negotiations offering the advantages of informality to the formal sector. King (2006, page 111) notes that the byelaws in Kumasi are 'largely ineffective'. She suggests that this is both because of the dominance of personal relations over bureaucratic rules (whereby some traders benefit from personal links and exchange information and political support for non-interference) and because of ambiguities in the byelaws themselves. However, she also notes that the lowest paid and smaller traders are disadvantaged by such practices. Although street traders pay daily tolls, they continue to be harassed for non-compliance. Blundo (2006) describes similar processes of informal negotiation in the case of Dakar, Senegal in his study of officials and their relations with public users of state services.

Horn (2011) reports on the views of workers with respect to formalization, drawing on a survey of 219 informal workers in 15 cities undertaken by a range of workers' organizations in Chile, Colombia, India, Indonesia, Kenya, Malawi, Pakistan, Peru, South Africa and Thailand. She notes that, while most street vendors and waste pickers wanted to register and be integrated into the formal regulatory environment, some expressed their concerns about these processes. Waste pickers in Colombia and India in particular valued their autonomy as well as their association with other informal workers. They wanted to engage with municipalities through agreements and regular meetings with their member-based organizations, and not necessarily through compliance with externally determined rules and regulations.

Finally, it should not be assumed that such informal negotiations and informal politics only take place in the Global South. It has been recognized for a long time that corporate bodies and other elite groups negotiate exemption from rules and regulations in the Global North. This might be related to tax settlements or special support. The most notable recent example has been state support for the financial sector in the context of the global banking crisis. These arrangements reflect social realities, and the interconnectedness of elites and their willingness to support each other; however, they also reflect economic realities and systemic interrelationships between significant sectors, and hence the need to offer support in particular contexts.

The scale of the informal economy

There is much more data on the proportion of the working population employed in the informal sector or in informal employment than there is on the incomes earned, the hours worked or the working conditions. However, because of the different definitions used, the statistics are often not comparable and should be treated with care.

In the ILO study mentioned previously (ILO 2011), consistent definitions were used in assembling data from 46 low- and middle-income nations. This analysis shows the high proportion of the non-agricultural working population in informal employment. Data are provided for two categories. The first is the proportion of non-agricultural employment in enterprises in the informal sector (i.e. with jobs in unregistered and/or small unincorporated private enterprises that are not separate legal entities, including own-account workers). The second is the proportion of non-agricultural employment in informal employment outside the informal sector, including employees holding informal jobs in formal sector enterprises and paid domestic workers employed by households in informal jobs. The sum of these, the proportion of non-agricultural employment which is informal, was high in almost all nations for which data were available (Table 4.4). It exceeded 80 per cent for India and Mali, and only in two nations (Serbia and Slovakia) was it below 10 per cent. Almost all the nations with relatively low proportions were in Eastern Europe, reflecting the historical development of their labour markets and the controls preventing informal sector development within communist states.

In all but two countries, the number of persons employed in the informal sector exceeds those in informal employment outside the informal sector. The exceptions are Moldova and West Bank and Gaza. The percentage of non-agricultural employment which is informal and outside the informal sector was particularly high in Bolivia, Ecuador, Lesotho, Madagascar, Mexico, Paraguay, Peru, Vietnam and West Bank and Gaza, where it exceeded 20 per cent. Disaggregated data are available for men and women in 37 countries: in 27, women outnumber men in informal employment; in Argentina, Armenia, Egypt, Macedonia, Moldova, Serbia, Sri Lanka, Venezuela, Vietnam and West Bank and Gaza this is not the case. In 39 countries this disaggregation was available for those persons employed in the informal sector, and in 25 there was a higher percentage of men than women in informal sector employment (with women more concentrated in informal employment outside the informal sector).

Generally, the higher the nation's GDP per capita, the lower the percentage of workers in informal employment within total non-agricultural employment, although there are some exceptions (both relatively low-income countries with low proportions of informal employment and relatively high-income countries with high proportions of informal employment). In addition, the higher the

Table 4.4 Percentage of nations' non-agricultural employment which is
informal employment

Percentage	Countries
> 70	Bolivia, Honduras, India, Madagascar, Mali, Paraguay, Peru, Zambia
50–70	Argentina, Colombia, Ecuador, Egypt, El Salvador, Liberia, Mexico, Nicaragua, Sri Lanka, Timor Leste, Uganda, Vietnam, West Bank and Gaza, Zimbabwe
30–50	Brazil, Costa Rica, Dominican Republic, Lesotho, Namibia, Panama, South Africa, Thailand, Turkey, Uruguay, Venezuela
< 30	Armenia, Azerbaijan, Macedonia, Moldova, Serbia, Slovakia

Source: Data from ILO (2011)

proportion of informal employment within non-agricultural employment, the higher the proportion of the population living below the national poverty line. But the validity of this analysis is in doubt, given the different criteria used by nations in setting poverty lines – for instance, do Mexico and Colombia really have much higher proportions of their population in poverty than India and Egypt? As explored in Chapter 2, there are many reasons why urban poverty assessments may be inaccurate. For these reasons, it is not clear that informal employment is correlated to high levels of poverty, although clearly this remains an area of concern.

There is some tendency for the proportion of a nation's non-agricultural employment in informal employment to be lower in nations that are more urbanized (Figure 4.1), although of course these are also nations with a higher proportion of their working population in non-agricultural employment.

Some other national studies show the high importance of informal employment. Mitullah (2010) reports that in 2002 the Kenyan informal sector provided 74 per cent of total private sector employment. In 2002, 5.1 million were informally employed, an increase from 4.6 million in 2001. Mitullah adds that, while the government introduced measures to improve informal sector performance in 1992 and 2005, many of these measures have not been realized. Brown and Lyons (2010) suggest that informal employment accounts for around 60 per cent of all urban employment in Africa, with home based workers the largest group, followed by street traders. Box 4.1 gives some examples of the importance of the informal economy to employment in particular cities.

Box 4.1 The role of informal employment in city case studies

- *Accra* Maxwell *et al.* (2000) note that in Accra the ratio of informal to formal workers is seven to one.
- *Yaoundé* Sikod (2001) reports that in Yaoundé, Cameroon 57.3 per cent of the population are employed in the informal sector.
- *Karachi* The Urban Resource Centre (2001) reports that 75 per cent of those employed in the city of Karachi work in the informal sector; however, it adds that there are close links to the formal sector.
- *Kumasi* Brown (2006b) suggests that the informal sector employs 75 per cent of the working population of Kumasi.
- *Dar es Salaam* 20 per cent of the urban population for Dar es Salaam are employed in the informal sector. As discussed, this perhaps surprisingly low figure may reflect legislation to allow for regularization of some informal trading (Brown 2006b).
- *Mombasa* Rakodi (2006) reports that in Mombasa the proportion of the labour force in formal employment fell from 53 per cent in 1979 to 46 per cent in 1989 and 43 per cent in 1999 (with about two fifths in the public sector).

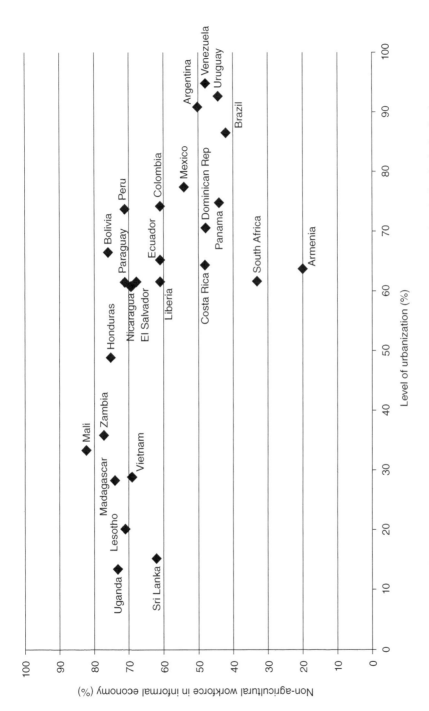

Figure 4.1 The proportion of a nation's non-agricultural employment in informal employment against the level of urbanization

Source: Data from ILO (2011)

Thus the relative inaccessibility of formal employment for much of the urban workforce is a consistent theme in studies of urban livelihoods. The trend towards informality is discussed in the section on 'Economies'.

Securing income

Regardless of whether their income comes from formal or informal employment, what matters to households is the scale of income and benefits, security of this income and benefits, and working conditions. Low, insecure incomes are a causal factor in much urban poverty. Both income levels and income security are discussed in this section.

Incomes from formal and informal employment

The dynamics of urban incomes and the consequences for poverty are explored in an unusual study which compares panel data sets for urban households in both Madagascar and Peru (Herrera and Roubaud 2005), and which shows the high proportion of the urban population that has been poor at least once, the importance of skilled work for avoiding poverty, and the problems of generalization. The analysis focuses on the late 1990s, some years after the governments of both countries had introduced neo-liberal economic policies. This was a period of recession in Peru and growth in Madagascar. The Peru three-wave panel data are from 1997, 1998 and 1999, while data for Madagascar are drawn from an annual labour force survey that took place between 1995 and 2001, supplemented by additional information gathered in 1995, 1998 and 2001. The focus is on household per capita income, including wages from work in primary and secondary employment, and formal and informal activities, as well as benefits in kind, social assistance benefits and pensions. Absolute poverty lines were set at $2 for Madagascar and $4 for Peru in 1998 and adjusted for inflation for 1997 and 1999.

A few notable points emerge from the study with regard to the adequacy of incomes. First, with respect to poverty transitions, about 17 per cent of individuals changed categories between poor and non-poor in Madagascar every year. In Peru, these 'crossovers' occurred in between a quarter and a fifth of sample households. Given the low level of incomes, this means that many households experience some poverty:

> Whereas the poverty rate in 1999 [in Madagascar] was 77%, 91% of Antananarivo residents had gone through at least one episode of poverty in the two previous years. In Peru, the proportions were 32% and 48%, respectively. However, regardless of the significance of these changes, a hard core of chronic poverty remains which, on the basis of our three-year panel, can be estimated at 13% in Peru and 65% in Madagascar.
>
> (Herrera and Roubaud 2005, page 28)

Second, the authors conclude that there are strong similarities between the urban populations in both countries, although there are also notable differences emerging in employment structure, with more qualified jobs in Peru both in industrial and office work, and in the quality of housing and public infrastructure. In terms of transitions, whether this involves managing to leave poverty or shifting between chronic (poor in all periods) and transitory poverty (poor in one or more periods), patterns are similar in both countries and larger, younger families are less likely to avoid poverty. The significance of the labour market is also supported by the findings in both countries: better-educated workers are more likely to exit poverty, as are those who are public-service employees or white-collar workers or who work outside the primary sector. Hence stratifications in the labour market are important but this is more nuanced than a simple divide into formal and informal employment.

Finally, Hererra and Roubaud (2005) emphasize that findings may differ between countries. In Madagascar households with working-age members employed in the informal sector are more likely to be among the chronically poor than the transitory poor; however, this is not the case in Peru, where there is no noticeable difference in the likelihood of being in chronic or transitory poverty for households with members working in the informal sector.

Chen, Vanek and Heintz (2006) argue that the relationship between the informal economy and poverty has to be assessed through a consideration of employment and earnings security together with the costs and benefits of securing work. They also argue that some of the costs are likely to be those associated with psychological and emotional responses to working in the informal sector, as it is socially determined to be of low status. In an assessment of three overview studies plus national-level analyses of India and Tunisia, the authors conclude that:

- There is limited information on relative earnings between the formal and informal sector; data from one of the overview studies suggests that in Egypt, El Salvador and South Africa earnings are higher in the formal sector while in another overview study data for Costa Rica and El Salvador suggest the reverse.
- There is considerable income disparity within the informal sector. For example, data from Tunisia suggest that average income of micro-entrepreneurs was four times as high as the legal minimum salary and 2.2 times the average salary in the formal sector; however, home workers are paid only 30 per cent of the minimum wage.
- Where data exist, evidence suggests that women earn less. Women are concentrated in the lowest-earning parts of the informal sector. However, within each employment sector, there is no systematic pattern in men's and women's poverty rates.

The authors explain that two labour force surveys – from 2002 in South Africa and 1999–2000 in India – find associations between household expenditure and employment data. Both found an overlap between being a 'poor household' and informal employment. The high level of informal employment in India makes strict formal and informal comparisons difficult. However, households that depend on 'regular' (as opposed to casual) informal wage employment have lower poverty rates relative to households that rely on self-employment, and households that depend on casual labour as their primary source of income are the most likely to be poor (Chen, Vanek and Heintz 2006).

The strong relationship between informality and income poverty has been noted by others. Analysing experiences in Honduras, Costa Rica and Brazil, Sinha and Lipton and colleagues (1999) suggest that poverty rates are higher among informal and unprotected workers. Alwang, Mills and Taruvinga (2002) report that the increase in urban poverty that took place in Zimbabwe in the early 1990s was particularly notable in those households dependent on earnings from the urban informal sector. Elaborating on the situation in Harare, Kanji (1995) explains that some income-earning opportunities within the informal economy became saturated as more workers entered specific sectors of informal production in which women were most involved (knitting, sewing and crocheting) and existing workers faced declining demand, increased competition and rising input costs. In Mombasa, Kenya adults classified by the government as poor (i.e. as living below their poverty line) are more likely to be working in the informal sector. In 2000, 59 per cent of adults in poor households worked in the informal sector, compared to 46 per cent of adults in 'non-poor' households (Rakodi 2006). About one third of Mombasa's residents were below the poverty line, according to a government report from 2000 (Rakodi 2006). Dutta with Batley (2000) offer a graphic illustration of the problem, describing falling earnings following the closure of textile mills in Ahmedabad. Monthly earnings excluding bonuses for mill workers had been between ₹1,500 and ₹2,500. A study of 1,729 mill workers who had been made redundant found that, for those in work, current monthly earnings were between ₹723 (from self-employment in manufacturing and repairs) and ₹1,156 (for auto-rickshaw drivers). Kundu (2011) analyses the NSS (National Sample Survey) data from India and notes that urban wage rates have declined significantly between 1999–2000 and 2004–05, despite national economic growth. The finding is that after two decades of increasing casualization for men, and somewhat erratic but generally slightly increasing casualization for women, wage rates fell significantly in the five years following 1999–2000, a period in which formal (regular) employment opportunities continued to decline for men but increased for women.

However, in an apparently rare example that warns once more about the dangers of generalization, Gilbert (1997) documents rising incomes together with increasing informalization. The percentage of informal workers in the labour market in Bogota grew from 22 per cent in 1976 to 27 per cent in 1995: 'the combined effect of economic growth and falling rates of unemployment has been to improve average incomes and cut the number of workers in particularly low-paid work' (page 29). Gilbert quotes an earlier study in order to show that the numbers 'living in misery' (i.e. those in acute need) in Bogota fell from 26 to 4 per cent between 1973 and 1991 (Londono de la Cuesta 1992, quoted in Gilbert 1997).

The World Bank's study of informal settlements in Nairobi and Dakar (Gulyani, Talukdar and Jack 2010) illustrates the diversity of relationships between poverty and employment status (Table 4.5) and provides evidence that these relationships are different in different locations. The level of poverty is calculated using national government poverty lines adjusted for inflation. Overall, the poor made up 77 per cent of working interviewees in Nairobi and 87 per cent in Dakar. What is notable is that employment status appears to differentiate poverty status more in Nairobi than in Dakar. In Dakar, for example, the percentage of those who are regular employees is 7.6 per cent of those below the poverty line and 9.1 per cent of those above it; the equivalent figures for Nairobi are 21.8 and 35.8 per cent – proportionately a much larger difference. In Nairobi, type of employment is much more likely to determine poverty status. Once more the dangers of generalization are exemplified.

More generally, there are few studies that deal directly with issues related to low pay, but there is evidence to suggest that earnings remain low at the lower ends of the formal sector or in particular professions. For instance, discussing poverty in urban centres in Zambia, Chibuye (2011) presents details of income ranges for various formal sector jobs, including for teachers, nurses, security guards and shop assistants. Many working in these professions have incomes below the poverty line, set for this study based on the costs of food and non-food needs. Studies of informal settlements frequently find some residents who are civil servants or professionals – this usually reflects both limited incomes and the high cost of formal housing.

The problems of both low incomes in formal and informal employment and income insecurity are elaborated by De Swardt *et al.* (2005) in their report on a random sample of 624 households in Khayelitsha and Greater Nyanga, two low-income settlements in Cape Town, in 2002: 'More than three-quarters (77 per cent) of households that had at least one wage earner still did not earn enough to

Table 4.5 Employment status and incidence of poverty among adult individuals in Nairobi and Dakar informal settlements, 2004 (note that data are rounded to the nearest tenth of a percentage point and totals to the nearest percentage point)

Employment status	Nairobi (%)		Dakar (%)	
	Poor	Non-poor	Poor	Non-poor
Unemployed	29.4	15.7	5.7	6.1
Regular employee	21.8	35.8	7.6	9.1
Casual employee	24.1	22.9	8.4	8.7
Own account/self-employed (non-farm)	18.3	21.1	23.1	22.7
Non-paid family worker	0.4	0.1	25.0	27.0
Student/apprentice	4.9	3.3	17.3	15.3
Other (e.g. pensioner)	1.0	1.2	13.0	11.1
Total	100	100	100	100

Source: Guylani *et al.* 2010, page 35

push income per adult equivalent over the poverty line of R560 per month' (page 103). This finding reflects both a lack of formal employment and low wages in both sectors. Even in the South African context, with a substantial formal sector, formal jobs were relatively scarce for the residents of these settlements. Only 23 per cent of adults reported earning a permanent (i.e. regular but not necessarily formal) salary and in 32 per cent of households the main breadwinner had lost his or her job at some point during the previous year, highlighting problems of labour market insecurity. The study also found, as noted in Chapter 3, that more than 70 per cent of households reported hunger and food intake lacking protein, fruit and vegetables.

De la Rocha (2007) highlights the importance of demand from those with formal incomes for the local economy, even if this demand is small in individual scale and does not reach many in the community. It enables a range of informal sector activities to thrive both because of regularity of income at the household level, and because of the consequent market for small goods within the neighbourhood. With a small permanent wage, women, for example, have money to make clothes for themselves with a potential additional trade in making clothes for others (thereby earning a small but useful income). This point is returned to in the section on 'Economies'.

In some countries, remittances from overseas are an increasingly significant source of household income. Their importance was noted by the World Bank in their poverty assessment for Nicaragua (World Bank Nicaragua 2008). While recognizing that remittance income is not equally spread, and a high proportion goes to the families of workers with skilled jobs and relatively high educational attainment, the report also notes that the remittances have a significant impact on poverty levels. For Nicaragua, the scale is considerable: an estimated 20,000–30,000 Nicaraguans migrate every year, and 10 per cent of Nicaraguans are resident outside the country. The report argues that 'Official remittances have increased 90 percent during the last ten years reaching $600 million in 2005 (or an amount equal to 40 percent of total exports and 12 percent of GDP)' (page 14). Sixty-eight per cent of remittances go to families in the upper two income deciles. However, remittances are a more significant component of incomes at the lower end of the scale, accounting for 15 per cent of income for households in the lowest decile. In terms of the impact on urban poverty, the report estimates that the urban poverty rate in 2005, based on household consumption, would have been 34.3 per cent without remittances, instead of the actual figure of 28.9 per cent; the equivalent figures for extreme urban poverty were 10.9 and 5.4 per cent respectively.

Labour and livelihoods

Labour and the neighbourhood

This section considers individual and household experiences in securing incomes in settlements where low-income groups are concentrated. It is limited by the relatively few studies that provide the depth and detail needed to show the diversity of ways in which households secure the funds they need to survive and, in some cases, prosper. The studies that do exist are important not just for their detailed accounts of how incomes are secured, but also because their descriptions and analyses begin to show how household incomes help to make up a neighbourhood economy. These neighbourhood studies elaborate on the different options for earning an income and comment on the advantages and disadvantages of different forms of employment. There is an overlap in spatial focus with some of the literature on city economies. In this section we cover literature that focuses on the employment realities for lower-income groups and on issues of poverty and vulnerability together with livelihoods. In the later section on city economies we cover material related more to the economy of spatial areas. Some authors cover both, hence we refer to their work in both sections.

Moser (2009) brings together the findings of longitudinal research from 1978 to 2004 on the households living within one community, Indio Guayas, in Guayaquil, Ecuador, with a particular focus on 51 families. She covers both settlement issues, including tenure security and access to basic services, and income earning. Consistent with the discussion here, Moser argues that it is more accurate to identify a continuum of income-generating activities spanning formal and informal sectors, noting that a clear distinction may not always be possible. With regard to income generation in the informal sector, Moser states:

> [T]he data showed that while for a few the informal sector provided a more profitable source of income than formal sector wage employment, for the majority it was a highly competitive sector characterised by small-scale enterprises producing petty commodities, and underpaid and irregular casual residual work.
>
> (page 121)

The household data show that about one third of all households worked from their homes, undertaking a range of informal sector activities including tailoring and dressmaking, taxi services and small shops. This percentage rises from 31 per cent in 1978 to 37 per cent in 2004 (a period from the beginning to the almost complete consolidation of the settlement). Within these households, the lowest income group were the most likely to use their home as a work base.

In more recent decades, informal sector economy activities have dominated income generation in Indio Guayas, with a gendered disadvantage as women have been pushed into the less remunerative sectors and in some cases been excluded from trading in areas that they previously occupied. Key activities in 1978 were domestic service, taking in washing (among those unable to leave children), retail selling, and dressmaking and tailoring. In 1992 two trends were evident: one was the intensification of labour, with more women working, and the other was the increasing casualization of male work. By 2004, casual work accounted for 49.5 per cent of all male workers, up from 31.5 per cent in 1978 and 41 per cent in 1992. Men began to leave the settlement for employment, both for activities such as construction labour and informal entrepreneurship. For the aggregate labour force (i.e. both men and women) the proportion with permanent employment was 24 per cent in 1978 and in 2004, but 35.5 per cent in 1992. Self-employment fell from 46 per cent in 1978 to 28.5 per cent in 1992, then increased to 32.5 per cent in 2004. As significant a change has been the increase in casual employment, from 30 per cent to 36 per cent and then 43.5 per cent in 1978, 1992 and 2004 respectively.

In terms of household well-being, the dependency ratio fell from 4.2 in 1978 to 2.6 in 2004; this is in part related to the trajectory of settlement development, with the younger families that moved to occupy the newly settled area on the periphery of the city becoming more mature households, with children at work and/or leaving the family home. Irrespective of this trend, Moser notes higher dependency ratios among the lowest income families, a long-accepted relationship (the same point was mentioned previously, in relation to Herrera and Roubaud's [2005] study of panel data from Madagascar and Peru): in 2004 the dependency ratio in non-poor households was 2.0 and in poor households it was 3.3. Education had opened up new employment possibilities for the children of the first settlers, some of whom have become skilled and professional workers. Household income diversification has also extended beyond employment income, with contributions from remittances, government transfers and rents. In 1995, 95 per cent of household income was from wages or income-generating activities, but by 2004 this figure had fallen to 81 per cent. Across the 51 households, inequality increased over the period, as some households managed to do better than others and the number of very poor households fell from 51 per cent in 1978 to 31 per cent in 2004. The Gini coefficient[70] for the households' incomes was 0.322 in 1978, 0.375 in 1992 and 0.416 in 2004. Moser points out that this final figure is close to the national coefficient for Ecuador of 0.437. Also notable is the increase in generational mobility and its gendered nature. In 2004, 4 per cent of fathers were in permanent regular employment compared to 30 per cent of mothers, 30 per cent of sons and 47 per cent of daughters.

One recent further source of income is the result of international migration. For residents of Guayaquil's informal settlements, the economic crisis in the late 1990s combined with relatively simple visa requirements to encourage migration to Spain; in the case of Indio Guayas residents, to Barcelona. By 2004, 2 million Ecuadorians (15 per cent of the total population) were working overseas. Without work permits and few social contacts, they struggled to find work. Amnesties and related opportunities to secure legal status in Spain offered some the opportunity to gain relatively highly paid employment. In general, men and women took up unskilled jobs but with higher levels of pay and state benefits than were possible in Ecuador. Among families in Guayaquil, more than three out of four migrants were sending back funds, and, of these, four out of five were doing so each month. An analysis for all 51 households shows that the average international migrants sent back in 2005 was US$143 a month, compared to monthly contributions of US$7.75 from children remaining in Guayaquil.

Perlman (2010) reports on another longitudinal study, this time from Rio de Janeiro. She follows what has happened to the residents of three *favelas* who she first interviewed in the late 1960s. Her follow-up research tracks down 262 of the original sample (of 600 random individuals plus 150 leaders) and also incorporates interviews with their children (a random sample of 394 of the 1,005 children identified) and grandchildren, where possible. She includes new random samples of 400 people and 25 community leaders for each of the three sites studied. The analysis includes incomes, employment options and enterprise development alongside discussions about housing consolidation and neighbourhood politics.

With regard to incomes, it is apparent from the life histories presented that households see education as an important avenue to social advancement, with some choosing smaller families to allow for greater investment. However, what also emerges from Perlman's research is that, for any given educational attainment, those who remained in the *favelas* earned considerably less than those who moved out. This was consistent with the census results for 2002: after 16 years of schooling, those who lived in the *favela* had an average income less than half that of those who lived outside the *favela*. In terms of securing success in life, 66 per cent reported that the key factor was jobs or work, with education cited by 50 per cent. This perspective is illustrated by another of Perlman's findings: 'about 60 per cent in each generation had better jobs than their own parents – this despite the fact that 85 per cent had more education than their own parents' (page 231). At the same time, the percentage of those in formal employment rose between 1969 and 2001, improving with each generation.

Banks (2010) provides many insights into the limited opportunities for livelihoods and the importance of social contacts in getting work for those living in informal settlements in Dhaka, Bangladesh. Low-income households are often excluded from economic opportunities because of a lack of skills, credit and connections. Banks analyses the livelihood strategies of a group of residents in two low-income settlements in Dhaka. The first is Gulshan, which is located advantageously close to the centre – close to garment factories and high-income areas with demand for domestic workers and security guards, for example. The second settlement is Mirpur, a peripheral location also close to garment factories but with only low-income neighbourhoods nearby. In each location, two neighbourhoods are studied, one without and one with legal basic services. Interviews with 76 households informed an understanding of employment in the informal and formal sectors, and livelihoods from small businesses (informal enterprises). The study focused on coping and improving households, i.e. those which were not destitute and were not on a downward income trajectory. In addition, Banks undertook a community survey within each of the neighbourhoods in which about 100 households within a confined spatial area were interviewed; the objective was 100 per cent coverage, and in total 420 households across the four areas were included.

Banks (2010) finds that female employment was high across all four communities, at between 46.4 and 59.4 per cent of households. The social acceptability of women's employment is an important factor explaining this, and the location with the highest proportion of women working is known for its home-based embroidery, a relatively high-status job as it enables the women to remain in the house. When households are stratified into three income groups, 69.3 per cent of households in the middle-income group include women who are employed compared to 50.3 per cent in the lowest income group and 42.6 per cent in the highest income group. These figures suggest that this additional source of income is significant in household well-being, as households with women working are more likely not to be in the lowest income group. As household incomes increase, there is social pressure for women not to work. Banks argues that there are two contrasting attitudes among interviewees, some arguing that women working is a 'necessary evil' while others perceive it to be of equal importance with male employment. The significance of gendered social relationships is a consistent theme in the literature and is returned to later in the section on gender and generation.

Unskilled labour is often considered to be a common source of male employment. It includes rickshaw pulling, construction and loading and unloading goods. The community survey found that only 38 per cent of household heads had unskilled labour as their sole or primary income source, of whom about two thirds pulled rickshaws. The main advantages of rickshaw pulling are the ease of entry, with low costs (a daily fee is paid to rent a rickshaw) and the relatively unskilled nature of the work. Personal connections are critical to being able to hire a rickshaw from a garage owner; however, many migrants to Dhaka have such connections or quickly acquire them by linking up with people from their areas of origin. Relations with the garage owner are important in part because of the risks of rickshaws being stolen and the high costs that have to be paid for their return. Interviewees explained that there is a citywide syndicate that steals rickshaws. The owners have to pay for their return (about 4,000 takas), with the driver who had been renting the rickshaw typically contributing about a quarter of this cost. Political contacts reduce this risk but are not easy to obtain, even for businessmen willing to invest money. Day labourers face problems securing regular work, and once more personal relations are necessary for obtaining employment. Advancement is very difficult in both rickshaw pulling (shifting from renting to owning) and labouring (becoming a labour contractor) due to the large amounts of capital needed (for investment and 'sweeteners') and multiple business risks. Alternative income-earning options such as small enterprise development also require access to capital. The same is true of other alternatives. Banks explains that 'lack of finance also prevents access to formal sector jobs, with household heads unable to accumulate a sufficient bribe to secure a job. Even with contacts in the right place they will ask for 3,000 taka to provide a service job' (page 116).

Factory work pays less than labouring (100 takas a day compared to 150 takas) but may be preferred due to the regularity of employment and hence greater income security. Fewer than 32 per cent of households across the four communities were engaged in formal or skilled work, and it is notable that not all formal workers had permanent contracts, with only those with permanent contracts able to access promotion and benefits. Banks concludes that this means 'only a small proportion being able to access these jobs on the best terms' (page 216).

Across the four neighbourhoods, 21 per cent of households were supported by small businesses. However, only 24 per cent of these households believed that their financial situation had improved in the previous five years and many households were struggling with debt from failed businesses. There was a significant difference between enterprises trading within the settlement and those trading outside it. For those trading inside the settlement, a major problem was people who did not pay, including those who needed help with cash-flow, those who were dishonest (i.e. who promised to pay but then absconded), and powerful local individuals (*mastaans* or strongmen) who demanded favours and who business owners could not afford to offend. There was even a local expression, *bhaki khay* – to eat without paying. A further problem facing these businesses was the limited size of their market. Those trading outside the informal settlement were generally able to secure greater profits as their clientele tended to include higher-income households, and non-paying customers were less of a problem. A particular problem that all faced at this time was rising prices, which in the case of non-essential products (such as flip-flops, chicken and haircuts) could not be passed on to customers.

Two substantive conclusions emerge from Banks's analysis. The first is the scale of vulnerability. Even if, for example, a household could manage to raise the 6,000–12,000 taka needed to purchase a rickshaw, they faced considerable risks, including damage and theft. Many households reported difficulties due to the high price of food, loan costs, rising prices, bribes and evictions. It is evident that even when households put together successful livelihood strategies, they recognized that these were not robust and there were numerous risks to be managed. Formal work may not be permanent and therefore remains insecure.

The second conclusion is the importance of informal networks and personal relationships. Such relations are needed to secure formal employment, but also for many other livelihoods; individuals need a *mamu* – an 'uncle'; a relative or non-relative, often from the same district – who acts as patron in securing a job or other assistance, for example political connections that prevent businesses having to pay protection monies. Reviewing the 76 household livelihood strategies that are subject to detailed analysis, Banks reports that 'all formal jobs require some form of relationship to secure employment. Furthermore, the *strength* of a relationship determines the kind of job accessed and the terms on which it is secured' (page 181). Access to these relationships does not appear to be easy, and interviewees discussed the costs incurred in trying and failing to build up social capital. Banks concludes that '[s]ocial connections take precedence over skills and experience in securing skilled jobs' (page 193) and discrimination is reported based on both religion and area of origin.

In another neighbourhood-level study from Asia, Bapat (2009) summarizes the results of surveys in seven 'slum' settlements in Pune, India for which data were collected in 1976, 1980 and 1988, with two of these settlements and one additional settlement surveyed in 2003. Overall, the study shows that residents had very limited opportunities to move from the 'slums', even though economic growth in the city as a whole was rapid and many saw some growth in income. Between 1976 and 1980, slum-dwelling households struggled, with little opportunity for income growth and increases in living costs. They increased their labour market participation (as Moser [2009] also found for her sample of households from Indio Guayas in Guayaquil); women were particularly affected and their labour participation increased as they found employment in low-remuneration jobs as domestic workers, petty traders and waste pickers, and from casual labour such as construction work. Between 1980 and 1988, the panel data suggest that households secured modest real increases in their incomes; this was a period of rapid economic growth for the city. But for the period 1976 to 1988, the proportion working in the factory and organized sector did not increase for men and fell for women. In the two settlements resurveyed in 2003, most women were still in unskilled work without job security or employment benefits.

A more elaborated picture of female employment emerges from Kantor's (2009) study drawing on panel data from 12 informal settlements in Lucknow, India, with three years of observations between 2001 and 2004. Of women over 12 years of age in each of the three years, one third were working. Of these, 36 per cent were sub-contracted workers (generally employed doing embroidery), 23 per cent were unpaid, working for the family business, 13 per cent were domestic workers, 12 per cent were own-account workers (artisans and vendors), 11 per cent had salaries and 5 per cent were casual workers. Lack of income was the main reason put forward for women entering the labour market and women of higher educational attainment were less likely to work; this is similar to Banks's (2010) conclusion from Dhaka that women's work is partly related to economic necessity. Sub-contracting work got the lowest remuneration, especially for those working through agents. Women faced constraints entering the labour market and were often limited to home-based work by social norms – this also meant lower quality work conditions and lower incomes.

Prior to moving on to the literature dealing with trades rather than neighbourhoods, it may be useful to consider what has been learnt from these studies focusing on spatial areas. First, there is an evident diversity of activities across the spectrum of formal and informal livelihood strategies. It is widely recognized that many urban poor households have multiple sources of incomes as they seek to secure their livelihood, although in some contexts opportunities may be more limited. Banerjee and Dulfo (2007, page 152) both elaborate on and warn against the dangers of over-generalization:

Many poor households have multiple occupations. Like the dosa women of Guntur, 21 percent of the households living under $2 a day in Hyderabad who have a business actually have more than one, while another 13 percent have both a business and a laborer's job. This multiplicity of occupations in urban areas is found in many other countries as well, though not everywhere. Among those earning less than $2 a day, 47 percent of the urban households in Cote d'Ivoire and Indonesia get their income from more than one source; 36 percent in Pakistan; 20.5 percent in Peru; and 24 percent in Mexico. However, in urban South Africa and Panama, almost no one has more than one occupation and only 9 percent do so in Nicaragua and Timor Leste.

In concluding this section, six further points can be highlighted. The first is that the literature on the informal sector has increasingly recognized the multiple forms through which informality can enter into both labour contracts and enterprise management, hence it is important to recognize the permeability of the boundaries between formal and informal and in some cases the creation of hybrids partly formal and partly informal.

Second, employment patterns for those living in informal settlements generally include formal employment, informal employment and some small enterprises trading inside and outside the settlement. They are connected, in numerous ways, with the urban centres within which they are located. Most of those living in informal settlements have low incomes and this may be the case regardless of the sector in which employment has been found.

Third, employment sectors are stratified by gender and the divisions are very much manifest at the neighbourhood level. This is returned to later, when we explore the relationship between access to labour markets and enterprises, and gender and generation.

Fourth, reviewing the limited number of studies of employment within informal settlements, casualization and informalization appear to have increased. But as some options have closed down, others have opened up and both education and remittances from family members who migrate may offer possibilities for enhancing incomes, albeit outside of the immediate neighbourhood.

Fifth, social relations and networks are seen as related to income-earning opportunities. 'Who you know' consistently emerges as important in explaining the position of individuals within the labour market.

Sixth, labour and micro-enterprise markets are dynamic and two longitudinal studies of livelihoods appear to suggest that they are improving for at least some households. It is difficult to identify the reasons for this. Is it because, as settlements consolidate during a period of urban expansion (including settlements that were peripheral when they were founded but are now no longer so), they are better placed within the city economy? Is it because households that are spatially stable build up the social relations that they need to secure the advancement of their members? Or is it because households are consolidating and moving from being a pair of young adults to becoming a more extended family with greater resources for livelihood generation, perhaps with children who are better educated than their parents and able to find better income-earning opportunities?

Trades

An alternative approach to understanding urban labour markets has been to focus on particular groups of low-paid and insecure workers. In this section we look at rickshaw pulling, street trading and waste recycling to gain a further understanding of the livelihoods of the urban poor.

Begum and Sen (2005) show the very limited possibilities for moving out of poverty for rickshaw pullers in Dhaka, drawing on interviews carried out in

2003 with 402 current and 98 former rickshaw pullers. Most had migrated from rural areas, but had been landless and had previously worked as casual day labourers in agriculture. The authors note that the group was 58 per cent uneducated, with a further 17 per cent completing only primary education. Rickshaw pulling appears to be the most easily available work for rural migrants but 87 per cent of them did not own rickshaws and had to hire them. On average, their daily income in 2003 was the equivalent of US$2.38; it accounted for 83 per cent of total household income; and it supported five people. Eighteen per cent had below-poverty-line incomes and 3 per cent were in extreme poverty (households with incomes of 60 per cent of the income poverty line). Poverty and extreme poverty levels were higher for long-duration pullers (27 per cent and 5 per cent respectively) than for recent joiners (of whom 10 per cent lived in poverty and none in extreme poverty). One of the problems workers face is increasing physical incapacity and exhaustion, and the heavy physical work is associated with declining returns; for example, while 82 per cent of recent pullers' households eat three meals a day, the figure is only 66 per cent for long-duration pullers. Health is the most common form of crisis: of the 75 per cent of rickshaw pullers who had experienced at least one crisis in the previous five years, 67 per cent had experienced a health-related crisis. In terms of intergenerational social mobility, the educational profile of rickshaw pullers' children was no better than that of their father. Most adult children worked, but were in occupations that 'provide neither sufficient income nor livelihood security' (page 15). Hence, there were few opportunities for social mobility or an upward career trajectory.

One of the most public and well-researched areas of low-income employment is street traders. While many such activities are informal, some are partially or wholly integrated into the formal sector. For example, individuals selling goods in front of a shop may be employees of the shop, and others work from formalized markets as registered businesses. The problems faced by street traders are widely recognized in the literature, in part perhaps because of the public visibility of at least some of their struggles and the significant numbers involved in the trade. Street traders (at least those who work in central areas) have to manage multiple and difficult relations as they negotiate for public space against competing demands. Brown (2006a) discusses different ways in which cities conceptualize and manage such space, and the challenges that arise for street traders. The significance of semi-formal trading activities is indicated by data from a census in the Central Business District of Nairobi which identified 3,488 traders, of whom only 6 per cent were on designated sites; three quarters (75.4 per cent) traded from pavements and 11 per cent were in bus stations (Mitullah 2010). Box 4.2 summarizes the findings of a study looking at the diversity of trading practices across Asia. It highlights the increasing numbers of traders following the financial crisis and the ambivalence of some governments towards the sector.

Box 4.2 Street traders in Asia

Bhowmik (2005) provides an overview of street trading in Asia, highlighting its scale and the increase in traders following the financial crash of 1998. She reports that:

- There are 90,000 street vendors in Dhaka even through the trade is considered illegal. A study of food vendors highlights the integration of gendered tasks: while men sell food, women prepare the food.
- In Sri Lanka, street trading may be legal, with a daily licence system for those willing to pay the daily tax. There were an estimated 8,000 to 10,000 street traders in Colombo in 2002. Food vending is more profitable than other forms, with an estimated daily average profit of SLRs575 (around US$6) in 2002.
- In Bangkok, there are 301 official demarcated areas for street trading and another 407 unofficial areas. In 1999 there were approximately 19,000–20,000 street traders. In 2005 there were likely to be over 100,000. The author suggests that the numbers have grown due to the Asian financial crisis.
- In Singapore the government seeks to ensure that all street traders are registered and working from designated areas. In 1988 there were 23,331 street traders, of whom 18,878 were selling food. In 2005 the number of traders was nearly 50,000. It appears that the street trader population is becoming both younger and better educated.
- In Malaysia there has been a national plan for street traders since 1990. The government estimates that numbers increased by 30 per cent between 1999 and 2000. In 2000 it was estimated that there were nearly 35,000 registered and more than 12,000 unregistered traders. About 35 per cent were thought to be selling food.
- In Manila the trade is also regulated, street vending having been legalized in 2001. It is estimated that there are 50,000 traders in the city, only a minority of whom have licences. A major problem is that there are no specified areas for trading in the city.
- Street traders in Vietnam are recognized as making an economic contribution but the state policy has been to encourage the formal sector. Most traders are women.
- Street trading is important in Cambodia. One study suggests that 97 per cent of street traders in Phnom Penh are women. One of the major problems is that they are not recognized and there are no permanent locations, resulting in continual harassment.

> • In Seoul, street traders face a very difficult situation. The main federation of trades unions estimates that the informal sector employs 57 per cent of all workers; however the sector is not recognized by the government. Seoul was estimated to have 800,000 street traders following the financial crisis, although the author mentions that these figures seem high.
> • In India, numbers of street traders increased significantly, especially after 1999, and it is estimated that 2.5 per cent of the urban population is engaged in this occupation. A number of studies in the late 1990s and subsequently suggest that daily earnings are between ₹50 and ₹80, with women earning ₹40–60. Women vendors face particular difficulties.
>
> One of the underlying issues emerging from this analysis is the changing composition of the group of street traders, as state regulation and associated formalization increases and as alternative opportunities in the formal sector decrease. While entry perhaps remains relatively easy, it may be that survival is becoming increasingly difficult as competition increases.

A survey of street traders in Kathmandu (Shrestha 2006) shows the complexity of their livelihood strategies and the importance of residential location. The survey identified more than 50 trading locations with an estimated 6,700 traders. Two areas were chosen for in-depth research, Dharaharra/Sundharra in a central city location close to a major bus station, and Anamnagar, an area serving a more local market. In Dharaharra/Sundharra the interviewees reported annual incomes of US$230, a figure which is very close to the national average income of US$240. Respondents emphasized the importance of having homes close by as most walk to work carrying their goods. The accounts of individual traders highlighted that their earnings are a part of more broadly based household economies which include other informal and formal incomes. Earnings in Anamnager were slightly higher than Dharaharra/Sundharra, in part because it is also a wholesale market, and the interviewees often sold others' goods with their own agricultural production. Shrestha suggests that:

> street trading offers a safety net from poverty, both for the elderly who were not supported by their families and for the vulnerable such as the unsupported mothers who had absent or polygamous husbands. It is also a means of advancement for those with entrepreneurial spirit .... For the young and enterprising, earnings were better than a government job.
>
> (page 171)

This conclusion is important in highlighting that the informal sector is both a survival economy and offers the possibility of advancement and social mobility (Brown 2006b). Shrestha (2006) did not provide information on the security of incomes, focusing rather on the challenges that traders face, including their vulnerability to harassment from authorities. Many are not formally organized and even when they are this may provide limited protection.

A different picture, with fewer opportunities for advancement, emerges from Iyenda (2005) and a 2001 survey of 125 street vendors in central areas of Kinshasa, DR Congo. Just over half were women and 33 per cent of these were heads of household; in total, 43 per cent of all interviewees had never worked in the formal sector. Only 6 per cent of the group earned money through other activities and they were very dependent on their trading income. Thirty-nine per cent earned less than US$5 a day from their trading activities; while this was more than might be earned in the formal sector, where government workers were paid about US$25 a month and those in the private sector between US$50 and US$100 a month, living costs were estimated at US$385 a month for a family of six. The conclusion is that 'street enterprises are not a panacea capable of improving people's living standards ... [they are] short-term, volatile and insecure employment opportunities, often with mediocre profits or achievements' (page 65).

Nnkya (2006) describes the activities of traders in two streets in Dar es Salaam. He notes a gendered differentiation in activities. Particularly notable, with the second street being less advantageously placed for trade, is the considerable range of earnings and profits. In Zanaki Street, the male traders had negotiated an agreement with shop owners and registered with the city council, and had an effective local association. Their daily profits were between TSh1,000 and TSh20,000 (US$0.7 and US$14). In Msasani there were both male and female traders, with women particularly involved in cooking and selling food and men in services such as plumbing and bicycle repairs. Most traders were not registered and profits ranged between TSh200 and TSh10,000 (US$0.13 and US$6.5). This illustrates the diversity of informal traders working just a few kilometres apart.

Another trade in which low-income groups are concentrated and for which there is some documentation is waste pickers and recyclers – those whose livelihood comes from sorting through the wastes from households or businesses to pick out items that can be sold to be reused or recycled. It is common for large cities to have tens of thousands of people working in the waste economy (Hardoy, Mitlin and Satterthwaite 2001). In Brazil's large cities, more than half a million people survive by collecting and selling solid waste,[71] and the recycling market has a turnover of more than US$1 billion (Fergutz, Dias and Mitlin 2011). In India, there are an estimated 1.5 million waste pickers (Chaturvedi 2010). In Karachi, the recycling industry provides a livelihood for some 55,000 families, and it recovers and recycles or reclaims a large volume of resources, greatly reducing the amount of waste that has to be disposed of (Hasan 1999). In Cairo, the Zabaleen – traditional waste collectors – have created what Fahmi (2005) suggests is one of the most efficient resource recovery and waste recycling systems. This includes not only waste collection and sorting but also many small and medium-size informal businesses processing the wastes (see Iskandar 2013). In Bangalore in the mid-1990s the municipal authorities only had to dispose of

335 tonnes of solid waste a day because around 2,700 tonnes were being recovered daily by waste pickers, households and the municipal collectors (Furedy 1994; Huysman 1994).

Most waste pickers work in (official or unofficial) solid waste dumps and on the streets, with little or no organization and very low returns. They are frequently exploited by those who purchase products from them. Not only are earnings low but, working individually, waste pickers do not have access to protective equipment or training, nor do they observe basic principles of hygiene, occupational health or correct waste handling. It is also common for some of the toxic or otherwise hazardous wastes generated by industries and hospitals to end up in solid waste dumps, increasing health risks for waste pickers. Ki Kim (1995) describes the conditions faced by recyclers in South Korea, and their extreme poverty, health problems and low social status, which led to difficulties in their children being accepted in school. Workers face these very poor conditions and have very low incomes in large part because they get such a small proportion of the revenue generated by the recycling industry. They get low prices from the intermediaries (formal companies and large networks of agents) who buy the recyclable materials and from city officials who manage collection services. In Bahia, Brazil, for example, PET containers are sold by waste pickers for R$0.15 per kilogram and are passed on by the intermediaries for R$0.90 per kilogram (Fergutz, Dias and Mitlin 2011). Their activities are even considered illegal in some nations.

This literature adds to our understanding of livelihoods at the neighbourhood level. First, even if entry is possible, it is evident that the opportunity for advancement in some trades is very low. As Begum and Sen (2005) describe, and as verified by Banks (2010), it is very difficult to move from being a rickshaw puller to a rickshaw owner because of the vulnerabilities involved. Even if the capital for the purchase of a rickshaw can be accumulated, the risks of theft are very great. The fact that older rickshaw pullers generally have lower incomes implies that rickshaw pulling is a useful entry point for a migrant with few alternatives but that households need to find a better source of income. Street trading may offer a source of advancement but this depends on location (and whether traders are permitted there) and the proximity to markets. While some traders identify and realize a good income, in other locations they really struggle. Particularly in cities with very low levels of economic growth, there are likely to be few opportunities. The ease of entry makes trading attractive to those with very low incomes but also means that during periods of recession others may enter the market, driving down returns (see the discussion in the section on 'Economies'). And markets themselves may be stratified, offering preferential access to some and systemically excluding particular groups and individuals. As discussed in the next section, gender is frequently associated with such segmentation.

Second, neighbourhoods are not isolated but are linked to the wider city economy. This is illustrated by the example of waste management. As has long been argued, the informal economy should not be seen as separate from the formal economy. (Although, despite their efforts, many waste recyclers face extremely adverse trading terms.) In addition to the reality that most households buy goods and services from both formal and informal sources, and that many households have incomes drawn from both, informal activities may have a direct input into the production processes of formal goods and services. In terms of the location of trades, it is evident that the residents of informal settlements find their incomes both within and beyond their own neighbourhoods.

Gender and generation

Whatever the spatial location of the employment or the particular trade followed, there is a significant body of evidence about the nature and scale of discrimination faced by some groups which disadvantages their participation in labour markets.

Gender differentiation in employment

With regard to gender differentiations in the labour market, as discussed, women work disproportionately in the informal and self-employed sector rather than in formal employment, and within these categories they work in those trades that are less well remunerated. Chen (2010) notes that women who work in the informal economy work disproportionately in low-paid or unpaid jobs, for instance as unpaid family workers, home workers, industrial outworkers and informal wage workers, with men disproportionately in better-paid work, as employers and regular informal wage workers, for example. Maxwell *et al.* (2000) note the association of women with informal employment in 'petty trade or street food vending' in Accra (see Box 4.4 on page 184). In this study, almost 60 per cent of men's primary income-generating strategies involved wage labour, while just under 80 per cent of women's primary strategies involved self-employment. Within this self-employment category, two thirds of women's activities involved petty trading and the preparation and sale of street food; both activities with low returns. Moser and Holland (1997) find that women's earnings in the informal sector in Chawama, a low-income district in Lusaka, Zambia, were generally lower than men's. Many women were street traders with a relatively low average daily income of 291 kwacha, while two thirds of men worked as market traders with an average daily income of 1,345 kwacha. Similar differences in employment patterns were observed in a study in Mexico in the 1990s, where the men were typically skilled, experienced and earning double what women earned while spending 20 per cent fewer hours at work (Latapí and de la Rocha 1995).

In a study of households in Nairobi's informal settlements, 73 per cent of interviewees had incomes below the government's poverty line; 78 per cent of female-headed households were poor compared to 71 per cent of male-headed households. However, among households with below-poverty-line incomes, female-headed households reported lower unemployment rates than both male-headed households and all households with incomes below the poverty line (World Bank Kenya 2006). As the proportion of women among adults in the household increased, the likelihood of being poor increased: '[F]emale slum dwellers are more likely to be unemployed, have a lower level of education, and are less likely to have a wage-paying job' (World Bank Kenya 2006, page 21). However, women were more likely to have a household micro-enterprise. Only 11 per cent of women had a regular job compared to 34 per cent of men, but 22 per cent had their own business or were own-account workers compared to 17 per cent of men, and it is evident that they put in considerable effort.

Drawing on overview studies, Chen, Vanek and Heintz (2006, page 2133) suggest that in general it is more likely that women in the Global South are informally employed:

> Other than in northern Africa, where 43 per cent of women workers are in informal employment, 60 per cent or more of women workers in the developing world are in informal employment (outside agriculture). In sub-Saharan Africa, 84 per cent of women non-agricultural workers are informally employed as compared to 63 per cent of men; and in Latin America the figures are 58 per cent of women in comparison to 48 per cent of men. In Asia, the proportion is 65 per cent for both women and men.

In terms of the balance between self-employment and informal wage employment, Chen, Vanek and Heintz (2006) suggest that the former in general constitutes 60–70 per cent of informal work. However, they elaborate on some specific differences:

> In northern Africa and Asia and at least half of the countries of sub-Saharan Africa and Latin America, more women in informal employment (outside agriculture) are in self-employment than in wage employment. By contrast informal wage employment is more important for women in Kenya, South Africa and four countries in South America – Brazil, Chile, Colombia and Costa Rica. In these countries more than half of women in informal employment are wage workers. Moreover, in all but one of these countries – South Africa – women are more likely to be informal wage workers than are men.
>
> (Chen, Vanek and Heintz 2006, page 2133)

The authors suggest that one reason for these differences is the significance of domestic work.

Gender differentiation within the informal sector

As already touched on, there are considerable gendered differences within both formal and informal work. Moser (2009) elaborates on those within the informal sector in Indio Guayas in Guayaquil, itself an informal settlement. Here, domestic work is largely the preserve of women and includes working in middle-class homes and taking laundry into the home, which Moser describes as 'the most desperately exploitative work' (page 123). Local shops trading from a room within the house are mainly established and managed by women, while men with a little more capital tend to set up corner shops, which are then run by both men and women. Bars are generally seen as being part of the male domain, and women who worked in bars were viewed with some disapproval. Mobile sellers – of fish, kitchen goods – are generally men; Moser suggests that this is both because of the difficulties of combining spatial mobility with childcare and associations of street work with prostitution (hence a need for women to work in a house or other fixed workplace). However, the consequences are that women find it more difficult to obtain a favourable trading space with few competitors. The sale of cooked food is carried out by both men and women; Moser suggests this is the trade with the greatest direct competition between genders. Tailoring is also done by both men and women, but women tend to make clothes for other women with cloth that the customer brings themselves while men tend to do contract work for companies. Gendered divisions within the informal sector are also noted by Brown (2006b), who discusses this in the context of street traders, and in terms of both the goods that men and women sell, and where they sell them. As noted previously, research on traders in Zanaki Street, central Dar es Salaam, found no women traders were operating there despite it being a major trading centre with its own trading association (Nnkya 2006). Box 4.2 on pages 177–8 also discusses gender-differentiated opportunities within street trading in Asia.

With limited openings and often with childcare responsibilities that further constrain their options, women do what is possible. Schlyter (2006) discusses the livelihood and shelter strategies of one woman, Esther, living in a formal town called Chitungwiza, about 25 kilometres outside Harare, Zimbabwe, to illustrate the challenges faced by women seeking to secure their livelihood (Box 4.3). This life history illustrates the dynamics between employment and locality discussed in the section on neighbourhoods. It also illustrates the difficulties that individuals have to overcome to achieve a degree of income security.

Box 4.3 Livelihood and shelter strategies of one woman resident of Chitungwiza, near Harare, Zimbabwe

Source: Schlyter (2006)

Schlyter begins her account when Esther moves with three children to Harare (then called Salisbury) in 1976 and finds a shack in a squatter settlement called Derbyshire. Her first livelihood strategy, once based in Harare, was vegetable selling, but this was abandoned after her forced move to Chirambahuyo, a settlement within Chitungwiza, following eviction in 1977, as there was an insufficient market. In Chirambahuyo she developed a livelihood strategy based on a lodger, a second-hand sewing machine and urban agriculture.

In 1980, following a further eviction, Esther secured a plot within a rent-to-buy development established in Chitungwiza. As a council tenant she was allowed to sub-let but was expected to register the lodgers (who paid a fee to the council); in practice, many such lodgers were not reported.

In 1987, the sewing machine broke but business had been bad and Esther decided to find alternatives. Urban agriculture was also being restricted by the state and had become a high-risk enterprise, as crops were sometimes destroyed by officials. Esther ran a shebeen (selling beer) which was profitable but illegal, and she was arrested twice.

In 1990 she took up an alternative trade, establishing a welding workshop, which contravened zoning regulations but, as was the case elsewhere, this was ignored by the local government. When two welders employed by Esther disappeared with some of her money, she relied on lodgers to keep the family going, even though the presence of backyard rental dwellings was restricted by the council from the early 1990s onwards.

The rental income consolidated slowly over the period of Esther's occupancy of the plot. In 1982, there was one rental room housing a single family; five years later, there were three rooms with two families and an adult couple. In 1992, Esther's own family had grown and was occupying three rooms, with an additional four rooms rented out (to three families and a single adult). The rental income was insufficient, however, and in the early 1990s Esther returned to the shebeen for additional income.

In 2000, 20 years after she first moved in, Esther was living in two rooms with her granddaughter and daughter, who had learning difficulties, and renting ten rooms (to five families, three adult couples and two single persons). By now, the council had abandoned earlier attempts to control rental practices. This was the year in which Esther died.

Esther's story elaborates on the vulnerabilities that women face as they attempt to secure their incomes. Similar findings emerge from a very different kind of research study, a sample of 559 households drawn from 16 urban and peri-urban enumeration areas in Accra, Ghana, all of which included a child below three years of age living with family (i.e. the sample excluded street children and the street homeless). The study was constructed by IFPRI and the Noguchi Memorial Institute for Medical Research with the aim of understanding the problems of urban food and nutrition. Box 4.4 describes the situation of women in the informal sector in Accra and highlights the relationship between informal work, low pay and poor nutrition.

Box 4.4 Informal work, low pay and poor nutrition in Accra

Source: Maxwell *et al.* (2000)

An estimated 23.6 per cent of Accra's population is food insecure, consuming less than 80 per cent of their calorie requirements but spending more than 50 per cent of their budget on food. A further 39.2 per cent are vulnerable, spending more than 50 per cent of their budget on food but with an adequate diet.

Of the quintile with the lowest expenditures, 62.2 per cent are food insecure. Twenty-two per cent of children in food insecure households are stunted. There are few opportunities for self-provisioning and urban agriculture, hence Accra's residents are heavily reliant on urban markets for access to food and their ability to purchase what they need.

Among individuals over 10 years, 53 per cent work (i.e. are engaged in some labour-based income-generating activity). Men's and women's income-generation activities differ markedly. Of those working, 46.7 per cent of women are in petty trading compared to 5.6 per cent of men, 20.2 per cent of women are in street food preparation and vending compared to 0.4 per cent of men, and 8.7 per cent of women are in skilled work compared to 35.8 per cent of men. Men are also more likely to be employed as casual labour (17 per cent of men compared to 6.2 per cent of women) and clerical professionals (16.4 per cent of men compared to 6.5 per cent of women). Overall the researchers estimate that 45.2 per cent of women work in marginal self-employed trades compared to 5.2 per cent of men.

Incomes for women are generally lower than those of men. Hence while female-headed households account for 35 per cent of the total sample, they account for over 40 per cent of households in the lowest income quintile and only 23 per cent of the households in the highest income quintile. More generally, those households in the lowest quintile for income are more dependent on self-employed marginal activities than other households. Unprotected waged work is more important for the two lowest income quintiles.

In terms of calorie availability alone, roughly 40 per cent of households in the sample can be categorized as food insecure. By occupational category, unskilled labourers and street food vendors have the highest proportions in the food insecure group. There is a strong relationship between expenditures and calorie adequacy. In the quintile with the lowest expenditures, 80 per cent of the households fall below 80 per cent of the calorie requirement. However, female-headed households spend more on food and buy cheaper calories, hence they are less food deficient.

Food is by far the largest item in household budgets, accounting for 54.5 per cent of all expenditures. Spending on infrastructure (fuel, health, transport) accounts for about 20 per cent of total expenditure. Housing costs are low, perhaps because many live in extended family compounds. Urban food consumption in Accra is heavily dependent on purchased food commodities, with 90 per cent of food expenditure going on purchased food, including a substantial amount for street foods. Little food is given or produced within the households. For the lowest-income households, 39 per cent of food expenditures go on purchasing snacks and meals away from home. One reason for this is that it is possible to buy a small amount and it reduces the time spent on food preparation at home.

Earning differentials in the informal and formal sectors

As described, the consequence of women working in the less favourable parts of the informal sector is lower incomes. Meagher (2010) argues that their relative disadvantage is more notable in the informal sector and she draws on an ILO study that shows Latin American women earn 64 per cent of men's wages in the formal economy but 52 per cent in the informal economy. Moser (1997) provides a further example when she notes that in Cisne Dos in Guayaquil, Ecuador women working in the informal sector earn less than women in the formal sector, the reverse of the trend for men. Meagher (2010) also argues that, while some proponents of deregulation suggest that fewer restrictions on informal enterprises will enable women's economic opportunities to flourish, evidence suggests that women are concentrated – both because of their childcare responsibilities and for reasons of discrimination – in those sectors that have the lowest returns and the least potential for growth.

Support for the significance of the type of work that women can secure in determining incomes is offered by research on 814 households in Surat, India (Kantor, Rani and Unni 2006). Surat is a city with growing prosperity and decadal economic growth of 93 per cent in the period 1981–91 and 60 per cent in 1991–2001. Four types of employment are considered: salaried work (which might be informal), casual work, self-employment and home-based piece-rate work. Salaried work accounted for 26.5 per cent of female employment (65 per cent of which was domestic service) and 18.2 per cent of male employment. Percentage shares for the other employment types were: for casual work, 21.1 per cent of women and 47.4 per cent of men; for self-employment, 21.9 per cent of women and 25.3 per cent of men; and for home-based piece-rate work, 30.5 per cent of women and 9.1 per cent of men. Median daily earnings were ₹120 for men and ₹36.5 for women. Casual work offered the best remuneration for women with a median daily earning of ₹51. Salaried work had the highest median average for men, with daily earnings of ₹144. In Nairobi women are also unlikely to work in the sectors with the highest remuneration (see Table 4.6 on page 194).

Liu (2010) draws on the Vietnam Living Standards Surveys and the Vietnam Households Living Standards Survey to analyse the ratio of male to female wages in Vietnam during a period of economic liberalization; the results span the formal and informal sectors. Between 1992 and 2002, the female to male wage ratio increased from 0.78 in 1993 to 0.80 in 1998 and 0.86 in 2002 (i.e. women increased their earnings relative to men). The following factors are identified as influencing this outcome: women are better educated than men (a factor influencing the ratio positively), market reforms are likely to increase competition and hence encourage employers to choose the most productive workers (positive), women are under-represented in the fastest growing sectors of the economy (negative), men are generally better paid except in the transport sector (negative), and market liberalization enables employers to return to traditional Confucian values which may discriminate against women (negative).

Whether in formal or informal work, low wages have been and continue to be a significant problem for women. In a study of 399 female migrants in Dhaka, 40 per cent were working as domestic servants and 38 per cent were working in the informal sector (Huq-Hussain 1995). About 40 per cent (42 per cent of recent migrants and 36 per cent of long-term migrants) did not receive any cash income and were paid with food or other goods; a further 21 per cent of recent migrants received less than 200 taka a month and 25 per cent of long-term migrants received less than 200 taka each month. In 2011, the gazetted minimum salary for a domestic worker in Zimbabwe was US$60 a month, in a context in which low-income communities estimate that US$150 is needed each month to purchase food for a household of two adults and four children (Chitekwe-Biti 2011, personal communication). These salaries, as with those in Dhaka, are based on the assumption that domestic servants have their day-to-day needs met by their employers (i.e. they are provided with food and accommodation).

Heintz (2010) argues that previous research has shown few systematic differences between the risk of poverty for men and women in specific employment categories. (It should be recognized that in many of the examples provided, women's lower incomes reflect their disproportionate representation in trades that are less well remunerated.) However, he cautions against putting too much focus on this conclusion. Of particular significance is that poverty is generally measured at the household level and households in which women are working in addition to men may have lower poverty levels than those in which only the male adult is working. He emphasizes that any analysis of gender and employment has to consider the composition of households, and the distribution of resources within them. Women-headed households may not be at greater risk of poverty because women are likely to have greater agency than in households headed by men, and hence may have more control over their incomes and strategies to improve their welfare. It is also important to recognize that there may be significant differences between countries due to a diversity of historical practices and social relations. Cultural differences in attitudes to women and their work are suggested in Herrera and Roubaud's (2005) study of urban poverty in Madagascar and Peru; their analysis suggests that women-headed households are not necessarily more likely to enter poverty. However, in some contexts women face an adverse situation: in Madagascar, 'households headed by women run a greater risk of finding themselves in chronic poverty ... whereas, in Peru, the gender of the household head is irrelevant' (page 42).

Barrientos (2010) argues that attention should also be paid to the vulnerabilities women face in employment in addition to adverse pay differentials. She discusses the UK Ethical Trading Initiative, which covers a number of trades and which attempts to establish codes of labour practice including improvements in working conditions. An evaluation in 2003 of the impact in six countries suggested that working conditions had improved, particularly in respect of health and safety, with 80 per cent of the 25 sites investigated showing improvements. But codes did not address other factors. There were no sites at which workers felt more able to join a trade union as a result of the code (in some cases trades unions existed already), and there was no evidence that discrimination against women in hiring, training and promotion had been reduced. Regular and permanent workers were the most likely to have benefited and casual and migrant workers were least likely to have had their working conditions improved. Kantor, Rani and Unni (2006) also consider these issues in their study of livelihoods in Surat, India. In terms of employment security, the study finds that 77.9 per cent of men and 72.2 per cent of women believe that they are likely to lose their current job; those doing causal work believe themselves to be the most vulnerable, although 75.9 per cent of women in salaried employment also expect to lose their jobs. Among those with salaries or casual work, 32.6 per cent of men and 37.5 per cent of women are not entitled to notice.

Gilbert (1997) remarks on the 'feminization' of the labour force in Colombia, as the informal sector is growing relative to the formal sector and the former has a higher percentage of women employees. There is broad agreement that, in some countries, women's labour has become more significant in the market in recent decades. However, as Heintz (2010) discusses, the usefulness of the term 'feminization' is disputed, as the implied link between increasing informalization and greater participation by women may not be found. Rather, both informalization and increasing participation by women may reflect a number of other trends, such as the greater use of sub-contracting by formal sector enterprises. There is some evidence of women's increased participation in all labour markets, however, and the next subsection considers why women work.

Women's work and its significance

The livelihood choices of women reflect opportunities and constraints. In some contexts, women's work has limited social acceptability. Both Kantor (2009), for the context of India, and Banks (2010), for the context of Bangladesh, describe the social restrictions that women face, both in terms of whether they work at all and whether their work is spatially constrained. What is evident from Kantor's (2009) study of Lucknow is that, regardless of the formal restrictions on women's work, reproductive responsibilities significantly restrict livelihood options. She finds that being married and the number of children under five reduces the likelihood of work, while being a lower-caste Hindu or Shia Muslim, being in a female-headed household, being older, and being in a lower-income household all increase the likelihood of women having employment. The study by Banks (2010) of four low-income areas in Dhaka suggests that a critical determining factor affecting household progression is the willingness of households to have women enter the labour market. In general, households view women's work favourably as long as it is in the home (the highest proportion of women's employment is in home-based embroidery) or considered to be 'prestigious' (teacher or shop assistant, for example). This study also showed that the highest income groups had the lowest proportion of households with women working.

In Kundu's (2011) summary of national survey results for India, he shows that women's participation in the labour market has not changed substantially in recent decades. Women's highest level of participation in the labour market was recorded in the recent 2004–05 survey, with figures of 30 per cent participation among illiterate women, 29 per cent among graduates and 49 per cent among those with diplomas. Those with intermediate educational qualifications were less likely to participate.

Moser (2009), in her study of residents in the informal settlement of Indio Guayas in Guayaquil, argues that women in relationships only tended to enter the labour market when their partners or husbands were finding it difficult to secure paid work, or when their relationships were breaking down.

Ferreira and Paes de Barros (1999) highlight the significance of shifts in labour market participation for understanding poverty in Brazil. Between 1976 and 1996, the self-employed formed a broadly consistent proportion of the labour market, at 27 per cent, but formal-sector employment fell from 57.8 to 31.5 per cent, and more people were informally employed. Per capita household income rose very slightly (less than 5 per cent) in real terms; inequality and the incidence of poverty were broadly unchanged, while the proportion of the population in extreme poverty increased from 7 to 9 per cent. Average years of schooling in urban areas increased from 3.2 in 1976 to 5.3 in 1996; moreover, while in 1976 girls were in school for an average of 2 months less than boys, by 1996 that had been reversed, with girls at school for a slightly longer period than boys. Labour-force participation for men was between 71 and 76 per cent throughout the period, while labour-force participation for women increased steadily, rising from 29 per cent in 1976 to 42 per cent in 1996. Ferreira and Paes de Barros (1999) suggest that female earnings remained lower than male earnings throughout the period but that the disadvantage is declining. Other influences that increase poverty were reducing remuneration for those in wage labour, and education and experience became less well rewarded during the period. More generally, larger families led to reduced participation in employment, and as education levels increased family size declined. Hence, despite wages falling, poverty levels were broadly consistent for those families above the fifteenth percentile, as more women entered the labour market, education levels improved (enabling better jobs to be secured) and family size decreased. Those below the twelfth percentile were not able to keep up, hence the increase in levels of extreme poverty. As in Banks's (2010) study, women's labour market participation is significant in improving household incomes.

This section has highlighted the many studies showing the increase in women's participation in urban labour markets; also that they earn less than men and usually have poorer access to formal sector or better remunerated jobs, or to better income-earning opportunities. It has pointed to some of the reasons for this, for instance social restrictions on where women work and what they can do, discrimination in hiring, training and promotion, and constraints on working due to women's reproductive role, childcare and household management. There are also other issues to be considered, for instance whether girls have the same opportunities as boys in education – for example whether they have the same options for staying in school – and whether women face more difficulties in obtaining capital to start or support businesses, or to buy housing or building land (Chant 2013). Women generally have a disproportionate share in unpaid work burdens, such as cooking, cleaning, laundry, shopping and fetching water and fuel, and the time and effort needed to fulfil these are often much increased by inadequacies in provision of water, sanitation and solid waste collection and by the lack of effective, easily accessed health care (it usually falls to women to cope with sickness or injury within households). Chant (2013) notes that the increase in the proportion of women in paid work has not led to increased engagement of men in domestic responsibilities and unpaid work.

Generation

Any consideration of livelihoods among low-income populations needs to consider the roles of children and youth and the opportunities and constraints they face. Using available statistics, it is difficult to identify the role of children and youth in income-earning activities and unpaid domestic work and the extent to which this constrains or prevents school attendance. There is also the distinction between children and youths living with family – so generally with adults earning incomes – and those who have left the family home, including those that have started their own families. This latter group includes children who have left their family home and live and work on the streets.

Many children in very low-income urban households work, usually within the informal economy for very low returns and often in occupations that expose them to many health risks (Bartlett *et al.* 1999). Access to formal sector employment may be restricted due to regulations that seek to prevent child labour. Most have no choice about whether or not they work, or about where and when they withdraw from school (Bartlett *et al.* 1999). Beall (2002, page 77) notes:

> In urban households, strategies to achieve long-term security involve investment in human capital and commonly this is directed at the education of children. When this is not possible for all the children in the household, a common pattern in poorer families is for older children to leave school early and engage in paid work.

However, many children combine a contribution to household income with school attendance (Bartlett *et al.* 1999).

Amis (2006) reports on data from 1996 on two informal settlements in Nairobi, in which only 50 per cent of children attend school either due to a lack of places or because they need to work. In Kibera, one of the largest informal settlements in Nairobi, a study of youth between the ages of 10 and 19 found that a quarter of boys and 14 per cent of girls were working for pay (Urulkar and Matheka 2007, cited in Sommers 2010). Generalizations need to be approached carefully, and there are examples of low-income settlements where few children work. Moser and McIlwaine (1997) note that in Commonwealth in Metro Manila, in the Philippines, only 2.5 per cent of children between the ages of 7 and 15 were working, despite low household incomes. But comparisons are hindered by the lack of agreement on the age ranges that the terms 'children' and 'youth' apply to. Perhaps if the data on Commonwealth included 16 to 19 year olds, it would show a significantly higher proportion working.

Studies of particular settlements or trades give some insight into children's incomes and livelihoods, the remuneration they receive, and the working conditions they are exposed to. Hunt (1996) reports on a study of children aged 5 to 15 living in informal settlements in Bangalore. One third of the children are waste pickers, 12 per cent are domestic workers, 21 per cent go to formal school and the remainder neither do paid work nor go to school. For those children who are waste pickers, their average earnings are ₹10 (US$ 0.21) a day and they work five days a week, seven hours a day. Begum and Sen (2005), in their discussion of rickshaw pullers and their families in Dhaka, report that the school attendance rate of the children between the ages of 5 and 15 is 58 per cent for those living with their parents in Dhaka and 73 per cent for those living with other family members in rural areas. With regard to work, 9 per cent of the 10–14-year-olds and 40 per cent of the 15–19-year-olds in the sample are regularly employed, with the figures for irregular employment being 2 and 11 per cent respectively.

There are a few other studies that give insights into the (very limited) income-earning opportunities open to children, whether they are members of households or have tenuous or no links with parents or relatives. The paper by Sheela Patel (1990) on street children, hotel boys and children of pavement dwellers and construction workers, published more than 20 years ago, reveals categories of children's employment that often go unnoticed, for instance the scale of employment of children in cheap eating places, and the children of construction workers who often live on the construction sites and also work there to supplement family incomes.

Conticini (2005) describes a problem faced by children, particularly girls, living on the streets in Dhaka, in the form of high levels of bribes paid to public officials and community leaders. Reporting on research with just fewer than 100 children (both girls and boys), the author notes that daily incomes range between 40 and 70 taka. However, the children have to pay bribes (taxes) to be allowed to carry on their work. Conticini explains that 'the taxes paid by girls reached 50–60 per cent of their income. The boys' taxes were between 30–50 per cent varying according to the nature of the work' (page 75).

Youths generally face higher levels of unemployment, fewer job opportunities and lower incomes than adults. The worldwide youth unemployment rate (among those actively seeking work) for 2006 was estimated by the ILO to be three times that of adults (ILO 2006). Youths are likely to be engaged in a very large range of informal, irregular and often illegal activities, many of which yield very little money (Sommers 2010). Interviews with youth in Mali, Nigeria, Tanzania and Vietnam had to include questions about first, second and third occupations and the ways in which time was allocated to each to make sense of youth livelihoods (Tacoli and Mabala 2010). Some detailed local studies give insights into the perspectives of youth with regard to employment. For instance, interviews with youths engaged in waste management in Nairobi suggested that they saw their work as being better than wage labour, which involved being 'someone else's donkey' (Thieme 2010).

But, again, it is difficult to identify the level of age-related discrimination faced by youths, in part because circumstances differ depending on whether or not they still live 'at home', in part because of the ambiguity in what is considered 'youth', which can indicate an age of as low as 10 years and up to 35 years.

The scale and nature of children's income-earning activities may also change to reflect changing economic circumstances. Latapí and de la Rocha (1995) argue that, during the economic crisis in Mexico in the 1980s, families responded by increasing women's participation in the labour market and that of young males (aged 14 and younger); in the city of Guadalajara, for example, young males increased their participation in the labour market by 25.9 per cent.

Childhood is typically seen as a time to gain an education to prepare for adulthood and employment, and higher levels of educational attainment are frequently associated with higher and more stable incomes. For instance, the World Bank notes that in Bolivia individuals with more education have less likelihood of being poor (World Bank Bolivia 2002). In the main cities, 'individuals ten years or older with no education at all had a probability of being poor of 60.9 per cent, as compared to 19.5 per cent for individuals with more than 12 years of schooling' (page iv). Haddad and Ahmed (2002) suggest that in Egypt the better educated are less likely to be poor. However, they also point to gender discrimination, as 'for women the returns to more education in urban areas are especially poor as public sector jobs have dried up' (page 19). In Accra education is also significantly and positively associated with higher per capita income levels (Maxwell *et al.* 2000). Maternal schooling brings more comprehensive benefits: higher levels of household food availability, higher quality diets, better care practices and behaviours, and better nutritional outcomes (Maxwell *et al.* 2000). But there are also studies showing that in particular places social contacts or relations have more importance than levels of education in getting jobs (for example Banks 2010, as described previously). Some of the research cited elsewhere in this chapter is relevant here: even with education, the remuneration received by *favela* residents in Rio de Janeiro is considerably less than that received by others who are similarly educated (Perlman 2010); and education may not help to secure employment, as was found to be the case in the Cape Flats area of Cape Town, although for those in work wages increased with educational attainment (De Swardt *et al.* 2005).

Gender can be as important a distinction as age. The experience of young men and young women can be very different. 'As Mabala points out, many young women, formally in the category of youth, tend to lose access to the programmes and opportunities made available to "youth" once they have children – a status that applies to probably more than half the women under the age of 24' (Bartlett 2010, page 308). Women's patterns of migration are different, and the economic opportunities available to them tend to be far more limited – and often more dangerous, as they are more likely to end up in hidden occupations such as domestic labour. Because of their narrower range of choices and lesser negotiating power, they are more likely to have to rely on sexual exchange as a means of survival, as reflected in their considerably higher rates of HIV (van Donk 2006).

Economies

This section explores what we know and understand about the nature of aggregated urban livelihoods as they make up the economics of informal settlements and cities. The previous sections in this chapter have looked at the specificities of urban work, both employment and its associated remuneration and working conditions, and enterprise activities. Here we consider what we know about the balance of livelihood and economic activities for particular urban centres or settlements within centres. Clearly it is not possible to disassociate the economies of urban centres from the wider economy. Such settlement economies are neither static nor autonomous from national and global economic trends. Montgomery *et al.* (2003, page 337) provide a summary of developments in urban economies in the Global South:

> In the 1980s and 1990s, macroeconomic crises and restructuring had the effect of curtailing wage-earning employment in many public and private enterprises. International assistance was often extended on terms that required reductions in government expenditures, a commitment to privatization and the imposition of cost containment measures in state-owned enterprises. Where such programs were implemented, parastatal enterprise and many private firms cut employment; in many cases recruitment to the civil service all but ceased. Some formerly protected subsidized traditional industries shrank as governments cut tariff protections and exposed their economies to the world markets .... [T]hose who lost wage employment in the formal sector often had little recourse but to take up informal employment. At the same time, however, informal sector entrepreneurs moved aggressively into fields that had been largely abandoned by the public sector such as transportation.

The authors also note the rise in sub-contracting and outsourcing among large firms, with many contracts being awarded to enterprises in the informal sector. The growth in the informal sector has already been discussed in this chapter. The broader themes highlighted by Montgomery *et al.* (2003) are echoed below, as commentators discuss the dynamics of urban economies in recent years.

In terms of understanding the totality of city economies, the economic significance of informal employment and the informal sector more generally emerges as a consistent theme, particularly for sub-Saharan Africa and some Asian nations. The section in this chapter on the informal economy highlights the scale of informal employment within nations in terms of the proportion of non-agricultural employment in informal sector enterprises or informal employment outside this sector. It also presents figures for particular cities, showing the many cities with a high proportion of informal employment. In this section, we explore the scale and distribution of formal and informal economic activities.

Understanding city economies from the bottom up

Research studies on two Kenyan cities point to some of the complexities. An enumeration of informal settlements in Kisumu in 2005–06 which included a survey of businesses shows the range and number of enterprises located there (Karanja 2010). Kisumu is Kenya's third largest city, with 355,024 inhabitants in the 1999 census. The informal settlements included 72,443 residents. In these areas, 3,059 enterprises were identified, of which more than half were retail and 19 per cent were services. The survey also illustrates the difficulties of differentiating formal and informal activities. Twenty per cent of the businesses were 'shops' (i.e. semi-permanent structures often having some kind of permit), 22 per cent were stalls (removable wooden structures generally without licences), 45 per cent were kiosks (mud or wattle, or iron sheet structures also without licences), 8 per cent were mobile and 5 per cent did not specify premises. Also notable is that only 12 per cent of the economically active population worked within the settlement, with the rest finding employment in the formal areas of the city, meaning that there was a strong dependency on employment and income earning outside of the immediate neighbourhood.

A study of informal settlements in Nairobi using a structured sample of 1,755 households (World Bank Kenya 2006) provides considerable insight into the livelihood strategies of low-income residents in 2004. Ninety-seven per cent of households had at least one income-generating activity. Income-generating activities were diverse, but as many as 30 per cent of households had an enterprise, and these households were less likely to be classified as poor.[72] Table 4.6 shows that the non-poor and men were more likely to have regular employment than women and the poor. Women's relative lack of participation in the labour market is particularly notable, as is the association between regular employment and being in a non-poor household. A comparison with aggregate figures for Nairobi's residents from the 1999 census shows that the proportion of individuals unemployed and seeking work is 9 percentage points higher in the 'slums' compared to Nairobi as a whole. Thirty-five per cent of Nairobi residents reported themselves to be 'not active' in the labour market because they are students,

Table 4.6 Employment in Nairobi's informal settlements (3,455 respondents; note that not all columns total 100 due to rounding of data)

Employment status	All (%)	Poor (%)	Non-poor (%)	Men (%)	Women (%)
Unemployed	26	29	15	10	49
Regular employee	24	21	35	34	11
Casual employee	25	25	24	34	12
Own account/self-employed	19	19	21	17	22
Student/apprentice	4	5	3	4	5
Other (e.g. pensioner)	1	1	1	1	1

Source: World Bank Kenya (2006), page 28

incapacitated, retired, or for some other reason; this falls to 24 per cent in the 2004 study of informal settlements (World Bank Kenya 2006).

Elaborating on the diversity of household activities, the survey found that, of 1,755 households, 544 had been involved in at least one income-generating enterprise in the previous two weeks and 75 reported two or more enterprises (World Bank Kenya 2006). The average household-level enterprise had been in business for 4.1 years and employed 1.6 people (including the owner). Just over half sold outside of their settlement, drawing in income from other parts of the city to their household economies. In terms of production and service process, households with enterprises were slightly more likely than average to have electricity (26 per cent compared to 22 per cent). Two categories of enterprise, manufacturing construction and repair, and bars and entertainment, had considerably better access to electricity, at 32 per cent and 54 per cent respectively. Such findings point to the importance of government in improving access to basic infrastructure and services.

A study of Sapu, an informal settlement in the municipality of Kilamba Kiaxi in Luanda, Angola, offers a further example of the significance of state investment. Prior to the construction of a bridge linking the settlement with a national main road, there were 10 enterprises along the road. Two years after the investment in the bridge, there were 44 new income-generating activities and the 10 existing businesses had expanded (Baskin and Miji 2006).

In terms of the nature of business activities in Nairobi's informal settlements, Table 4.7 illustrates the diversity of trading and services, showing that just under two thirds of enterprises are retail trading and about 20 per cent are related to manufacturing, construction and repairs.

Table 4.7 Household enterprises in Nairobi's informal settlements – primary activities

Type of enterprise	Percentage
Retail – general and food (including small trade, hawking, kiosks)	*64.0*
Selling fruits and vegetables	17.6
Food preparation, sale and processing	14.2
Selling clothes and shoes	11.8
Kiosk selling various items	7.5
Water kiosk	0.6
Small retailers/hawkers – cereals, household supplies, household fuels and miscellaneous	12.3
Small manufacturing/production, construction and repair of goods	*22.2*
Sewing and textiles	10.1
Shoe making/repair	3.3
Furniture making	2.6
TV/video/electronics/cell phone sales and repair	1.8
Metal welding/fabrication	0.7
Building contractor/plumber/electrician/painter	1.3
Automotive repair	2.4

Type of enterprise	Percentage
Services – hairdressing, laundry, transport, medical, photography, etc.	*8.1*
Hairdressing	4.0
Dry cleaning, washing, ironing, carpet cleaning	0.7
Medical clinic	0.2
Transportation – boda-boda (motorcycle taxis), cargo carts, etc.	1.7
Photography	0.6
Medicine – traditional	0.9
Services – bars, entertainment, and brewing	*2.4*
Brewing	1.7
Bar/entertainment (pool tables)	0.7
Farming and livestock	*0.9*
Other	*2.4*
Total main household micro-enterprises	100.0

Source: World Bank Kenya (2006), pages 32–3

The World Bank undertook similar analyses of informal settlements in Dakar and Johannesburg (Gulyani, Talukdar and Jack 2010). The results are indicative of the different levels of formalization within the cities' economies, with distinct differentials in levels of unemployment, formal employment and enterprise activities. More specifically, the authors highlight different patterns of work based in part on the wider economy:

> Unemployment is widespread among Johannesburg's slum residents, where every other adult is unemployed. That compares to an unemployment level of 26 percent in Nairobi and only 6 percent in Dakar. Within households the story is much the same: a typical household in Johannesburg slums will have one-third of adult members unemployed, compared to one-fifth in Nairobi and only one-twentieth in Dakar.
>
> (page 7)

Patterns of employment reflect the relative predominance of the formal economy in South Africa:

> Johannesburg also has the highest proportion of regularly employed adults (28 percent) compared with 25 percent in Nairobi and only 8 percent in Dakar. Self-employment or work in household-owned microenterprises is uncommon in Johannesburg but prevalent in Nairobi and Dakar, where about one in five report that they work in their own household microenterprise. Nairobi's slum residents report the highest level (24 percent) of casual employment, followed by Johannesburg (10 percent) and Dakar (8 percent)
>
> (page 7)

Overall, comparing the three cities, residents in Johannesburg's low-income settlements are the most likely to be either unemployed or regularly employed and the least likely to be working in a household microenterprise. Table 4.5 on page 167 shows the importance of working in family enterprises (even if non-paid) and being in education (as a student or apprentice) for informal settlement dwellers in Dakar. This data points again to the importance of social relationships in creating opportunities for work.

In terms of the specificity of trades within the informal sector in other cities, in Mombasa, Kenya a 1999 survey suggests the following trade division within the informal sector: 62 per cent were involved in retailing, 20 per cent in services, 9 per cent in transport and 5 per cent in water vending (Rakodi 2006). Bromley (1997, cited in Pratt 2006) studied street-based economic activities in Cali, Colombia and reports that the most common such activity was retailing, at 33 per cent, followed by small-scale transport (16 per cent) and gambling (16 per cent). Personal services (such as shoe shining), security services, recycling and waste management, prostitution, begging and property crimes each represented less than 10 per cent of activities.

The city of Mombasa, Kenya's second largest city, exemplifies the difficulties that urban centres may face in developing their economies and providing livelihoods for their citizens. Located on the coast with the best natural deep-water harbour in East Africa, the city has particular advantages of location (Rakodi 2006). However, it has faced economic decline since the 1980s due both to global trends and regional dynamics. From 1979 to 1999 the percentage of the labour force in formal wage employment fell from 53 per cent to 43 per cent. Trade through the port fell during the 1980s both because of a lack of demand from the hinterland and the level of investment (or lack of it) in port facilities. During the 1990s trade began to grow once again. Tourism has been of increasing importance but it remains vulnerable to violence and insecurity both within Kenya and in the wider region. Moreover, much of the investment in tourism is foreign, hence relatively little of the earnings are spent locally. While some industrial growth has taken place, Rakodi (2006) suggests that this was undermined by structural adjustment policies followed by the national government during the 1990s. Municipal capability has been weakened by central government control over revenues, self-interested politicians, a lack of qualified senior staff, and insufficient financial resources. These factors all contribute to a lack of effective economic planning.

Hasan (2002) describes the scale of informal sector activities in the case of Karachi, emphasizing that most of the population lives in informal settlements and receives informal services. For example, some 72 per cent of the population were estimated to travel in informal minibuses. Hasan discusses the broader economic impacts that Pakistan's structural adjustment programme has had, and its ramifications for livelihood strategies during recent decades. In summary, duties on imports have been reduced, the costs of public services have increased and devaluation to ensure that exports are cheaper has increased the cost of living and resulted in inflation. As a consequence, Hasan argues, the light manufacturing business in Karachi has failed to compete with other Asian locations. Rising electricity prices are further reducing outputs, and increasing living costs have resulted in many people searching for additional part-time work. The author suggests that the links between the formal and informal sector will decrease, except in those areas with export potential, and the informal sector will increasingly serve lower-income households.

Hasan's (2002) analysis draws attention to the links between informal and formal enterprises. The example from Nairobi shows the importance of electrical supply for enterprises within informal settlements. But the informal sector is not just a consumer of public services, it is also a provider, including in the area of waste management. The waste economy is present in all urban centres and is an example of such a trade. The scale and range of informal employment within waste collection, recycling and waste management were discussed in a previous section. The solid waste sector illustrates the choices that cities face in managing their economy, including the choices that governments make in favouring certain modalities of public service provision with implications for both those receiving the services and workers. This includes how the work of waste pickers and informal enterprises involved in using or processing wastes are viewed and what provisions (if any) are made to include or support this work within policies and measures related to collection, management and disposal of wastes (see, for instance, Fahmi 2005; Iskandar 2013; Menegat 2002). In most cities, there is little appreciation of the scale of the 'waste economy' in terms of the economic and environmental value of materials recovered and the costs saved to city and municipal governments. For the informal waste pickers, the returns they receive do not reflect the value of the services they provide, the wastes they recycle, the money they save for city governments (reducing waste volumes and extending the life of landfills), or their contribution to cleaner cities and to reducing greenhouse gas emissions.

In some cities, there has been a switch away from municipal services (which may tolerate informal livelihood activities) towards the formal commercial sector. Fahmi (2005) and Iskandar (2013) describe this in Cairo and highlight its impacts on livelihoods for the waste pickers and recycling firms. Similarly, in 2009, the Ahmedabad Municipal Commission gave a new municipal waste contract to a private recycling firm which now collects waste twice a day along routes previously used by informal recyclers (Horn 2011). However, this trend is not inevitable. The Brazilian government has recently begun to respond to waste pickers' needs by launching a financing line through the Brazilian Development Bank which aims to generate 39,000 jobs for waste pickers in 199 cities, primarily through supporting investment by waste picker co-operatives. These practices aim to contest the exploitative relations that exist where workers are embedded within vertical trading relations and returns are low.

Other cities have invested in alternative modalities for waste management that favour low-paid workers earning their living through recycling waste. In Brazil, 327 of the 5,560 municipalities have adopted selective waste collection systems to enable the recycling of waste materials, and 142 of these (approximately 2.5 per cent of all municipalities) maintain partnerships with waste picker associations and co-operatives (Fergutz, Dias and Mitlin 2011). In Londrina, a city in the south of Brazil, a partnership between city officials and waste pickers results in the daily collection of 100 tonnes of recyclable materials, 25 per cent of the city's total daily waste. One innovation is the door-to-door collection, which builds a bond between waste pickers and the community, emphasizing their skilled contribution. This increases the quality of the materials collected and reduces the collection of waste which cannot be recycled (Fergutz, Dias and Mitlin 2011). The programme started in 2001, in part to remove waste pickers from the city landfill. Twenty-nine sorting centres were set up to allow 500 waste pickers to work together to sort and sell their product. The creation of these centres has been instrumental to the success of the project, as it reduces the distance covered by waste pickers. The centres are used for the temporary storage of the collected materials, which are then taken by city trucks to another centre where they are pressed and sold. Eighty per cent of waste pickers taking part in this initiative are women. Since the quality of the materials is now higher, so are the prices obtained. This example shows that city governments can choose to invest in waste management systems that help to improve the livelihoods of low-income households.

Economic development, government policy and the consequences for the urban poor

The contribution of the state to economic development is a vast subject, spanning the developmental states of East Asia, controversies over Keynesian and neo-liberal economies and the economic consequences of structural adjustment programmes. Due to the scale of such debates, this section does not attempt to summarize these literatures; rather the discussion brings together four themes that are important in understanding the current interface of the economy with urban poverty. These themes are: the ways in which city governments seek to restructure urban space to attract inward investment; recent perspectives on the shift from formal to informal employment; the financial crises and their impact on urban populations; and what such trends might mean for the livelihood strategies and struggles of the urban poor.

Attracting inward investment

Livelihood opportunities in cities reflect the vision, will and capability of the state as well as the dynamics of capital investment. Urban policies and economic outcomes influence the kinds of employment and livelihood opportunities that emerge and expand, and those that close down. Government policy may be influenced by the perceived and actual nexus between a city's spatial appearance and private investment. Specifically, it appears to be common for governments to believe that they can influence inward investment by changing the visual appearance of their urban space. This has a further impact on economic opportunities and related inequalities when manifest in evictions of informal dwellers and the clearing of informal vendors from central city areas to create a 'modern' city. Chatterjee (2011) illustrates the relationship between economic investment and visual appearance in the context of India, emphasizing how urban beautification has been associated with a set of neo-liberal economic values, including competitive labour markets, and has resulted in the spatial exclusion of low-income groups. In this case, the policies of the city government in Ahmedabad were influenced by national legislation favouring more flexible land markets and offering greater support for entrepreneurship.

The material response to such ideas is illustrated by events in Mexico City and the decision to remove street traders from the city's central areas. Once more there is a link to a particular vision of the city, in this case a modernist exclusivity that defines and enforces legal and illegal activities (Crossa 2009). More generally, contested access to public space is part of the daily reality of street traders, who spend time and resources negotiating for space to carry out their work. City governments may adopt improvement programmes that favour powerful economic interests; Mexico City has the Programa de Rescate, which has sought to remove 9,000 street traders from the historic centre to 'revitalise and beautify' the city (Crossa 2009). The motivation to clear the traders in part reflects a wish to improve security and a belief that traders increase crime, but the programme is closely linked to large-scale corporate business interests. As Crossa (2009) explains, this is not a conflict between formal and informal traders as there is frequently a symbiotic rather than competitive relationship between the two. Formal traders may encourage informal vendors to occupy the space in front of their shops as they help to draw customers into the area.

The interrelationships between capital and state policies also emerge from studies that focus on general economic trends and consider their impact on urban centres. Fernandes (2004, page 2423) discusses the restructuring of urban space in Mumbai in the context of national government policies that favour economic liberalization:

> [R]ising real estate prices have ... accelerated the shift from older declining manufacturing industries such as the Bombay textile industry, one of India's oldest manufacturing industries, to new economy industries such as the services sector and media enterprises. The 1990s, the first decade of India's new economic policies, produced steep speculative rises in Mumbai's real estate .... [S]hifts from manufacturing to service industries have also served to skew the benefits of India's new economy towards the new middle classes and away from the working classes .... According to one estimate, employment in the textile industry has dropped from 250 000 in 1980 to 57 000 in 2000 .... One consequence is that unemployed mill workers are often forced to turn to alternative forms of employment such as hawking in order to support themselves.

As Fernandes illustrates for Mumbai, these processes involve complex interactions between state policies and citizen responses. In this case, as middle-class households gain a stronger identity and grow in number, the objectives for the management of urban space by the government change. Fernandes (2004, page 2424) describes the potential conflicts of interest that emerge:

A clear pattern that runs through the state strategies deployed in the management of urban space is one that restructures the space in ways that cater to the wealthier segments of Mumbai and to the lifestyles of the new Indian middle classes – for instance, by transforming spaces to cater to joggers …. In one such plan, for instance, the BMC developed a Rs6 000 000 beautification project that would transform one of Mumbai's most well-known public spaces, Shivaji Park, by constructing seven gates, 'VIP' parking, tiled jogging tracks and elaborate fountains and pavilions.

Fernandes (2004) suggests that economic restructuring has influenced the way in which the middle-class residents of Mumbai perceive their own interests, producing a different kind of politics as they seek to protect their interests as consumers (see also Chakrabarti 2008). Bhan (2009) elaborates on the ways in which those living in low-income neighbourhoods have been removed from the centre of Delhi to create a 'modern' city. Economic dynamics are partly determined globally but the specific outcomes for a city economy may also reflect local politics and, in the case of Mumbai, the strategies adopted by the elite to undermine workers' interests and union power (Harris 2008).

The shift away from formality

Irrespective of the economic activities favoured by restructuring in specific countries, there are some consistencies in the nature of the economic restructuring. It is almost universally agreed that the informal sector is increasingly significant as an employer of labour, and many examples of this have already been provided. Agarwala (2006) analyses the increasing trend towards informality in Indian labour markets and suggests that it has been adopted as a deliberate strategy to increase the profitability of the formal productive sector:

> [B]y the end of the 1990s, India's informal sector was estimated to account for over 60 percent of gross domestic product. In 2002, the Indian government recognized the informal sector as the primary source of future employment for all Indians.
>
> (page 421)

Agarwala (2006) estimates that about 54 per cent of non-agricultural informal sector workers are micro-entrepreneurs or otherwise self-employed, and the remaining 46 per cent are employed within the informal sector.

The shift in employment patterns towards informality is illustrated in Dar es Salaam, with Nnkya (2006) reporting that the percentage of the labour force employed by government and parastatals declined from 21.4 per cent to 6.9 per cent between 1991–92 and 2000–01. The category of 'self-employment with employees' also fell significantly from 17.3 to 5.9 per cent during this period. Other significant shifts were an increase in the share of the labour force being private employees, from 9.7 to 16 per cent, and a growth in 'self-employed without employees' (i.e. very small enterprises), from 1.1 to 17.4 per cent. In Zambia, employment in the formal sector declined from 25 per cent of total employment in 1970 to less than 10 per cent in 1990 (Chibuye 2011). The trend in Latin America is illustrated by Ferreira and de Barros (1999), who study the very significant increase in urban poverty in Brazil between 1976 and 1996 and who note that the proportion of workers with formal documentation halved from just under 60 per cent to just over 30 per cent.

Kundu (2011) illustrates both this trend and the dangers of a simplistic understanding in his recent analysis of urban trends in India. In this case, the percentage in casual employment (i.e. those employed without any regular job contract and social security benefits) in India rose from 13.2 per cent in 1977 to 18.5 per cent in 1997 before falling back in the years to 2004–05. The percentage in self-employment rose slightly and consistently during this period, from 40.4 per cent in 1977 to 44.8 per cent in 2004–05. The percentage of male employees in regular employment (both formal and informal) fell consistently from 1977–78 to 1998, when it reached 39.5 per cent of the urban labour force, at which point it broadly stabilized. Figures for female employment show very different trends. Casual labour was static at between 25 and 30 per cent of female employment between 1977–78 and 1998, but it then began to fall, and in 2004–05 it was 16.7 per cent. Numbers in regular employment increased consistently from 24.9 per cent in 1977–78 to 33.2 per cent in 1995–96. Since then, the figure has fluctuated, increasing slightly to 35.6 per cent in 2004–05. Self-employment began this period at 49.5 per cent and fell back to a low of 38.4 per cent, in 1998 but increased again to 47.7 per cent in 2004–05. Kundu (2011, page 30) warns against simplistic interpretation of these trends, noting that 'regular employment' for women includes domestic work, which, he argues, has 'working conditions only marginally better than those available for casual workers'.

Financial crisis

Whether securing a livelihood in the formal sector or the informal, the urban poor are vulnerable to general economic trends and they have faced difficulties in recent years due to periodic financial crises. Fallon and Lucas (2002) study seven countries experiencing financial crises in the late 1990s and argue that life became increasingly difficult for the urban poor as inflation reduced the value of real wages. Drawing on data from Argentina, Malaysia, Mexico, Indonesia, South Korea, Thailand and Turkey, the authors analyse the impact of financial crises on labour markets and incomes. They suggest that in urban areas both the self-employed and waged earners suffer. For example, in Indonesia, male employment in urban areas fell by 3.1 per cent (although self-employment and family work increased, wage labour fell substantially) and female employment fell by 1.9 per cent (in this case both wage labour and self-employment fell). These shifts in employment opportunities have also had impacts on migration trends. In Indonesia, 'some 6 per cent of all prime-age adults moved from urban to rural areas in just one year from 1997 to 1998; just half that number moved in the opposite direction'

(Fallon and Lucas 2002, page 30). A further response of some national governments was the repatriation of foreign workers in an effort to support the domestic labour force; for example, the government of Malaysia failed to renew migrant work permits.

While there were reductions in migration and rising unemployment, Fallon and Lucas (2002, page 31) suggest that 'the main crisis in labour markets was in wages .... [R]eal wages fell by 44 per cent in Indonesia and 31 per cent in Turkey in a single year'. Faced with difficulties in finding livelihoods and with rising inflation and unemployment, many workers seem to have accepted such wage reductions, particularly those who are the lowest paid. In addition to the difficulties faced by Indonesians with waged incomes, the authors also note that self-employment earnings fell in urban areas and suggest that this was because of increasing competition and declining demand. Higher-income urban households benefited from women entering the labour market and increasing their work in family enterprises. In terms of the impact on poverty, Fallon and Lucas (2002) argue that this calculation depends critically on the inflation adjustment. (This conclusion is also relevant to the discussion in Chapter 2 of the importance of accurate price adjustments to the measurement of urban poverty.) The authors note that:

> when the increase in the official cost of living is used to deflate expenditure, the overall rise in poverty is not very dramatic .... Price data collected in association with the Indonesia Family Life Survey suggest a much higher rate of overall inflation and a sharper rise in poverty.
>
> (page 36)

To understand the impact of the more recent global recession on urban informal livelihoods, Horn (2009, 2011) gathers both individual and group perspectives from those participating in worker organizations and networks. The networks include waste pickers, street traders and home-based workers (both contracted and own-account or self-employed workers). In 2009, the study included just over 50 interviews within each category and 79 per cent of interviewees were women. Street vending data were drawn from Kenya, Malawi, Peru and South Africa, data for home-based work from Indonesia, Pakistan and Thailand, and data for waste picking from Chile, Colombia and India.

Overall, 65 per cent of respondents reported that trade had declined, with the figure rising to 85 per cent in the case of waste pickers. More than half (55 per cent) of sub-contracted home workers reported that their work had been reduced; however, experiences were varied and 27 per cent of self-employed workers reported that business had improved. Both street traders and home-based workers (86 per cent) reported that the costs of business had risen and interviewees explained that they faced a difficult situation in competitive markets:

> 91 per cent of home-based workers spent more on business costs in June 2009 than they did in January 2009, the majority of home-based workers, both

self-employed and sub-contracted, had seen the sale price of their goods decrease over the same period.

(Horn 2009, page 10)

Horn (2009) reports that, while waste pickers have not faced increasing costs, the prices paid for recycled products have fallen significantly and systematically, particularly in Latin America. Fifty-five per cent of interviewees reported that there were more people entering the sector, with most of those entering being women. Cohen (2010) also reports increasing competition in the case of street traders in Johannesburg. Many of Horn's interviewees saw this increased competition as an outcome of retrenchment in the formal sector. Seventy-seven per cent of those interviewed reported that profits fell between January and June 2009. Horn concludes:

> Global recession is leading to increased numbers of informal workers and thereby contributing to increased competition within the informal economy. This is undermining the livelihoods of the traditional informal workforce and the ability of new entrants to find shelter in the informal economy.
>
> (Horn 2009, pages 13–14)

A follow-up study interviewed an overlapping sample early in 2010 to reassess trends for those working in the informal sector (Horn 2011). High prices for household items continued to put pressure on budgets at a time when a lack of employment in the formal sector meant that people continued to enter the informal sector. In this second study the interviewees included 63 street vendors from India, Kenya, Malawi, Peru and South Africa; 54 waste pickers from Colombia and India; and 102 home-based workers from Indonesia, India, Pakistan and Thailand. Perhaps reflecting the recovery in global trade, informal workers were seeing higher demand. For example, home-based workers in Indonesia saw business slump between November 2009 and February 2010 but had observed improvements since then. Sub-contracted workers appear to have done better than self-employed: 46 per cent of the former reported that the number of customers grew between mid-2009 and early 2010 and 39 per cent reported more purchases; the figures were 14 per cent and 26 per cent respectively for the self-employed. In the case of waste pickers, there was no notable increase in demand for high quality waste between the two periods. Pickers agree that general economic conditions have improved but argue that in their case this has not translated into increased demand because of a structural change in the market, specifically 'a rise in individuals competing for waste, the industry downturn among important waste sources such as local factories, and the privatization of municipal collection routes' (Horn 2011, page 10). Horn (2011) also reports further falls in demand for street vendors' products. Across all sectors within the research, six out of ten respondents reported that there was more competition with a continuing flow of new entrants. In terms of the costs of production, only 7 per cent of those interviewed thought that costs had fallen and 63 per cent reported an increase.

Turning to incomes, across the full sample, 30 per cent of respondents increased their profit levels between mid-2009 and early 2010, 18 per cent saw no change in profits and for 52 per cent profits declined. The majority of both home-based workers and street vendors had begun to look for alternative sources of income; most appeared to have been successful and only 17 per cent experienced reduced income. Rising food prices created additional difficulties for households: 16 per cent of the sample report withdrawing one or more children from school (of whom 50 per cent withdrew female children, 30 per cent male children and 20 per cent both).

These overviews offer a snapshot of the situation in some countries and some trades over the last 15 years. The picture emerging is one of continuing economic difficulty, with workers adjusting their income-earning strategies so as to minimize reductions in their standard of living. The next subsection draws on another set of studies to understand the implications of these trends for household incomes and livelihood strategies.

The consequences for households

The previous subsections have discussed three distinct but related economic dynamics affecting urban households, with their dependence on urban labour markets. The structural adjustment processes taking place over recent decades have reduced formal employment, particularly in the public sector, and encouraged the casualization of labour markets. Financial crises have brought further shocks to many city economies and, while their impacts are cyclical, the repeated occurrence of these events suggests that increasing numbers of households will be affected (albeit temporarily). And the desires of middle- and upper-income groups and of city politicians for a 'modern' city landscape has led to the exclusion of some informal activities (and other manifestations of informality) and the destruction of more visible and better-located informal settlements. The discussions in this subsection concentrate primarily on Latin America, where urbanization and industrialization have long been established, and where considerable economic restructuring has taken place in recent decades. Perhaps reflecting a difficult context, there are several studies that are available to help us understand the consequences of such changes.

Nearly two decades ago, Minujin (1995) identified the 'new poor' in Latin America, where sharp falls in real incomes impoverished many previously middle-income households. He suggested that a new group had emerged alongside the 'structural poor', with very low incomes but with characteristics of higher-income groups, in that they did not live in informal settlements, were generally better educated and maintained middle-class social and cultural values. The 'structural poor' are those who had long lived in informal settlements lacking basic services, whereas the 'new poor' generally lived in homes with basic services, but had incomes that could not cover the cost of a basic basket of goods and services.

Minujin (1995) illustrates the scale of problem in Buenos Aires, Argentina where, in 1980, 20.6 per cent of the population were poor, and over 80 per cent of this group were classified as the structural poor. By 1990, the percentage in poverty had risen to 34.5 per cent and the poor were almost evenly divided between the new poor and the structural poor, at 53 and 47 per cent respectively. Auyero (2000) reports on a study from Beccaria and Lopez (1996) which suggests that this had taken place at a time of considerably widening inequality, with the 30 per cent of households with the lowest income having their share of total income reduced from 13.2 per cent in 1974 to 8.1 per cent in 1995, and the share of the middle 60 per cent of households falling from 61.5 per cent to 55.4 per cent over the same period, while the 10 per cent of households with the highest incomes saw their share of total household income increase from 25.3 per cent to 36.5 per cent. Whatever the increases in inequality, there is some reason to believe that a higher proportion of this 'new poor' group will find it easier to move out of poverty because relatively high levels of services reduce their exposure to health problems and higher levels of education better equip them to take up the opportunities that emerge – although an exception is older age groups who have retired and have difficulties returning to work. While many discussions of the 'new poor' have concentrated on Latin America, Maxwell *et al.* (2000) make use of a similar concept when analysing vulnerable groups in Accra, Ghana.

De la Rocha (2007), in discussing the implications of global economic trends for women in Mexico's urban labour markets, identifies both informalization and falling real wages to be of considerable importance. Drawing on her earlier research, she argues that there has been a significant change in livelihood opportunities with households facing increasing difficulties in securing sufficient earnings. In the 1980s, both men and women found low-paid jobs through a variety of strategies. They augmented formal work by investing in micro-enterprise activities (both petty trading and skilled construction work such as carpentry), producing goods and services for consumption (i.e. enhancing the production of the family through activities such as dressmaking, which de la Rocha refers to as 'self-provisioning') and using reciprocal exchange through networks and social support systems to improve their access to resources. However, with the growing significance of informal work and declining real wages (for example, a 35 per cent fall in real wages in Guadalajara between 1982 and 1985), they have faced considerable difficulties in securing sufficient income for their families. Self-provisioning – making rather than buying clothes, for example – has increased, despite the additional burdens on women, as households have sought to save money. The data also suggests that unpaid work in family businesses has increased.

Following continuing macro-economic difficulties and the financial crisis in 1994, responses appear to have changed significantly, as opportunities for families to respond by increasing their hours worked have declined. While women's labour market participation has continued to increase, '[male] unemployment soared .... Unemployment among male youth reached unprecedented levels in 1995, touching almost 30 per cent in the main metropolitan areas during that year' (de la Rocha 2007, page 56). Part of the reason for growing unemployment has been trade liberalization, with small Mexican firms unable to compete in global markets in the context of fewer restrictions on trade and market access.

In terms of wage employment, the study found that women work longer for less and young men are more likely to migrate or become involved in illegal activities. The reduction in permanent employment has made it more difficult for other family members to secure an income from petty production. Households find it more difficult to use self-provisioning because this requires some income to initiate the activities (the materials must be purchased and transported). If there is sufficient income to begin then there are opportunities both to reduce the cost of household goods and services and to make money through the sale of surplus stock to neighbours. However, without even the income to begin, these opportunities cannot be realized. Social networks have been a less effective source of support because money has become scarce everywhere and reciprocal exchanges could not function without at least some cash. De la Rocha concludes that, without a source of formal income as an essential component, the survival model is significantly less effective in securing household income. As a consequence:

> The second half of the 1990s[,] … marked by scarcity of job options for the majority, has seen a process of real deterioration of income and survival sources. A huge gap is opening up between the very privileged, who can access permanent employment, and the excluded.
>
> (de la Rocha 2007, page 61)

The generalizability of these findings is difficult to assess. In a very different context, Gaerlan *et al.* (2010) examine the impacts of financial recession on women's work in Calabarzon, in the Philippines. The authors describe the reduction in the viability of some industries due to increased international competition, the continuing and sustained casualization of labour (even within free-trade zones) and the difficulties in finding work. However, the women interviewed are still able to diversify their income sources through acquiring additional informal work, drawing on family networks and continuing to cut back on household consumption – that is, they can manage with responses that worked for the urban poor in Mexico in earlier decades.

The two recent longitudinal studies in Latin America discussed previously provide a further opportunity to consider whether de la Rocha's findings are observable elsewhere, and they are broadly supportive in this regional context.

Perlman (2010) analyses trends across the city of Rio de Janeiro, drawing on interviews with residents she had previously interviewed in the late 1960s, also with their children and grandchildren. Between 1969 and 2003, long-term unemployment (defined as those out of work for more than six months) rose, while the number of interviewees reporting they had no income increased. More generally, inequality in Rio de Janeiro had been similar to that in Brazil as a whole – static and high, with a Gini coefficient in 2003 of 0.57. While Perlman's respondents had secured improved access to basic services and more household assets, in 2003 interviewees were pessimistic about economic conditions, including real wages and employment opportunities. An analysis of the labour market showed a decline in the availability of manual work. In 1960–64 just under 90 per cent of men between 16 and 31 who were employed were working in the manual trades; by 2000, this proportion had fallen to 60 per cent, reflecting reduced opportunities for the unskilled. Perlman adds that unemployment had also increased because changes in legislation had reduced demand for some kinds of casual workers, such as domestic workers. She concludes:

> material conditions of life are much better today than they were four decades ago and educational levels are much higher. But unemployment is also much higher and educational gains have not translated into proportionately better jobs. The jobs people do get pay what lyrics to a popular samba call 'a salary of poverty' meaning that even among families with a working person, going to bed hungry is not uncommon.
>
> (Perlman 2010, page 232)

In her study of Indio Guayas in Guayaquil, Ecuador, Moser (2009) notes that any analysis of household employment strategies in the settlement is constrained by the paucity of empirical data. Within the neighbourhood she studied, employment rates for men declined from 84.9 per cent in 1978 to 75.9 per cent in 1992 and 74.8 per cent in 2004, while rates for women in the same years increased and then fell back, going from 34.6 per cent to 43.8 per cent then 36.5 per cent. Women's labour market participation reflected changing culture, improved educational opportunities and the need to work to secure living standards. In terms of employment categories, for men, manufacturing and the retail trade fell in significance with the rise in services employment from about 5 per cent to 25 per cent of the sample between 1978 and 2004. Women have also seen a 20 per cent rise in the share of employment in the service sector with falls in the significance of manufacturing (10 per cent) and the retail trade (7–8 per cent). The most significant trend within overall employment patterns is that between 1978 and 2004, casual temporary work increased for both men and women. In terms of total employment it increased from 30 per cent of those employed in 1978 to 36 per cent in 1992 and to 43.5 per cent in 2004. This casual labour – daily work – is the most uncertain. Moser also describes how over the 30-year period 'more traditional occupations such as tailoring and shoemaking declined, with older artisans finding it difficult to make ends meet' (2009, page 131).

Monthly real incomes fell very significantly from US$117.3 in 1978 to US$73.6 in 1992 and then increased to US$101.6 in 2004 (this average figure is for both men and women and all employment categories). These income dynamics mask two different trends, with male incomes falling significantly, and women's incomes falling slightly at the beginning of the period and then showing a real increase of about 38 per cent over the full period, 1978 to 2004. The falls in income have been mitigated by an increase in non-wage income, including both social transfers from the state and remittance income from overseas migrants. By

2004, 35 per cent of surveyed households had some level of remittance income.[73] While rental income was not yet significant, Moser notes that by 2004 households were constructing rooms to rent.

Some concluding thoughts on the economies of the urban poor

This section has shown that finding incomes appears to be increasingly difficult, although clearly the general health of the economy is critical to the scale and nature of income-earning opportunities. A number of conclusions emerge. First, earnings secured from those also living within the immediate settlement are important for household members, particularly women who have to be home-based either because of domestic responsibilities or due to social constraints, but economic interactions between informal settlements and the formal city are considerable. Next, while the relationship between educational attainment and income levels is observed in a number of studies, findings from both Rio de Janeiro and Cape Town suggest that access to this route may be limited for the most disadvantaged citizens. And the reorientation of economies away from formal to informal work has been substantive in many of the studies considered here. While recent data from India suggests that this shift is now complete, studies that enable us to conclude that this finding can be generalized do not exist. From the perspective of individual traders and own-account workers, the level of competition from new entrants into their informal sectors continues to grow.

At the same time, and despite the level of interconnectedness between informal low-income workers and the city, urban governments are seeking to formalize the economic activities taking place in central city streets, with less opportunity for both informal settlements and informal trading. The context for those embedded in these activities and places is difficult and the studies suggest to us that this trend is continuing. As low-income households are expelled from central areas, their livelihood struggles are likely to intensify.

Accounts of livelihood activities draw our attention to the impacts of economic and financial crises. There is evidence both of the difficulties of finding work and falling wage rates. While some households are able to increase the number of members working, in other contexts this appears to be difficult.

In terms of livelihood activities, the presence and importance of income drawn from diverse sources emerges from a number of the studies cited. In a context in which income insecurity is considerable, those households who are able to follow a number of earning strategies are better able to weather the difficulties faced by those working in any specific sector. Households with multiple income-earners following different livelihood strategies – enterprises, formal jobs, contract work and casual labour – are less vulnerable if and when they have to respond to adversity. However, while that has long been appreciated, what is less well understood is how the different kinds of incomes combine to provide an adequate standard of living. The studies suggest that livelihood opportunities may be shifting so significantly that previous combinations of strategies are no longer as effective in addressing household needs. However, as some possibilities close down others may open up; in many cities, remittances from migrants overseas have become an increasingly important source of income in recent years. The current recession in Europe may now jeopardize such livelihood strategies. The changing structure of household livelihoods requires an integration of the analysis of individual incomes with that of household economic interactions.

Many of the activities followed within informal low-income settlements reflect the lack of opportunities and scarce incomes. Residents make their living selling daily amounts of products because they and their neighbours lack the capital to purchase in bulk. Other entrepreneurs provide access to basic services such as water vending because of a lack of public provision. We know remarkably little about the ways in which income circulates in low-income settlements, and the nature of economic relations with the wider city and the critical drivers of economic growth. Many documents suggest a need for 'pro-poor' growth but there is not much understanding of how this can actually be achieved.

Conclusion

What matters

Almost every low-income person or household in urban areas makes choices about where to live based on where they can or may be able to earn an income. They make multi-factor trade-offs involving location (especially with regard to the proximity of income-earning opportunties) and type and quality of accommodation (which also influence home-working possibilities). There is also the ingenuity of how they use the limited spaces to which they have access; this is evidenced if you look into the tiny homes of pavement dwellers in Byculla in Mumbai and see the organization of space to provide for the domestic needs of household members and income-earning possibilities. What we would class as some of the most crowded and dangerous forms of accommodation may have very high economic value for those living there because of the access to income-earning opportunities it provides. Again, one of the most dramatic examples of this is provided by the pavement dwellers in Byculla: a high proportion work within a short walk of their 'homes', their incomes being too low to afford either local rents or daily transport to and from cheaper rental locations further away. To have no transport costs and require very little travelling time allows them to survive on lower incomes. Similarly, for low-paid construction workers, living within the construction site may be dangerous and lacking in basic amenities but it cuts down the time for and cost of getting to and from work. However, such locations are becoming increasingly rare and those continuing to live in well-placed neighbourhoods are likely to be under pressure to move, particularly in cities with rapidly growing economies. The likely consequence will be increasing segregation of urban space. This is considered further in Chapter 5.

Certain factors may enhance income-earning opportunities – for instance the availability of credit and a bank account, the extension of a reliable supply of piped water and electricity to a settlement, good social contacts, literacy and completion of secondary school (although there are instances in which most of these factors are not effective). Other factors can constrain income-earning opportunities – for instance gatekeepers to better jobs or incomes who require payment or favour particular groups, the societal constraints on what women can and cannot do and controls on entry into some livelihoods or their practice. Competition for income-earning opportunities can drive down the incomes these provide, or require longer working hours. Each individual or household will also face particular economic constraints and opportunities related to their home and location, the number and age of their children, their social contacts, and so on. Clearly the scale of economic growth plays a role, and this is increasingly influenced by global trends such as the price of oil, also by governments' own macro-economic strategies including exchange rate policies. The particular circumstances prevailing in a region, such as levels of security, prosperity, and the occurrence of natural events, also ultimately influence household economies.

What we should know but frequently don't

There are evident difficulties in drawing comparisons between studies of different cities or different settlements within cities, as each study uses different categorizations in describing activities within different types of income-earning strategies. However, the discussion of urban economies highlights more fundamental problems. There are very few studies that bring together information about the multiplicity of trades and labour market outcomes for particular urban districts and centres. In the majority of cases, there is very little understanding of what matters for the livelihoods of the urban poor. Without such information, it is not possible to conceive of effective interventions to improve incomes and reduce poverty. It also makes it difficult (or impossible) to ascertain how infrastructure and service provision can best contribute to poverty reduction. For a large number of cities and countries there is also very little information about which economic activities are undertaken and their relative significance. Those countries with the more developed economies are more likely to have better information, but this is probably of limited relevance to the residents of cities in low-income countries. So it is difficult to ascertain the relevance of what Moser (2009) documents for Indio Guayas, Perlman (2010) documents for *favelas* in Rio and de la Rocha (2007) documents for Mexico's labour markets (for instance) to cities or smaller urban centres within the least developed nations.

One of the keys to understanding the scale and depth of urban poverty must be to understand income-earning possibilities and constraints for different individuals, households and groups in any city or city district. This also means gaining an understanding of the labour market and the opportunities for self-employment (and who has these opportunities). But this is complicated. For most cities, there is little data – especially for those in informal employment. For some cities, there may be more detail from particular studies – sometimes quite a lot of detail – but still without much insight into income levels, working conditions and priority needs among the urban poor. We do obtain valuable insights into these issues from the few detailed studies of the lives and livelihoods of individuals and households in particular settlements where low-income groups are concentrated (especially where these have been studied over time). We also get insights from studies of particular low-income groups (defined by occupation, for instance). But studies with this kind of detail and depth are rare. And, as is evident from the findings presented above, they also caution against generalizations.

Then there is the need to understand how income-earning opportunities have changed and are changing, and how this change is related to and influenced by changes in city economies, the scale and composition of in- and out-migration, changes in land and housing availability and whether deficits in public provision or support for infrastructure and services are increasing or decreasing. Change may also be related to specific government policies – for instance cutting public sector jobs or reducing wages – that in turn may be related to conditions imposed on governments by external funding agencies. Or change may be related to decisions made by city governments, such as those made in Ahmedabad and Cairo to contract private sector firms to collect waste previously collected by informal recyclers. What is evident is that both the level and predictability of income are important. As households seek livelihood strategies that reduce risk, they need to be able to secure their basic needs, even if there is little possibility for advancement.

Next, there is the need to understand key influences on the access each individual or household has to different kinds of income-earning opportunities, including where they live and the accessibility of income-earning opportunities, in terms both of time and monetary cost. What is evident from the discussion in this chapter is that personal relations are critical, or, put another way, in a context in which opportunities are scarce, social networks are key to allocating resources and establishing obligations. Unfortunately, the result is reduced social mobility and increasingly divided urban spaces. In most cities there are more or less explicit or implicit forms of discrimination against women which limit income-earning opportunities, although the character and extent of discrimination varies.

Again, better understanding of the links between income-earning opportunities, neighbourhoods and housing is needed. These links are obvious and clear in discussions with low-income groups but become obscured in the general literature. There are parallels here with the inaccurate over-simplification of housing issues (the poor live in 'slums') and income-earning opportunities (the poor work in informal employment).

Finally

There are issues around our responsibilities as researchers: we are meant to have the capacity to better understand the issues facing urban poor groups in terms of incomes and livelihoods – do we spend enough time actually discussing these issues with low-income groups and understanding which issues they prioritize and which responses would best serve them? Many development interventions in this area have concentrated on micro-finance, but access to credit, while important, is only one component of livelihood expansion. Such schemes may assist particular enterprises but do little to address the lack of new markets or income-earning opportunities. One question here is why many 'slum' and shack dwellers' organizations do not prioritize initiatives to address incomes. This is not a reflection of the absence of need; rather it is, at least in part, a reflection of the difficulty of identifying measures that will increase incomes while maintaining a collective orientation. In some locations, residents compete against each other in labour and product markets, and an emphasis on income generation may favour some households more than others. In most high-income nations there have been measures that have helped – for example setting minimum wage levels – but these are hardly realistic in nations where so much employment falls outside the reach of regulations or where government capacity to set and enforce regulations is limited. Acting on other deprivations – for example creating safer, more secure housing and easily accessed, good quality affordable health care, emergency services and schools – and lowering the cost of services – for instance replacing water vendors or kiosks with piped water supplies, replacing pay-to-use toilets with community toilets and providing forms of credit that reduce debt burdens – can act to reduce poverty without increasing incomes.

The need to understand, in an integrated fashion, the different dimensions of urban poverty is addressed in Chapter 6, while experiences with poverty reduction are analysed in the companion volume to this (Satterthwaite and Mitlin 2013).

5   Critical issues in
urban inequality

Introduction

Inequality can be considered and measured in all nine aspects of urban poverty noted at the end of Chapter 2 (see Box 2.2 on pages 89–90). In terms of this disaggregation, six aspects relate to the role of the state. Four are about what governments should provide or ensure provision of – public infrastructure, basic services, safety nets and the rule of law. One is about governance – the extent to which political systems and bureaucratic structures help reduce or increase urban poverty. Finally, there is the key role and influence of the state in housing conditions – not so much what government builds but what it provides and supports through infrastructure and service provision, land-use planning and management, and building and land-use regulations. Inequality can also be considered in terms of health outcomes – see the discussion in Chapter 3. Of course, there is the complication of the multiple connections between these different aspects of poverty. Improvements in one can bring improvements in many others. But worsening conditions in one can also prompt worsening conditions in others.

This chapter overlaps in some respects with Chapter 3, on health and poverty, which provides examples of inequalities in terms of social differences (for instance contrasts between richer and poorer groups in infant or under-five mortality rates) and spatial differences (contrasts between informal settlements and other areas in health or housing indicators). Chapter 3 also includes examples of the greater health burdens associated with low income. However, these are presented as part of the evidence base on the health problems faced by those with inadequate incomes and assets. This chapter rather focuses on what causes such unequal access, and hence complements the understanding developed in the earlier chapter.

Much emphasis is placed in discussions on development on the numbers in absolute poverty and the nature of such poverty. But the experience of low-income households, including the deprivations they face, is also related to their relative position in society.[74] Inequalities in, for instance, income, quality of living and working conditions or status are central to an understanding of the ways in which injustice and exclusion take place. Building on the discussions of absolute poverty in Chapter 2 and the health burdens associated with poverty in Chapter 3, this chapter considers why inequality is an important factor to understand and address both in terms of poverty reduction and of a broader agenda for securing improvements in the quality of life for urban citizens. As we show in this chapter, inequality matters for understanding and addressing poverty, as well as in its own right.

In keeping with previous chapters, this chapter continues to recognize the multiplicity of aspects of poverty. We consider inequality in terms of five specific categories, the first four of which correspond to categories already considered: income, which in an urban context is primarily market income but which may include income from migrated family members and other private transfers; assets, particularly those related to shelter, including housing and security of tenure; entitlements, for example access to state services such as health care and education, the rule of law and state transfers such as pensions; and capacities for political agency. The fifth dimension we consider is that of social status, which may be tied to spatial location, for instance, in informal settlements, and which directly affects people's well-being as well as influencing their ability to secure income and assets and claim their entitlements (either individually or in groups). In some cases, such inequalities also have an impact on people's ability to develop their capacities, as unequal social relations act to constrain opportunities.

Inequality in urban areas in the Global South has not received consistent and systematic attention. In part this reflects the available data and how they are used. Censuses should provide the basis for a very detailed analysis of inequality, based on the data they collect, including the quality of housing and levels of overcrowding, and the quality of facilities within the house (e.g. water, sanitation, energy supply and equipment), but only rarely is this potential realized. Data from censuses are so often only published at high levels of aggregation. In theory, census data should allow comparisons between small areas or even streets; such comparisons are possible in many high-income nations. This should serve both to highlight inequalities and to provide the basis for addressing them, with census data pinpointing the districts, sub-districts or even streets where provision for infrastructure and services is most inadequate, for example. But it is rare for the census authorities (or perhaps the politicians that oversee them) to provide this, even to local governments whose effectiveness could be much improved by access to census data for small areas.

Previous chapters have described how, in most low-income nations, external support for 'data for development' has focused on surveys designed to cover a sample that is nationally representative. These surveys are far cheaper and easier to implement than censuses and can also be done more frequently, so aiding monitoring of changes and trends. But their sample sizes are too small to allow for a detailed look at inequality. So in their measurements they provide little or no scope for examination of, for instance, inequalities within either national urban populations or particular cities. As we will see, disaggregated information is often unavailable, or samples can only be disaggregated into very broad categories, such as national rural and urban populations. These tell us nothing about inequalities within urban (or rural) populations. Thus, all discussions of inequality, including the discussion in this chapter, are limited by the predominant forms of data collection, which reflect only a limited interest in urban inequality. We recognize that there are many inequalities that are not fully captured by the discussion below; this is due in part to these data deficiencies.

Why inequality matters

While the need to raise incomes or living standards for the 'absolute poor' can be recognized as an imperative, it is not so evident why levels of inequality should matter, once those at the lowest income levels have sufficient to meet their basic needs, including adequate living conditions. Hence, for some, an initial question is: why a concern with inequality?

The ways in which poverty was defined and measured in Chapter 2 are in absolute terms. So an individual or household experiences poverty if their diet is below a norm considered to be the minimum for health; or if their income is below the absolute level considered necessary to afford sufficient food and meet other basic needs; or if their asset portfolio is too small or limited to help them cope with stresses and shocks. They live in poverty if their housing conditions fall below some set of absolute norms (in terms of space per person, tenure or quality of building materials, for example). Other aspects of absolute poverty were also considered, for instance the absence of a just rule of law, a lack of voice and inadequacies in access to good quality schools, health care services and emergency services, although in many nations these are deprivations also faced by groups who would not be considered poor.

But all these aspects of poverty can also be considered and measured in relative terms. So, for instance, the focus is not on absolute incomes but on the income levels of the poorest – say the poorest 2 or 10 or 20 per cent of the population compared to the income levels of the wealthiest 2, 10 or 20 per cent. Relative incomes can also be used to set income-based poverty lines, an approach widely applied in high-income nations but much less evident in low- and middle-income nations.[75] Similarly, measures of health outcomes, such as premature death, including infant, child and maternal mortality, and illness or injury, can also be presented in relative terms, for instance by comparison to the health of wealthy groups or some average (national, rural, urban). Or comparisons can be defined by geographic area, for example health-related indicators can be compared for those living in different states or provinces, or indicators for informal settlements within a city can be compared to averages for the city or nation as a whole. It is also possible to consider all the social and political determinants of health discussed in previous chapters in relative terms – so housing size and quality, the nature of tenure, the quality of infrastructure and services can be considered for different population groups, and can be defined by geographic area or by income or asset levels.

Income or resource poverty can be considered as a function of both the total resources within a given society and the distribution of such resources. Looked at another way, if there is sufficient national income to meet every citizen's basic needs but no more, then inadequate access to income for some will only arise when others have more than the amount required to meet their needs. In this case, poverty is related to the level of inequality in society and the social relations that determine who has access to and control over resources. The significance of unequal income distribution for the extent of poverty is highlighted in a report by the Asian Development Bank (2007) which shows the extent to which income poverty in Asia has increased because of growing income inequality. In Bangladesh, 35 per cent of the population were below the (absolute) poverty line in 2005, 9 per cent higher than would have been the case if income inequalities had been maintained at their 1991 level. In Nepal, 25 per cent of the population had incomes below the poverty line in 2003 and it was calculated that less than 15 per cent of families would have been below the poverty line if income inequality had not increased between 1995 and 2003. Such figures illustrate why development agencies have become increasingly interested in what they term 'pro-poor' economic growth (although there are multiple definitions of this term). For those who work in urban areas, it may appear that there is little evidence of poverty reduction in cities with rapid and sustained economic growth, and this too is likely to be related to increasing income inequality.

It is worth noting that there are reasons why inequality may be a source of concern which are not specifically linked to issues of poverty. One notable area is the relationship between inequality and growth. At the level of the macro-economy, lower-income households spend a higher proportion of their income than higher-income households (i.e. for every given dollar added to their income, they spend more and save less than higher-income households), hence income that is allocated to them will result in a higher level of economic demand for goods and services than if the income was allocated to families in higher-income groups. In the case of low- and middle-income countries, the higher-income groups may be spending on luxury items imported from abroad with few direct benefits for the local economy. In this context, measures resulting in a more equal income distribution support economic growth. Birdsall and Londoño (1997) summarize some ways in which high inequality in low-income countries in the Global South adversely affects economic growth, suggesting that it 'generates policy and macroeconomic instability, leads to higher fiscal deficits reflecting the median voter's interests, and given weak capital markets and resulting liquidity constraints for the poor, reduces savings and investments, especially in human capital' (page 34). They suggest that higher levels of inequality are, for these reasons, negatively associated with long-term growth.

However, an argument related to urbanization suggests that inequality is not a source of concern for economists. Kuznets (1955) suggested that, as labour moves from agriculture to industry (so mostly from rural to urban areas), inequality increases simply because wage rates are higher in urban areas. Higher wage rates may reflect both increases in the returns on labour (i.e. a more productive labour force) and a higher degree of commodification, with more basic goods and services needing to be purchased (the former captures a real income inequality; the latter does not and may be misleading, as those outside of a monetized economy may secure the same benefits – they just don't have to pay for them). Once most people have moved from rural to urban areas, Kuznets's argument is that inequality will decline because fewer people will be reliant on low-paying agricultural jobs and subsistence agriculture. However, while this argument suggests that increasing inequality (measured at the national level) may be a temporary phenomenon associated with urbanization, it makes no reference to inequalities within urban areas, nor does it say anything about the extent to which inequality falls as the society becomes urbanized.

At the local level, there are likely to be multiple dynamics between economic growth, inequality, entrepreneurship and aspects of deprivation. Some of these complexities are captured in Copestake's (2002) study of micro-finance and inequality in Zambia's Copperbelt. He discusses the outcomes of a micro-finance initiative (CETZAM) which operated in five Copperbelt towns between 1998 and 2001, securing 12,000 clients. Copestake argues that CETZAM enabled some residents to secure loans and build up businesses but that new enterprises tended to compete with each other and in this context only some could succeed. While the scheme was initially successful in drawing in some of the lowest-income households to become members, higher-income households took the largest loans and were the most successful in terms of the acquisition of profits. The lower-income members tended to leave the scheme, with the loan groups claiming that a major reason was loan default. Copestake argues that '[t]he overall picture that emerges is of a minority of generally richer clients doing well and remaining loyal to CETZAM, while the majority left after one or more cycles, wiser perhaps, but financially poorer' (2002, page 753).

Copestake (2002) suggests that long-term impacts on both economic growth and poverty reduction are related to what those who acquire wealth do with it, particularly the proportion that is profitably invested. If the more prosperous enterprises bring new job opportunities either directly or through the creation of a more affluent group within low-income settlements then there may be benefits for the lowest-income households. While he suggests that there may be a level of frustration felt by those who are not able to access and use opportunities, he also notes that those outside the low-income settlements may be doing even better, and hence that programmes such as CETZAM may help to alleviate some of the social pressures arising from neo-liberal economic inequalities. What he does not discuss is how these processes of increasing income inequality may result in perceived divisions within local communities. If local residents believe that their interests differ from those of their neighbour, this may make it more difficult to work together to address collective problems such as infrastructure and service deficiencies. The macro-economic analysis of Birdsall and Londoño (1997) has some resonance here, as investment propensities vary across households and are partly determined by income; in addition the will to invest (and decide where investment is made) depends on social relationships and on the scale of public provision (which may also be influenced by local social relations and the ability of community organizations to negotiate with the state).

Whatever the relationship between inequality and economic growth, there is a concern that high levels of income inequality may result in an increasingly divided population and elite decisions that further penalize the disadvantaged. Velez, de Barros and Ferreira (2004) discuss how elites may influence political outcomes to underprovide public goods (despite negative impacts on growth) so as to minimize their own tax burden and maximize their personal incomes. In Delhi, resident welfare associations formed by those living in apartment blocks or legal housing colonies have organized to ensure their priorities are addressed and to file public interest litigation to try to get rid of nearby informal settlements and illegal commercial enterprises (see Joshi 2008; Chakrabarti 2008; Bhan 2009; Baud and Nainan 2008). An analysis of how changes in urban governance in Delhi over the last two decades have influenced the provision of health care services found little interest among resident associations in government-provided local primary health care because their members had private health care; as one resident commented, 'we are not concerned with this dispensary, we don't use it, only the servants go there' (Lama-Rewal 2011, page 576).

In addition to such explicit self-interest, Hulme and Green (2005, page 876) argue that:

> as the gap between the rich and the poor grows, it becomes easier for elites to assert a conceptual distance between themselves and those living in poverty, whose poverty is blamed on their culture, their ignorance, lack of skills or their farming practices.

A further concern is raised by Hurtado (2006) when he suggests that, at least for Latin America, there is a strong relationship between income distribution and/or equitable growth and democracy. He argues that higher levels of inequality result in a reduced satisfaction with democratic government.

It is recognized that income inequalities are likely to affect relations within society – both generally and specifically for lower-income groups. The two most common contexts in which this has been discussed in the literature are in relation to issues of violence and health. While neither is solely related to living in towns and cities, both are frequently considered within the urban context. Wilkinson (2005) discusses the health-related consequences of inequality with a particular emphasis on psycho-social pathways and, in the context of violence, low social status and low self-esteem. Fajnzylber, Lederma and Loayza (2002) study the relationship between violent crime and inequality and conclude that 'an increase in income inequality has a significant and robust effect of raising crime rates. In addition, the GDP growth rate has a significant crime-reducing impact' (page 7).[76] With reference to our specific interest in the urban context, the authors conclude that, despite the common assumption that there is more crime in urban areas, the level of urbanization is not significantly correlated with violent crime; that is, the more urbanized societies within their sample were neither more nor less violent. Although much of this research is for the Global North (particularly the USA), the arguments have a relevance to the Global South (see also Stewart 2001).

Moser's (2004) review of violence and urban areas suggests that poverty and inequality frequently overlap to generate conditions in which some people resort to crime and violence. The structural causes of violence generally relate to unequal power relations and so also to inequality in terms of the lack of power, voice and agency among low-income groups. Social exclusion is one manifestation of inequality and this too can be a strong indirect catalyst of urban violence. Areas of a city with high levels of violence also mean high levels of fear and insecurity that in turn bring serious implications for trust, well-being and social capital among individuals and within communities. Spatial manifestations of inequality can also be linked to crime – for instance urban areas within the city or on the city periphery which concentrate low-income groups may lack policing or appropriate policing (see Roy, Jockin and Javed 2004) or contain unsafe spaces that reflect poor infrastructure and design, for example isolated and unlit areas, including streets, lanes, bus stops and public toilets (see Moser 2004).

In summary, despite the lack of interest in inequality shown by most discussions of urban poverty in the Global South, the literature suggests multiple and complex links and interactions between dimensions of inequality and poverty. Levels of poverty, its prevalence and depth, are a function of the distribution as well as the totality of resources. In addition, the evidence suggests that there is a dynamic relationship between economic growth and income inequality. When seeking to understand the relationships between inequality and poverty, there is a need to recognize the multiple forms of inequality which, in the urban context, relate to incomes, access to material assets including public goods, and social relations. The interactions between such inequalities and the extent to which they may exacerbate or alleviate each other are explored further in this chapter.

In the specific context of inequalities in social relations, highly differentiated societies may lead to further inequalities, with elites who are self-interested and unaccountable and who have little understanding of the livelihood realities of those far below them on the income scale. Hence inequalities are linked to levels of social integration and the ability of societies to manage collective decision making. The negative experience of being disadvantaged by unequal social relations manifests itself in many ways; one of these is poor health, which further increases the difficulties faced by the urban poor (see Chapter 3).

Approaches and frameworks

Before considering in detail the ways in which inequality is manifest and the consequences that emerge, this section looks briefly at the ways in which commentators have sought to understand and then measure urban inequality. It considers three primary frameworks, focusing on income (including income before and after state transfers), assets (including inequalities in land, housing and capital wealth), and social status.

Incomes

Most urban income is earned through labour markets, and hence the returns to labour, which in part reflect the nature of labour markets, are a major influence on the scale of income inequalities. Earned income can be differentiated from returns on investments (such as profits from business activity or rental incomes from land holdings) secured by those who own enterprises and other productive assets. While a high proportion of the labour force in towns and cities in the Global South works within the informal sector, in many cases this involves wage labour rather than entrepreneurship, as these individuals are employed by those running informal enterprises. Understanding inequalities that emerge from labour markets requires consideration of the nature of the labour market, the distribution within the labour market of jobs with different skill and experience requirements, and the relative returns on jobs with different levels of skill and experience.

To understand the processes through which income inequalities are established and maintained, it is necessary to go beyond the broad aggregate of household income to examine several different kinds of income, each of which may have a different distribution and hence make a different contribution to inequality in household incomes. The major kinds of income are:

- income earned through wages – income earned from the assets or incomes of others, and related to the informal and/or formal labour markets
- income earned by the assets held by the household – profits from production or trade of goods and services, or income earned from investments, including rental income
- private transfers – for example, remittances from national or international migration
- net income received from the state – direct and in-kind grants and transfers minus direct taxation.

The rest of this section considers issues related to income inequality in more detail. It introduces different measurement indicators for income inequalities. These are generally measured using the Gini coefficient, although specialists also use a range of other measures, based on logarithmic functions. These different measures offer different bases for analysis and this section elaborates on the particularities of some of the most popular measures and their significance for our understanding of urban inequalities. The conceptual basis of the measures themselves is not considered here and is left to the literature on methodology.[77]

The Gini coefficient is the most widely used measure as it offers quick comparative analyses of income inequalities between spatial areas (countries, cities, regions) and over time. The Gini coefficient varies from perfect equality (0) to perfect inequality (1); Figure 5.1 on page 224 shows the Gini coefficients for particular cities.

An alternative approach is the use of Theil indicators, which offer important additional understandings of value to those studying inequality. Theil indicators use logarithmic transformations to analyse income inequalities and consequently have two particular qualities: they are more sensitive than the Gini coefficient to extremes of inequality (i.e. inequalities at the top and bottom of the income distribution) and they enable sub-groups to be separately analysed within total populations. As Leite, McKinley and Osorio (2006) show in a study of incomes in South Africa, the ability of Theil measures to decompose populations into groups, and then measure inequality 'between groups' and 'within groups' is an important research tool that is particularly significant when studying heterogeneous urban populations. The 'between group' component is that inequality which would arise if everyone had the average income for their group and compares the difference between group means, while the 'within group' is a measure of this more focused level of differentiation:

> The first component, *between group inequality*, indicates how much of total inequality would remain if incomes were equalized within each population sub-group. The *within group* component captures the amount of inequality that would remain if differences between groups in their average incomes were eliminated, and thus only *within groups* differences remain.
>
> (Leite, McKinley and Osorio 2006, page 31)

Confusingly, there is not one Theil indicator but three.[78] Like the Gini coefficient, Theil indicators run from 0 to 1.

Leite, McKinley and Osorio (2006) seek to understand the relevance of factors such as age, education, gender and race to income differentials in South Africa. The context is one in which educational opportunities and hence attainment have been significantly better for the 'white' section of the population, incomes have been rising at the top of the income scale and increasing numbers of women have entered the labour market (generally as unskilled workers), resulting in increasing competition in this part of the labour market. Inequality measures indicate fluctuating changes in terms of levels of earnings. Leite, McKinley and Osorio (2006) compare indicators showing that the Gini coefficient on earnings income increased from 0.57 in 1995 to 0.62 in 2000 and then fell to 0.6 in 2004, while the Theil GE(0) coefficients for the same years are 0.61, 0.71 and 0.7 respectively. The higher values and greater range in the Theil GE(0) index indicates that income differentials are particularly adverse for the lowest income group.

Turning to the analysis of the significant factors behind these aggregated figures, between-group differences in income related to educational categories declined from 30 per cent in 1995 to 27 per cent in 2004 while between-group differences in race declined from about 30 per cent to 23 per cent over the same period. This reflects the declining significance of educational qualifications, perhaps because of a limited job market for some levels of qualifications, and hence education being no guarantee of a job; and the de-racialization of the labour force, with increasing openings for limited numbers of African and Coloured workers. At the same time, there were increases in some other aspects of between-group inequalities: urban wages rose faster than rural wages (i.e. location explained more of the observed income inequality) and employment status differentials also increased, reflecting greater inequalities among those in work, with professional classes having higher wage increases than unskilled workers.

For an urban context with highly differentiated populations divided by multiple characteristics, including incomes, race, ethnicity, gender, and the status attached to spatial residency, this ability to decompose data may be particularly useful for analysing the changes taking place over time and hence provide the information needed for policy interventions.

A further example is provided by Akita and Miyata (2007) in their study of Indonesia, in which they seek to understand the significance for educational attainment of incomes and of urban or rural residency (referred to as urban and rural 'sectors'). The study covers the years 1996 to 2002 and includes the financial crises of the late 1990s. Their conclusions highlight a number of factors, including the increased significance of 'between sector' inequality over the period. Between 1996 and 2002, the researchers observed two factors of significance: average urban incomes rose faster than average rural incomes and urban inequalities increased, with incomes for those at the top of the labour market increasing significantly more than for those on very low wages; as can be seen from the discussion of Leite, McKinley and Osorio (2006), this is very similar to the situation in South Africa. The authors conclude:

> As the economy continues to develop, it is likely that even more people will obtain higher education, and more specialized jobs requiring different skills will become available in urban areas. As a result, urban inequality is likely to remain high, given current policies and economic trends.
>
> (Akita and Miyata 2007, page 21)

Such methodologies enable a detailed analysis of what is happening at different points of the income scale and for social groups with specific characteristics. In this case, the authors suggest that to reduce inequalities the aim should be to increase the numbers of those who are the most qualified, i.e. those with the highest earnings; measures might include, for example, the expansion of tertiary educational opportunities to increase the labour supply, or adjusting migration policies to encourage workers to come to Indonesia and provide support in certain sectors. While this may bring down the numerical indicators, it will do little to address the needs of the lowest-income citizens.

Despite the advantages of more disaggregated analysis, Gini coefficients continue to be widely used, perhaps because of their simplicity. Figure 5.1 gives Gini coefficients for a range of cities. What is perhaps worthy of note is that many of the cities with the highest income inequality have much lower levels of infrastructure and service inequality than cities with low levels of income inequality. For instance, Cape Town, Johannesburg, São Paulo, Curitiba, major US cities and Santiago, among the most unequal cities in terms of income, have far less inequality in provision for piped water into people's homes and connection to sewers than the less income-unequal cities of Dar es Salaam and Addis Ababa.

It is also likely that Dar es Salaam and Addis Ababa have much higher levels of inequality with regard to key health outcomes (life expectancy at birth, and infant, child and maternal mortality rates) than many of the cities with higher levels of income inequality. This is a reminder of the multiple aspects of urban poverty and inequality, and the danger of emphasizing the measurement of one aspect to the exclusion of others. It also illustrates the potential role of the state in reducing some key aspects of inequality.

However, these indicators and related discussions are based on the assumption that comparisons are between accurate measures of real wages. As discussed in Chapter 2, the lack of information on price differentials between regions within countries can make the comparison of inequality between urban and rural areas and across urban centres very difficult (Aten and Heston 2005). If, for example, urban living costs have not been accurately incorporated into real wage assessments, then the conclusions above may be misleading, with the finding of growing urban–rural inequality not reflecting the actual situation. This is not the only information which may be missing. Leite, McKinley and Osorio (2006) use earnings income in their analysis but they recognize that in some cases income inequalities are compared across total incomes. Hurtado (2006) makes the point that there is no internationally agreed or applied approach for including social transfers and other expenditures in household surveys and, as reported in Atkinson's (1999) study of inequality in OECD countries, the lack of such an approach can make international comparisons problematic.

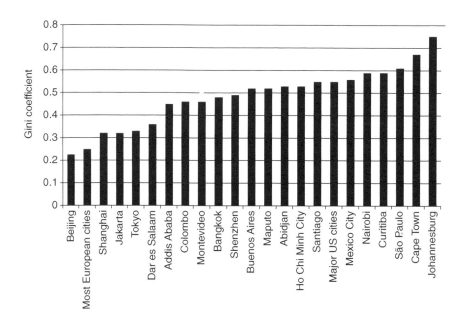

Figure 5.1 Gini coefficients for cities

Source: Data from UN-HABITAT (2008)

Assets

As an alternative to income measures of inequality, some analysts consider the unequal distribution of assets (sometimes called 'capitals'). Such analyses are considered to be complementary to those related to income, helping to reveal some of the dynamics behind income inequalities as well as being directly relevant in understanding aspects of poverty and social exclusion. In addition, surveys may be more likely to get accurate data from households on assets than on income levels. Such assets include those that are directly income generating (i.e. productive capital, such as sewing machines) but go beyond this to consider consumer goods such as radios. Goods such as fridges meet domestic needs and may also be used in (and make possible) a small enterprise. Bicycles or motor bikes can allow more distant income-earning opportunities to be tapped. Hence asset portfolios include a range of goods that add directly to income and which can also be important for understanding social and economic inequalities, both in terms of income-generating capacity and other aspects of well-being.

Asset comparisons measure the distribution of the stock of any one of a number of capitals across the population. For example, the World Bank's poverty assessment for Zambia contrasts the asset ownership of the 20 per cent of the urban population with the highest incomes with that of the 20 per cent of the population with the lowest incomes, for 31 different assets (World Bank Zambia 2007). Their list, developed in a participatory process, includes cell phones, electric and non-electric irons, and bicycles. These capitals generally reflect those identified within the Sustainable Livelihoods Framework[79] and include: physical capital, such as productive equipment and housing; financial capital, such as financial savings; human capital, such as educational attainment; natural capital, usually meaning productive land and access to water, sometimes also the quality of the local environment; and social capital, for example membership of networks and institutions such as the church.

In a detailed study illustrative of the ways in which the asset approach to urban inequality may help our understanding, Menon, Ruel and Morris (2000) analyse Demographic and Health Surveys for 11 countries, examining intra-urban and intra-rural health differentials. A key concern of the study is to explore the validity of the common assumption that child undernutrition is worse in rural than in urban areas. They found that the prevalence of stunting is lower in urban areas of all countries but also that the gaps between high and low socio-economic status are greater in urban areas, hence that intra-urban differentials are significantly higher: 'In most countries, stunting in the poorest urban quintile was almost the same as that among poor rural dwellers' (page 282). The authors explore the correlation between socio-economic assets in urban areas and stunting. They create an asset index (indicating socio-economic status, or 'SES') based on dwelling characteristics, access to water and sanitation, and ownership of assets such as bicycles, televisions and radios. They then consider the relationship between this asset index and undernutrition. In this case, inequalities in the distribution of assets within urban areas are correlated to inequalities in stunting. They conclude:

Our analysis clearly shows that across the developing world, there are large socio-economic differentials in stunting among 0- to 36-month-old children, that these differentials are commonly greater in urban than in rural areas, and that the most disadvantaged urban children have rates of stunting that are on average only slightly lower than those of the most disadvantaged rural children …. Our study showed that the risk of stunting may be up to 10 times higher for urban children of low SES than for urban children of high SES. The fact that such strong socio-economic gradients are consistently found in urban areas of developing countries implies that reliance on global average statistics to allocate resources between rural and urban areas could be dangerously misleading.

(Menon, Ruel and Morris 2000, pages 287–8)

Agarwal (2011) looks at intra-urban inequalities in India, in health, health care or key social, housing or health care-related determinants of health. He uses a wealth index constructed from 33 assets (including ownership of a mattress, chair, bed, table, electric fan, radio, television and sewing machine) and housing characteristics (electricity connection, water source, and type of toilet facility and flooring) to allow comparisons between the poorest quartile and the rest of the population for a number of states and for India as a whole. Some of his findings are presented in Chapter 3. His analysis highlights that the poorest quartiles generally have much higher under-five mortality rates and children under five who are stunted, and much poorer provision in their homes for water and sanitation. The poorest quartiles also have much lower percentages of children completely immunized, mothers with at least three antenatal care visits and births assisted by health personnel. Large differentials in these are evident for urban India in general and across all the states for which data are available.

One of the methodological challenges is that of aggregating different kinds of capital assets such as radios, televisions, housing quality and services. Intuitively, this is difficult because such assets are measured in very different units. A range of statistical procedures have been used to address this and facilitate comparisons between households (see Moser and Felton 2007a; Booysen *et al.* 2007). In their study, Menon, Ruel and Morris (2000) use principal components analysis to identify the assets to be included in the index and the relative importance of each, and Moser and Felton (2007a) repeat this methodology.

Moser (2007) is illustrative of the insights that asset accumulation can offer our understanding of inequality. Her work explores the accumulation of physical assets by a group of low-income residents in what began as an informal settlement in Guayaquil. The residents of Indio Guayas moved into a low-lying mangrove swamp over 30 years ago. At the time of occupation, all the families had very similar levels of wealth. The research examines a panel data set of 51 households interviewed using the same questionnaire in 1978, 1992 and 2004. Over time, income inequality increases and the Gini coefficient rises from 0.32 in 1978 to 0.375 in 1992 and 0.416 in 2004. The study considers the development of the area and analyses the acquisition of social and physical infrastructure, including the consolidation of a community organization (social capital) able to secure access to social grants from international NGOs. Residents secured tenure in a mangrove swamp that was taken over by professional squatters who

> sold off [land] as 10- by 30-meter plots to settlers anxious to escape high rents in the inner city. The young population arrived living on the water and lacking not only land but all basic services such as electricity, running water, and plumbing, as well as social services such as health and education.
>
> (Moser 2007, page 18)

Moser and Felton (2007b) suggest that understanding changes in household income growth may be assisted by an analysis of the patterns of asset accumulation. In particular, they investigate the significance of housing improvements, consumer durables such as electronic goods, productive capital (such as sewing machines), rental income, educational attainment, and participation in community groups, churches and sports clubs. They conclude:

> In terms of the relationship between assets and income mobility, it is useful to identify whether those poor who moved out of poverty started out with better assets. Examination of the average starting level of each household experiencing upward mobility between 1978 and 2004 shows that households that experienced upward mobility did not necessarily start out with higher levels of capital than households that remained stuck in poverty .... However, households that remained non-poor between 1978 and 2004 started out with significantly higher levels of financial-productive capital and smaller households than those that started out non-poor but sank into poverty. Households that experienced upward mobility acquired significantly higher levels of human capital and financial-productive capital than households that remained stuck in poverty.
>
> (Moser and Felton 2007b, page 33)

The authors find that the most important assets for income improvement are financial and human capital, and note that another factor in maintaining relatively high family incomes is a small family size. However, they also argue against over-reliance on any single asset in analysing income changes, and suggest that it is 'the slow appreciation of the entire asset portfolio' that is of primary importance (Moser and Felton 2007b, page 35). The longitudinal nature of the study enables a comparison of generations and it is the second generation of settlers (i.e. the children of the first generation) that significantly improve their human capital with more education. The authors also note an apparent generational shift in accumulation strategies, with the second generation securing consumer goods prior to housing improvements; this reverses the pattern of the first generation, which prioritized housing. The significance of these trends will only become apparent over time.

While Moser and Felton (2007a and b) are interested in how assets have led to changes in income poverty and inequality, other contributions focus on asset inequalities themselves, generally with a focus on a particular asset. Particularly notable are discussions about inequalities in access to education, nutrition, health care and the incidence of ill-health (and/or serious injury and/or early mortality), and other service inequalities. These all affect human capital and the ability of individuals to make best use of their abilities and capacities. In its overview report, the Asian Development Bank (2007), for example, notes that 5 per cent of the children of those in the top 20 per cent of income earners in Asia are severely underweight, compared to 27 per cent for those in the lowest 20 per cent.

Social status

A further approach to measuring inequality is to focus on differences in social status, the way in which these difference are constructed, the establishment of social hierarchy, and the scale of the differences that develop. In general, researchers place emphasis on how social categorizations (by race, gender and age for example) affect access to assets and incomes, rather than on the more subtle ways in which inequalities in social status affect well-being and life opportunities.

Studies that have focused on the various manifestations and dynamics of social status directly (rather than on income proxies) have generally been long-term and draw on ethnographic and anthropological methodologies within the study of broader social and political trends. In this context, they rarely offer the numerical precision that is possible with income and asset measures, and they do not rely on statistical verifications. These arguments rely on their narratives and conceptual frameworks for their powers of persuasion, as they seek to capture the ways in which social relations both create and close off possibilities for inclusion and advancement.

Perlman's 2010 book *Favela* presents a longitudinal analysis of life for low-income households in Rio de Janeiro through a study of the residents of three areas first researched by the author in the late 1960s. Her discussion contains many details of the lives of these residents and augments these with reflections on city-specific and urban processes. The study uses mixed methods and, as illustrated elsewhere in this volume, she provides a wealth of evidence to offer insight into processes of exclusion and inclusion. In seeking to capture some of the processes related to social status, she devotes a closing chapter to 'The importance of being *gente*' and elaborates thus: 'The term *gente* means "somebody" – a *person*, a *human* and to be gente is to be accorded the dignity and respect that is automatically conferred on the "we" of the human community and denied to the "they"' (page 316). The chapter synthesizes the multiple ways in which social relations confer a secondary status on particular socially defined typologies of citizens. Perlman's primary focus is on the consequences of living in a *favela* for an individual's social status. The discussion highlights both the subtleties of such discrimination and its longevity: 'If having local status, assets, livelihood, and the requisite appearance is not enough to ensure being a person, neither is exiting the favela and moving into a *conjunto* or legal neighbourhood' (Perlman 2010, page 321). She captures the experience through life histories used to illustrate both the nature of discrimination and the creation of social status, as well as through drawing on a wider literature that examines similar processes.

The micro-politics of urban settlement development and the influence of race are explored by Myers (2003), who studies how the fabric of urban space is produced and the roles of colonizer, bureaucrat and resident in four African cities, and by Scheper-Hughes (1992) in her seminal book *Death Without Weeping*. Myers (2003) discusses the development of low-income neighbourhoods such as Ng'ambo in Zanzibar, the racism embedded within the design of the colonial city and African residents' sense of disempowerment and frustration with their appalling living conditions. As he describes for the case of Zanzibar, even post-colonial redevelopment failed to address the needs of the urban poor, as the areas in greatest need were passed over in favour of those with greater public visibility. Scheper-Hughes (1992) seeks to understand how women, as mothers, came to terms with the very high levels of infant mortality and the chronic hunger, sickness, death and sense of loss associated with it. She describes the context of an informal settlement in a small town in the north-east of Brazil in the late 1980s, in which women are subject to overlapping forms of disadvantage in their social relationships with more powerful groups and their mostly male leaders. Among themselves – their family, kin, co-workers and friends – they are egalitarian and collectivist. To their patrons, bosses and superiors who oppress and exploit them, they are servile and loyal because they so often need their favour. They have also seen how popular protest has long been crushed. The medical profession fails to address the malnutrition their children are experiencing (prescribing pain killers and sleeping tablets), street children and young men disappear and the police are prime suspects, young children are locked up when their mothers are absent for fear of body and organ snatching, others are 'borrowed' and sent for adoption, their community organization is dominated by a self-interested male leader, and liberation theologists argue for new and more radical approaches but fail to address questions of sexuality and reproduction. In 1987, infant mortality in the town was 211 deaths for every 1,000 births. Of the total deaths in the town in 1987, 38.2 per cent were those of children younger than five.

Alvarez, Dagnino and Escobar (1998) discuss a different manifestation of inequality when they argue that neo-liberalism means that state responsibilities and democratic politics are being reduced and citizenship is increasingly being redefined by the market. They argue that cultural politics is important in understanding the level of inclusion in debates and policy making. They are concerned to draw attention to the ways in which a range of agencies including social movements challenge exclusionary boundaries and contest political power. The issue of social change and transformation is not the focus of this chapter but the scale of political exclusion is, we argue, central to understanding patterns and trends in inequality. In the final section we return to the ways in which political inequalities are constructed and maintained in an urban context.

In concluding this section, it should be recognized that the multiple dimensions of inequality are, of course, related. However, inequality is rarely studied in its multiple facets. One publication that sought to do this is the Institute for Policy

Studies' assessment of race in the United States in 2009 (Rivera *et al.* 2009). The authors document multiple manifestations of inequality between blacks, *latinos* and whites, touching on unemployment rates, incomes, proportion of population below the poverty line, assets, private pensions, living in 'poverty' neighbourhoods and social mobility (for instance the chances of children born in the poorest quintile reaching the top 5 per cent of income earners).

Having reviewed the ways in which inequalities are measured, analysed and understood, the remaining sections of this chapter consider the experience of inequalities in urban areas of the Global South in more detail.

The experience of income inequalities

As noted above, any discussion of income inequalities needs to consider a number of aspects, including the nature of the economy, sources of income and wage differentials, as well as the way in which the tax regime influences net household income. This section discusses inequalities in wage income, the influence of state redistribution of income inequalities and the significance of other sources of income. It begins with a discussion of income inequalities in urban and rural areas.

Understanding urban and rural inequalities

Traditionally, 'urban' and 'rural' categorizations have served as a crude distinction between the locations of secondary and tertiary economic activities (manufacturing and services) and primary activities (including agriculture, mining, fishing and forestry). Over time, and due in part to the dynamics of both livelihoods and commercial choices regarding locations, the precision of this differentiation between urban and rural has been undermined. Manufacturing and service enterprises have developed in many rural areas and the importance of agricultural activities to some urban dwellers has continued or even expanded, reflecting urban or peri-urban agriculture, and farmers and agricultural workers living in urban areas. In most areas in high-income nations and in wealthier areas in some middle-income nations only a very small proportion of rural dwellers work in the primary sector; however, this is not the case for most of the Global South.

In this context, distinctions are of degree rather than absolute. In urban areas, it is more likely that citizens will be dependent on wage labour rather than subsistence agriculture or smallholder farming. In aggregate, urban economies and related livelihoods are overwhelmingly non-agricultural (although they may be associated with the processing of agricultural products or with providing goods and services to rural-based consumers and producers); they are based primarily around the economies of scale and proximity of capitalist production processes and the associated concentrations of population. But note that in rural areas there are also many who are dependent on wages, being landless labourers or unable to make sufficient income from the land available to them.

With a significant proportion of all urban incomes determined through the market, there is likely to be a higher degree of differentiation and greater income inequality than might be observed within a rural population primarily dependent on subsistence agriculture. As noted previously, this observation and the associated debate about the relationship of inequality, growth and changes in the economy to urbanization is longstanding. Kuznets (1955) argued that the shift from an agricultural to non-agricultural population will be associated first with increasing inequality, as some citizens move to urban areas and receive waged incomes (rather than being dependent on at least partially non-monetized subsistence incomes). Over time, Kuznets's model suggests, this inequality will decrease, as people's share in higher-income non-agricultural activity increases and the population becomes urban and integrated within the modern economy. However, the reality may be considerably more complex. In practice, income differentials are changing considerably due to a large number of factors, including new sources of income such as remunerations, state transfers, the share of wages and profits, and changes in relative prices. In many Latin American countries – Bolivia, Brazil, Chile, Colombia, Nicaragua, Panama, Peru – there have been reductions in income inequality (as measured by the Gini coefficient) in the last 10 to 15 years. However, for others, such as Costa Rica, the Dominican Republic, Ecuador, Mexico, and Paraguay, this trend is not evident.[80]

With respect to urban and rural differentials, the evidence is somewhat mixed, perhaps reflecting difficulties in income measurement as well as differences in economic structure and the scale of economic growth, discussed later. Comparative figures on inequality are reported in a number of poverty reduction strategy papers (PRSPs). Inequality appears to be higher in urban than in rural areas for most of the countries for which strategy papers were available up to 2004 (and in some cases is increasing), although this is related to the structure of the economies in these countries, and this finding cannot be generalized (Mitlin 2004). There are also concerns that overall inequalities appear to be rising, for example in Vietnam (World Bank Vietnam 2003). But at least in countries with rapidly growing economies, given that most new investment and employment is in the more successful cities, it would be expected that incomes would rise for a proportion of these cities' workforces (for example for professionals and most entrepreneurs) and that income inequalities would increase. Some examples are given in Box 5.1.

Most of the examples in Box 5.1 show inequalities are growing at national level and are higher in urban than in rural areas. For most of those nations for which data are available on changes in rural and urban inequalities over time, inequalities in urban areas grew more than those in rural areas. To look at this in more detail, we analysed data from 37 countries for which there was some comparative data in the form of Gini coefficients for either trends in urban inequalities or urban and rural inequalities, and in most cases both. This data came from a variety of sources but primarily UN agencies, supplemented by PRSPs and World Bank poverty assessments. A first point to make is that estimations of Gini coefficients for the same country in the same year can differ according to the source of the information. Elbers *et al.* (2005) discuss some of the problems of comparison in their study of local inequalities. Data may be drawn from surveys or censuses, and may be income or consumption based. Notwithstanding these difficulties, we have carried out an analysis to examine the frequency with which urban inequality exceeds rural inequality and to see the trends related to urban inequality. We have not completed a statistical exercise because this would imply a degree of validity that is unwarranted, given the mixed sources used and the extent to which data change over relatively short time periods, suggesting a degree of volatility potentially related to a large number of factors.

Box 5.1 Urban and rural income inequalities compared

- *Bangladesh* Between 1995 and 2000, the Gini coefficient for rural inequality rose from 0.24 to 0.27 and that for urban inequality increased from 0.31 to 0.37 (World Bank Bangladesh 2002).
- *Cambodia* The Gini coefficient was 0.37 in Phnom Penh, 0.43 in other urban areas and 0.34 in rural areas in 2004 (World Bank Cambodia 2006).
- *Ethiopia* The strategy paper for Ethiopia concludes that economic growth led to increasing inequality in urban areas. Inequality fell slightly in rural areas between 1995–96 and 1999–2000, from a Gini coefficient of 0.27 to 0.26, but increased significantly in urban areas, from 0.34 to 0.38 (Ethiopia, Federal Democratic Republic of and Ministry of Finance and Economic Development 2002).
- *Malawi* Inequality was much higher in urban areas in 2000, with a Gini coefficient of 0.52 compared to 0.37 in rural areas (Malawi, Government of 2002). In 2005, urban inequality was lower, at 0.48, with rural inequality being 0.34 (World Bank Malawi 2007).
- *Mozambique* The Gini coefficient for Maputo rose from 0.44 to 0.52 between 1996–97 and 2004–05, while the national coefficient rose from 0.4 to 0.42 (World Bank Mozambique 2008).
- *Nicaragua* Inequality in urban areas fell, with a Gini coefficient of 0.45 in 1993, 0.41 in 2001 and 0.38 in 2005; figures for rural areas were 0.43, 0.35 and 0.34 respectively (World Bank Nicaragua 2008).
- *Senegal* The 2002 strategy paper for Senegal argues that: 'The Gini Index was 0.50 in 1996 in Dakar, which denotes a significantly high level of inequality. It is estimated at 0.30 for the country as a whole' (Senegal, Republic of 2002). The analysis for 2004–05 suggests that inequality in Dakar has fallen to 0.42 while inequality in rural areas remains at 0.30 (Senegal, Republic of 2006).
- *Sri Lanka* Between 1995–96 and 2002, urban inequality rose, with a Gini coefficient of 0.38 and 0.42 in these years, respectively, while rural inequality also increased, with coefficients 0.33 and 0.39 (World Bank Sri Lanka 2007).
- *Uganda* The national Gini coefficient rose from 0.35 to 0.43 between 1997 and 2002–03, with the urban and rural coefficients increasing from 0.35 to 0.48, and 0.31 to 0.36, respectively (World Bank Uganda 2006).

- *Vietnam* The national Gini coefficient increased from 0.34 in 1993 to 0.37 in 2002 but there was no change in either urban or rural levels of inequality, with Gini coefficients of 0.35 and 0.28, respectively (World Bank Vietnam 2003).
- *Zambia* The Gini coefficient at the national level was 0.61 for 1996, rising to 0.66 in 1998. In 2003, the national level coefficient was 0.57 with urban and rural figures being 0.61 and 0.42, respectively (Zambia, Republic of 2006).

Of the 73 observations of urban trends (based on comparison to urban Gini coefficients from previous periods), inequality increased in 26 cases, it stayed the same in 7 cases and it declined in 40 cases. The majority of these observations were made by comparing data for a period lasting from the mid-1990s to 2008–10. The trends for Latin America are different from those for Africa, also from those for the small number of Asian countries in our sample. In Latin America, 60 per cent of observations show a decline in urban inequality, in 10 per cent it stayed the same and in 30 per cent it increased. In the other observations, predominantly for sub-Saharan Africa, the sample was evenly split between increasing and declining inequality.

For our comparison of urban and rural inequality, we examined 93 cases involving 28 countries. In 71 per cent of observations, urban inequality was higher than rural, in 9 per cent it was the same and in 20 per cent it was lower. In 64 per cent of Latin American comparisons, urban inequality was higher.

In respect of the relative inequality between urban and rural areas we should be cautious about generalizing, as there are examples that show that rural inequalities can be higher than urban inequalities, and that levels of inequality are not increasing in every nation. In the case of Honduras, for example, the PRSP concludes that inequality is declining slightly in urban areas but has increased in rural areas (Honduras, Government of 2001). Here, the structure of the economy may be key, with Honduras having a plantation economy. In Nicaragua, as reported in Box 5.1, inequality fell in both urban and rural areas between 1993 and 2005.

A comparative study of urban and rural inequalities in Africa also highlights the dangers of generalization. Comparisons were made for eight countries and two time periods. (It should be noted that the time periods do not match with any degree of precision but in all but one case fall during the 1990s.) In four of the eight countries, inequalities fell in both urban and rural areas. For the first period, urban inequalities are greater in four countries, rural inequalities are greater in three countries and urban and rural inequalities are the same in one country. for the second period, inequality is higher in urban than in rural areas in five countries, while inequality in rural areas is higher in three countries.

However, it is apparent from the data that figures change considerably from year to year even. The data in Table 5.1 have been drawn from a series of studies on the dynamics of poverty using consumption measures, while the information in

Box 5.1 is drawn from PRSPs and equivalents, and poverty assessments. For example, for Ethiopia, the information provided in Table 5.1 is drawn from a panel data set of 3,000 households collected by the Department of Economics, Addis Ababa University, in collaboration with University of Oxford and Göteborg University (Bigsten and Shimeles 2004). Poverty was measured using per capita consumption. The information provided in Box 5.1 is drawn from two national Household Income Consumption and Expenditure surveys carried out by Ethiopia's Central Statistical Authority (CSA), with a sample of first 12,000 households and then 17,000 households for the two survey periods. This also focused on consumption expenditure.

In explaining reasons for changes in levels of income equality, Christiaensen, Demery and Paternostro (2005) point out that these changes have taken place during both growth and decline, hence to understand the trends beneath these figures there is a need to break down the impact on poverty into that which reflects the changing distribution (with the consumption mean kept constant) and that which reflects the changing mean (with the distribution kept constant). The authors conclude that in most of the countries studied the change in incidence of absolute poverty has had relatively little to do with changes in distribution of

Table 5.1 Africa – comparative consumption inequalities

| | Gini coefficient | |
	Year 1	Year 2
Ethiopia 1994–97		
rural	0.39	0.43
urban	0.40	0.45
Ghana 1992–98		
rural	0.33	0.33
urban	0.34	0.31
Madagascar 1993–99		
rural	0.42	0.36
urban	0.41	0.38
Mauritania 1987–95		
rural	0.43	0.37
urban	0.40	0.36
Nigeria 1992–96		
rural	0.51	0.44
urban	0.51	0.51
Uganda 1992–2000		
rural	0.33	0.32
urban	0.39	0.40
Zambia 1991–98		
rural	0.61	0.48
urban	0.47	0.43
Zimbabwe 1991–96		
rural	0.58	0.57
urban	0.60	0.59

Source: Christiaensen *et al.* (2005), page 215

income. In periods of recession in Madagascar, Nigeria and Zimbabwe, they found that reductions in inequality tended to reduce the effect of increasing poverty (i.e. falling average incomes). This conclusion, that urban inequalities fall during recession, is supported by evidence from other studies (see, for example, Friedman 2005). In both Ethiopia and Uganda, growth (rather than decline) had occurred, but in Uganda there had been no significant change in inequality, while in Ethiopia there had been a significant increase. Christiaensen, Demery and Paternostro (2005) examine possible reasons for this with reference to wider economic trends. In Ethiopia, agricultural reforms, the devaluation of the currency and liberalization of foreign exchange markets created new prospects for farmers with export goods. In Uganda, liberalization in agricultural markets, foreign exchange and trade also took place, with associated benefits to a similar group of farmers. In Ethiopia, however, some rural households struggled to participate in these opportunities because they owned little or no land, or were poorly located and lacked access to markets. In Uganda, the authors suggest, based on research, that households that did better from the economic reforms were more likely to be educated and have land; those that remained poor were more likely to have poor health and lack access to electricity. The lack of increase in Uganda's inequality figure may be due to the relatively high proportion involved in export agriculture. However, reflecting the major interest of development agencies, the authors focus more on what reduces poverty rather than what improves income distribution.

With regard to understanding the capacity for income growth, the authors emphasize that reducing remoteness from markets is key, and their discussion is oriented towards addressing rural challenges. They make relatively few references to the urban context, although they note that, while poverty in Accra fell significantly, 'in the Savannah zone poverty even *increased* in the urban areas, while it fell only marginally in the rural Savannah' (Christiaensen, Demery and Paternostro 2005, page 226; emphasis in the original). Here, the authors are associating the fortunes of urban centres with the agricultural productivity and prosperity of their rural hinterlands and, in so doing, they emphasize that aggregated national figures may not be helpful in understanding the underlying dynamics. The economies of most urban centres are influenced by demand for producer and consumer goods and services from nearby rural populations and enterprises; for many, this is the main basis for their economy (see, for instance, Hardoy and Satterthwaite 1986a, 1986b, 1989; Manzanal and Vapnarsky 1986; Blitzer *et al.* 1988). These examples highlight the limitations of discussing rural and urban poverty as if they were not linked.

Earlier studies of Ghana suggest a less positive assessment of the poverty situation in Accra. Maxwell *et al.* (2000) note that the Gini coefficient for income data on households in Accra increased from 0.43 in 1987–88 to 0.50 in 1992. This was a period in which middle-income households saw their living standards fall and the numbers below the poverty line in Accra increased significantly 'from less than one in ten to almost one in four' (Maxwell *et al.* 2000, page 4). So here, income inequality was rising while absolute poverty was rising.

In the case of Indonesia, Friedman (2005) illustrates the significance of the economic cycle on changing levels of inequality, and the relative significance of the monetized economy for income inequalities in urban areas. Friedman (2005) analyses panel data with information from six periods between 1984 and 1999; broadly this is a period in which poverty indicators fell fairly consistently in both urban and rural areas until 1996 and then rose sharply in response to the financial crisis. Considering the provincial data, he finds that 'Gini coefficients in 1987 range from 0.25 to 0.35 in urban areas and from 0.21 to 0.31 in rural areas' (page 173). The trends are mixed. In about a half of the 26 provinces, urban inequality increased during the period up to 1996. However, in only two provinces did it increase during the period of recession between 1996 and 1999. In general, inequality decreases in rural areas throughout the period considered, although this trend is more pronounced during recession.

Akita and Miyata (2007) also investigate inequality in Indonesia and highlight the particularly important role played by the high-income end of the labour market as economic growth created a demand for qualified personnel, pushing up wages. For Vietnam, the World Bank (2003) poverty assessment also concludes that income inequalities increase during periods of economic growth and fall during recession. The picture of increasing incomes for those who are highly paid resulting in increasing inequalities within urban areas is also suggested by Balisacan and Fuwa's (2004) study of the Philippines. The Gini index suggests a small increase in urban inequality and a smaller increase in rural inequality between 1985 and 2000. In both cases, inequality dips twice (in 1988 and 1994) before rising again (see Table 5.2). The Theil T[81] index (particularly sensitive to changes among those with higher incomes) shows a more significant increase, with the coefficient rising by 0.032 between 1985 and 2000 in urban areas, compared with a rise of 0.013 in the Gini coefficient. Such factors may relate both to the specific nature of economic growth in some countries, and to the more generalized impacts of growth. For example, if financial services are gaining increasing importance in the economy and associated employment is for high-wage skilled workers, then inequality may increase. During periods of economic growth it is likely that supply may be lacking in particular sections of the labour

Table 5.2 Philippines – inequality estimates (based on per capita consumption adjusted for provincial cost of living differences)

Measure	1985	1988	1991	1994	1997	2000
Urban inequality						
Gini	0.410	0.390	0.421	0.392	0.425	0.423
Theil T	0.327	0.286	0.355	0.295	0.379	0.359
Rural inequality						
Gini	0.352	0.350	0.359	0.336	0.352	0.360
Theil T	0.226	0.217	0.238	0.205	0.230	0.242

Source: Balisacan and Fuwa 2004

market, enabling them to secure wage increases. The positive correlation with rising inequalities suggests that higher skilled workers are in short supply and hence doing better in these circumstances. This reinforces the argument that education is an important investment associated with better income-earning opportunities in the Global South.

In conclusion, research suggests that rural and urban income inequalities need to be compared with care but that in most cases urban inequalities exceed rural inequalities. Notably, recession seems to be associated with declining urban inequality, but this is not always the case.

These aggregate studies of urban and rural differentials in incomes are enhanced by a more detailed household study that considers a broader range of inequalities. Du Toit (2005) compares the situations of those with very low incomes in a study of three areas in South Africa, using data gathered through 1,898 household interviews. The study highlights similarities and differences between an area with an economy based on subsistence agriculture, an urban economy and a commercialized agricultural area. The interviews were completed in Mount Frere, a remote area in one of the former homelands of the Eastern Cape, in Cape Town, with households living in the ex-African townships of Khayelitsha and Nyanga East, and in Ceres, an area of highly mechanized fruit export agriculture. What is notable is that Gini coefficients are remarkably similar for the three areas (these coefficients are significantly lower than national figures because they compare income differentials within relatively localized areas). Notable differences between urban and rural areas are the high level of households reporting that they are without clean drinking water in Mount Frere and the number without shelter in Cape Town (see Table 5.3).

Table 5.3 Comparative poverty and inequality in three sites in South Africa

	Mount Frere	*Cape Town*	*Ceres*
Average monthly expenditure per adult equivalent	R164.55	R252.10	R399.47
Households with expenditure below R280 per adult equivalent	85%	49%	49%
Gini coefficient for household expenditure	0.40	0.43	0.41
Households with food expenditure of more than 40 per cent	93%	94%	90%
Households often experiencing			
going without food	23%	31%	17%
going without medical care	16%	12%	8%
going without clean drinking water	40%	9%	6%
going without sufficient fuel for heating and cooking	5%	20%	15%
going without shelter	13%	38%	12%
feeling unsafe due to crime	2%	9%	13%

Source: Du Toit (2005), page 9

Inequality in the labour market – and why labour market structure and relative labour market rewards matter

In most urban areas, most households have little or no possibility of secure livelihoods through growing their own food so the labour market is the primary determinant of their household income.[82] We know that household incomes often include multiple sources of earnings, including waged income, enterprise incomes, rents and remittances. Especially in the case of the lowest-income workers, the primary source of income is wages. The problems associated with low pay have been discussed in Chapter 4; here we consider the nature and scale of income inequalities, and what this means for our understanding of absolute poverty.

The significance of market structure for labour market inequalities is illustrated by the case of Chile. Hurtado (2006) shows how the persistence of considerable income inequality in Chile (despite reductions in the numbers living below the poverty line) is related to the structure of the labour market. Following a difficult economic and social period between 1974 and 1989,[83] with average per capita growth in income of only 1.5 per cent a year and significant levels of poverty, democratization is widely considered to have achieved growth with equity. Over the last 20 years, average annual per capita income growth has been 4.2 per cent and the percentage of the population below the poverty line has fallen from 38.6 per cent in 1990 to 18.8 per cent in 2003. However, between 1990 and 2003 there was no change in inequality and the Gini coefficient was between 0.56 and 0.58 throughout. The ratio of the average income of the top 20 per cent of income earners to that of the bottom 20 per cent of income earners was virtually unchanged, at 14.0 in 1990 and 14.1 in 2003.

Hurtado puts forward three reasons to explain why inequality did not fall. The first is related to the nature of economic growth. Chile's economic model has encouraged trade through low tariffs on imports with strong monetary controls and fiscal rules to keep inflation low and prevent the budget deficit rising. The pro-market nature of economic policy is reflected in a strong emphasis on privatization and competition in service provision. Low inflation has maintained low interest rates and facilitated international borrowing. Investment in human capital has been high and total expenditure on education equalled 7.3 per cent of GDP (compared to an OECD average of 5.4 per cent). By 2004, foreign direct investment was equivalent to 7.1 per cent of GNP, and this accounted for 60 per cent of the increase in investment. However, while exports accounted for a third of GNP in 2004, these products were generally of low value and they made no contribution to reducing unemployment. The expansion of employment took place in the informal sector, small and medium enterprises and personal services. The second reason, Hurtado suggests, is Chile's labour market participation rate, which is the lowest in Latin America, and also in part the country's high dependency ratio (highest for the lowest income households at 4.7). The third reason is the continuing significance of informal employment, which accounted for 36.9 per cent of total employment in 1990 and 37.6 per cent in 2000.[84] In 2000, informal workers were estimated to have only 25 per cent of the average productivity of formal workers, with significantly lower remuneration. While informal employment increased more than formal employment from 1990 to 2000, family income did not increase as much (4.4 per cent compared to 5.4 per cent) as wage growth was lower (3.3 per cent for informal workers compared to 4.7 per cent for formal workers). Hence the lowest-income households could not close the gap on higher-income households. Moreover, income inequalities were exacerbated for informal workers as they had less employment security and did not receive the benefits of formally employed workers:

> The poorest 20 per cent have very precarious jobs .... They also have higher unemployment rates (they represent 41.6 per cent of all the unemployed) and higher dependency ratios (twice as large as the average) .... The incidence of poverty among [informal] workers is 26 per cent, while in formal jobs it is 8.5 per cent .... Only 50 per cent of informal workers have a formal contract (and thus access to social benefits) while 86.5 per cent of formal workers have such a contract.
>
> (Hurtado 2006, page 9)

As this example illustrates, labour inequalities reflect both the remuneration paid to different groups within the labour market and the structure of the labour market (that is, how many well-paid and poorly paid jobs there are). In Chile, higher productivity helped to reduce poverty for those in formal employment, with the minimum wage increasing by 70.1 per cent in real terms between 1990 and 2004. Wages for those at higher levels of income increased by 20 per cent more than wages for the low-paid, so inequality was not reduced despite reductions in absolute poverty.

Ferreira and de Barros's (1999) study of urban poverty in Brazil also emphasizes the significance of the informalization of the economy (particularly for the employees with the lowest skills) in maintaining and potentially extending income inequalities. Their study is a further example of the importance of understanding exactly what is taking place within different parts of the labour market to understanding changes in inequality and poverty. The authors consider the reasons for a significant increase in figures for extreme urban poverty (defined as household income below US$30 a month) from 6.8 per cent to 9.2 per cent of the population between 1976 and 1996, although the national Gini coefficient remained the same at 0.59. While urban poverty fell for some households, this fall was only realized by those above the fifteenth income percentile. Ferreira and de Barros conclude that the rise in levels of absolute urban poverty was caused by adverse changes in urban labour markets and reduced participation in the labour force. Structural changes taking place during this period included an increase in urbanization from 68 to 77 per cent and a halving of the proportion of workers with formal documentation, from just under 60 per cent to just over 30 per cent. National mean incomes increased by 22 per cent but much of this 'improvement' was related to rural-to-urban migration and higher wages in urban areas; there was very little change in average urban incomes, just 5 per cent. The authors suggest that apparently stable inequality is explained by the problems faced by the 'very poor' group being avoided by those with slightly higher income levels. Those slightly further up the income ladder (the fifteenth percentile upwards) managed to maintain their incomes through investing in more education (in some cases) and reduced family size. A further factor of significance was that women's participation in the labour market increased significantly between 1976 and 1996, from 29 per cent to 42 per cent, and helped raise household incomes. Hence the population share below a higher poverty line of US$60 a month was more or less stable at 22 per cent between 1976 and 1996. But urban residents from the twelfth percentile downwards lost income as they were faced with declining returns on education and experience and they reduced their participation in urban labour markets.

Dutta (2005) looks at labour market changes in India. She analyses changes in male earnings in both formal (regular) and informal (casual) labour markets between 1983 and 2000, in particular to see if the increase in waged income inequalities observed elsewhere have also taken place in India. (Note that the definition of casual workers used includes those working in agriculture so her conclusions are not specifically urban.) The period covered by the study was one of considerable economic growth – between 6 and 7 per cent each year throughout the 1990s. The author notes that, throughout, average wage levels favoured the regularly employed, with an increasing ratio of regular-to-casual workers' wages of 2.9, 3.1 and 3.3 for 1983, 1993 and 1999 respectively. She argues that:

> there are striking differences in the evolution and structure of wage inequality for the two groups of workers. Wage inequality among regular workers is not only considerably higher than that among casual workers it has also risen between 1983 and 1999, particularly during the 1990s. ... Human capital (as embodied in age and education) is one of the major factors explaining both the level of and change in wage inequality. For casual workers, geographic location plays an important part in determining wage inequality.
>
> (Dutta 2005, page 24)

Broadly, this picture is consistent with increasing stratification and growing inequality among workers, with higher returns going to the most highly trained workers; however, there was also growing inequality within groups with the same level of education. Among regular workers wage inequality grew during the 1990s. This is not true of casual workers, but since many are unskilled and have little education there is less opportunity for differentiation within the group.

Agarwala (2006) highlights the growing importance of the informal sector in India and notes that it was thought to account for over 60 per cent of GDP by the end of the 1990s. In terms of the urban labour force, the informal sector accounts for 82 per cent of all workers of whom just over half (54 per cent) are entrepreneurs or self-employed and the rest are employees. Agarwala undertook 140 interviews with low-income informally employed women working in Mumbai, Kolkata and Chennai. She argues that many of their efforts to improve their lives focus on accessing a range of state benefits rather than pressing for an increase in their daily wages (which are between US$0.25 and US$2), and that this move is strategic. She argues that, though the experience of previous decades was that protection in the workplace and wage increases could be secured, the result has been growing informalization and a reduction in the number of registered industrial disputes, with most workers 'too frightened to risk losing their jobs by making demands on their employer' (Agarwala 2006, page 432). The next subsection examines the significance of state interventions, both direct and indirect, in addressing income inequalities. Before we consider this, a final example discusses South Africa and the slow reduction in income inequalities in a context characterized by democratization and greater globalization.

In South Africa, as noted previously (see Figure 5.1 on page 224), income inequalities are particularly high. Such inequalities are determined primarily by labour market outcomes. In recent years, the South African labour market has been characterized by increasing productivity and this is most evident at the higher end, with a growing demand for skilled workers. Pauw and Mncube (2007) argue that the post-democratization economic model has been one in which the low-income groups have suffered as 'the direct employment effect of liberalization has been biased against low-skilled workers' (page 37). Van der Berg, Louw and Berger (2007) warn against attributing too many of these changes to globalization, however, whatever the cause, these authors also agree that there was a 'decline of the share of employment of unskilled labour in the total from 31 per cent in 1995 to 27 per cent in 2002' (page 9). This has resulted in increasing difficulties for those with low educational attainment who are looking for unskilled work. One further factor is that the non-wage costs of employment have risen since 1994 due to stricter labour market legislation, and this has also encouraged employers to favour the more productive skilled workers as unskilled workers have become relatively more expensive (Pauw and Mncube 2007). Whatever the specific reasons for limited employment opportunities, 5 million individuals entered the labour market between 1995 to 2000 but only 1.6 million found employment (Van der Berg, Louw and Berger 2007). As Van der Berg, Louw and Berger (2007) describe, black Africans are disadvantaged by the increasing demand for skilled workers due to their limited historic access to education:

> blacks joined the ranks of the unemployed in disproportionately large numbers. The cause of this perpetuation of racial inequality in the labour market can be traced to the interaction between the skill-based nature of recent economic growth in South Africa and racial human capital stock: firms increasingly demand employees with high levels of education. Between 1995 and 2003, 64 per cent of individuals with tertiary education found work … and a mere 14 per cent of individuals with incomplete secondary education. … In 2004, white labour force participants had an average of 12.4 years of schooling, compared with a much lower average of 8.6 years for black labour force participants.

(pages 9–10)

While this discussion relates to the formal labour market, in most towns and cities in the Global South the informal sector has an important role in providing work (as discussed in Chapter 4), albeit often poorly remunerated and with difficult working conditions. However, in South Africa the informal sector is unusually small (Van der Berg *et al.* 2005) due to the attempts of the apartheid state to force the black labour force to buy from the corporate sector and maximize the income generated by the white elite. Attempts to catalyse micro-enterprise growth in recent years have struggled in part because a capital-intensive formal sector provides significant competition and existing buying habits remain oriented to the formal sector. While the informal sector may not provide particularly good employment opportunities, in many contexts it does provide a place to gain skills and experience; some income is earned, some mobility may take place and some informal enterprises may prosper and grow. However, this is not the case in South Africa. A further factor to consider, as shown above in the case of micro-enterprises in the Zambian Copperbelt (Copestake 2002), is that entrepreneurship may result in growing income inequalities between different households, with those businesses that were initially better placed gaining most from a micro-lending programme. Hence informal businesses may provide a route for some entrepreneurs to gain upward mobility and improve their incomes; however, the lowest-income traders and producers may not be included in this trajectory.

The contribution of the state

In addition to earnings income, household incomes may include other cash transfers. Some of these transfers are received from government, which also supports households through non-cash benefits such as investments in water networks and the costs of building and operating schools and health care centres. These non-cash benefits can be poverty-reducing – through reducing costs (so more income is available for other goods or services) or helping household enterprise activities – but they do not directly augment household income. There may be a tension between these two methods of support – direct and indirect – relating to their influence on the social relations within low-income communities and between low-income communities and the state. Debates about the most effective strategies for addressing poverty and inequality are not the major focus here, however (such debates are discussed in this book's companion volume). Here, our focus is on elaborating the major sources of inequalities and describing their scale and nature. This subsection and the next consider the net impact of state taxation and transfers (as well as other household revenue-raising strategies) on income inequalities. The unequal impacts of state investments related to basic services and other capital expenditures are considered in the section that follows.

There is relatively little data on the significance of state redistribution in countries in the Global South, and no data is available for the city level. Box 5.2 demonstrates its potential significance using an example from the UK.

Box 5.2 What happens when the state gets involved?

Source: Seager (2006)

Average income of richest 20% is 16 times that of the poorest

Tax and benefit changes in the past few years have reduced income inequality between the richest and poorest people in Britain, but inequality remains high by historical standards, official data showed yesterday. The Office for National Statistics said inequality had narrowed since 2001–02, reversing the rises of the late 1990s, but the fall is not big enough to reverse the huge rise in the late 1980s when Margaret Thatcher was prime minister. The ONS data showed that in 2004–05, the average gross income of the richest 20% of families in Britain, at £66,300, was 16 times that of the poorest 20% who earned £4,300 on average. After adjusting for taxes and benefits, however, this ratio fell sharply to four-to-one. The ONS said cash benefits such as income support, child benefit, incapacity benefit and the state pension play the largest part in reducing income inequality.

Atkinson (1999) considers illustrative data on inequality in the UK, Canada and Finland, concluding that in 'all three countries there have been substantial periods of time when the government has succeeded through fiscal policy in offsetting rising inequality of market incomes' (page 19). In the UK between 1977 and 1984, the Gini coefficient for market incomes rose by 0.06, while inequality in disposable income rose by only 0.01, as fiscal redistribution took place. However, between 1984 and 1991, the redistributive contribution of transfers and benefits (the difference between the Gini coefficients on market incomes and market incomes net of transfers) fell from 0.19 to 0.11. This fall is made up of a smaller impact from cash transfers (by 0.05), less progressive direct taxes (0.01) and more regressive indirect taxes (0.02) (Atkinson 1999). This points to the critical contribution of the state; however, it ignores the scale of state investment in basic services and changes in the scale and allocation of expenditures on basic services such as water, sanitation, drainage, health care and education, which might be income enhancing or simply improve well-being.

The significance of such policies in at least some countries in the Global South is illustrated by Hurtado (2006), who argues that state redistribution policies can have a role in mitigating the worst effects of labour market outcomes. Comparing the experiences of Brazil and Chile, he notes that both countries saw similar falls in the percentage of their population below the poverty line but suggests that this was primarily due in Chile to economic growth (and associated improvements in labour productivity) and in Brazil to income redistribution. South Africa is also a country with a commitment to state redistribution, and the state has a demonstrated capacity to realize these goals. The discussion that follows expands on the nature of state redistribution in South Africa, illustrating some of the issues involved. However, this should not be taken to imply that the South African interventions are typical; it appears that few governments are adopting such policies.

Despite the government's commitment to redistribution, South Africa remains one of the world's most unequal countries, with an estimated Gini coefficient for per capita income of 0.673. Pauw and Mncube (2007) point to the increase in the ratio of the average annual per capita income ratio of the highest income quintile to that the lowest income quintile: in 1995 it was 36 and five years later in 2000 it had increased to 45. This is indicative of the inability of the lowest income group to keep pace with the financial achievements of high-income individuals. Pauw and Mncube analyse a number of studies, reporting ambiguous results in terms of changes to poverty levels but a consensus that inequality has increased. Table 5.4 shows the impact of state transfers and direct taxes on income inequality. 'Poor' here indicates those households in the two lowest household income quintiles. The average net transfer for low-income people has fallen in its absolute value, although it should be noted that Table 5.4 does not include the most recent period and the introduction of a Child Support Grant.

What is evident from Table 5.4 is that inequality is being reduced by the transfers from government. However, the potential impact of state measures is reduced by non-take-up of cash transfers. It has been estimated that perfect take-up would reduce the Gini coefficient of household per capita expenditure from 0.67 to 0.62 (Woolard 2003, cited in Pauw and Mncube 2007).

Van der Berg (2005) argues that poverty in South Africa has fallen since 1999 (see Table 5.5) and that this is largely attributable to social grants. But he also notes that inequality has not fallen because of the continuing importance of wages in determining household income. In analysing the significance of government transfers on redistribution, he highlights some of the difficulties that governments face in shifting allocations in service provision and argues that 'expenditure on social grant was by far the best targeted of all public spending' (page 17). Social grants are heavily targeted at those with low incomes and hence are redistributive:

Table 5.4 Income redistribution in South Africa

	1995		2000		Gini coefficient		
	Poor	Non-poor	Poor	Non-poor	1995	2000	Change
1 Gross per capita income (GCI)	R1,553	R20,853	R1,456	R22,110	0.67	0.72	6.9%
2 GCI after tax	R2,177	R21,412	R1,921	R22,674	0.65	0.70	6.9%
3 Net per capita income (i.e. after taxes)	R2,108	R18,326	R1,896	R21,128	0.64	0.68	6.6%
Percentage change, 1–3	35.7%	−12.1%	30.2%	−4.4%	−5.7%	−5.9%	

Source: Pauw and Mncube (2007), page 32

Table 5.5 Poverty in South Africa, 1993–2004 (poverty line of R3,000 per year per capita, held at 2000 value)

	1993	*2000*	*2004*
Poverty headcount	0.406	0.413	0.332
Poverty gap ratio	0.200	0.205	0.146
Poverty gap squared ratio (severity)	0.126	0.127	0.085
Number of poor (millions)	16.2	18.5	15.4
Number of non-poor (millions)	23.7	26.2	31.0

Source: Van der Berg *et al.* (2005), page 17

'Compared to their overall income before grants of R22.5 billion, the value of social spending of R52.3 billion to the poorest four deciles of households dramatically increased their access to resources' (page 31).

There has been considerable change in the distribution of state expenditures in South Africa. In 1993, black populations received 77. 2 per cent of state transfers and white populations received 7.8 per cent; by 2004, these percentages were 85.1 per cent and 3.6 per cent respectively (Van der Berg *et al.* 2005). Van der Berg *et al.* (2005) argue that much of the increase of R22 billion in the social grant payment expenditure has been allocated to low-income households, amounting annually to more than R1,000 per low-income person and, with a per capita poverty line of R3,000 a year, this scale of redistribution is likely to be significant. The authors suggest that two further factors have been significant in assisting the reduction in poverty: real remuneration has increased for those in work and the income distribution in 2000 included a large number of households clustered on the poverty line that have now been raised above it. Despite this, the authors note that the Gini coefficients show increasing inequality over the period to 2004. In other words, it appears that the government is redistributing income and enabling the poor to keep pace with a labour market which is rewarding those at the top more than those at the bottom, but the redistribution is not sufficient to reduce inequality.

In addition to redistribution through transfer payments, there are numerous other direct state expenditures that relate particularly to the problems associated with urban poverty: 'household surveys show a strong increase in access to housing, electricity, water and sanitation' (Van der Berg *et al.* 2005). Van der Berg (2005) argues that the distribution of state expenditures has shifted, such that the benefits are now more likely to be received by low-income households, or are at least more equally distributed. Between 1995 and 2000, per capita growth on expenditure for health clinics, social grants and housing was 194 per cent, 40 per cent and 206 per cent respectively. However, it should be noted that the 2000 budget for tertiary education (R6.5 billion) remains about twice that of housing (R3 billion) and equals about one third of the expenditure on social grants (R19 billion). In terms of the distribution of these benefits by income group, in 2000 the 40 per cent of the population with the lowest incomes received 60 per cent of the school education expenditure, 14 per cent of the tertiary education expenditure,

78.3 per cent of the social grants expenditure and 47.2 per cent of the housing expenditure. The 20 per cent of highest income earners received 8.8, 38.2, 3.9 and 8.1 per cent of these expenditures, respectively (Van der Berg 2005). According to Van der Berg (2005, page 32), 'in terms of population groups, all groups other than blacks experienced a small decline in per capita social spending.' However, actual access to needed services may remain very unequal. Membership of medical aid (private health insurance) is much more likely for the higher-income groups: in 2003 only 8 per cent of the black African population had medical aid, compared to 65 per cent of the white population.

Neighbourhood realities are considered by De Swardt *et al.* (2005), who report on research in Khayelitsha and the neighbouring settlement of Nyanga in Cape Town. From a random sample of 624 households, 52 per cent reported that they had no income from wages, and 67 per cent of individuals between 18 and 25 reported that they were neither employed nor in further education. Seventy-seven per cent of those households with at least one adult working did not earn enough for their income to exceed the poverty line of R560 per month adult equivalent. Fifty-five per cent of households received at least one cash grant (old age pension, child support, disability), with an average monthly value of R166. Hence the overall picture is one in which government transfers are important in addressing issues of poverty.

Analyses of inequality in South Africa are concerned both with the absolute level of inequality and its racial composition. Changes in the distribution of income across the population take place alongside the mobility experienced by particular households. There is evidence of a degree of de-racialization of the labour market. Van der Berg *et al.* (2005) analyse changes in incomes for two groups, the higher middle class (those with incomes above R40,000 a year) and the lower middle class (or those with incomes between R25,000 and 39,999). The proportion of the black African population within the higher middle group rose from 12.3 per cent in 1994 to 24.7 per cent in 2004, at the same time as the size of this group increased from 8.1 to 10.4 per cent of the total population. The proportion within the lower middle group increased from 21.1 to 33.3 per cent over the same period, while the size of this group increased from 13.5 to 16.5 per cent of the population. In summary, there have been growing employment opportunities for those with skills, including black Africans.

The importance of governments' direct investment in basic services in addressing poverty and inequality in Brazil is highlighted by Velez, de Barros and Ferreira (2004). This report discusses the aggregate situation of state transfers and benefits and concludes that, although public expenditure in Brazil is regressively distributed, it is less so than household income and hence reduces inequality. Of major significance in determining this outcome are pension payments that go to those previously employed in the formal sector, which are more evenly distributed than incomes; pensions, the authors calculate, reduce the Gini coefficient by 1.85 percentage points. However, only 15 per cent of the public pension expenditure is allocated to the lowest 40 per cent of income earners, while 51 per cent is allocated to the highest 20 per cent.[85] Non-pensions public expenditure is allocated more evenly but is still very slightly regressive, with the lowest 40 per cent of income earners enjoying 38 per cent of the total expenditure and the highest 20 per cent of income earners securing 22 per cent of total expenditure. The authors conclude that investments in *favela* upgrading, kindergartens and crèches are among the most progressive of public expenditures (that is, they have the most redistributive impact). A more specific breakdown of five categories of total urban investment expenditure shows that only *favela* upgrading is highly redistributive, with 61 per cent of expenditure being received by the lowest 40 per cent of income earners. Expenditures in the other four categories – water connections, sewer connections, urban public transport and housing – are less progressive with, respectively, 27, 18, 24 and 0 per cent being secured by the lowest 40 per cent of income earners.

However, it might be argued that this analysis and those of state redistribution in South Africa are somewhat hasty. Velez *et al.* (2004) argue that the positive redistributional impact occurs because low-income households benefit from kindergartens, children's services, *favela* upgrading, maternal nutrition, basic education and childcare. Their analysis is that some sectors (tertiary education, pensions, sewer connections and housing) are more regressive while others (public health care, unemployment insurance, water connections, urban public transport, secondary education) are more moderately progressive. However, it appears that these findings are based on expenditure inputs, rather than the ways in which local communities perceive and value the benefits. For example, for two upgrading programmes with similar cash inputs, one may be more participatory, encouraging residents to play a major role. We return to the theme of which state interventions in urban poverty are most effective in this book's companion volume.

More recently, income inequalities in Brazil have fallen significantly, with a national Gini coefficient of 0.59 in 2001 and 0.52 in 2009. Hailu and Soares (2009) suggest that improved access to education together with demographic factors such as falling family size account for a third of the improvement, direct cash transfers to low-income families account for a further third and the remaining third is unexplained, but may be related to the transfer of incomes to low-income households boosting the local economy and hence growing labour demand (unemployment fell 22 per cent between 2004 and 2007).

China is another country in which there has been, relatively speaking, a significant level of research on urban poverty and inequality, partly as a result of concerns about the scale of growth in inequality. Gao (2006) notes that official statistics show the Gini coefficient for income in China rising from 0.33 in 1980 to 0.4 in 1994 and 0.46 in 2000; throughout this period, urban inequality was lower than rural inequality but grew more quickly, narrowing the gap. The importance of waged income in determining inequality is shown by Knight, Shi and Renwei (2004): in 1995 (the most recent date for which figures are available), 77 per cent of household income was wage income.

To understand some of the dynamics behind the aggregate inequality figures, Gao (2006) considers both waged income and social benefits from employers and the state in more depth, with a focus on urban areas. She considers post-transfer income and includes all market income (such as rental income), social benefits (such as child-related transfers and hardship allowance) and private transfers received by households (such as housing and health benefits). Her conclusion is that 'excluding the bottom decile, social benefits were distributed by and large regressively across income groups in 1988 .... [I]n 2002, by contrast, leaving the bottom decile aside, the distribution of social benefits fluctuated ... without a clear pattern' (page 16). Cash transfers, she suggests, may be focused on those with the lowest incomes because of the high proportion of pensioners in the lowest income groups, also the unemployed. In terms of the overall impact, she concludes that:

> [A]lthough social benefit transfers in both years did help to reduce the gap somewhat, post-transfer income inequality levels in 2002 were still higher than in 1988, indicating that the increase in social benefit levels was not sufficient to close the gap caused by increasing market income inequality during the period.
>
> (Gao 2006, page 26)

Indicative figures are available to show the extent to which the lowest income households benefited from different types of state expenditure in China. The average per capita state expenditure in 2002 secured by the 40 per cent of the urban population with the lowest incomes, as a percentage of the average expenditure secured by the 20 per cent with the highest incomes, was 59 per cent in the case of education, 328 per cent in the case of cash transfers, and 56 per cent in the case of housing. The broader picture is that cash transfers are redistributive, other expenditures much less so (Gao 2006).

The effectiveness of tax and transfers in China is indicated by the fact that the Gini coefficient for urban (not national) inequality fell from 0.27 to 0.22 between pre- and post-transfer incomes in 1988 and from 0.38 to 0.33, respectively, in 2002 (Gao 2006). The underlying economic context and its impact on income inequalities is indicated by the fact that the pre-tax and pre-benefit dispersion ratio (the ratio of the income of the top income decile to that of the lowest income decile) was 3.10 in 1988 and rose to 7.37 in 2002, indicating a considerable increase in inequality. Social benefits reduced the ratio to 2.52 and 4.11 in the respective years (Gao 2006).

However, Gao (2006) notes that these data do not include rural migrants to the city – meaning one of the lowest income and most vulnerable groups living in towns and cities was excluded from the analysis. Solinger (2006) also highlights the poverty faced by this migrant population, estimated at over 100 million, noting that it is also not included in official statistics on urban poverty.

In summary, in none of three countries considered above is there a state that redistributes on the scale of governments in Europe. In South Africa, where the lack of an informal sector and smallholder agriculture reinforces the importance of formal urban incomes, increasing waged income inequality has to some extent been offset by the scale of state redistribution. In China, urban inequality is increasing, although on a smaller scale than would have been the case if public transfers did not take place. And in Brazil during the 1990s the most significant transfers reaching the lowest-income households were the investments of the state in social services, although more recently cash transfers have also played a significant role. However, the quality of services is likely to be of critical significance in determining the effectiveness of this spending.

Other transfers

In addition to state transfers, there are a range of other transfers, including remittances from migrants. One of the notable trends in recent years has been increasing remittances in some countries, with migrants making up a significant proportion of the population (see Chapter 4).

'Urban' inequality: The nexus between income, access to infrastructure and services and residential areas

As discussed in Chapter 4, most urban households are dependent on incomes determined by the labour market to secure their basic needs and the labour market is an important source of income inequality. It also influences inequality in living conditions, as land sites, housing and building materials, water, fuel and access to toilets, which may be secured for free or at low cost in rural areas, are all commoditized in most urban contexts and, at least in the cases of land sites, shelter, water and fuel, may only be secured at a considerable cost. Chapter 2 described this in some detail. It also described how accessing education and health care in urban areas may require payments that take up a considerable proportion of household income, especially where low-income urban households are unable to get their children into government schools or access public health care. It is often assumed that urban households have better access than most rural dwellers to services because of much greater physical proximity – but proximity does not mean access. There are many examples of large water mains running through or beside informal settlements which provide no water to the residents. Access to water and sanitation and other basic services depends on the nature of investment in particular residential locations.

For those living in peri-urban areas or some distance from the centre of a large city, or in other areas where income-earning opportunities are concentrated, transport costs may add considerably to the cost of living. Because urban incomes and expenditures are more monetized, they are likely to be more affected by government tax regimes. For example, formal employment is more likely to be taxed than informal employment, and informal enterprises operating in central locations may have to pay for trading licences (or make informal payments to police or local groups). For urban populations, fewer essential goods are obtained by direct production or informal exchange and some goods may be taxed at the point of sale. In some cases, the revenue extracted by the state through taxation may be balanced by improved access to state benefits, transfer payments and subsidized goods and services.

This section considers inequalities in access to essential urban goods and services linked to urban 'space', particularly local neighbourhoods. Examples are provided which illustrate what might be termed 'spatial inequalities' – differentials in health status, housing quality or provision for infrastructure and services between different neighbourhoods, districts or municipalities within a city or metropolitan area. The section describes the ways in which governments structure urban space, hence how they affect spatial inequalities, and discusses the reasons why spatial inequalities occur.

The structuring of urban space

While the provision of basic needs and associated services is more likely to be commoditized in urban areas, access to and exclusion from such services is likely to be associated with particular residential locations. Urban residential areas are usually highly stratified with regard to housing price and quality, tenure security and access to water, sanitation and waste management services, as well as quality of public transport and proximity to health clinics and schools. Different kinds of markets for these services prevail in different areas.

In the past, governments have restricted access to urban areas; one of the more extreme examples is South Africa during the apartheid era, when very significant numbers of citizens were denied access to urban areas, hence livelihood opportunities and a range of services and facilities, because of racial and ethnic differences. Comparable exclusionary political regimes were imposed by colonial powers in other African nations. However, today, controls are more likely to operate through the market and the cost of access to particular residential areas, with different levels of infrastructure and services. Despite this emphasis on the market as a means of allocation, the nature of urban space remains dependent on the state. Governments have a major influence on the physical components of spatial inequalities through the differential scale of infrastructure investment in particular neighbourhoods. Even with the last 20 years of pressure from international agencies for privatization, less than 10 per cent of the world's population is provided with drinking water through private operators (OECD 2003). In most contexts governments remain responsible for the management of such infrastructure, deciding the overall scale of investment, and the distribution of investments between different spatial areas and between solutions of varying complexity and cost. If provision is privatized, governments still influence the quality and extent of provision through contracts or other forms of agreement.

This potential for investment draws attention to the positive role of the state; inequalities in access to piped water, sanitation and drainage, for instance, can be reduced or removed by provision to all neighbourhoods. This highlights the redistributional impact of infrastructure investment compared to other forms of state expenditure, such as pensions linked to formal employment.

This role is complex. In addition to investing in infrastructure, governments also set the rules by which residential occupation takes place. Planning codes (including regulations on minimum plot sizes and infrastructure standards) and building standards influence the cost and hence affordability of legal urban residency. The creation of different kinds of areas through the imposition of different density standards takes place in urban centres across the world. In Southern Africa, for example, neighbourhoods are commonly talked about as being 'low density' (synonymous with high incomes) or 'high density' (synonymous with low incomes). The particular rules for different areas, their distribution and their service provision structure urban space. Here we use the term 'distribution' to refer both to the proportions of areas with different rules and to the physical location of such areas. There is nothing inherently fixed about the nature of this distribution or the particular regulations governing occupation, but their implications for structuring urban space and populations are profound. For example, Windhoek in Namibia is divided into a number of distinct areas, with low-income housing in the north-west of the city and high-income settlements just to the east of the central area. In 2001, the city authorities introduced a new development and upgrading strategy with a number of 'development levels'. This policy enables residents to settle legally in groups on land for which they have collective tenure with communal services such as a single water point and toilet block. Over time, families are able to upgrade access by extending services to their individual plots, which are created when they sub divide the land. The use of a single collective title enables them to have smaller, cheaper plots than is permitted by the regulations governing individual stands. With this policy, the cost of legal tenure has been significantly reduced (Mitlin and Muller 2004). However, the plots associated with these lower-cost development levels are being made available in only Katatura, the traditional location for the black African population.

Regulations are also used to remove urban residents from areas they have long occupied when more powerful groups decide that they are no longer able to stay. The mass evictions that took place in Zimbabwe in 2005, Operation Murambatsvina, were justified by the government as allowing removal, it was claimed, of only those buildings that were illegal and in contravention of regulations. Many evictions are justified based on the 'illegality' of structures (see, for instance, Bhan 2009).

In addition to the government, the market is also usually an active agent in creating spatial divisions, structuring investment in such a way as to produce large differences between higher- and lower-income residences, and these differences may extend to neighbourhoods or to whole settlements. It may be argued that such differentiations occur as the market responds to consumer choice and demand, but in practice the issues may be more complex, with commercial interests responding to a spatial planning framework that itself reflects public sector investment priorities.

The creation of urban spatial inequality through public policy is highlighted for the case of China by Liu and Wu (2006). They document the shift from a planned to a more market-oriented economy and the associated growth of spatial differentiation processes. They argue that, within the previous socialist, planned economy, residency was largely determined by the location of workplace and the practice of providing workplace housing to employees at a subsidized rate. The authors suggest that, although this resulted in the creation of some concentrations of wealth and poverty related to occupation and, by association, social status (for example, intellectuals who lived close to universities), it also produced relatively large numbers of mixed-income neighbourhoods. However, the withdrawal of housing subsidies together with increased levels of income inequality in urban China has resulted in increasing differentiation between neighbourhoods. The authors study the implications for settlement status and the quality of housing in three low-income neighbourhoods in Nanjing, a relatively prosperous city on the Yangtse River. One feature of this particular city is an inflow of migrants in search of job opportunities; by 2002, this group accounted for 17 per cent of the urban population. Liu and Wu (2006, page 624) conclude that both state and market have contributed to the creation of some neglected areas:

> In sum, the existence of three typical neighbourhoods of poverty concentration indicates that the spatial distribution of urban poverty is not just dependent upon market-based real estate development. All of these poverty neighbour-hoods are de facto the derelicts of the state-led urban redevelopment and urban sprawl.

Most notable is the concentration of low incomes; the three settlements studied, Pingshijie, Wubaicun and Xiyingcun, have, respectively, 70, 65 and 82 per cent of households with incomes below 1,000 yuan (US$120) a month. While not directly comparable, the high concentration of families with low incomes is shown by the fact that, across the city of Nanjing, only 1.6 per cent of residents have a monthly per capita income below 220 yuan (US$26; the government minimum living standard). The neighbourhoods studied are characterized by overcrowding (Pingshijie has only 6 square metres per capita) and a very poor quality of construction and services (Liu and Wu 2006).

The occupation of 'informal settlements' and informal housing

Chapter 2 gave many examples of the high proportion of the population in many cities living in informal settlements, while Chapter 3 provided many examples of the inadequacies in infrastructure and service provision and of the much higher levels of premature mortality and morbidity in these settlements. Comparisons between formal and informal housing show inequalities in the quality and size of housing, the extent and quality of infrastructure and service provision, health outcomes and the extent of protection from forced eviction. As described in Chapter 3, many informal settlements are also on land sites at high risk from extreme weather and other disasters. Of course, there are often considerable differences among informal settlements in any city, and effective upgrading programmes in some cities have improved conditions in some settlements, and may indeed have changed their status from informal to formal.

In addition to informal land occupation, informal occupation of formal settlements also takes place. This may take the form of construction of shacks, additional buildings in the grounds of formal areas or extensions to existing buildings (which may or may not contravene building regulations). Or it may involve increased numbers occupying existing housing (including housing counted as part of the formal stock) and so increased overcrowding. In South Africa, it has become evident that the efforts of the state to restrict development of informal settlements has resulted in a shift from illegal land occupation to occupation of illegal structures within existing, mostly legal plots. Between 1996 and 2007, the total number of households residing in informal dwellings grew by 24.4 per cent, from 1.45 million to 1.80 million. Within this, the number of households living in backyard informal dwellings rose by 46 per cent, from 403,000 to 590,000; by comparison, the number of households staying in freestanding informal settlements grew 16 per cent, from just over 1 million to 1.2 million (South African Institute of Race Relations 2009). Numbers of backyard informal structures in formal settlements grew as a proportion of total informal dwellings by 18 per cent, while numbers built in informal settlements declined by 7 per cent. In effect, there has been a shift away from households living in informal settlements towards the renting of shacks within formal areas, including settlements constructed with state-subsidized finance.

In most cities, the effects of state and market combine with shelter needs to result in a range of low-income settlements housing a significant proportion of the population on a small fraction of the city's land area. In Nairobi, for example, half the population live in informal settlements, estimated in 1995 to cover only 4 per cent of the land area (Alder 1995). In Mumbai, around half the population live in informal or illegal settlements representing only few per cent of the city's total area.[86] Perhaps in cities with governments more tolerant of informal settlements these are less constrained: a paper on informal settlements in Xalapa, Mexico reports that informal settlements cover nearly half the city land area (Benítez *et al.* 2012).

The spatial structuring of inequality in housing conditions in terms of plot sizes and quality of infrastructure was characteristic of colonial urban planning in Asia and Africa. King (1976) describes developments related to colonial rule when the city of Delhi was developed as the capital of India. He reports densities in 1931 of 50,000 people per square mile in the old city and suburbs, 1,800 per square mile in the area of the Civil Station and land allocated through three durbars (the nineteenth-century colonial settlement), 2,000 per square mile in the twentieth-century colonial urban settlement of New Delhi and 500 per square mile in the cantonment (military camp). Also described by King is the way in which the colonial government allocated space based on status and a rigid hierarchy linked to employment, which determined both the amount of land allocated and the funds available for construction.

Whatever the source of differential investment and the risks associated with individual settlements, residential densities in terms of number of persons per room and housing space per person are generally higher in central city locations, reflecting the greater value attached by the market to land. It is common for three- to five-person households to live in a small single room and it can mean that indoor space can be as little as 1 square metre per person.[87] Even formal, legal housing in cities such as Mumbai can provide as little as 25 to 30 square metres of space and house five or more persons. There are obviously numerous consequences for poverty and inequality arising from these high densities.

Inequalities and inequities in access to basic infrastructure and services

Chapter 3 gave many examples of the inadequacies in provision for infrastructure and services among low-income populations. But, in general, differential needs for essential services – relating to population density, for instance – are rarely measured. There are large differences in the needs of settlements with regard to the quality of provision for water and sanitation, related to population density and size. For instance, a public standpipe within a few metres of the dwellings of the five households it serves is not the same as a standpipe serving 200 or more households, which will be far further away for most and mean long queues (although both standpipes would be counted as 'improved' provision in UN statistics). Similarly, a pit latrine in a low-density setting – well-constructed, serving only one household, located so as to avoid contaminating water sources and with access for regular emptying – can provide good quality sanitation, but this is not the case in high-density settings, where space is limited and the number of users is much higher. It is surprising that provision for water and sanitation is still measured and monitored using the same criteria for rural and urban areas.

In countries where there has been progress in improving provision for water and sanitation, it would be revealing to see which income groups have benefited most. A study of three nations (WHO and UNICEF 2011) showed that in India and Nepal the least wealthy quintiles benefited little or not at all, while in Bangladesh the least wealthy did benefit. The data were not broken down for urban and rural households, however.

Of particular interest is the overlap between different forms of inequality. Tables 5.6 and 5.7 illustrate the ways in which low incomes are associated with poor access to basic services and infrastructure in two Central American cities. The data, from a World Bank study, demonstrate the scale of these interrelationships.

Table 5.6 highlights the almost perfectly consistent correspondence between access to improved housing and basic services in San Salvador and income quintiles, with low-income households more likely to be disadvantaged than higher-income households. In terms of access to water services, most higher-income households (73 per cent) acquired access through a developer which provided the connection prior to the purchase of the plot. Low-income groups had to lobby within the political system and communal action was the major route of access for the lowest income quintile, helping 60 per cent of families (World Bank

Table 5.6 Housing in San Salvador metropolitan area, 2000

	Quintiles*					
Households' housing and services	*Q1*	*Q2*	*Q3*	*Q4*	*Q5*	*Overall*
No vehicle access (%)	73	58	37	30	17	43
In non-asphalt street (%)	22	13	4	4	0	9
Showering in backyard or outside property (%)	31	18	8	6	2	13
Sharing shower with neighbours (%)	6	2	2	1	0	2
Sharing bathroom with neighbours (%)	7	4	2	3	1	3
With access to piped water network (%)	82	89	95	96	97	92
Using standpipes (%)	10	4	1	1	0	3
Waiting more than five years for water connection (%)	30	29	25	16	8	21
Using sanitary facility connected to public sewer (%)	73	83	89	96	98	88
Persons per bedroom	4	3	2	2	1	2
Amount paid for installation of water connection (US$)	72	86	46	34	29	53
Acquisition cost for connection to public sewer (ANDA** only, US$)	69	51	15	11	11	32

* Q1 is the lowest income quintile, Q5 the highest
** The national water and sanitation agency

Source: Data from World Bank Central America (2002)

Central America 2002). Water consumption is broadly similar for all income quintiles and the tariff is also broadly similar, hence low-income households have to spend a much higher proportion of their incomes on water. A programme supported by UNICEF and the government of Luxembourg has assisted low-income households in San Salvador to gain access to the piped water network. Between 1996 and 2001, over 20,000 households in 125 communities were connected. Communities provided labour to reduce the costs, but despite this, the study argues, the connection fees do not recover the investment costs. Table 5.6 shows that low-income households pay more for connection to the public sewer. This cost differential is explained by a lack of sanitation when many low-income households first move into their properties; this is not the case for higher-income households, who benefit from historic investment.

Moreover, the report provides further evidence that the locations in which low-income households find accommodation are particularly disadvantaged. Comparing the lowest and highest income quintiles, it finds that all income groups are similarly affected by flooding, with an overall average of 10 per cent of residents affected and very little difference between income groups. However, low-income residents were more likely to be affected by landslides, with an incidence of 18 per cent of households affected in the lowest income quintile compared to 5 per cent in the highest income quintile (World Bank Central America 2002). But the inequalities in the infrastructure in San Salvador are actually much smaller than in most cities in low-income nations, for instance only 10 per cent of households in the lowest income quintile use standpipes, 82 per cent have access to the piped water network and 73 per cent have toilets connected to public sewers. Comparing figures from a study of urban areas in Zambia, only 15 per cent of the lowest income quintile there have their own tap, for example, compared to 59 per cent of the highest income quintile; for use of unprotected water sources, the proportions are 32 per cent and 8 per cent, respectively; for access to a flush toilet, 17 and 61 per cent. The study's authors note particular problems with high densities and a lack of space for pit latrines in the older urban settlements (World Bank Zambia 2007).

World Bank Central America (2002) includes a review of the situation in Tegucigalpa, Honduras, where there are larger differentials in access to basic services. A notable characteristic emphasizing the differences in quality of accommodation is the percentage having to shower in a backyard or outside of their property: 80 per cent for the poorest quintile, zero per cent for the wealthiest. Similarly, the average paid by households in the lowest income quintile to have a toilet connected to the public sewer was roughly six times the amount paid by households in the highest income quintile. As in San Salvador, a special programme has sought to assist the lowest income households to gain access to water and sanitation. Under this scheme, water is brought to community holding tanks several times a week. However, 'the program is far from perfect. Households served through the program pay a higher rate for water and receive less than those connected to the aqueduct although they represent a lower income population' (World Bank Central America 2002, page 47).

Table 5.7 Housing and infrastructure in Tegucigalpa, Honduras, 2000

| Households | *Quintiles** | | | | | |
	Q1	*Q2*	*Q3*	*Q4*	*Q5*	*Overall*
No vehicle access (%)	35	36	42	32	29	35
In non-asphalt street (%)	87	65	36	14	5	41
Showering in backyard or outside property (%)	80	50	21	6	0	31
Sharing shower with neighbours (%)	6	2	2	1	0	2
Sharing bathroom with neighbours (%)	8	4	1	0	0	3
With access to piped water network (%)	62	81	95	98	98	87
Using standpipes (%)	3	1	0	0	0	1
Waiting more than five years for water connection (%)	22	20	11	12	7	14
Using sanitary facility connected to public sewer (%)	37	66	90	98	99	78
Persons per bedroom	4	3	2	2	1	2
Amount paid for installation of water connection (SANAA,** lempiras)	363	313	98	131	26	165
Acquisition cost for connection to public sewer (SANAA,** lempiras)	1,404	1,244	978	987	229	1,102

* Q1 is the lowest income quintile, Q5 the highest
** The national water and sanitation agency

Source: Data from World Bank Central America (2002)

Table 5.8 shows differentials in access to water and sanitation within the city of Bangalore, India in 2000. Again, differentials are shown in relation to social inequality, although in this instance social inequality is represented by an assets index rather than by income.

The table shows that, for almost all the indicators, the more wealthy the socio-economic category, the higher the proportion of households with good quality provision for water, sanitation and solid waste collection. So, for example, 60 per cent in the wealthiest category had individual connections to the official water network, declining to 19 per cent for the least wealthy. Similarly, 96 per cent in the wealthiest category had a toilet at home, declining across the other categories to 32 per cent in the least wealthy category. Also, defecation in the open was recorded only for the two least wealthy categories and public toilet use only for the three least wealthy categories, with the figures being highest for the least wealthy category (see Figure 5.2). Other studies for Bangalore highlight just how poor provision for water, sanitation and solid waste collection is in informal settlements or 'slums' (see, for instance, Benjamin 2000; Achar, Bhaskara Rao and de Bruijne 2001; Schenk 2001).

Table 5.8 Water and sanitation in Bangalore, 2000

	Population within Bangalore Municipal Corporation by socio-economic category (%)*						
Characteristics	*Overall*	*SEC-A*	*SEC-B*	*SEC-C*	*SEC-D*	*SEC-E*	*'Slums'*
Proportion of all households	100	16	20	27	20	17	17
Individual connection to official water network	36	60	45	35	23	19	25
Shared connection to official water network	36	32	40	40	36	30	29
Any public water supply	29	5	14	27	45	55	61
Toilet at home	66	96	85	69	50	32	34
Shared toilet outside home	28	4	14	28	43	52	44
Public toilet	4	—	—	3	6	12	19
Defecate in open	1	—	—	—	1	5	5
Tap in toilet	47	73	58	39	23	14	9
Carry water to toilet	45	14	32	56	71	81	86
Drainage connection to municipal sewers	81	91	89	83	73	70	75
Household collection of solid wastes	34	45	45	35	25	20	12

* SEC-A is the wealthiest socio-economic category, SEC-E the poorest; 'Slums' is a separate category comprising households from each income group living in dwellings designated as being in slums

Source: Sinclair Knight Merz *et al.* (2002)

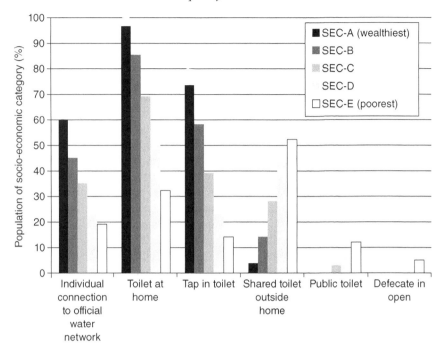

Figure 5.2 Provision for toilets by socio-economic group in Bangalore, 2000

Source: Data from Sinclair Knight Merz *et al.* (2002)

Another set of statistics on inequities in access to infrastructure and services in India comes from a comparison of provision for the poorest quartile with that for the rest of the population in selected states and some cities (Agarwal 2011). These have already been discussed in relation to asset inequality earlier in this chapter and in relation to health outcomes associated with poverty in Chapter 3. What the author's analysis highlights is that the lowest income quartiles generally have much poorer provision in their homes for water and sanitation, and worse health outcomes.

Understanding inequalities in basic infrastructure and services

Examples of differential access to basic infrastructure and services are commonplace across cities in low- and middle-income countries, although there are large differences in the proportions of their populations with very poor provision. Those unable to afford to rent, buy or build formal housing find themselves renting, buying or building in neighbourhoods with inadequacies in access to basic infrastructure and services. In each locality there is a complex mix of reasons that defines or influences the scale and scope of these inadequacies. While some argue that it is lack of capacity to pay which ensures low-income households are less well served than higher-income households, the installation of piped networks reflects choices made by public bodies about whether investment will take place. In

Guayaquil, Ecuador, where in the early 1990s 40 per cent of the population consumed only 3 per cent of the water, Swyngedouw (2004) finds that there is no scarcity of water, rather the problem is one of unfair distribution. The situation worsened over the period 1974 to 1990, with the rate of coverage of the piped network falling by 9 per cent, and by 1990 only 45 per cent of households had piped water with indoor plumbing, leaving almost 600,000 dependent on water vendors. Swyngedouw suggests that the occupation of land without infrastructure by migrants from rural areas was encouraged by a combination of interests, including those seeking to benefit from land speculation and those seeking to establish clientelistic relations with the incoming populations. While the land was low cost because of the lack of services, 'what was saved on land rent [was] spent many times over on the purchase of water' (Swyngedouw 2004, page 70).

Swyngedouw elaborates on the nature and extent of exclusion of low-income populations from piped water, referring back to the historical development of the city. In the second half of the nineteenth century, cocoa production became established in the coastal zone of Ecuador and wage labour in cocoa plantations replaced peasant subsistence agriculture. Guayaquil became a central point for the export of cocoa, with a range of economic activities and a growing population. The ruling political elite in the city sought, among other things, to invest in a water and sanitation network. While in the early decades of the twentieth century the network expanded, from the second decade the increase in population, with continuing opportunities for income earning through vending, outstripped the growth of the network. Whatever the intentions of the state, the collapse of cocoa farming resulted in a lack of municipal investment capacity. Large numbers of plantation workers came to the city in search of work and landowners sought to make money through rental accommodation as their earnings from cocoa fell sharply. Between 1928 and 1939, there was no increase in the quantity of water supplied through the piped network, but the number of urban residents almost doubled. The municipality controlled the water supply and the price was significantly below cost, offering the higher-income households on the network a subsidy and preventing the expansion of the system. Although Ecuador's economic fortunes improved with the introduction and expansion of banana production and further investment in the water network took place, the areas in which the network expanded became sites for middle- and high-income neighbourhoods. As the nature of agricultural development excluded low-income rural residents and encouraged migration, population growth in Guayaquil again resulted in low-income urban neighbourhoods without piped water:

By 1974, 63 per cent of the total population of 823,000 inhabitants and 71 per cent of the urban area had to be supplied by tankers or community taps. The now endemic exclusionary water practices laid the foundations for a thriving private water economy monopolized by water vendors whose exclusive control over the distribution of a key element of nature in the non-serviced urban areas enabled the appropriation of considerable water rents.

(Swyngedouw 2004, pages 108–9)

A study in Nairobi also elaborates on the processes through which low-income households are disadvantaged due to their unequal access to positions of political influence. Gulyani and Talukdar (2008) examine a stratified sample of 1,755 households from 88 of the identified 1,263 informal settlements in the city. They find that 92 per cent of these households are rent-paying tenants, 6 per cent own land and housing and 2 per cent own their own dwelling but not land. Conditions are extremely poor: only 12 per cent of units have permanent external walls and an average of 2.6 persons occupy each room. Eighty-one per cent of the sample have no access to piped water, only a quarter have access to a private toilet and 87 per cent have no access to public sewer or soak pit, instead using an informal connection to a public sewer or a pit latrine. Solid waste disposal systems barely exist. The authors argue that rents are high relative both to the incomes of low-income households and to the capital investment in housing – on average, rents are US$11 a month and account for 12 per cent of income – and they conclude that 'the market does not offer cheaper, or more affordable units' (Gulyani and Talukdar 2008, page 1925). They estimate that for investment in a single room the payback period from rental income is 20 months.

However, this situation (and that described for other informal settlements in Nairobi in Chapter 3) is far from accidental. The high returns from being a landlord are indicative of significant barriers to market access, barriers which include the role of political connections in accessing land and the payment of illegal fees which enable landlords to build. In Nairobi during the 1980s, land was allocated to a range of powerful individuals by the government. These individuals use agents to manage their properties within informal settlements, renting either land or, more frequently, an already constructed shack to households in need of accommodation (see Amis 1984). Syagga *et al.* (2002, cited in Gulyani and Talukdar 2008) found that, of 120 landlords, 41 per cent were government officials and 16 per cent were politicians; these and other landlords were very likely to be absentee landlords, with little interest in upgrading their properties. A further disincentive to improving the appalling infrastructure is that landlords provide services, for example water kiosks, yard taps, in-house connections and toilets, and 'all of these are known to be good businesses' (Gulyani and Talukdar 2008, page 1931). In other words, the politically well-connected landlords have an interest in ensuring a continuing lack of infrastructure investment. Gulyani and Talukdar (2008, page 1931) conclude:

> Together these factors have created severe disincentives for action and investment for all three of the key stakeholders in Nairobi's slums – landlords, tenants and government .... [I]n Nairobi, the problem is that the *tenure mix* is highly unusual with too many tenants and too few owner-occupiers and resident landlords.

A third example illustrates similar exploitative processes. In Karachi, one reason for deficiencies in piped water provision is the large sums of money made by those who own and operate water tankers and the municipal officials that benefit from providing tankers with access to municipal supplies (Rahman 2008). In many low-income settlements, households buy from donkey cart suppliers and unofficial tanker providers, often at considerable cost. In 2007, some 665 million gallons of water per day (MGD) were potentially available for domestic consumption in the city but only 293 MGD reached residential areas. Several low-income districts received only 30–57 per cent of their intended quota. With Karachi's population at 16 million and an assumed minimum requirement of 20 gallons per person per day, a total of 320 MGD is required by domestic consumers, with another 123 MGD for industries and 110 MGD for other uses. These figures suggest that supply should be sufficient for all. The amount supplied through nine official hydrants was 25 MGD, double their official allocation, and the prices charged were in excess of the official rates (Rahman 2008). In addition there are 161 unofficial hydrants, and a survey of nine of these showed that they were being used to supply 20 MGD; hence a considerable amount of water was being sold through unofficial hydrants. An estimated 185–222 MGD was distributed by tanker (supplied by these and other hydrants), with 70 per cent of this going to industries. Rahman (2008) concludes that the shortfall in bulk supply of about 300 MGD is supplied by tanker with a total annual income of Rs49.6 billion. The result of illegal siphoning is that many consumers cannot access piped supplies and pay more than necessary, and the Karachi Water and Sewerage Board are denied the trade that they require to cover costs and reinvest. If all water was supplied through the piped system, sufficient water could be provided for a household at a cost of about Rs200 a month, approximately one third of the present cost (Rahman 2008).

What is evident in Guayaquil, Nairobi and Karachi is that inequalities in access to infrastructure reflect inequalities in both income and political power. While housing markets, and in particular lack of affordability, may be put forward as explanations for poor access to infrastructure in low-income settlements, these case studies highlight that infrastructure investments are essentially political decisions (rather than market transactions) and that the interests of political elites are primarily responsible for the lack of access to essential services such as piped water and sanitation. Not discussed here but also important in terms of the interrelationship of public investments, housing inequalities and private gains are political choices made in relation to transport services. The final section in this chapter considers the role of political inequalities in urban poverty.

Social status and residency

Residence in low-income areas may itself be a determinant of low social status, and result in further disadvantage. As suggested previously, there is some evidence that residency in low-income settlements is itself a categorization which is associated with other forms of social discrimination, in addition to inadequate access to basic services. For example, Perlman (2007) reports on the differences in pay between *favela* residents and non-*favela* residents, with the former being paid only 40 per cent of the income of the latter for an identical investment in education of 16 years' schooling. In her longitudinal study, she argues that the residents in the community she originally studied are doing better than newer residents to the city, that is, they have been more socially mobile. However, she also reports that residents perceive themselves as facing continuing discrimination, in part due to skin colour but also because 'simply living in a *favela* may be equally stigmatizing, and many people told of being afraid to give correct addresses on job interviews, knowing that eyebrows would be raised and the interview terminated if this were known' (Perlman 2004, page 135). In addition, she concludes that those *favela* residents who were moved (in some cases forcibly) to formal accommodation in the early 1970s have done better than those who remain in the *favelas* because they have had improved access to jobs and education (Perlman 2010).

Perlman's research highlights some of the adverse consequences for social status of living in low-income settlements. In so doing, it draws attention to the spatial dimensions of inequality. Residents in informal settlements have fewer opportunities, and these difficulties are compounded because of social relations that associate physical differences between geographic areas with differences in social status. Perlman (2010) seeks to measure the level of adversity faced by constructing an index of socio-economic status and comparing households according to their residency. She documents the distinct disadvantage of those remaining in informal settlements. Similar findings emerge elsewhere, for example Marx and Charlton (2003), in their study of housing conditions in Durban in 2003, explain that 'In discussions with residents of informal settlements, each of them referred to the fact that they felt that friends and relatives from formal areas look down on those who live in informal areas' (page 8).

One of the difficulties faced by those living in informal settlements is a representation of these neighbourhoods as 'dirty'. There is a particularly striking relationship between ideas of cleanliness and social stratification; put another way, powerful associations are made by external observers between dirt, poverty and moral delinquency. At the global level, a report by the Centre on Housing Rights and Evictions (COHRE 2006) identifies examples of evictions justified by governments on the grounds of settlements failing to meet health and safety standards. Some of these evictions were specifically linked to allegations of criminal activities taking place in informal settlements. Others were not associated with criminal acts, but simply with the presence of low-income informal development. Bhan (2009) offers an example of the kinds of discourse and opinions that lie behind these views. He discusses the increased incidence of eviction in Delhi in the last 15 years, and quotes high court judgements which argue that the displacement of low-income settlements is necessary if the city is not to be 'allowed to degenerate and decay' (page 128). Bhan adds that the court argued that 'cleaning up the city' (page 135) was a priority, meaning that evictions should be allowed. He describes how those living in informal settlements were portrayed as encroachers or trespassers and so unworthy of legal protection or of any state help in resettlement.

The association between low-income informal settlements, a lack of cleanliness and moral inadequacy forms part of a longstanding discourse which for those living in informal settlements leads to adverse spatial and social stratification. The scale of social discrimination against the residents of low-income settlements, rationalized in part as being due to lack of cleanliness, forms a context in which any discourse involving such associations disadvantages low-income residents. This is particularly the case for women, due to their gendered responsibilities for the household. Songsore and McGranahan (1998, page 410) note that 'During Accra's colonial period, for example, there were times when the work of the lower courts was dominated by cases of women accused of sanitary offenses.' Obrist (2004) updates and extends an analysis of the consequences for women of the public campaign for hygiene in a recent study of women living in a lower-middle income neighbourhood in Dar es Salaam. Although the interviewees emphasize the importance of cleanliness, they explain that it is difficult to achieve because of lack of water, related both to the uncertain supply and the cost of water purchased through informal venders. Obrist illustrates the contradictions that the women have to live with:

> While we chatted with Anna, her daughter Mariamu passed and went to the toilet with bare feet. Anna says, she feels ashamed seeing her children walking barefoot, especially entering places like the toilet. She simply cannot afford shoes for them. Sometimes she instructs them to wash their hands after going to the toilet, but when she remembers that they do not even wear shoes, she just keeps quiet 'because what they get via their feet is much worse than what they get from not washing their hands.'
>
> (Obrist 2004, page 52)

Obrist argues that such situations, combined with understanding of the importance of hygiene for good health, mean that

> women who are committed to health development carry not only a practical and intellectual but also an emotional burden. To them it really matters whether they can put key elements of these discourses into daily practice, and they feel distressed, if they do not manage to do so.
>
> (Obrist 2004, page 53)

In part such distress is caused by social attitudes which emphasize the importance of cleanliness and which implicitly – and sometimes explicitly – judge low-income women (in particular) for failing to maintain such conditions. Nations and Monte (1996) describe a particularly extreme example of criticism in their discussion of cholera and cholera prevention in Fortaleza, in the north-east of Brazil. They argue that (as also illustrated for the case of Delhi in Bhan [2009]) there is a well-established discourse in Latin America which blames low-income and disadvantaged citizens for their own problems. One of the communities studied by Nations and Monte is in an insecure settlement with a history of multiple evictions, no sanitary facilities and serious health problems; the other is a resettlement area with poor quality housing and toilet facilities limited to pit latrines on only some of the plots. The authors argue that so-called patient 'non-compliance' – mocking cholera prevention messages, lashing out at medical authorities, threatening powerful politicians, shunning doctors' advice, spitting-up medication, and resisting hospital rehydration, etc. – is popular resistance against, not so much cholera care, but social practices of defamation and discrimination.

(Nations and Monte 1996, page 1010)

The labelling or classification of a settlement as a 'slum' is also a way of stigmatizing those who live there. Call or classify a settlement as a slum and this suggests that it needs replacing and helps legitimate its clearance by the eviction of its inhabitants. There are also examples of informal settlements being given derogatory names, for instance the informal settlement of Old Fadama or Agbogbloshie in Accra is often referred to by outsiders as 'Sodom and Gomorrah' and is judged to be a centre for criminal activities. Informal settlements in Cairo are termed *ashwa'iyyat* and this is often understood as a derogatory term. Bayat and Denis (2000) note that some see these as 'unnatural' communities which trigger 'social disease' and 'abnormal behaviour' such as lack of privacy, overcrowding and violence: 'The informal cities are perceived by many in Egypt as representing a Hobbesian locus of lawlessness and extremism, producing a "culture of violence" and an "abnormal" way of life' (page 185). Many of these informal settlements have multi-storey buildings and the residents include middle-class professionals. As a counterpoint to this, some informal settlements are given names that either reflect their aspirations or are comments on what they are not: Paradise, Where Angels Tread, Garden Flower of Spring …

In addition, the term 'slum' is often used as a general term for a range of different kinds of housing or settlements, including those that serve low-income groups well; in any city, there are a range of different housing sub-markets through which those with limited incomes buy, rent or build their homes (see Hardoy and Satterthwaite 1989; *Environment and Urbanization* 1989). However, it is difficult to avoid the term 'slum' for at least two reasons. The first is that some urban poor groups have organized themselves as 'slum'-dweller organizations or federations, including one of the most successful and innovative of these, the National Slum Dwellers Federation in India. In India there are also advantages for residents of an informal settlement in their settlement being recognized officially as a 'slum' and becoming a 'notified slum'; indeed, residents may even lobby to gain this official classification. Second, the only global estimates for deficiencies in housing collected by the United Nations are for 'slums'. Where the term is used, it means an urban settlement characterized by at least some of the following features: a lack of formal recognition on the part of local government of the settlement and its residents; the absence of secure tenure for residents; inadequacies in provision for infrastructure and services; overcrowded and substandard dwellings; and location on land less than suitable for occupation (UN-HABITAT 2003b).

The social associations between location and status may also be used to attribute positive values to high-income settlements, reflecting a perceived need to protect their residents from the rest of the city. This is not new; there is even a neighbourhood in Brazil called Higienópolis ('city of hygiene'), built initially in the 1920s when 'modern' cities were seen as addressing key public health issues. Arguably, the growth of gated communities reflects in part the extent to which higher-income groups have lost their ability to contain low-income residents within specific 'poor' parts of the city, and their felt need to formalize protection of their own neighbourhoods, as a response. Gated communities are often promoted for their healthiness and standard of public order. Once more, social discourse appears to draw on negative associations that go beyond income levels to reflect ideas of cleanliness and moral virtue to legitimate such exclusionary practices.[88] As discussed by Pow (2007) in his study of gated communities in Shanghai, one issue is how to prevent lower-status social groups gaining access:

> a strong moral order prevails in Shanghai's gated communities where an air of tranquillity, harmony and civility seems to pervade social life behind the gates. Such a wholesome environment and social atmosphere are not to be taken-for-granted and are the results of the concerted efforts by residents and estate management companies to construct a civilised moral enclave that keeps at bay 'undesirable outsiders' from trespassing in the neighbourhood and 'polluting' its pristine environment. In trying to maintain the wholesomeness of their living environment, residents often draw upon moralising discourses to construct moral geographies of exclusion/inclusion that shape and structure territoriality and social life in gated communities.
>
> (Pow 2007, page 1544)

This subsection has not attempted to provide a comprehensive analysis of the kinds of social processes that embed multiple forms of inequality. However, in describing both the ways in which access to basic services is stratified and social discrimination based on the settlement in which people live, it has sought to illuminate some of the processes at work. The examples illustrate how such factors result in forceful exclusion, adverse treatment in relation to employment opportunities, resettlement locations and services, and negative social values, with further impacts on self-belief and self-respect among those discriminated against, and the reinforcement of unequal relations.

This section provides an overview of spatial differentiations and inequalities but gives less attention to other differences and their associated needs. In the case of sanitation, for example, in addition to spatial differences relating to the neighbourhood and (for example) type of tenure, there are also differences in need related to personal characteristics such as age, health and gender. Differences in the nature of provision may also be required to ensure that groups with different belief systems about the way in which human waste should be treated do not face particular difficulties of access and use. Young children need smaller toilets and may be frightened to use conventional pit latrines because of the large pits and the fact that they are dark (Bartlett 2003). Older people may require more frequent access to toilets and hence need a greater intensity of provision and easy access.

In some cases, needs may be socially determined. Women and girls, for example, may be vulnerable because they are harassed or attacked when using public toilets in the evening or at night. These dangers are highlighted in an Amnesty International (2010) report entitled *Insecurity and Indignity: Women's Experiences in the Slums of Nairobi, Kenya*, which includes a significant focus on the lack of adequate sanitation. The report documents the major risk posed to women by lack of proximate facilities, with most having to walk more than 300 metres to a toilet. The women interviewed spoke about how it is dangerous for them to walk alone in the settlement after seven in the evening. Issues related to menstruation add to the particular needs of women and girls.

The next section seeks to capture some of the ways in which political structures manage and constrain attempts by low-income residents to secure social justice. Why do market mechanisms and government intervention do so little to address the needs and interests of the urban poor?

Political inequalities

Unequal access to government goods, services and cash transfers, and, at least to some extent, disadvantageous positions within labour markets, reflect inequalities in power and social status. Social inequalities may be created and reinforced based on race, gender, ethnicity and age, in addition to the differential access related to residential location and occupation described previously. Class and caste remain important factors influencing social relations and related inequalities. Such factors may be relevant in explaining the local incidence of various dimensions of inequality, that is, the sectors in which inequality is manifest, such as residential location, access to basic services and access to labour markets or particular jobs. They also help to explain the structure and level of inequality, that is, the nature of the distribution and the degree of disparity between, for example, predominantly high-income and low-income neighbourhoods, or the top and bottom deciles for employment income. Social relations also help to explain the degree of mobility; mobility enables individuals to move up particular kinds of social scale, ensuring that inequalities associated with social positions are not passed on from one generation to another.

This section considers inequalities in political influence in an urban context. We do not discuss national political processes, which are relevant to determining issues of taxation and benefits, as this is somewhat outside the scope of this volume. Rather we focus on differential access to urban governance processes which are critical to policies related to urban land (residential and commercial), infrastructure, services and housing. Political outcomes that are adverse for low-income and disadvantaged groups emerge from a number of distinct processes. Most notably, there are unrepresentative processes which give rise to unequal access to positions of political power and unequal levels of influence over those with power, there are discriminatory policies, such as those requiring significant investment in residential plots which make housing unaffordable for low-income households, and there is discriminatory enactment of reasonable policies, resulting in unfair practices.

Politics and political power

In the context of democracy, governments are expected to be responsive to their citizens, treating them equally. However, there is considerable evidence to show that, even in democratic societies, governments respond to more powerful, well-placed elites, in terms of both their priorities and policy responses. In other cases, governments may be more well meaning but lack the capacity to deliver.

Political exclusion may be explicit in the case of those living in informal settlements. In Thailand, for example, residents of informal settlements do not have a valid address for electoral purposes and those that wish to vote have to negotiate the use of a formal address with a relative or friend. In India, lack of a legal address can bar individuals or households from getting on the voters' register, getting a ration card (which provides access to some staples at subsidized prices) or getting children into public schools. In urban China, those without urban registration make up a large and particularly vulnerable group denied access to a range of goods and services. As Gao (2006) notes, it is not possible to assess how they are faring in urban areas because of a lack of data, but their inclusion in research would increase the scale of the inequalities found and greatly change our understanding of the scale and depth of urban poverty in China.

However, these explicit forms of political exclusion of low-income urban residents are only part of a much more significant issue. Low-income residents struggle to gain access to the resources they need and to negotiate with political elites to have their interests addressed. Crossa (2009) discusses the fortunes of different organizations seeking to address the needs of street traders in Mexico City during a period in which the city government was seeking to regularize the city centre and exclude them from trading. There were an estimated 9,000 to 30,000 traders and 71 networking organizations in the city. Crossa considers the strategies and successes of two of these organizations, highlighting the differences that emerge due to differences in their political connections.

> The first organization, which I refer to as TAP, was formed in the early 1980s and is one of the largest street-vending organizations in the Historic Center. It is affiliated with the PRI. The TAP organizational structure is kin based and hierarchical. TAP authorities claim the organization has over 2,500 members located in different areas of the Historic Center; it also has members based in other areas of the city. ... The second organization, which I refer to as UMC, is a small organization with 800 members in the Historic Center and no members in any other part of the city. UMC was created after the leader of another organization of street vendors died and that organization was dismantled.
>
> (Crossa 2009, page 53)

The PRI is the political party that dominated the Mexican state for decades, with its power only challenged from the mid-1990s. It is recognized to be highly clientelistic, establishing vertical relations with a number of popular organizations to build the base required for political domination. Crossa (2009) discusses how the different political relations established by these two groups affected their tactics as they sought to maintain a presence in the central city in the face of pressure from the city council to prevent them trading, from 2001 onwards. For example, TAP had the relationships and resources to monitor police activities and hence facilitate mobile trading, while UMC traders were considerably more vulnerable and had to carry all their goods with them to enable them to move immediately. Crossa shows how the political relations that individuals and collectives of the urban poor are able to establish – relations which manifest the extent and nature of systemic political inequalities – are directly linked to the security of their livelihoods.

Also illustrated by Crossa's example are stratifications in power within and between citizen groups and social movements. Although there is a strong consciousness in many grassroots organizations in the Global South of the need for access to basic services including water and sanitation, perceptions of needs and interests continue to differ. Perreault (2006) discusses resistance to water privatization in Cochabamba, highlighting the fact that the struggle to keep prices low addressed the needs of those connected to the piped water network but did little to address the needs of those unable to connect due to a lack of public investment. Those not connected may have much more of an interest in private sector involvement, particularly if it comes with requirements to extend the networks and secure more customers. However, such diversity of interests may not be attended to when movements challenge the shift towards private sector involvement in water companies; in part this is because those most disadvantaged do not publicly challenge their disadvantage. Such examples demonstrate the very real difficulties that grassroots organizations face in ensuring political outcomes that address the needs of informal settlement residents, both within neo-liberal regimes and among those contesting such regimes.

Participatory budgeting sought to address structural disadvantage in at least some parts of the political realm and offer low-income communities the opportunity to influence decision making and resource allocation. Cabannes (2004) reviews the experience with participatory budgeting in 25 municipalities in Latin America and Europe. While the nature and extent of these initiatives varied considerably (as might be expected), there were some commonalities:

- Participation rates varied from 2 to 7 per cent of the relevant population (Cabannes 2004).
- Participatory budgets were focused on spatial areas; some cities also introduced committees specific to disadvantaged groups (such as women and ethnic minorities), while others practised affirmative action and used a quota system for such groups.
- There are few investigations that measure changed investment priorities. The data reported show that greater investment takes place in low-income areas, but evidence of changed priorities in local infrastructure improvements is not available.

Cabannes (2004) is positive about the impact of these initiatives on political inclusion through increases in participation. However, Avritzer (2006) studies a number of cities in which participatory budgeting has been undertaken in Brazil, and is more cautious. He argues that it worked well in Pôrto Alegre because of the existing strength of social organizations, and suggests that if this institutional presence is not established then the political benefits do not emerge. He analyses a number of dimensions of participation, finding that the lowest-income citizens are less likely to participate, and the greatest participation is among those with average incomes. He reports that, even in Pôrto Alegre, the lowest-income participants were significantly less likely to speak or to speak frequently in the regional and thematic assemblies to debate priorities. Avritzer (2006) agrees that there is evidence to support the redistributional impact of participatory budgeting, with increasing capital investment in low-income neighbourhoods. He also suggests that the problems of clientelistic politics may be reduced, with fewer 'political mediators' used to access material benefits. However, he argues that without a strong associative movement gains in democratization do not take place (though there may still be positive distributional impacts). His conclusions are broadly consistent with the research of Houtzager, Acharya and Lavalle (2007), who are pessimistic about the capacity of existing associational forms of community and grassroots organization to change political outcomes in favour of the poor. Following a study of 1,200 households in both Mexico City and São Paulo, they conclude that, in general, relationships continue to be those of dependence and clientelism.

Rodgers (2010) links the outcomes of participatory budgeting in Buenos Aires to patterns of political exclusion. He analyses the introduction of participatory budgeting at a time of considerable political tension related to the economic crisis in Argentina, suggesting that existing parties faced a lack of credibility which enabled new political configurations to press for the scaling up of participatory budgeting. While he believes that initial efforts were successful in drawing citizens into a participatory process at the neighbourhood level, he also describes a context in which politicians sought to use the process for their own ends through attempts to control the local process, changes in the local authority staff and a reduction in the significance of participatory budgeting in the city's budget. The picture that emerges is one in which low-income citizens either individually or through their representative organizations have little influence over the government of the city.

There is a wide-ranging literature on the ubiquitous presence of clientelistic politics, although opinions about its impact differ. There is an acknowledgement that it offers benefits to low-income groups, particularly those within specific neighbourhoods or voting constituencies (Benjamin 2000; Auyero 2000; Almansi *et al*. 2011). However, it is also argued that the material benefits which result are at the cost of a reinforcement of political inequalities and the strengthening of vertical and personalized links between political elites, state authorities and low-income citizens (Wood 2003). Even the material benefits secured may not be sufficient to challenge the more substantive resource inequalities in terms of public infrastructure investments, as described in previous sections.

Valença (2007) describes how such a politics functions to reinforce existing inequalities in an exploration of housing programmes in Brazil during the early 1990s and the Collor government. The housing secretariat established a programme intended to benefit the lowest-income households, particularly those with less than five times the minimum wage. Valença does not criticize the design of the programme but rather argues that the orientation of its implementation was towards enterprise development and profit-making rather than reaching the lowest-income households. In 1990 and 1991 there were 340,000 housing approvals and 264,000 starts. The processes for decision making on projects enabled the government to determine its own priorities in part through the Ministry for Social Action but also through the President's Office. Allocations depended on political relations between elites rather than the needs of citizens. There appear to be similarities with the processes of land allocation in Nairobi described previously. Valença (2007, page 406) concludes that 'although client-patronage was nothing new in Brazilian politics, during the Collor term it acquired a concrete organizational form'.

Bayat (2000) describes the ways in which the urban poor are excluded from access to the resources they need. He argues that existing analyses have failed to capture the response of these residents. Most significantly, he argues that responses may reinforce the stability of the existing system as much as they may seek to challenge political disadvantage. He documents how individuals negotiate urban governance outcomes in cities of the Middle East. He argues that the occupation of streets by informal traders, the expansion of housing against formal regulations and the non-payment and illegal tapping of basic services are all part of a quiet encroachment that reflect an inability to challenge disadvantageous outcomes.

> The notion of 'quiet encroachment' describes the silent, protracted but pervasive advancement of ordinary people on the propertied and powerful in order to survive and improve their lives. This is marked by quiet, largely atomized and prolonged mobilization with episodic collective action – open and fleeting struggles without clear leadership, ideology or structured organization. While the quiet encroachment cannot be considered a 'social movement' as such, it is also distinct from survival strategies or 'everyday resistance' in that the struggles and gains of the agents are not made at the cost of fellow poor or themselves, but at the cost of the state, the rich and the powerful (Bayat 2000).

Bayat suggests that it is helpful to see such activities 'not as a deliberate political act; rather, they are driven by the force of necessity – the necessity to survive and improve a dignified life' (2000, page 547). In so doing he highlights the extent to which exclusion from resources and from influence over the rules that control access to resources create difficulties in the struggle to secure urban livelihoods.

In no sphere is this sense of being trapped in exploitative political relations without the ability to challenge them more clearly expressed than in attitudes to security and the police. Garrett and Ahmed (2004) talk about the reluctance of community members in Dinajpur, Bangladesh to report crime to the police: this happened in only 8 per cent of the cases identified in a survey of 585 households. They conclude that 'the poor do not get justice. Their interaction with the formal security services and legal institutions is practically non-existent' (page 149). Women living in informal settlements in Mumbai also highlighted the lack of assistance they got from the police when they sought to report a crime (Roy, Jockin and Javed 2004).

Conclusion

There are many aspects of urban inequality and they are often severe in their implications for the quality of life, health and well-being of urban dwellers. Five of the most important inequalities emerging from the literature are those related to income (particularly earnings from labour markets), housing quality, differential access to secure tenure and basic infrastructure and services, political exclusion, and social status, including the stigma frequently attached to living in informal settlements. One of the often-repeated themes of this discussion has been the ways in which the different inequalities reinforce each other. For instance, low incomes result in residence in locations viewed negatively by members of better-placed social groups, and those locations are often not well provided with infrastructure and services, or may indeed have no such provision. Such areas may house a concentration of groups that experience social disadvantage as well as being relatively poorly placed to compete in labour markets, and who face discrimination on grounds of gender, race and ethnicity, or for other reasons. At the same time, those with low incomes are likely to lack political power, especially in situations in which they are not well organized, and hence find it difficult to challenge the deficiencies in provision affecting them. Many aspects of poverty are related to the refusal or incapacity of the state to treat all citizens equally in respect of state-funded infrastructure and services. Whatever the rhetoric associated with the modern democratic state, all citizens are not equal.

The overlap between inequality and absolute poverty remains in almost all towns and cities in the Global South. There seems to be a common pattern, in which economic growth is associated with increasing levels of income inequality as skilled workers and professionals are able to secure increasing rewards. At the same time, the impacts of economic downturn may be greatest for those with the highest incomes, as inequalities in income distributions are reduced, perhaps in part reflecting the fact that wages for the lowest-income households are at or below subsistence level. Income inequalities appear to be higher in urban areas in most countries, although this pattern is not universal and there remain countries in which rural income inequalities exceed those in urban areas. The basic dynamics suggested by Kuznets's (1955) model – an increase in inequalities followed by a decrease, as labour from subsistence agriculture is absorbed into the 'modern' economy – appear to be overtaken by economic and social specificities that prevail in particular circumstances. For example, plantation economies with waged labour may increase income inequalities in rural areas at the same time as continuing informalization in urban labour markets is associated with continuing high differentials in these areas. The state has evident potential to redistribute incomes (including through cash transfers and pensions) and provide households with access to infrastructure and services, sometimes also to better quality housing, but their expenditures often do not favour and sometimes do not even reach the lowest-income households. Extending the rule of law and ensuring those in informal settlements can get onto the voters' register lessens inequality in these two areas. Inequalities in access to safe homes and residential neighbourhoods and to infrastructure and services may be as high or higher in urban areas than in rural areas. In many urban areas this is partly driven by the high standards enjoyed by wealthier groups.

Comparing rural and urban populations, it is evident that the simple association of rural areas with agriculture and urban with manufacturing and processing industries has changed in most places. Many rural livelihoods are no longer dependent on subsistence or smallholder agriculture and a range of further 'off-farm' and 'non-farm' activities create opportunities to augment incomes. For a proportion of the urban population, their livelihoods have long incorporated an element of subsistence and trading agriculture; while urban agriculture is likely to be constrained in the larger and more successful cities, it may still exist in small spaces, often focusing on high-value goods,[89] while it remains more significant on urban peripheries and in smaller and less successful urban centres. Of course, access to the land and water needed for successful urban or peri-urban agriculture is influenced by income level and by social or political influence. There are also multiple interchanges between rural and urban family members that affect urban and rural incomes. There is considerable diversity of income in many urban contexts, with exceptionally low wages in some cases being found alongside internationally comparable formal sector salaries, especially in larger or primary urban centres. As noted previously, wage labour is the major source and primary cause of income inequality in urban areas.

These urban income inequalities are severe, with the structure of the economy providing an insufficient number of adequately paid jobs and hence making it difficult for households to increase their earnings. In Brazil, China and South Africa, parts of the population have experienced some degree of economic prosperity, with rising real incomes. This has been enjoyed mostly by those with the required level of education and skills. For those at the less skilled level of the labour market, incomes remain inadequate and do not appear to be improving, and may be getting worse. Analysis of income inequalities highlights the structural constraints on poverty reduction. There is consistent evidence that informal work has increased, with negative implications for wages and benefits (see Chapter 4). Mobility can address the needs of individual families but limited opportunities for higher-paying jobs places absolute constraints on the numbers who can advance, helping to explain why increased investment in education may not always be associated with improvements in income.

While much emphasis is placed on both the market (in respect of income) and 'society' (in respect of discrimination and prejudice) as sources of inequality, the discussion here has highlighted the contribution of the state. The state clearly has a direct responsibility to ensure that the tax system collects resources fairly and that benefits are distributed according to need. State policies can contribute to alleviating income differentials among the population. State fiscal redistribution has helped to reduce income inequalities in Brazil, China and South Africa. It is notable that these are all countries in which the state has a clear developmental policy agenda. However, the degree of the redistribution in Brazil and China is relatively low, suggesting that it is difficult for the state to act at scale. Even in South Africa, where considerable investment has been made, the impact on inequality appears to be minimal (although more recent figures may indicate a more positive impact). This can be attributed in part to the balance of incomes in these countries, as many have incomes too low to make a contribution to revenue from direct taxes. Moreover, in many countries, including Brazil, tax avoidance remains high and the revenue contribution from high-income earners is limited. A similar picture emerges for the Central American economies. Indirect taxes are likely to impact more heavily on those with low incomes, as they spend a higher proportion of their incomes (although the exact impact will depend on which goods are taxed). In Brazil, for example, the 40 per cent of earners with the lowest income received less than 10 per cent of total income but paid 15.5 per cent of total indirect tax in 1991 (Velez, de Barros and Ferreira 2004). A further constraint on the scale of redistribution of income is the limited influence of the state on the labour market and the income that labour receives.

Low-income citizens may be further disadvantaged by the inadequacies in government redistribution through expenditure. If a major component of state redistribution is limited to formal workers, for example pensions or access to health care, then informal workers will not benefit. If a major component of state redistribution is implementing or funding provision for infrastructure and services (such as piped water, sewers and drains and all-weather roads and paths), those living in informal settlements which receive little or none of this are obviously disadvantaged. Benefits distributed through social and educational services may not fully advantage the lowest income groups, who may find themselves unable to access these or facing stigma in claiming them, or that only a low quality of service is available to them. The scale of state investment can be a poor indicator of the benefits received by low-income groups. This is exemplified by South Africa's housing policy, which allocates funding to providing low-income households with their first home on a very large scale, but in practice often produces small, poor quality, poorly located units. Some of these are soon abandoned by families due to their distant location, poor quality or associated costs (Bradlow, Bolnick and Shearing 2011). In Chile, housing conditions have improved considerably for large sections of the low-income urban population, yet dissatisfaction with the units is evident in concerns about neighbourhoods, housing quality and distance from urban facilities (Rodríguez and Sugranyes 2007).

As indicated in Table 5.9, income distribution (whether the outcome of labour markets or enterprise activities) is a major source of income inequality. At the same time, low incomes reduce the likelihood of the individual social and economic mobility that can reduce the rigidity of economic differentiation and give rise to new opportunities. Low incomes also make educational investment less likely at the household level, disadvantaging the next generation. As noted in a previous chapter, taking children out of school is a common response to economic difficulties for low-income households. For documented examples, this is in part because of the costs saved (for instance in school fees, costs of books and uniforms, and transport to and from school), in part because of the extra income or other support that children can contribute. Low incomes also reduce the capacity of the state to raise revenue, thereby making it difficult for education services to expand and for the economy to move to an alternative trajectory involving fewer low-skilled and low-paid jobs.

As summarized in Table 5.9, political, social and spatial dimensions of inequality appear to be important in maintaining adverse distributional outcomes

Table 5.9 The interaction between inequalities, and their causes and consequences

Inequality	*Cause*	*Consequences leading to further inequality*
Labour market, employment	• Income from employment is a major source of income inequality. • The structure of the labour market is critical. • Many small-scale enterprises have low levels of capital investment and low returns.	• Lack of income underpins inequality in housing quality, infrastructure, services and access to employment opportunities. • Lack of income makes educational investments difficult and makes it harder for children of low-income households to participate in the labour market. • Informal workers and traders may face discrimination, reducing future earnings. • Informal employment is likely to be associated with poorer health, lack of pension arrangements and other disadvantageous conditions, leading to a high risk of future income inequality.
Spatial	• Living in low-income settlements means that access to basic services is likely to be limited. • Low-income settlements or resettlement areas may be located far from work opportunities and essential services.	• Living conditions in informal settlements usually have serious consequences for health (and, as discussed in Chapter 3, contribute to large health inequalities). • Social stigma attached to those living in informal settlements encourages an 'us and them' attitude among the elite, and may make it more difficult for redistribution policies to secure support to address disadvantage. • Residency in low-income settlements may lead to discrimination in labour markets. • Lack of access to education may make it more difficult for the next generation to secure social mobility.

Inequality	Cause	Consequences leading to further inequality
Social	Discriminatory views based on, for example, gender, race, informal employment status or residence in a particular location.	• Differential access to incomes and/or higher expenditures may make it difficult for individual households to purchase the goods they need for immediate survival and make it harder to achieve mobility. • Lack of social status may lead to bribes and other illegal activities being required to access basic services. • Social attitudes, and the social stigma attached to particular groups as well as to those living in particular locations, maintaining unequal social structures.
Political	• Some groups may be treated systematically less well than others. The apartheid state is among the most extreme examples. • Living in informal settlements without the formal address needed for electoral registration. • The lowest-income groups cannot afford to take time off from earning money to participate in political processes.	• Social differences may be used to justify discriminatory policies, such as local governments refusing infrastructure and access to services for those living in informal settlements. • Lack of flexibility and inappropriate service delivery will lead to ineffectual social programmes even if finance is provided. • Clientelism in political processes results in unrepresentative and unaccountable community leadership. • Consultative processes may be dominated by the articulate and well educated.

– including the concentration of those with inadequate incomes in low quality neighbourhoods with poor housing, disadvantageous locations and inadequate, often expensive, services. Inequalities in access to multiple goods and services are of major significance in influencing the kinds of employment that low-income households can secure, their other income-earning opportunities and the extent to which they can benefit from health and education provision. The influence of the state over where low-income households locate and the transport access associated with these sites is evident, and governments can and do determine the scale and extent of the disadvantage that low-income households face when the only affordable accommodation is in inaccessible sites. As illustrated by a number of cities in Latin America that have improved public transport and increased the number of city neighbourhoods with a good service (World Bank Central America 2002), governments can act to improve transport services. This can reduce a range of inequalities, for instance by reducing the time and cost of access to income-earning opportunities and services for residents of many low-income districts and widening the geographic area they can afford to travel to. It may make transport safer. It can help reduce the cost of land for housing by bringing large new areas of land within reach of centres of employment, in terms of the affordable daily limits of travelling time and cost.

The considerable social stigma that may be attached to residence in low-income settlements appears significant. This is likely to be related to both the extent to which populations locate in these areas and the scale of differences in living conditions between low-income and higher-income neighbourhoods. Where incomes are universally low and government provision for shelter inadequate at scale, social stigma is likely to be less, as many households find themselves in such locations. Living conditions may be very difficult but households do not find themselves having to deal with the additional burdens of social inequality and low social status. However, in middle-income countries, where higher-income households have access to full services, as is the case in South Africa and much of Latin America and the Caribbean, the inequalities are much greater and the stigma attached to residency in low-income areas may similarly be greater.

Unequal access to the political system also has implications for inequality, although arguably these are universal and not specifically urban. There are concerns that inequality undermines democracy and social democracy (in which the state takes on an obligation to address the needs of all citizens). The essential role that state redistribution can play in mitigating inequalities in waged income and enterprise earnings has already been considered. Even without income redistribution, the state can significantly improve the situation of the lowest-paid urban dwellers by investing in essential basic services. However, state expenditure is not necessarily redistributive and political inclusion (not just in terms of democracy but also in terms of ongoing engagement with the political system) may be important in ensuring that state expenditures support equity. The reality is often far from this. Political relations are established which function in the interests of political elites and in some cases in the interests of those responsible for supplying informal commercial services to informal areas. Shelter and access to basic services are essential for survival in urban areas, but in scarce supply. The result is exploitative political relationships, with powerful elites controlling local political outcomes through clientelistic networks, generally offering partial allocations of basic services to selected individuals and groups, sometimes with financial benefits for a select few. As explored in the companion volume to this, a critical step in reducing poverty and inequality is to challenge such processes and their outcomes.

Other forms of inequality are also part of the social mix in towns and cities in the Global South. Discrimination and unequal social relations exist on multiple bases, including race, ethnicity, gender and age. These have not been dealt with in detail in this chapter as they are not exclusively urban, but this is not to say they are unimportant. Prejudice within the formal financial sector, for example, is one reason why low-income households from informal settlements find it difficult to register for bank accounts (Solo 2008), secure loans and upgrade their homes.

Within this, there is evidence to show that the more significant reasons for denying access to housing loans are related to lack of formal employment (meaning income earned is not formally documented), and building and land-use regulations that distinguish between 'legal' and 'illegal' dwellings (Calderón 2004).

Thus, urban inequality is characterized by the differing dimensions of and interactions between political, spatial, social and labour market inequalities.

In summary, the available evidence shows rising inequality in incomes in most urban contexts in the Global South. This usually brings with it increasing social and spatial segmentation of towns and cities, as those with limited incomes concentrate in the neighbourhoods most disadvantaged in terms of housing quality and infrastructure and services provision, often also location in relation to income-earning opportunities. This poses general problems, but has particularly negative consequences for those on the lower rungs of the social and economic ladders. However, there is nothing inevitable about this in any respect. Urban centres are places of social change and opportunity. Social and political relations between lower-income groups or groups living in informal settlements and the wider city can be transformed. Job opportunities do exist, albeit they sometimes have limited value. Governments do act and do invest, but not always in the interests of society. An understanding of the many different factors that create and exacerbate inequality will better inform the response to it, suggesting routes by which it can be reduced.

6 Broadening the understanding and measurement of urban poverty

Introduction

This chapter begins by reconsidering the multiple deprivations associated with urban poverty that were listed at the end of Chapter 2 and elaborated in Chapters 3 to 5. It then discusses the implications of incorporating these into poverty assessments and measurements. There is also a discussion of how addressing non-income aspects of deprivation can in effect provide a 'hidden income' as these reduce costs directly (for example, cheaper safe water) and indirectly (for instance through reducing health burdens or income lost because of injury, illness and premature death). This complements the focus of Chapter 2 on what is needed to have poverty lines set to levels that reflect the minimum income that urban dwellers need for food and non-food items, and adjusted to reflect spatial differences in the costs of necessities. This chapter also considers how understanding of health issues and inequality shapes an understanding of urban poverty and what is needed to address it. It discusses whether a focus on urban poverty might distract attention from rural poverty. And it ends with key conclusions for a post-MDG world.

Understanding the multiple deprivations associated with urban poverty

Discussions of basic needs and human development and how they came to be incorporated into discussions of development (including into the MDGs) seem almost to be from a different world to the poverty assessments and poverty reduction strategy papers discussed in Chapter 2. For instance, poverty assessments rarely recognize the limitations of defining and measuring poverty only in absolute terms and of basing the definition and measurement on 'expert' judgement. There is little recognition of the need to incorporate in definitions of poverty consideration of living conditions and of whether individuals or households have the resources to allow them to participate in society. In most poverty assessments, little mention is made of relative poverty lines (although some include information on inequalities) and assessment of 'needs' other than 'expert' judgements. Many poverty assessments do include some consideration of participatory poverty assessments, but they are not used to amend the primary focus on incomes and expenditures and a poverty line based on a monetary value calculated from the cost of a required food intake plus a simple non-food costs adjustment. It is as if the broader perspectives on poverty in the writings of, say, Townsend, Chambers or Sen over the last 25 years had never arisen (see for instance Townsend 1993 or Chambers 1995). Ruth Lister's comment that it is generally the understandings held by more powerful groups, rather than those of people who experience poverty, that are reflected in how poverty is conceptualized and defined has particular relevance here (Lister 2004).

Broadening the definition and measurement of poverty beyond absolute poverty lines based only on income or consumption should help change fundamentally the basis for understanding and action. In Chapter 2, we elaborated other aspects of poverty or of the deprivations associated with poverty (see Box 2.2 on pages 89–90), beyond inadequate and often unstable income, under the following headings:

- Inadequate, unstable or risky asset base
- Poor quality and often insecure, hazardous and overcrowded housing
- Inadequate provision of 'public' infrastructure
- Inadequate provision of basic services
- High prices paid for many necessities
- Limited or no safety net
- Inadequate protection of rights through the operation of the law
- Voicelessness and powerlessness within political systems and bureaucratic structures.

One key aspect of deprivation, part of the denial of political voice and rights, is lack of documentation needed for individuals or households to assert their rights and access entitlements (Patel and Baptist 2012; Appadurai 2012). Perhaps as many as 1 billion people live in informal settlements in urban areas and most lack not only infrastructure and services but also official identity documents or documents confirming their address and, beyond this, their right to live there. To have no such documents may mean being denied connections to piped water supplies and sewers, or services to collect household wastes, or policing, or even access to schools and health care. It often means there is no possibility of opening a bank account, obtaining insurance or getting on the voters' register (see Szreter 2007). A legal address can also provide some protection against homes being bulldozed or, should this be unavoidable, it can provide access to rights such as being given notice, getting support to find alternative accommodation and getting compensation.

There is an astonishing lack of data about informal settlements – their scale, boundaries, populations, buildings and enterprises, and the quality and extent of their infrastructure and services. This contributes to the needs of their inhabitants being ignored. It leads to their contributions to the urban economy (and to the services enjoyed by higher-income groups) being forgotten or greatly understated. The lack of documentation serves as an excuse for government agencies not to provide infrastructure and services. It also means there is no counter to the claims of politicians or civil servants that those living in informal settlements are law breakers or unemployed migrants who, they suggest, should go back to rural areas (although many were born in the city or have lived there for years).

Many groups that have adequate incomes may face some of the deprivations listed in Box 2.2 – in countries in which it is not only low-income groups that lack voice and influence, or adequate provision for infrastructure, services and the rule of law. But, as emphasized in this chapter (and more broadly in this book), competent, effective and accountable urban governments greatly reduce many of these deprivations – while incompetent, ineffective and unaccountable urban governments greatly increase them. Much of this deprivation, and especially that related to public infrastructure and services, the rule of law and lack of voice, is not primarily the result of households' inadequate incomes but instead is rooted in inadequacies in local government and governance. This is shown in Figure 6.1, which illustrates the many factors that cause or contribute to urban poverty; good policy and practice in urban government address not only the deprivations but also many of their immediate external causes.

Implications for incorporating the many dimensions of deprivation into poverty assessments and measurements

It may be difficult for those who are used to equating poverty with consumption-based criteria to accept this broader view, and it is difficult to incorporate some of the aspects described into quantitative measurements of poverty. But there are many examples of government, NGO or community-driven programmes that show it is important,[90] for the following reasons:

- *It helps shift official perceptions of 'poor people' from being 'objects' of government policy to being citizens with rights and legitimate demands.* It also implies a greater engagement with groups facing deprivation. The definition and setting of income- or consumption-based poverty lines described in Chapter 2 makes little or no provision for consultation with low-income groups. And so there is no scope for those who suffer deprivation to define their own needs and priorities. No scope for them to challenge the inaccurate and often unfair stereotypes used by politicians, officials, the media and others in discussions of poverty (Lister 2004; Escobar 1996). No possibility of these people holding governments and international agencies to account for inaccuracies. Some of the considerable inaccuracies in statistics on levels of urban poverty would have been avoided if those setting the poverty lines had actually walked through informal settlements and talked to their inhabitants.
- *It provides more entry points for poverty reduction and makes explicit the contributions that a much wider group of governmental, private sector, non-governmental and community-based organizations can make to poverty reduction.* Figure 6.1 lists 21 different immediate causes of deprivations – this means 21 different areas in which action can help reduce deprivations.

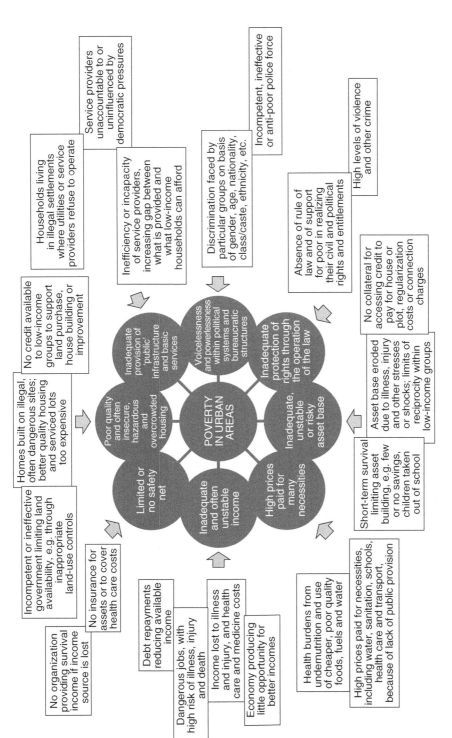

Figure 6.1 Deprivations associated with urban poverty and their immediate external causes

Figure 6.1 illustrates a constantly recurring theme: the degree to which the scale and depth of deprivation is caused by local governments not meeting their responsibilities. It also emphasizes the degree to which these deprivations can be reduced where local governments do fulfil their role. Local governments have responsibility for the provision of most infrastructure and services related to needs and they influence their availability and cost, either as providers or as the managers of provision through contracts. Local governments usually influence whether infrastructure and services can be provided to those living in informal settlements. They influence the availability, price and location of land for housing, house prices, the quality and extent of provision for basic infrastructure and services and whether low-income groups can buy, build or rent legal and good quality housing. This in turn influences the proportion of people living in informal settlements and on dangerous sites. So the extent to which low-income groups have a voice and influence within political systems and bureaucratic structures (including service providers) affects how much attention is given to their housing, infrastructure and service needs. It generally also falls to local government to ensure health and safety in workplaces and to have measures in place that limit discrimination on the basis of, for example, gender, age, nationality, class or caste, or ethnic group with regard to access to income, housing, credit, services, etc. Those of us living in high-income nations perhaps forget the contribution competent and accountable urban government makes to poverty reduction and the political organization and contestation needed to achieve this. The companion volume to this (Satterthwaite and Mitlin 2013) will explore how local government can contribute to poverty reduction, and the various implications of alternative approaches by state agencies.

There are many local services that may be under the jurisdiction of higher levels of government, for instance in some nations this applies to health care (or parts of the health care system), education (or higher education), safety nets and policing, sometimes also water. Getting the documentation needed to assert rights and obtain entitlements may also involve the local offices of higher levels of government. Addressing these areas can be a very important part of poverty reduction, for instance policing in order to reduce violence and other crime within the settlements where low-income groups are concentrated, or provision for the rule of law in order to help low-income citizens realize their civil and political rights and entitlements.

There is also a range of financial services that can support those with limited incomes to meet their needs, for instance the provision of credit to support land purchase and house building or improvement, safety net incomes for those with very inadequate incomes or who lose their incomes, and insurance for homes and assets, also for life and health care, where relevant. Local governments may have no direct role in these services but they often have important indirect roles, for example determining whether or not those who live in informal settlements have or can get legal identity documents.

The different aspects of poverty included in Figure 6.1 highlight the importance of factors other than income. Many case studies show that the deprivations associated with low income can be much reduced without increasing incomes, through increasing assets or safety nets, improving housing conditions and basic services, or through political changes allowing low-income groups to negotiate more support and less harassment. Urban governments, NGOs and grassroots organizations generally have relatively little scope to directly increase poorer groups' incomes (see Chapter 4), but have much more scope to address the other aspects of poverty, by, say, improving or extending basic services, removing constraints to finding or building better quality accommodation, or reducing police harassment. Piped water provided to the homes and rooms where low-income groups live, for example, can directly add to disposable incomes by significantly reducing costs incurred.

Box 2.2 and Figure 6.1 also emphasize the multiple roles that housing and neighbourhoods can have in urban poverty – and in poverty reduction. Housing in urban contexts generally has more influence on the incomes, asset bases, livelihoods, vulnerability, health and quality of life of low-income groups than external poverty reduction specialists recognize. It not only provides accommodation, it is also:

- a location for getting to and from income-earning opportunities and services, with some low-income groups having to put up with very poor quality accommodation because it is close to these resources;
- often a significant cost in individual or household budgets (as described in Chapter 2). Reducing this cost can mean there is more income available for other necessities;
- for many, a location where income-earning activities take place, in the form of home-based work or renting out space;
- the primary defence against most environmental health risks, which are more serious in urban than in rural contexts if there is no provision for water, sanitation, drainage or household waste collection, because of the greater concentration of people and their wastes. As discussed in Chapter 3, for the hundreds of millions of urban dwellers living in poor quality accommodation, the health burdens they face from diseases and injuries originating in the home and home neighbourhood are a very large part of their total health burdens, and much greater than the burdens faced by those in good quality accommodation;
- a valuable asset for those low-income households who are 'owner-occupiers' (even if in an illegal subdivision or squatter settlement where ownership is not officially recognized);
- for many low-income groups, the place where social networks are built. These have great importance for households, helping them avoid poverty or cope with shocks and stresses.

Safer and more secure housing also provides households with more protection against the loss of their household assets from theft, accidental fire, extreme weather or disasters such as floods, landslides or earthquakes. As described in Chapter 3, it is almost always lower-income groups in urban areas that bear most of the costs of disaster, and climate change adds to the urgency of addressing the vulnerabilities of and risks to low-income groups and their settlements.

One important aspect of poverty for large sections of the urban population with low incomes is the insecurity of their accommodation, either because they are tenants and have little legal protection from instant eviction or other unfair practices or because they live in illegal settlements under threat of eviction. It is interesting to note the degree to which organizations and federations formed by the urban poor or homeless in many different nations prioritize better quality or more secure housing. Increasing incomes is very important, but organizing and working to address housing and neighbourhood conditions usually represents the best response to their poverty that is possible locally, particularly for the women that make up the majority of members.[91]

It may be assumed that higher incomes are the best way to help low-income households buy, build or rent better quality, safer, more secure housing. But there is often more possibility of achieving this by making housing cheaper, for instance through addressing the many constraints that unnecessarily increase the cost and reduce the supply of housing and of inputs into housing (land, materials, credit, infrastructure, etc.). There are often many untapped resources that can help low-income households get better quality accommodation without increasing their incomes, in particular unused or under-utilized land on which they can secure their homes, incrementally developing shelter if and when it is affordable.

The key point is that good local governance, including support and space for urban poor organizations, can considerably reduce poverty, even if incomes among the urban poor are not increasing.

Implications for reducing poverty

- *Actions taken to reduce poverty can have multiple interrelated effects on different aspects of deprivation.* For instance, improved basic service provision – for instance, water piped into the home replacing a long trek to fetch and carry water from a standpipe or kiosk – improves health, reduces time burdens and fatigue and increases real income (by reducing medical costs and time off work due to illness or injury).
- *Acting on other aspects of poverty often increases incomes for poorer groups.* Better quality housing and basic infrastructure and services can increase households' incomes through the mechanisms described in the previous point, for example. Similarly:
  - it can enhance income-earning opportunities for home enterprises, the potential scope and scale of which is often much improved by the provision of electricity, more space, better water supply and sanitation, and solid waste collection;
  - a good quality piped water supply not only greatly improves the quality and quantity of water available to a household but, in many low-income settlements, it also reduces the daily or weekly bill for water; for low-income households this often translates directly into increased food intake.

- *Local resources and space for urban poor groups' own initiatives is important.* Many of the more successful poverty reduction programmes have been delivered through urban poor groups' successfully negotiating resources, room for autonomous action or a halt to harassment from local authorities – often with little or no foreign funding involved,[92] also often without much funding from local authorities. If this is generally true, it greatly widens the scope for local actions that can help reduce poverty. It is also important that governments and international agencies are able to recognize the resources and capabilities of those with low incomes or living in informal settlements, who can contribute much to more effective poverty reduction programmes.

   Where people's capacity to pay for improved services and for safer housing is limited, their capacity to negotiate with local authorities for reduced harassment (for example to remove the threat of eviction) and very modest resources (such as the loan of equipment to help dig or clear drainage ditches, or a weekly collection of solid waste) can bring considerable benefits at very low cost.

- *Long-term support is needed from governments and international agencies for 'good' local governance in urban centres.* In many urban centres, provision for urban infrastructure and services is so limited and the capacity to expand it so lacking that many of those with 'above poverty line' incomes, including even middle-income groups, cannot find housing with adequate water and sanitation and protection against natural disasters. 'Good' local governance is important both for what it can contribute to poverty reduction and for what it can prevent. In particular it can prevent local governments from implementing programmes to bulldoze informal settlements and 'resettlement' programmes that cause, exacerbate or deepen poverty.

- *There is a need for the urban poor to have influence on local processes related to poverty reduction.* As in many aspects of development policy, specialists need to shift away from recommending what should be done and towards recommending what local processes should be supported to influence what is done.[93] It is difficult to generalize about which poverty-reduction measures should receive priority because this depends on local circumstances and on whose needs are being considered; it is easier to generalize about the local processes needed that enable local choices in which urban poor groups have influence, mobilize local resources and remove local blockages. One cannot generalize about which of the different aspects of poverty shown in Figure 6.1 should receive priority – it depends so much on local circumstances and capacities, and has to be guided by what is possible. Obviously, all households with low or unstable incomes want higher and more stable incomes, but there may be little scope for boosting these, and at the same time there may be considerable local capacity for working with urban poor groups to extend basic services, support improvements to housing and provide more secure tenure for those in illegal settlements. The problem of what to prioritize is reduced if local authorities and other agencies involve urban poor groups in discussions of what to prioritize and why. Most successful poverty reduction initiatives strive to ensure that urban poor groups have more influence on what is done and how it is done, and often this leads to actions or programmes that address more than one aspect of poverty at the same time.

*   *If poverty is measured using only consumption-based poverty lines, it must be clear what is omitted.* The points made here do not invalidate the utility of a poverty line, but its correct use depends on recognizing that it does not measure all aspects of poverty. Factors omitted include public goods without a market, such as law and order, and civil and political rights, negative externalities such as pollution, and those essential goods and services the quality and extent of which depend to a large degree on good governance.

The opportunities for enhancing income, consumption and services

Chapter 2 showed that most urban households need substantially higher cash incomes to avoid poverty than most rural households, especially if they live in larger or more prosperous cities. But in most or perhaps all low- and middle-income nations, a proportion of low-income urban households will enjoy better quality infrastructure and basic services than most low-income rural households. These can be considered an important 'hidden additional income' (or perhaps, more correctly, hidden consumption) associated with urban areas, and include goods and services which are and are not delivered through the market (including public goods). They may arise because:

*   infrastructure and services are provided by governments or local institutions (for instance, NGOs or charities) free or below their actual cost
*   goods may have prices lowered through subsidies (for instance, government subsidies may lower the price of certain staple foods or fuels)
*   services or credit are available at prices lowered through subsidies (for instance, for some public transport systems or housing finance)
*   there is a wider range of public goods and goods and services provided by private enterprises which have lower prices and are of better quality because of agglomeration economies.

Poverty lines fail to capture most of these cost savings. If poverty is measured only by consumption expenditure, a household living in a home with secure tenure, piped water, connection to a sewer and solid waste collection will appear just as poor as a household with none of this if it has the same expenditure level. The same is true for access to 'public' services provided free or below cost, especially schools, health centres and emergency services. At one extreme, in well-governed urban centres where the potential agglomeration economies in the provision of infrastructure and services are realized, most households with incomes close to the poverty line may not 'live in poverty'. They can send their children to school and use official health care services because these are free or efficiently provided, so costs are kept down. They can live in legal housing where they are not in constant fear of eviction, and where they are served with regular, safe, piped water supplies and adequate sanitation, drainage and waste removal. At the other extreme, in urban centres with very poor or inadequate governance, households with incomes close to the poverty line may have none of these. Indeed, many households with incomes significantly above the poverty line may 'live in poverty' because provision for infrastructure and services is so inadequate.

Chapter 2 gave many examples in which the measurement of poverty fails to incorporate important aspects of individual welfare, including the consumption of public goods such as schools, health services and provision for water and sanitation. Khusro (1999) notes the difficulty of calculating expenditure on public goods, as people typically do not 'purchase' their literacy, education and health in the same manner that they purchase food and other necessities. But in nations and cities where schools and health care are either subsidized or supplied at the state's expense, personal expenditure data do not capture the (often large) costs avoided. Thus a focus on measuring and monitoring poverty using poverty lines can greatly understate the potential to reduce poverty through provision of public goods, including those provided by non-governmental organizations and private companies. As examples given in Chapter 2 indicate, many low-income urban dwellers do in fact purchase education, literacy and health goods in the absence of public provision; however, there are no data on how widespread or common this is. What is more common, as described in Chapter 3, is a lack of public provision for water and sanitation, which often means high costs are paid for these services, even where their quality is poor.

It is likely that sections of the urban population benefit substantially from cheaper, more readily available or better quality infrastructure, services and goods, both public and private – but:

- the data show that few or even none of those with low incomes benefit; and
- it is difficult to separate out benefits that arise from 'urban bias' – in the sense of government investment, expenditure or other measures benefiting urban dwellers more than rural dwellers – from a higher level of investment in urban areas because of higher population densities, more concentrated demand, and agglomeration economies in the supply of infrastructure and services.

Certainly, public agencies responsible for the provision of piped water and sewers often fail to cover their costs through connection fees and user charges, and this means that those who receive connections are receiving subsidies. But, as described in detail in Chapter 3, a large proportion of the urban population do not receive either piped water to their homes or connection to sewers. Indeed, most urban centres in sub-Saharan Africa and many in Asia have no sewers and a limited or no piped water network; for those urban centres that do, it is largely middle- and upper-income groups that are served. This is the case even in large cities, where it might be assumed that 'urban biases' would be most evident. Urban populations generally benefit more from publicly funded schools (as can be seen from, for instance, higher enrolment rates in schools for urban populations) and probably hospitals and clinics, but, again, in most nations large sections of the urban population are ill-served or are not served at all, as evidenced by the examples of low-income households having to pay for private schools, private health care and private water supplies. The inhabitants of illegal settlements in cities often face difficulties not only in getting their children into schools but also in accessing other 'public goods' because these require a legal address or official documentation. And, as reported in Chapter 5 for the case of Central America, when low-income households are connected the charges may be higher, justified on the grounds of the higher costs involved in servicing informal settlements.

Lama-Rewal (2011) notes that in large cities in India low-income groups often display a preference for private medical practitioners, even though public health care is in theory free, because public provision is so poor – under-staffed, with inadequate supplies and inconvenient opening hours. This mirrors what Misra (1990) has observed in informal settlements in Allahabad. Agarwal (2011) documents the inadequacies in the coverage of health care services for the poorest quartile of urban populations for India as a whole and for selected states, including the low proportion of urban children fully immunized and the high proportion of mothers with inadequate antenatal health care.

Thus, although the literature on 'urban bias' assumes that urban populations are better served by infrastructure and services than rural populations because they are much closer to schools, hospitals, water mains and sewers, the extent to which this benefits urban dwellers (especially low-income urban dwellers) is not clear – proximity does not mean access.

The other difficulty with regard to 'urban bias' is separating out urban advantages from urban biases. Most urban contexts provide agglomeration economies that reduce the unit cost of providing good quality infrastructure and services. Average incomes are also generally higher in urban areas than in rural areas, and this means greater capacity to pay. The unit cost of providing piped water to each housing unit and a connection to a sewer or drainage network falls as density increases, while the cost per person of many elements of a water and sewer network (such as water storage and treatment and sewage treatment) comes down as settlement population increases. So the cost of removing deprivations associated with a lack of provision for piped water, sanitation and drainage is usually less per person in urban areas, and if incomes are higher the gap between the cost of good quality provision and the cost that can be afforded is also reduced. There are similar cost savings or economies of scale or proximity for public transport and for many educational, health and emergency services, although rural contexts may allow for less expensive forms of adequate sanitation.[94]

One example of what is possible in urban settings is the community-managed sewer construction programme in Orangi in Karachi, which provided a model subsequently implemented in other urban areas in Pakistan. Here, sewers and drains were constructed in low-income areas with full cost recovery from those who were connected (Hasan 2006). Clearly, in most rural contexts the unit cost of constructing comparable sewers, with connections to each house, would have been much higher. Yet the provision of these sewers in Orangi does not represent urban bias but rather good use of demand and innovation to keep down unit costs. The households paid US$20–30 for their household connection and share of the costs of sanitation.[95] It might also be argued that providing urban populations with better quality infrastructure and services using funding drawn from urban tax bases does not represent 'urban bias'.[96]

The proportion of urban dwellers who benefit from 'urban advantages' and the extent of this benefit depend heavily on the quality of local governance. In well-governed cities, these potential advantages are realized, often with funding drawn only from the city's own tax/revenue base. Efficient public, private or community action can lower the income that a household requires to 'avoid' poverty, or some aspects of poverty. Well-managed city or municipal systems for water and sanitation, drainage and waste removal (generally more common in urban than in rural areas) can greatly reduce the cost of adequate accommodation with basic services. Or an upgrading programme to provide or improve water supplies, sanitation, drainage, paved roads and paths in existing low-income settlements can, in effect, move many inhabitants out of 'living in poverty', as their costs are not increased and the quality of their homes is greatly improved.[97] Effective public or non-profit private provision for schools, health care and childcare can also reduce the household income needed to avoid poverty. An efficient public transport system can cut the costs of access to employment and widen employment opportunities. There are also many examples of relatively low-income urban households gaining access to land for housing at below-market prices, through invasion, illegal occupation or purchasing illegal subdivisions – although the opportunity to acquire a secure land site below the market price is now less common, as even informal or illegal means of obtaining land for housing have become highly commercialized in many cities.

Thus, if efficient public, private or community action to improve housing and basic services is concentrated in urban areas, this could lower the 'poverty line income' needed for those urban households who benefit from such action, enabling them to avoid living in poverty.

However, while urban populations can benefit from indirect 'income' or consumption where there is 'good' governance, they can also suffer where there is 'bad' or 'no' governance. The advantages of larger and more concentrated populations for the provision of infrastructure and services turn into disadvantages, particularly with regard to environmental health risks, if there is no provision. This may help explain why, as described in Chapter 3, under-five mortality rates are not much lower in urban than in rural areas in many nations, and actually higher in some nations. Here, the potential urban advantage of cheaper and better quality infrastructure and services is not realized. As noted, there are hundreds of millions of urban households who have no access to safe and sufficient water supplies, and no provision for sanitation and drainage. Many have inadequate or no access to schools and health care services, even if they have incomes that are above the poverty line. Many urban governments are, in effect, anti-poor, and help create poverty through unnecessary rules and regulations, including harassment and penalties for informal enterprises, and eviction and resettlement programmes. Amis (1999) notes that even if local governments have a limited capacity to reduce poverty they have a much greater capacity to create or exacerbate it.

Thus, many low-income urban dwellers suffer from forms of deprivation generally associated with poverty which are not caused by low income, but rather the incapacity of public, private or non-profit institutions to ensure provision[98] and the capacity of government institutions to contribute to impoverishment. Here, we return to the issue highlighted earlier: the importance of recognizing the extent to which many forms of deprivation faced by low-income households – and often many non-poor households – are the result more of weak, ineffective, unrepresentative or corrupt government than of low income levels. It follows that many forms of deprivation associated with poverty can be addressed by more competent and effective public or private institutions, and in many urban areas this can be done with little or no subsidy. Thus in most urban centres there is scope for improvement in housing, living conditions and basic services for lower-income households, at low per capita cost and with a considerable degree of cost recovery. This highlights the need for poverty measures to include assessments of the quality and extent of provision for public goods. Minujin (1999) argues that provision for basic needs should be measured directly because it is not captured in a money-metric index. Certainly, in many Latin American nations it is relatively common for official statistics used by governments to monitor poverty to include assessments of 'unsatisfied basic needs', and there is some indication that this is also becoming more common in other nations.

Implications for the measurement of urban poverty

The implications of the discussion in Chapter 2 regarding the definition of poverty lines should be self-evident:

- *There is a need to ensure that poverty lines reflect the actual income households need to avoid poverty (that is, to pay for the goods and services required to avoid poverty).* This means evaluating the validity of the measures currently used to define non-food needs or to calculate what allowance should be made for non-food needs. It includes considering whether equivalence scales used are appropriate, for instance with regard to the assumptions they make about the costs of meeting the food and non-food needs of children. It also requires that greater attention be paid to adjusting poverty lines by location, so that they take into account geographic variations in the income needed to avoid poverty and do not understate the scale of poverty in high-cost locations. This recognizes the extent to which the income needed to avoid poverty varies between urban centres, meaning a single 'urban' and 'rural' adjustment is inadequate. One particular difficulty is setting a realistic poverty line when a high proportion of low-income individuals and households in urban areas have to pay high prices for, for instance, water, sanitation, private health care and schools, because of deficiencies in public provision.

- *There is a need to pay particular attention to incorporating more consideration of housing conditions and tenure, including the quality and extent of provision for water and sanitation or the income needed to obtain better quality housing.* There needs to be more correspondence between figures on who is 'poor' and who is living in poverty, including recognition that the quality of local governance will influence the extent of the association between income levels and housing and living conditions. It would be worth considering another way of addressing this, by setting some standard for adequate housing for each city, reflecting secure tenure and adequate water, sanitation and drainage, and investigating how much households would need to spend to get to this standard (see Chandrasekhar and Montgomery 2010; Chibuye 2011). This is in effect doing for key non-food needs what is often done for food needs. Of course, how 'adequate housing' is defined will influence its cost: in investigating the cost of minimally adequate housing in urban areas and the degree to which the poverty line would have to be revised upwards to take account of this, Chandrasekhar and Montgomery (2010) set a lower standard for urban India than Chibuye (2011) does for urban centres in Zambia. Again, it is important that low-income groups are part of the discussion to decide what is considered 'adequate'.
- *There is a need to incorporate non-income aspects of poverty into official measures and monitoring, including those with little correlation to income.*
- *The US$1-a-day or US$2-a-day poverty line should be avoided, unless its use can be demonstrated to have validity for a nation or its urban population.* These poverty lines are particularly inappropriate for nations or cities where low-income groups face high costs and for nations where there are large differences in the incomes needed to avoid poverty. Applying the dollar-a-day poverty line to India assumes that the income needed to avoid poverty is the same in India's villages, small towns, cities and mega-cities, and the same in poor cities as it is in wealthy, booming cities.

The implications for the measurement of poverty of some of the other aspects of deprivation are less certain. It is clear that there are many aspects of poverty that poverty lines do not measure – and cannot measure. Some may be addressed by household surveys and censuses that pay more attention to housing and living conditions and to the quality and extent of infrastructure and service provision. If discussion about how poverty should be measured is brought more into the public domain, especially within low- and middle-income nations, this should encourage innovations to make measurement more effective. As a review of urban demography noted:

As China and other poor countries become more urban, the limitations of urban poverty estimates cannot be left to delicately worded footnotes and rueful caveats. Urbanization underscores the need for rigorous justification of the basis for urban poverty estimates and clear statements of the limits and uncertainties that surround such estimates.

(Montgomery *et al*. 2003, page 184)

However, perhaps a more pressing need for most urban centres is for attention to be paid to improving and expanding the local information base for the measurement of all aspects of poverty. This will support local actions for poverty reduction and local processes for determining what should be done and how, including those providing more space and scope for urban poor groups and organizations and for local government.

Here we return to another theme that comes up continually throughout this book: the over-reliance on national sample surveys for data on deprivations. Household surveys based on representative samples for national populations (including Demographic and Health Surveys and Living Standards Measurement Studies) are of little use at the local level because they do not identify who is suffering from deprivation and where they live. They may have sample sizes large enough to indicate conditions in 'urban areas' or even in cities in different size classes (see Montgomery *et al.* 2003), but this is still of no use to city and municipal authorities who need local detail. Local authorities need to know not only the proportion of people in their jurisdiction who lack provision but also where they live. You cannot start a programme to extend provision for piped water if you do not know which households need it.

There is surprisingly little consideration of the data needed to support local action on poverty reduction or of the potential role of local authorities or other local bodies, including organizations made up of those living in informal settlements, in formulating a better understanding of poverty and more effective actions to reduce it. Many national governments and international agencies may have supported decentralization and local democracy but they have not supported the changes these require in official statistical services. There are at least five possible ways to address this:

1   *Ensure that census data are available to local authorities and other local bodies in a form that allows them to be used in identifying and acting on deprivations.* That is, make certain that small-area data are available. It is not clear how many national governments ensure that local governments get census data in a form that is useful to them, but this appears to be rare (see Navarro 2001). Of course, there is the problem for many sub-Saharan African nations and some other low-income nations that censuses are rare and, for those that have been held, often inaccurate.

2   *Complement national household surveys with surveys of particular cities that can produce the detail needed about informal settlements.* See, for instance, the many insights provided about poverty, health and living conditions through the survey of Nairobi's informal settlements, which the African Population and Health Research Center designed to fit within and complement the national Demographic and Health Survey (APHRC 2002). Perhaps the most surprising aspect of this and of the other detailed work of this centre in informal settlements in Nairobi is how few other cities have comparable research under way.

3   *Support local initiatives to generate the detailed data needed for action, including those that urban poor organizations and federations can undertake themselves.* There are now examples from many different nations and cities of citywide 'slum' surveys, very detailed 'slum' enumerations and censuses, and 'slum' mapping undertaken by urban poor organizations and federations and the local NGOs that work with them, for instance in Ghana (Farouk and Owusu 2012), Kenya (Karanja 2010), India (Livengood and Kunte 2012), Namibia (Muller and Mbanga 2012), South Africa (Baptist and Bolnick 2012), Thailand (Archer 2012), Uganda (Makau, Dobson and Samia 2012) and Zimbabwe (Chitekwe-Biti *et al.* 2012).[99] The similarities between the tools and methods used in the different cities and nations are no coincidence, as most of the work has been undertaken by city and national federations of 'slum'- or shack-dwellers who are members of Slum/Shack Dwellers International (SDI). The federations and NGOs formed SDI in part to help them to learn from each other, including about community-led documentation. Federations chose to undertake this work because of the lack of surveys or the exclusion of informal settlements from surveys, and community-led documentation has become part of how 'slum'- or shack-dwellers and their organizations demonstrate their capacities to local government. In this work they have drawn on the longstanding approaches of the Orangi Pilot Project – Research and Training Institute and its extensive mapping activities in the city of Karachi (OPP-RTI 2002; Hasan 2006).

These initiatives provide very strong information bases for planning and implementing housing improvement, regularization of tenure and improvement of infrastructure and services, and high levels of accountability and participation are built into them. Many have also been catalysts for large-scale initiatives for poverty reduction, in which representative urban poor organizations and local authorities work in partnership. Community-led surveys and mapping in informal settlements are also central to the work of the Asian Coalition for Community Action, a programme of the Asian Coalition for Housing Rights[100] that is supporting more than 700 community-driven upgrading activities in 150 cities in 19 different Asian nations (see Boonyabancha and Mitlin 2012). The residents' engagement in mapping their settlement helps them identify and analyse pressing issues. Their influence on citywide processes is then much increased as all the communities in a city that are taking action share their experiences and discuss how to work together.

There are other examples of local organizations that make it their task to draw together all available data which, supplemented with consultation and discussion, provide a much stronger local information base; this may be done by local government or by other local institutions.[101] City or municipal governments often have a range of information that could be used to support better policies and actions (see Navarro 2001; Velasquez 1998), but it is usually scattered among different departments. With recognition among international agencies of the need for more civil society engagement in defining, measuring and monitoring poverty, and in discussions of how to address it, perhaps all cities should have local 'urban resource centres'.[102] These are the kinds of local institutions that could help develop more valid and detailed poverty statistics rooted in local realities, working with urban poor groups.

4　*Deepen and make more relevant the questions asked in household surveys and censuses with regard to the quality and security of housing and quality and extent of provision for infrastructure and services.* Knowing who has access to a piped water system does not mean much if there are no data on the quality and regularity of the supply and the ease of access. It may be obvious that accessing piped water from a standpipe 100 metres from the home which is shared with 1,000 other households is not the same as having a connection in the home, but many statistics on water provision do not distinguish between these.

5　*'Ground-truth' poverty statistics and poverty lines.* For instance, look at housing conditions for households with incomes close to the poverty line to see if their housing needs are met. Also, quick pilots can be carried out to test the validity of a newly developed poverty line or any other measure meant to contribute to understanding of urban poverty. James Garrett from IFPRI has commented that poverty lines or measures need 'a sniff test' – as in the quick and most basic test of whether food is edible. It does not take much time or many resources to arrange discussions with grassroots organizations about the validity of what is proposed or the feasibility of its application. This need for ground-truthing is particularly important for academics or institutions who want to compare poverty levels between nations or between rural and urban areas within nations, to avoid producing poverty statistics that bear no relation to local realities.

One possible criticism of these recommendations is that they reflect an unrealistic or even a romantic view of what the 'urban poor' can do, and give too much weight to insisting that they be fully involved in discussions about how best to define, measure and then reduce poverty. Any agency that has worked at grassroots level with poor groups knows that it is difficult to mesh the institutional concerns of their funders with more open, transparent and participatory ways of working. Often it is not easy to work in participatory ways with urban poor groups – indeed, such groups are often full of complex conflicts that make any consensus on priorities difficult to achieve. Many individuals and groups among the urban poor have a profound distrust of all external agencies, often rooted in their previous unsatisfactory experiences. But the recommendations made here are based on methods that have been tried and tested in many different nations; these are also at the centre of the companion book to this (Satterthwaite and Mitlin 2013). These experiences show that, when one seeks to reconcile what is the most effective way to reduce urban poverty with what is possible within a locality, one of the critical determinants of success is the quality of the relationship between 'the poor' and the organizations or agencies which have the resources or powers to help address one or more aspects of the deprivations they suffer. As we will show in the companion volume, the collection of information about the nature and extent of deprivation forms a basis on which organized groups can prioritize, strategize and engage with authorities.

Obviously, the extent of success also depends on:

- the extent to which organizations or agencies have resources or decision-making powers that can support urban poor groups;
- the space given by such organizations to urban poor groups in defining priorities and developing responses;
- how urban poor groups are organized, and whose interests they represent – most of the examples of success are drawn from nations where organizations and federations of the urban poor have developed in ways that make them representative of and accountable to their members (and have women in key roles).

Obviously, the quality of the relationship between those with low incomes and/or living in informal settlements and all local or external agencies is influenced by these agencies' transparency and accountability to such groups. The experiences of urban poor federations and of many other government or international initiatives that have worked with urban poor groups show how much low-income groups and their community organizations can achieve with limited resources, where relationships with local (and other) organizations are good and there is appropriate support for their actions. Those concerned with the definition and measurement of poverty need to consider how their work can support this.

Urban poverty and health

Chapter 3 describes the very large health burden faced by men and women (and boys and girls) in households with inadequate incomes in urban areas, and how much of this can and should be avoided. It emphasizes how one key characteristic of a badly governed city is very large differentials between high- and low-income populations in a range of health-related indicators, including infant, child and maternal mortality rates, access to good quality health care services and quality of provision for water, sanitation and household waste collection. A key characteristic of a well-governed city is the absence of such differentials or much smaller differentials, with figures comparable to other safer cities being achieved.

Income-based poverty lines give no clues about health burdens experienced by low-income dwellers, other than who has incomes or consumption levels likely to be inadequate in relation to food costs and needs, and perhaps some non-food costs and needs. In a large and increasing number of urban centres in middle-income nations, most households with incomes close to the official poverty lines have regular water supplies piped into their homes, good provision for sanitation and household waste collection. In urban areas in high-income nations, there is close to 100 per cent coverage. Elsewhere, most or all urban households with incomes close to the poverty line get none of these. However low their income is, a household in a high-income nation, does not expect to spend hours a day fetching and carrying water from distant standpipes or kiosks, to have no toilet in their accommodation or to have no collection of household wastes. Chapters 3 and 5 also show how health problems, like poverty lines, can be viewed in absolute and in relative terms.

Chapter 3 highlighted the many ways in which different health problems contribute to poverty and how, in turn, different aspects of poverty contribute to illness, injury and premature death. This makes clear the very large range of factors that are termed health determinants because they directly or indirectly influence health outcomes. As Figure 3.4 on page 100 shows, there is an enormous range of economic, social and environmental determinants of health in urban areas, from how the prosperity of the national economy and the policies and priorities of national governments influence the resources and capacities of urban governments, to local land and labour markets, to living and working conditions, to the extent to which those with limited incomes can influence government action and develop their own social support networks. This range of health determinants also means that there are many ways in which addressing health problems can reduce poverty and many ways in which reducing poverty can improve health.

Chapter 3 again raises the issue of the lack of relevant data. There is an astonishing lack of basic data on health and health determinants to inform and support good policies. As with data on income or consumption poverty, there is, in particular, very little information to support local policies and investments, even though most of the responsibilities for addressing health and its determinants fall to local (city or municipal) governments. For instance, for most urban centres, there are no data on infant, child and maternal mortality rates by district, or for the informal settlements where these rates are likely to be highest, nor are there such data for hunger or indicators of malnutrition such as stunting and wasting, and often there are no such data for provision of water and sanitation. Chapter 3 also highlights how, where there are detailed local studies, they often show the quality and extent of provision is much poorer than official statistics suggest. There are usually few data on the quality and coverage of health care and the availability of emergency services; if these are included, they are not available by district or settlement. Thus there is little to inform city and municipal governments about where (spatially) or who (socially) faces the most serious health risks, or how these risks differ by age group or sex. There is also astonishingly little information available on disasters and their impacts, as most disasters are not recorded in national or international disaster databases (although, as described in Chapter 3, this is beginning to change). Chapter 3 includes a short section on climate change: in general, those within the urban population who are most exposed to and at risk from environmental health hazards and least well-served by provision for water, sanitation, health care and emergency services are those who are most at risk from the direct and indirect impacts of climate change.

Finally, with health, as with the setting of poverty lines, there is very little engagement of those who collect and use data with those living in informal settlements. Yet we have a few studies which show how much can be learnt about risk and vulnerability by working with and supporting people who live in informal settlements to produce the data needed to address the health burdens they face.

Comparing urban and rural poverty?

We began this book with the claim that the scale and depth of urban poverty is ignored or given insufficient attention within most low-income nations, many middle-income nations and globally. We noted that this reflects the considerable misrepresentation and underestimation of urban poverty, which occurs because of the very narrow ways in which poverty is usually defined and measured. We hope that the evidence presented in Chapters 2 to 5 substantiates this. But, as stated in Chapter 1, we also need to be very clear that this book is not making the case for reducing the attention given to rural poverty.

One of the great mistakes in development policy over the last 40 years has been to treat 'rural' and 'urban' poverty as somehow separate and to assume that they are in competition with each other for resources. In part, this is due to a failure to recognize how many aspects of rural and urban prosperity are linked, with more prosperous farmers and rural families supporting local urban development and drawing on urban-produced goods and urban-based markets and services. As international development assistance agencies recognized that insufficient attention had been given to agriculture and to rural development during the 1970s – encouraged and supported by Michael Lipton's book *Why Poor People Stay Poor: Urban Bias in World Development* (Lipton 1977) – so rural proponents developed the data and the justifications for giving them greater priority. Chapter 2 describes how poverty statistics came to support this by understating and misrepresenting the scale and nature of urban poverty, sometimes so badly that in many low-income nations there seemed to be no urban poverty. Those who worked on rural or agricultural issues welcomed the statistics and data sets that supported their case and this helped create the myth that almost all poverty (and extreme poverty) was in rural areas. This myth was sustained by faulty data and weak conceptual frameworks.

Giving priority to rural development was also assumed to address urban poverty as it would slow or stop migration to urban areas, as such migration was judged to be a sign of rural underdevelopment. The fact that most new investment and a large and growing proportion of GDP and jobs came from urban-based enterprises was not acknowledged. Many governments saw rural-to-urban migration as something to be controlled or stopped, even as almost every successful economy urbanized (and most less successful economies did not). The importance of remittances for rural households' income and consumption that came from household members working in urban areas was not acknowledged. And even where there was recognition of the increasing importance of 'non-farm' and 'off-farm' work for rural livelihoods and incomes, what was almost never mentioned was that a high proportion of this work was in urban areas. Similarly, little attention was given to the fact that successful rural and agricultural development will usually stimulate and support urban development and vice versa – an issue we sought to document and highlight during the 1980s (Hardoy and Satterthwaite 1986a, 1986b, 1989; see also Manzanal and Vapnarsky 1986). Fortunately, there is now a large literature on rural–urban linkages and their implications for rural and urban poverty (and prosperity) among different groups.[103]

Thus, while striving to ensure poverty measures capture the scale and nature of deprivations linked to urban (and rural) characteristics, it is also important to seek more integrated understandings of poverty, including the linkages between rural and urban dwellers and rural and urban economies, and the underlying causes of poverty that often contribute to both rural and urban poverty. As Wratten (1995) notes, discussions about whether rural or urban poverty is worse can distract attention from the structural determinants that affect both. These include determinants internal to the nation, such as the distribution of assets, socially constructed constraints on opportunity based on class, gender, race and age, and macro-economic policies (though these are often influenced by external agencies). They also include determinants external to low- and middle-income nations, such as terms of trade, external debt burdens, and the barriers to accessing the world's wealthiest consumer markets and unfair practices within these markets. Discussions about how much farmers in low-income nations lose out to rich-world farmers because of trade barriers and subsidies usually forget how much this also affects urban-based enterprises that serve export agriculture (providing transport, credit, farm inputs, storage, processing, etc.) or which rely on rural households' demand for goods and services.

Now that more attention is being given to urban poverty, it may be that urban development proponents will also use inaccurate statistics to bolster their case. That this book is concerned with urban poverty is not meant to draw attention away from rural poverty. It is clear that, globally, the number of people suffering hunger and other effects of poverty is still larger in rural areas than in urban areas, especially in most low-income nations (which are also generally the nations with the lowest levels of urbanization). However, there are likely to be more urban than rural dwellers suffering the effects of poverty in more urbanized (mostly middle-income) nations and there are also very substantial numbers of urban dwellers in poverty in low-income nations. The proportion of the world's poor that live and work in urban areas is also likely to be increasing. This would become evident if more realistic poverty lines were set and applied. Chapter 2 describes how the construction and application of poverty lines came to understate urban poverty, in large part by making insufficient allowance for the costs of non-food needs in urban areas (or in particular urban areas – generally the largest and most successful cities). Chapter 1 also noted the change in the relative proportion of the population in rural and urban areas in the last 30–40 years. Since 1975, the urban population in the Global South has grown by 1.8 billion people, compared to rural population growth of 848 million.

Previous chapters have presented many examples of the very large and mostly preventable health burdens suffered by low-income urban dwellers; also of the inadequacies of their incomes, homes and infrastructure and services provision. When confronted with the scale and depth of deprivation in urban areas, it is difficult to conceive of there being an urban bias – or, if there is such a bias, clearly it does not benefit large sections of the urban population. We have also stressed the extent to which urban deprivations are hidden because much of the information comes from national sample surveys which tell us little about deprivations among lower-income urban dwellers.

Even if indicators for urban populations are generally better than for rural populations, it does not imply that there is no need to address urban problems. Under-five mortality rates may be lower in urban areas than rural areas – sometimes a lot lower. For instance, in Mali in 2006, the under-five mortality rate was reported as 158.2 deaths per 1,000 live births for its urban population and 234.2 for its rural population. For Liberia in 2009, the figures were 138 deaths per 1,000 live births in urban areas and 170 in rural areas. Though they make clear the urgent need to act on under-five mortality rates in rural areas, these findings do not imply that there is no need to act in urban areas. And, reviewing the findings from the most recent Demographic and Health Surveys and reproductive health surveys, there are actually nine countries for which under-five mortality rates were reported as being higher in urban than in rural areas, and several where there was very little difference, while the lower urban rates reported for some countries represent a relatively recent development.[104]

If we had an accurate basis for assessing who was poor in rural and urban areas, and it was shown that 60 per cent lived in rural areas, it hardly means that the 40 per cent in urban areas should be ignored. In some ways the scale of under-five mortality among urban populations is more shocking, given how much easier and cheaper it is to provide the services that reduce such rates in most urban contexts. Well-governed urban areas should have an advantage that is not derived from higher subsidies or other biases, but simply from using the potential of agglomeration economies.

Some studies on differentials in mortality rates and malnutrition show that there is less urban bias than has long been assumed. Using data from 47 low- and middle-income countries, it was found that urban populations' lower child mortality rates and improved nutrition largely vanished after researchers controlled for wealth, education and other socio-economic factors. An urban child health advantage was only identified 'in a little more than one-third of the countries studied' (Van de Poel, O'Donnell and van Doorslaer 2007). A study of maternal health care in 30 countries in the Global South concluded that poor and marginalized urban sub-groups compare unfavourably with other urban dwellers with respect to mortality, and groups such as the poorest migrants from rural areas and 'slum' dwellers may have maternal, newborn and child mortality rates as high as or even higher than the rural poor (Matthews *et al.* 2010).

Several studies have compared rural and urban populations with regard to malnutrition. An analysis of Demographic and Health Survey data from 11 countries on stunting among children up to three years of age (Menon, Ruel and Morris 2000) found that the most disadvantaged urban children had rates of stunting that were on average only slightly lower than those of the most disadvantaged rural children. As mentioned in Chapter 5, this study also found that the risk of stunting may be up to 10 times higher when comparing urban children of low and high socio-economic status. A study on childhood stunting also based on Demographic and Health Survey data found that the 'urban advantage' in child health disappears for all but one nation once the socio-economic status of households is accounted for (Fotso 2007). A study of disparities in childhood nutritional status in Angola, Central African Republic and Senegal found that, when using a simple urban–rural comparison, the prevalence of stunting was significantly higher in rural areas. But when the urban and rural populations were stratified using a measure of wealth, '[p]oor children in these urban areas were just as likely to be stunted or underweight as poor children living in rural areas' (Kennedy *et al.* 2006, page 187).

A study of the world's most deprived (Ahmed *et al.* 2007) noted that the rural disadvantage apparent when applying the same dollar-a-day poverty line to rural and urban areas is less evident when looking at rates of food energy deficiency. The authors suggested that this may in part be due to urban households having higher costs for non-food needs such as housing, health and transport. In 12 out of 18 low- and middle-income countries (in all of which nationally representative household surveys were carried out between 1996 and 2003), the incidence of hunger (food energy deficiency) in urban areas equalled or exceeded rural levels. In seven of these nations (mostly in Asia), the incidence of food energy deficiency was substantially higher in urban areas.

Chapter 5 also summarizes the findings of a study which compared poverty in a remote rural area, an informal urban settlement in Cape Town and a settlement in a highly mechanized agricultural export area in South Africa. The proportion of households reporting going without food was highest in the informal urban settlement; in addition, the proportion of households reporting deprivations such as going without medical care, clean drinking water, shelter and sufficient fuel was lower in the export agriculture area than in the informal urban settlement (du Toit 2005).

This does not mean that urban poverty is worse than rural poverty, but the findings of these kinds of studies caution against quick, simple generalizations or assumptions that there is an urban advantage or an urban bias. These studies also show that the problems of ill-health and malnutrition may be very serious among lower-income groups in urban areas, but hidden in any urban average because of the concentration of well-fed middle- and upper-income groups in urban areas.

It is also worth recalling the points made in Chapter 2 about the need for caution in comparing rural and urban poverty because of the different contexts and needs involved, and thus the different kinds of interventions needed to improve health and reduce deprivation. For instance, there are probably more homeless people in urban areas than in rural areas. Most low-income urban dwellers are likely to be closer to water sources than most low-income rural dwellers, but they may have greater difficulty accessing these, due to long queues, irregular supplies or cost. Most urban dwellers are closer to health care services but here, too, access may be limited by queues or costs. It may be that a higher proportion of urban dwellers than rural dwellers face harassment, eviction or arrest because their homes and livelihoods are illegal. Most urban dwellers have far less opportunity to grow their own food or to forage for it (which for many rural dwellers is an important safety net), although urban and peri-urban agriculture have importance in many urban contexts. More urban dwellers have to pay for their housing, especially tenants, also for water and often for access to toilets; as Chapter 2 shows, these costs often take up a large proportion of their household incomes.

Of course, a high proportion of low-income rural dwellers also face profound disadvantages, such as very large time and energy costs – rather than heavy monetary costs – for fetching and carrying water from distant sources, also greater inaccessibility of services, including schools, health care and emergency services.

Further, there are large numbers of individuals and households which have both rural and urban components to their livelihoods, assets, incomes and social networks, which again cautions against simplistic 'rural-versus-urban' comparisons.

Addressing inequality

Involving the organizations formed by 'slum'- or shack-dwellers in the assessment and analysis of poverty not only improves the depth, detail and relevance of findings; through such interactions with government authorities, these organizations can begin to challenge the scale of the political inequalities described in Chapter 5. As discussed there, low-income and otherwise disadvantaged households may be denied the right to vote because they live in informal settlements. In many more cases, lack of basic infrastructure and basic services combines with insecure tenure to make the residents of informal settlements dependent on politicians and sometimes officials for favours. A situation of resource scarcity combines with a lack of state accountability and dysfunctional high-cost models of urban development imported from the North and results in significant underinvestment in a limited number of residential areas. Faced with such structural disadvantage, exercising democracy does not involve any ideological choice but is simply a way in which the urban poor seek to negotiate access to essential goods and services.

Chapter 5 also discusses the scale of spatial inequalities reflecting the neglect of informal settlements. It shows that such spatial inequalities are neither accidental nor neutral. They result from systemic disadvantaging of the urban poor by political elites, through exclusion of the urban poor from decision making. This is reinforced by negative, discriminatory social attitudes which are in part due to the stigma associated with residency in informal settlements. The documentation of outcomes in cities such as Guayaquil, Karachi and Nairobi makes it clear that the high costs of informal shelter advantage some elite groups.

Politicians have to allocate resources within a context of resource scarcity and usually with an emphasis on the prevailing high-cost Northern models of development. The structural pressures of limited budgets and a limited range of acceptable solutions means that they are able to address only a few of the many areas of need. Their response is to do this in a way that matches their self-interest (that is, they take advantage of the situation). However, more organized urban poor communities are able to recognize that these structures are based on partiality, with some settlements favoured over others to reward them for acting as 'vote banks'. Gaining understanding of the situation through engagement in enumerations and surveys enables communities to challenge these inherently discriminatory practices and work with the state to change them.

Addressing urban poverty and inequality requires the involvement of the state. The state cannot act to address all deprivations – for instance, its potential contribution to increased incomes is limited, particularly if a high proportion of the working population is in the informal sector. But Chapter 5 also points to the importance of economic structure in determining what is possible for the urban poor, whose income earners may be 'trapped' within low productivity sectors of the economy with very few opportunities for social mobility (see also Chapter 4). State revenue-raising through taxation thus represents an opportunity to support households in need and to make essential investments to provide more equal access to basic services. Not all state expenditures are redistributive, however. Investments in pensions restricted to formal workers, improvements in infrastructure favouring higher-income households and educational investments favouring secondary or tertiary education are all examples of regressive state expenditures. But recognizing these problems is a first and necessary step in working out what to do next.

Inequalities combine with absolute poverty across towns and cities in the Global South. This book argues that this is insufficiently recognized, and hence not addressed. Despite their stated intent, both the development assistance agencies of the Global North and national and local governments in the Global South – are unable to respond to development needs at the required scale due to lack of information. Moreover this lack of information results in poor conceptual models and inadequate frameworks that compound ignorance and the ineffectiveness of policies and programmes.

We argue that another, better future is possible, and should be pursued. A more just, inclusive world is possible, and just and inclusive cities are needed to achieve it. For these to become a reality, there must be recognition of what it means to have a low income, be without basic services and face discrimination and exclusion, and recognition that this is the experience of hundreds of millions of urban households. Also key is the capacity of the urban poor to bring their perspectives and abilities to bear in addressing the deprivations they face – both in terms of what they themselves do and in terms of their influence within local government and beyond. To underpin understanding of and action on urban poverty, a joint endeavour is needed to source and analyse supporting data – data of a very different type than that currently used to define and measure poverty.

What is needed in a post-MDG world

- *Greater attention given to urban poverty and to its economic, social and political underpinnings.* This includes recognizing the many dimensions of urban poverty, which include inadequate incomes; inadequate, unstable or risky asset bases; poor quality and often insecure, hazardous and overcrowded housing; inadequate provision of 'public' infrastructure and basic services; high prices paid for many necessities; limited or no safety net; inadequate protection of rights through the operation of the law; and voicelessness and powerlessness within political systems and bureaucratic structures. Recognizing urban poverty's many dimensions also highlights the many entry points through which it can be reduced.
- *Recognition that the role of the urban poor, individually and collectively, is key to poverty reduction.* There is a need for far greater understanding of the competencies, capacities and priorities of the urban poor, and of the extent to which a real commitment on the part of local governments to working with the urban poor can remove one of the most profound deprivations associated with poverty – the lack of voice and recognition.
- *Recognition that competent, accountable, adequately resourced urban governments can contribute enormously to poverty reduction.* This is so even if they have limited capacity for directly increasing incomes, as their contribution can take the form of ensuring provision of infrastructure and services, and working with urban poor groups. It should also be recognized that, conversely, incompetent, unaccountable, inadequately resourced urban governments enormously increase urban poverty and reduce or even remove health advantages for urban dwellers.
- *Commitment to a dramatic improvement in local-level documentation, in its depth, detail and coverage, so that local governments, citizens and civil society organizations can be provided with a basis for key decisions and actions.* As discussed earlier in this chapter, organizations and federations of the urban poor have demonstrated their capacity to help governments do this. The availability of more accurate and useful indicators will also allow for international comparisons of who falls below income-based poverty lines, who does not have water, sanitation and other basic services that reduce health risks, and who lacks the resilience needed to cope with disasters, or with economic, social and political change – and now also climate change.
- *If the post-MDG landscape still includes targets, for example for reductions in infant, child and maternal mortality rates, international agencies need to devise frameworks to support local governments in addressing these targets and to develop the capacity to collect the data needed to monitor results at a local level.*

Notes

1. Why this book?

1 The Demographic and Health Surveys are national surveys that collect data from a representative sample of households on issues relating to population, HIV, health and nutrition. See http://measuredhs.com/

2 We use the term 'informal settlement' instead of 'slum' for the settlements that have developed in so many cities that have some aspects of illegality and so often house a large proportion of the low-income population. They include a great range of settlements in terms of the nature of their illegality (from illegal occupation of the land, for instance, to legal ownership of the site but contravention of development regulations), the extent of provision for infrastructure and services, the extent of protection from eviction and the likelihood of being legalized (see Hardoy and Satterthwaite 1989 for more discussion on this). In some Latin American nations they are referred to as 'popular settlements'.

3 See the discussion of the term 'the poor' in the final section of this chapter.

4 Poverty reduction strategy papers can be downloaded from the International Monetary Fund's website at http://www.imf.org/external/np/prsp/prsp.aspx

5 In addition, most rural areas have been 'urbanized' in terms of employment structures, as most of the rural population does not work in agriculture, forestry or fishing, with many commuting to urban jobs or to industry and service enterprises that locate in rural areas, or telecommuting.

6 Here it is important to distinguish between growth in urban populations and growth in levels of urbanization. Nations' urban populations can be growing rapidly from natural increase even as the level of urbanization increases slowly or not at all.

7 The full text of these is available online at http://eau.sagepub.com/

8 These were published in the two 1995 issues of *Environment and Urbanization* – see http://eau.sagepub.com/

9 Satterthwaite 1995, 1997a, 2004; Mitlin 2000, 2001, 2004; Jonsson and Satterthwaite 2000 (an unpublished background paper prepared for the US National Research Council's Panel on Urban Population Dynamics, whose report *Cities Transformed* was published in 2003 – see Montgomery *et al.* 2003); Mitlin and Satterthwaite 2001.

2. Measuring poverty

10 Sahn and Stifel (2003) suggest 1.2 per cent in 1998; official statistics suggested three different figures in 1997: hard-core poverty 7.6 per cent; food poverty 38.3 per cent; absolute poverty 49 per cent (Kenya, Government of 2000).

11 This book draws on so many poverty assessments by the World Bank that, following the conventional referencing system, it would mean some years would have many

publications listed as 'World Bank'. To avoid this, where the World Bank report is on a particular country, we add the name of the country to the reference.

12 See Tacoli 1998; Satterthwaite and Tacoli 2003; Tacoli 2003, 2006; Tacoli and Mabala 2010. See also special issues of *Environment and Urbanization* on rural–urban links, 15(1) in 2003 and 10(1) in 1998, and, on migration and mobility, 22(1) in 2010; these are available at http://eau.sagepub.com/

13 There are important exceptions – for instance, the lively debate in India about the setting of poverty lines, also recent discussions in Zambia.

14 See Corbridge and Jones (2005), also the discussion in Hardoy and Satterthwaite (1989) which suggested that if there was urban bias it was likely to be 'large-city middle and upper income group bias', as it clearly brought little or no benefit to most of the low-income urban population.

15 From 1977 to 1998 our research programme monitored the proportion of funding allocated to different aspects of urban poverty reduction for a range of international agencies, based on analyses of each of their project commitments (see Satterthwaite 1997b, 2001; Hardoy, Mitlin and Satterthwaite 2001). But it always proved difficult to get funding to support this work and we could not sustain this monitoring. In addition, as more development assistance was allocated to sector support or basket funding, so it became more difficult to analyse what proportion of funding went to urban poverty reduction.

16 This subsection is an updated version of the first section in Satterthwaite (1997a).

17 Assuming around 1.4 billion urban dwellers in low- and middle-income nations at that date (see United Nations 2012).

18 The official UN statistics for water and sanitation provision may not show this but, as discussed in Chapter 3, this is because they are not based on data showing who has adequate or safe provision.

19 Chen and Ravallion (2007) suggest that 752 million urban dwellers were poor in 2002 if a $2-a-day poverty line is used.

20 The authors of this paper have worked for many years with the inhabitants of informal settlements in addressing household and community needs. In the interviews they undertook, they chose to focus on nine women they knew and had worked with and of whom they felt able to ask sensitive questions, and go into detail about income and goods purchased (see Hardoy with Almansi 2011).

21 The Millennium Development Goals are discussed in more detail in a later section in this chapter. The extent to which these help reduce urban poverty depends on the extent to which governments and international agencies acknowledge the urban components of the deficits in terms of malnutrition and inadequate income, and in provision of water, sanitation, maternal and child health care and disease control

22 We reviewed how poverty is defined and measured in 59 low- and middle-income nations, and also how the definition of poverty lines changed over the last 15 years for some of these nations (details and sources by country are provided in an annex available at http://www.routledge.com/books/details/9780415624671/). Of these nations, 27 are in sub-Saharan Africa, 13 in Asia and 19 in Latin America and the Caribbean. 23 are low-income nations including 16 in sub-Saharan Africa. The nations covered represent two thirds of all low-income nations and three fifths of all nations in sub-Saharan Africa.

23 GTZ (Deutsche Gesellschaft für Technische Zusammenarbeit) is the German Agency for Technical Cooperation, now part of GIZ (Deutsche Gesellschaft für Internationale Zusammenarbeit), the German Agency for International Cooperation.

24 There are also debates and discussions regarding the adequacy of the methods used to establish or estimate the incomes needed to afford sufficient food – see, for instance, Ravallion (1998); Wratten (1995); and Reddy and Pogge (2003).

25 See, for instance, Grootaert (1996) for Côte d'Ivoire; Ghosh, Ahmad and Maitra (1994) for four cities in India; Maxwell *et al.* (1998) for Accra; Dinye (1995) for a

sample of households within a low-income settlement in Kumasi; Malawi, Government of (1994) for Lilongwe, Blantyre and Mzuzu cities; Huq *et al.* (1996) for the urban poor in Bangladesh.

26 The exclusion of these is usually justified by pointing to the difficulty in determining how these affect income, because they are large but occasional expenditures.

27 Renters or tenants may be reluctant to say that they are paying rent, or to reveal how much they pay – see Weru (2004), for example.

28 See Grootaert (1996) for a discussion of this with regard to Côte d'Ivoire.

29 Other public toilets charge more for defecation than for urination.

30 In the UK, those who live in London and other higher-cost locations often get a considerable upward adjustment in their income (a 'weighting allowance') in recognition of the higher costs.

31 For reviews, see WHO (1992); UNCHS (1996); Hardoy, Mitlin and Satterthwaite (2001). Documentation goes back to the 1960s and 1970s, however, including for example Abrams (1964); Ward (1976); Turner (1976).

32 See Swaminathan (1995), which reports on different estimates for the proportion of 'slum' households and 'pavement dwellers' in Mumbai who have below-poverty-line incomes. The main surprise is that, in surveys made during the 1970s and 1980s, 30–45 percent of pavement dwellers are reported as having incomes above the income poverty line. This could be taken as a confirmation that many non-poor households live on the pavements, but given the very poor conditions, the insecurity and the lack of basic services for those who dwell on the pavements (Swaminathan 1995; SPARC 1985), more likely explanations are the lack of provision for non-food needs when setting poverty lines and the high cost of housing in Mumbai.

33 In the USA, adjusting for housing costs alone would significantly shift the US poverty profile, with the likely effect of raising estimates of poverty in metropolitan areas (Citro and Michael 1995); it may be that locational cost-of-living adjustments in low- and middle-income countries would need to be larger than in the USA, because living costs for poorer groups are increased by poor governance, as discussed in Chapter 6.

34 For discussions of how allowance has been made for spatial variations in costs, see Datt and Jolliffe (1999) for Egypt; Grootaert (1996) for Côte d'Ivoire; Ministry of Planning and Finance, Government of Mozambique *et al.* (1998) for Mozambique; and Lanjouw, Prennushi and Zaidi (1999) for Nepal.

35 Deaton and Tarozzi (2000) list the 228 commodities for which expenditure data were collected in India's National Sample Survey, fiftieth round. It shows the careful and detailed attention given to food expenditures (most items are food items) and to fuel expenditures (all non-food items are for fuel or energy). By implication, 'the poor' only need food and fuel. This is not an appropriate basis for gauging the income that poor households need in locations where many other needs are monetized and where the cost of meeting these needs would represent a significant proportion of the income for low-income households (and often more than they can afford, meaning these non-food and non-fuel needs are not met).

36 As discussed later, the quality and availability of education, health care, piped water, good quality sanitation, drainage and garbage collection is generally better in middle-income nations than low-income nations; where there are competent, effective and accountable urban governments (which are more common in middle-income nations), these may bring both better provision and lower prices for large sections of the urban poor.

37 Many low-income households have to purchase water from vendors which is very expensive per unit volume. When the water is expensive, they will generally use cheaper but less readily available and poorer quality water sources for most household tasks (see UN-HABITAT 2003a).

38 This may not indicate that these are more expensive in urban areas but rather that urban households or low-income urban households choose to spend more on them,

though in most instances urban poor households' expenditures on these are more likely to be related to need than choice. This section's focus is on whether sufficient allowance is made in poverty lines for non-food costs for urban populations, not about whether non-food costs are higher in urban areas than in rural areas. Some non-food costs are likely to be higher in rural areas than in urban areas; income-based poverty measures also fail to highlight some serious rural deprivations, such as the very inadequate access to public services and (producer and consumer) markets. However, some discussion of rural–urban differences in non-food costs is necessary if poverty lines use national or rural household survey data to calculate non-food needs, and thus make little or no allowance for those non-food items that are generally more expensive in urban areas (or in particular urban centres or districts).

39 Despite evidence that a high share of household expenditures in urban areas goes on non-food items such as transport and housing, the poverty line was still set at only 1.3 times the cost of a basic food basket.

40 Kanji (1995) also documents that in Zimbabwe in 1992 primary school fees were introduced in urban but not in rural areas, and that fees for secondary schools were higher in urban than in rural areas. Devas and Korboe (2000) note the introduction of charges for health and education in Ghana.

41 The proportion of total expenditure going to education also increased in rural areas – from 0.8 to 2.8 per cent.

42 This is hardly ever acknowledged in the general literature on poverty, although it has been one of the main themes of the literature on urban development from the 1960s onwards (see Abrams 1964; Turner 1976; Ward 1976; Hardoy and Satterthwaite 1989; UNCHS 1996; UN-HABITAT 2003b).

43 See, for instance, Barbosa *et al.* 1997; Richmond 1997; UNCHS and World Bank 1993; UNCHS 1993; UNDP 1998; Rakodi and Withers 1995. It is worth noting that rent accounted for 17–21 per cent of the 'poverty-line income' that Rowntree calculated was necessary for minimum necessities in York in 1899 (Rowntree 1902). The allowance varied according to the size of the household.

44 Of course, many other local factors were also present, including rent increases that had taken place because the government had removed rent controls, and the weakening of the military dictatorship, which gave low-income households more hope that the settlements they rapidly built would not be bulldozed (see Cuenya, Armus, *et al.* 1990; Cuenya, Almada *et al.* 1990).

45 See UN-HABITAT 2003a. See also Cairncross 1990; Devas and Korboe 2000; Ghosh *et al.* 1994; Aegisson 2001; Moser 1996; Etemadi 2000 for other examples of low-income households paying high costs or high proportions of their income on water and/or sanitation.

46 This literature is reviewed in Hardoy, Mitlin and Satterthwaite (2001); see also Burra, Patel and Kerr (2003); UN-HABITAT (2003a).

47 See Devas and Korboe (2000) for an example in Kumasi; and Patel, d'Cruz and Burra (2002) for an example in Mumbai.

48 There is a very considerable literature now on the cost of evictions for low-income households and the extent to which this creates poverty – see, for instance, the publications of the Asian Coalition for Housing Rights over the last 24 years; also the publications of the Centre on Housing Rights and Evictions (COHRE); and the papers in *Environment and Urbanization* 6(1) from 1994 on evictions, especially Murphy and Anana (1994) and COHRE (1994). See also Bhan (2009) and Bartlett *et al.* (1999).

49 See http://www.chronicpoverty.org/

50 This list has been developed and modified since it was first drafted for the editorial of the October 1995 issue of *Environment and Urbanization*, and earlier versions of it have been published in various papers (for instance, Satterthwaite 1997a, 2001; Mitlin and Satterthwaite 2004). It has drawn on many others' work, especially Moser,

Herbert and Makonnen (1993), Amis (1995), Chambers (1995), Wratten (1995), Baulch (1996) and Moser (1996, 1998).

3. Why is health so poor among low-income urban dwellers?

51 Often through an asset index, because interviewees are reluctant to report their incomes or give inaccurate data; see Agarwal (2011) for a discussion of this method and its application.

52 An exception are cities where local governments have sought to identify and act on important health risks or determinants of health; see Llorca (2011) for an example.

53 Some interesting insights into this are discussed in Chaplin (1999, 2011) and McGranahan (2007), including the ways in which middle- and upper-income groups supported large investments in provision for water and sanitation in Europe and North America in the second half of the nineteenth century because their health and businesses were impacted by cholera epidemics; now middle- and upper-income groups know how to protect themselves from infectious and parasitic diseases without having to contribute to the costs of extending such protection to low-income groups.

54 Statistics on infant and child mortality are generally given as 0–1 year (infant), 1–4 years (child) and under-five mortality rates per 1,000 live births. It is also more common now for infant mortality rates to be divided into neonatal (0–28 days) and post-neonatal (28 days–1 year). This kind of disaggregation is useful, as there are considerable differences in the range and relative importance of risks and responses for these different age groups (see Arrossi 1996). A study in two informal settlements in Nairobi found that perinatal causes accounted for 28 per cent of the life years lost among under-fives (see Kyobutungi *et al.* 2008).

55 Statistics for infant and child mortality rates for individual cities are rare; it is likely that many cities in middle-income nations have low rates, as provision for water, sanitation and health care have improved greatly in most urban areas.

56 All high-income nations and many middle-income nations have achieved this, and many have rates below five per 1,000 live births. WHO data on under-five mortality are available at http://apps.who.int/ghodata/?vid=180#

57 Stillbirths contributed 16.3 per cent; perinatal causes overall contributed 28 per cent.

58 See, for instance, WHO (1989, 1992, 1996). UNICEF published a newsletter, *Urban Examples*, for several years, and had a full-time senior urban advisor.

59 This list draws on and updates Satterthwaite (2007b).

60 The WHO guidelines are based on the annual mean concentration of particulate matter with particles smaller than 10 microns ('PM_{10}') and smaller than 2.5 microns ('$PM_{2.5}$'). These guidelines are 20 µg/m³ for PM_{10} and 10 µg/m³ for $PM_{2.5}$ (WHO 2011d).

61 Further details and the WHO's database on outdoor air pollution in cities can be accessed at http://www.who.int/phe/health_topics/outdoorair/databases/en/.

62 Electricity, for example, is a very clean fuel at point of use but it may make large contributions to air pollution where it is produced, as it does, for instance, in the case of a coal-fired power station with inadequate or no air pollution control.

63 The dates of the figures on access to electricity and modern fuels vary by country, with most between 2003 and 2007.

64 Such surveys rarely ask questions about incomes because of the unreliability of reporting, but they can use asset indexes as a proxy for income levels.

65 This point and list of cities was first developed in Hardoy and Satterthwaite (1984). It has been further developed and elaborated since; see Hardoy, Mitlin and Satterthwaite (2001).

66 This paragraph draws on Satterthwaite (2011).

4. Incomes and livelihoods

67 There may be a few exceptions, for instance, those who grow crops on vacant land without opposition from the landowner or government. However, there are often better returns from growing crops for sale rather than for domestic consumption.

68 Again, there are exceptions, for examples agricultural labourers in rural areas who have to pay rent for accommodation.

69 Own-account workers are those who are working on their own with one or more partners, hold the type of job defined as self-employed, and do not have regular employees.

70 The Gini coefficient is a measure of inequality, with 0 being perfect equality and 1 perfect inequality; see the subsection on 'Incomes' in Chapter 5.

71 According to an estimate of the National Movement of Recyclable Materials Waste Pickers (MNCR).

72 The 'poor' are defined as those with incomes below the government's 1999 poverty line, adjusted for changes in consumer prices; this equalled KSh3,174 (US$42) per adult equivalent per month, excluding rent (World Bank Kenya 2006).

73 The growing importance of remittances is recognized by Hasan (2010) in the context of Pakistan. He argues that high remittance values are correlated to high levels of GDP growth because remittances are the third most important source of capital for economic growth in the country.

5. Critical issues in urban inequality

74 This has long been recognized in many high-income nations, where more attention is given to relative poverty. Surprisingly little attention has been paid to relative poverty in development discussions, however.

75 For instance, a poverty line may be set not based on the costs of food and non-food needs but on, say, 50 per cent of the median income for the particular nation.

76 For homicides, their data set of 39 countries is made up of about 50 per cent industrialized countries, 25 per cent Latin American countries and one African country, with Eastern Europe and Asia providing the remainder. For robberies, there is greater representation of Asia and less of Latin America.

77 On the Gini coefficient, see Sen (1973); on the Theil measure see Conceição and Ferreira (2000).

78 These three are Theil L and Theil T, respectively known as Theil GE(0) or E(0) and Theil GE(1) or E(1). In addition, there is GE(2) or E(2). These numbers refer to the mathematical construction of the index which produces different sensitivities. Theil L index, or E(0), is particularly sensitive to the distribution where incomes are lowest and hence to income transfers from poor to the rich (Conceição and Ferreira 2000). For this reason it is used by those concerned with inequalities for the lowest-income and most disadvantaged citizens. E(2) is sensitive to the higher-income part of the distribution and Theil T, or E(1), is neutral (Ferreira and de Barros 1999).

79 The Sustainable Livelihoods Framework was popularized by the UK Department for International Development to assist with identifying effective strategies for poverty reduction (Rakodi with Lloyd-Jones 2002).

80 These conclusions draw on data from UN-HABITAT (2011), Christiaensen, Demery and Paternostro (2005), and Economic Commission for Latin America and the Caribbean (undated).

81 Also referred to as GE(1) or E(1).

82 Urban and peri-urban agriculture can be important for substantial proportions of the urban population in many cities, although it may mostly be better-off groups that have access to the land needed for this to be their main source of livelihood; see Lee-Smith (2010).

83 This period followed the overthrow of democracy by the military, headed by General Pinochet, in 1973; it was only in 1990 that power was returned to a democratically elected government.

84 Hurtado's (2006) analysis uses the definition of the informal sector used by International Labour Organization: workers in firms with five or fewer employees and self-employed workers who are not technicians or professionals, or who provide domestic services.

85 The finding that public financial intervention may not be progressive, or may only be partially progressive, in its impact on income distribution is not unique to Brazil. Agosin *et al.* (2005) analyse data for three countries in Central America and conclude that the Gini coefficients related to after-tax incomes are higher than those of pre-tax incomes in El Salvador and Honduras, and the coefficient is not significantly changed in the case of Costa Rica.

86 Of course, comparisons between cities need to be made with caution, as the city boundaries upon which these calculations are based may be set in different ways, for instance by reference to built-up areas, municipal boundaries beyond which a city has grown or wider planning region boundaries which encompass much more than just built-up areas.

87 For women pavement dwellers in Mumbai, it is even less than this, as their tiny dwellings are only large enough to store household goods, to cook and perhaps to sit with a sewing machine.

88 Ironically it now appears that the medical profession thinks that young children in high-income households may be overprotected and may require greater access to 'dirt' to ensure good health (see, for example, Brody 2009).

89 Urban agriculture often involves what might be considered unusual goods. When one of the authors visited a low-income inner city district in Surabaya, three common 'urban agriculture' products were: fighting cocks, who fended for themselves; singing birds, in cages that could be kept on roofs, with the value of the bird enhanced if it sang well; and the inhabitants' favourite chillies, grown in tiny beds incorporated into the top of walls in front of the residences. In a study of urban agriculture in Mexico City, some households were cultivating turf to sell to middle-class households for their gardens (Losada *et al.* 1998).

6. Broadening the understanding and measurement of urban poverty

90 The evidence to support this is assembled in the companion volume to this (Satterthwaite and Mitlin 2013), which focuses on reducing urban poverty. In addressing the dimensions of urban poverty, it draws on many case studies illustrating the possibilities. See, for instance, Boonyabancha (2005, 2009); Boonyabancha and Mitlin (2012); Bolnick (1993, 1996); Schusterman and Hardoy (1997); Schusterman *et al.* (2001); Hasan (1997); Porio *et al.* (2004); Stein (2001); Alimuddin, Hasan and Sadiq (2004); Baumann, Bolnick and Mitlin (2004); Patel and Mitlin (2004); Weru (2004); Mitlin (2008); Mitlin and Muller (2004); Cain, Daly and Robson (2002); Mitlin and Satterthwaite (2004); Satterthwaite (2005); Satterthwaite, Patel and Mitlin (2011).

91 We return to this issue in the companion volume to this (Satterthwaite and Mitlin 2013).

92 This is the case for most of the case studies cited in note 90.

93 This also raises issues of responsibility and accountability for researchers and staff from official agencies who make judgements about who is 'poor'. Their judgements can influence who benefits and who does not from, say, infrastructure and services or safety nets. This is why our work has long emphasized the need for local judgements and decisions that are accountable to local populations and subject to their influences.

94 The cheapest forms of 'improved' sanitation, such as ventilated improved pit latrines, become inappropriate at higher population densities and with larger settlements.

95 Other examples appear in the companion volume to this (Satterthwaite and Mitlin 2013).

96 This may still be contentious, with rural proponents arguing that cities' larger tax base is in part the result of terms of trade or government policies favouring urban areas, and urban proponents arguing that it arises from the fact that cities concentrate a much higher proportion of economic activities than of population, and emphasizing how much city enterprises and populations contribute to national tax revenues.

97 Household costs may be increased where cost recovery is sought, but major improvements can often be made at low cost with cost recovery achieved through community-managed schemes; for example the sewers installed in Orangi supported by the Orangi Pilot Project (Hasan 1997, 2006). Costs may also be reduced, for instance where inhabitants have previously been purchasing water from vendors and the household payments made for upgrading are less than those made to the vendors.

98 One study in the Indian city of Aligarh found that there were serious deficiencies in infrastructure and service provision throughout the whole city, and that a higher income level did not necessarily correspond to a significant diminution in household-level environmental problems. For instance, in the cases of drainage provision and waste collection, there were only marginal improvements in quality of provision as household income rose. Open defecation (due to lack of provision for sanitation) was not restricted to areas where the population had below-poverty-line incomes. This points to serious environmental problems at the household level prevailing across the whole city, irrespective of economic circumstances or size and quality of housing; see Aziz, Singh and Siddiqi (1995).

99 Most of the studies cited here are papers published in the April 2012 issue of *Environment and Urbanization*. See also Patel and Baptist 2012; Patel, d'Cruz and Burra 2002; Weru 2004.

100 http://achr.net/

101 See Navarro (2001) for an example of how this was done for two medium size Argentine towns, and Velasquez (1998) for how this was done by urban observatories in different parts of the city of Manizales in Colombia.

102 See, for instance, the programme of the Urban Resource Centre in Karachi (URC 1994; Hasan 1999).

103 Key references include Tacoli 1998, 2003, 2006; Tacoli and Mabala 2010. See also special issues of *Environment and Urbanization* on rural–urban links, 15(1) in 2003 and 10(1) in 1998, and, on migration and mobility, 22(1) in 2010; these are available at http://eau.sagepub.com/

104 Data from STATcompiler (http://www.statcompiler.com).

References

Abrams, Charles (1964), *Man's Struggle for Shelter in an Urbanizing World*, Cambridge, MA: MIT Press.

Achar, K.T.V., B. Bhaskara Rao and A. de Bruijne (2001), 'Organization and management of water needs in slums' in Hans Schenk (ed.) *Living in India's Slums: A Case Study of Bangalore,* Manohar, New Delhi: IDPAD, 161–86.

Adelekan, Ibidun O. (2010), 'Vulnerability of poor urban coastal communities to flooding in Lagos, Nigeria', *Environment and Urbanization* 22:2, 433–50.

——(2012), 'Vulnerability to wind hazards in the traditional city of Ibadan, Nigeria', *Environment and Urbanization* 24:2, 597–618.

Adelekan, Ibidun O. and A.T. Jerome (2006) 'Dynamics of household energy consumption in a traditional African city, Ibadan,' *Environmentalist* 26:2, 99–110.

Aegisson, Gunnar (2001), *Building Civil Society: Starting with the Basics*, London: One World Action.

Agarwal, Siddarth (2011), 'The state of urban health in India: comparing the poorest quartile to the rest of the urban population in selected states and cities', *Environment and Urbanization* 23:1, 13–28.

Agarwal, Siddharth, Vani Sethi, Palak Gupta, Meenakshi Jha, Ayushi Agnihotri and Mark Nord (2009), 'Experiential household food insecurity in an urban underserved slum of North India', *Food Security* 1, 239–50.

Agarwala, Rina (2006), 'From work to welfare', *Critical Asian Studies* 38:4, 419–44.

Agosin, Manuel R., Alberto Barreix, Juan Carlos Gómez Sabaini and Roberto Machado (2005), 'Tax reform for human development in Central America', *Cepal Review* 87, 79–94.

Ahmed, A.U., R.V. Hill, L.C. Smith, D.M. Wiesmann and T. Frankenberger (2007), *The World's Most Deprived: Characteristics and Causes of Extreme Poverty and Hunger*, 2020 Vision for Food, Agriculture and the Environment Discussion Paper No. 43, Washington, DC: International Food Policy Research Institute (IFPRI).

Akita, Takahiro and Sachiko Miyata (2007), *Urbanization, Educational Expansion and Expenditure Inequality in 1996, 1999 and 2002*, IFPRI Discussion Paper 728, Washington, DC: International Food Policy Research Institute.

Alam, Mozaharul and M.D. Golam Rabbani (2007), 'Vulnerabilities and responses to climate change for Dhaka', *Environment and Urbanization* 19:1, 81–97.

Alder, Graham (1995), 'Tackling poverty in Nairobi's informal settlements: developing an institutional strategy', *Environment and Urbanization* 7:2, 85–107.

Aliber, Michael (2003), 'Chronic poverty in South Africa: incidence, causes and policies', *World Development* 31:3, 473–90.

Alimuddin, Salim, Arif Hasan and Asiya Sadiq (2004), 'The work of the Anjuman Samaji Behbood in Faisalabad, Pakistan' in Diana Mitlin and David Satterthwaite (eds), *Empowering Squatter Citizen*, London: Earthscan Publications.

Alkire, Sabina and Maria Emma Santos (2010), *Acute Multidimensional Poverty: A New Index for Developing Countries*, OPHI Working Paper 38, Oxford Poverty and Human Development Initiative, Oxford: University of Oxford.

Almansi, Florencia (2009), 'Rosario's development: interview with Miguel Lifschitz, mayor of Rosario, Argentina', *Environment and Urbanization* 21:1, 19–35.

Almansi, Florencis, Ana Hardoy, Jorgelina Hardoy, Gustavo Pandiella, Leonardo Tambussi, Gaston Urquiza, Gordon McGranahan and David Satterthwaite (2011), *Limits to Participation: The Struggle for Environmental Improvement in Moreno*, Buenos Aires: IIED-America Latina.

Alvarez, Sonia E., Evelina Dagnino and Arturo Escobar (1998), 'Introduction: the cultural and political in Latin American social movements' in Sonia E. Alvarez, Evelina Dagnino, and Arturo Escobar (eds), *Cultures of Politics, Politics of Culture*, Boulder: Westview Press, 1–32.

Alwang, Jeffrey, Bradford F. Mills and Nelson Taruvinga (2002), *Why has Poverty Increased in Zimbabwe?* Washington, DC: World Bank.

Amis, Philip (1984), 'Squatters or tenants: the commercialization of unauthorized housing in Nairobi', *World Development* 12:1, 87–96.

——(1995), 'Making sense of urban poverty', *Environment and Urbanization* 7:1, 145–57.

——(1999), *Urban Economic Growth and Poverty Reduction*, Urban Governance, Partnerships and Poverty Research Working Paper 2, Birmingham: International Development Department, University of Birmingham.

——(2006), 'Urban poverty in East Africa: Nairobi and Kampala's comparative trajectories' in Deborah Fahy Bryceson and Deborah Potts (eds), *African Urban Economies: Viability, Vitality or Vitiation?* Basingstoke: Palgrave Macmillan, 169–84.

Amis, Philip and Sashi Kumar (2000), 'Urban economic growth, infrastructure and poverty from India: lessons from Visakhapatnam', *Environment and Urbanization* 12:1, 185–96.

Amnesty International (2010), *Insecurity and Indignity: Women's Experiences in the Slums of Nairobi, Kenya*, London: Amnesty International Publications.

Anand, S. and M. Ravallion (1993), 'Human development in poor countries: on the role of private incomes and public services', *Journal of Economic Perspectives* 7:1, 133–50.

Antai, Diddy and Tahereh Moradi (2010), 'Urban area disadvantage and under-5 mortality in Nigeria: the effect of rapid urbanization', *Environmental Health Perspectives* 118:6, 877–83.

APHRC (2002), *Population and Health Dynamics in Nairobi's Informal Settlements*, Nairobi: African Population and Health Research Center.

Appadurai, Arjun (2012), 'Why enumeration counts', *Environment and Urbanization* 24:2, 639–42.

Archer, Diane (2012), 'Community mapping and planning: the role of community architects in facilitating a people's process in citywide upgrading of informal settlements', *Environment and Urbanization* 24:2, 423–40.

Arrossi, Silvina (1996), 'Inequality and health in Metropolitan Buenos Aires', *Environment and Urbanization* 8:2, 43–70.

Asian Coalition for Housing Rights (1989), 'Evictions in Seoul, South Korea', *Environment and Urbanization* 1:1, 89–94.

——(2001), 'Building an urban poor people's movement in Phnom Penh, Cambodia', *Environment and Urbanization* 13:2, 61–72.

Asian Development Bank (2007), *Inequality in Asia: Key Indicators 2007*, Metro Manila: Asian Development Bank.

Aten, Alan and Bettina Heston (2005), 'Regional output differences in international perspective' in Ravi Kanbur and Anthony J. Venables (eds), *Spatial Inequality and Development*, Oxford: Oxford University Press, 15–41.

Atkinson, Anthony (1999), 'Is rising inequality inevitable? A critique of the transatlantic consensus', WIDER Annual Lecture 3, Helsinki: UNU/WIDER (World Institute for Development Economics Research).

Auyero Javier (2000), *Poor People's Politics*, Durham and London: Duke University Press.

Avritzer, Leonardo (2006), 'New public spaces in Brazil: local democracy and deliberative politics', *International Journal of Urban and Regional Research* 30:3, 623–37.

Aziz, A., A.L. Singh and R.H. Siddiqi (1995), *Aligarh Environment Study*, Aligarh: Aligarh Muslim University.

Balisacan, Arsenio M. and Nobuhiko Fuwa (2004), *Changes in Spatial Income Inequality in the Philippines*, Wider Research Paper No. 2004/34, Helsinki: UNU/Wider.

Banerjee, Abhijit V. and Esther Dulfo (2007), 'The economic lives of the poor', *Journal of Economic Perspectives* 21:1, 141–67.

Bangladesh Bureau of Statistics (1997), *Child Nutrition Survey of Bangladesh 1995–1996*, Dhaka: Ministry of Planning, Statistics Division, Government of Bangladesh.

Banks, Nicola (2010), 'Employment and mobility among low-income urban households in Dhaka, Bangladesh', PhD thesis, Manchester: University of Manchester.

Bapat, Meera (2009), *Poverty Lines and the Lives of the Poor: Underestimation of Poverty – the Case of India*, Poverty Reduction in Urban Areas Series, Working Paper 20, London: International Institute for Environment and Development.

Bapat, Meera and Indu Agarwal (2003), 'Our needs, our priorities; women and men from the 'slums' in Mumbai and Pune talk about their needs for water and sanitation', *Environment and Urbanization* 15:2, 71–86.

Baptist, Carrie and Joel Bolnick (2012), 'Participatory enumerations, in situ upgrading and mega events: the 2009 survey in Joe Slovo, Cape Town', *Environment and Urbanization* 24:1, 59–66.

Barbosa, Ronnie, Yves Cabannes and Lucia Moraes (1997), 'Tenant today, *posseiro* tomorrow', *Environment and Urbanization* 9:2, 17–41.

Barrientos, Stephanie (2010), 'Gender and ethical trade: can vulnerable women workers benefit?' in Sylvia Chant (ed.), *The International Handbook of Gender and Poverty: Concepts, Research, Policy*, Cheltenham: Edward Elgar, 440–5.

Barter, Paul A. (1999), 'Transport and urban poverty in Asia: a brief introduction to the key issues', *Regional Development Dialogue* 20:1, 143–63.

Bartlett, Sheridan (2002), 'The problem of children's injuries in low-income countries: a review', *Health Policy and Planning* 17:1, 1–13.

——(2003), 'Water, sanitation and urban children: the need to go beyond 'improved' provision', *Environment and Urbanization* 15:2, 57–70.

——(2008), 'Climate change and urban children: implications for adaptation in low and middle income countries', *Environment and Urbanization* 20:2, 501–20

——(2010), 'Editorial: responding to urban youth's own perspectives', *Environment and Urbanization* 22:2, 307–16.

Bartlett, Sheridan, Roger Hart, David Satterthwaite, Ximena de la Barra and Alfredo Missair (1999), *Cities for Children: Children's Rights, Poverty and Urban Management*, London: Earthscan.

Baskin, Julian and Daniel Miji (2006), 'Partnership for infrastructure in the *musseques* of Luanda, Angola' in Lucy Stevens, S. Coupe and D. Mitlin (eds), *Confronting the Crisis in Urban Poverty: Making Integrated Approaches Work*, Rugby: Intermediate Technology Publications, 39–62.

Baud, Isa and Nainan, Navtej (2008), '"Negotiated spaces" for representation in Mumbai: ward committees, advanced locality management and the politics of middle-class activism', *Environment and Urbanization* 20:2, 483–500.

Baulch, B. (1996), 'The new poverty agenda: a disputed consensus', *IDS Bulletin* 27:1, 1–10.

Baumann, Ted, Joel Bolnick and Diana Mitlin (2004), 'The age of cities and organizations of the urban poor; the work of the South African Homeless People's Federation' in Diana Mitlin and David Satterthwaite (eds), *Empowering Squatter Citizen*, London: Earthscan Publications.

Bayat, Asef (2000), 'From "dangerous classes" to "quiet rebels": politics of the urban subaltern in the Global South', *International Sociology* 15:3, 533–57.

Bayat, Asef and Eric Denis (2000), 'Who is afraid of Ashwaiyyat: urban change and politics in Egypt', *Environment and Urbanization* 12:2, 185–99.

Beall, Jo (2002), 'Living in the present, investing in the future: housing security among the poor' in Carole Rakodi with Tony Lloyd-Jones (eds), *Urban Livelihoods: A People-Centred Approach to Reducing Poverty*, London: Earthscan, 71–89.

Beard, Victoria A. (2000), 'Rethinking urban poverty: a look inside the Indonesian household', *Third World Planning Review* 22:4, 361–79.

Beck, Tony (1994), *The Experience of Poverty: Fighting for Respect and Resource in Village India*, London: Intermediate Technology Publications.

Begum, Sharifa and Binayak Sen (2005), 'Pulling rickshaws in the city of Dhaka: a way out of poverty?' *Environment and Urbanization* 17:2, 11–26.

Benítez, Griselda, Arturo Pérez-Vázquez, Martha Nava-Tablada, Miguel Equihua and José Luis Álvarez-Palacios (2012), 'Expansion and environmental effects of informal settlements on the outskirts of Xalapa City, Veracruz, Mexico', *Environment and Urbanization* 24:1, 149–66.

Benjamin, Solomon (2000), 'Governance, economic settings and poverty in Bangalore', *Environment and Urbanization* 12:1, 35–56.

Bhan, Gautam (2009), '"This is no longer the city I once knew": evictions, the urban poor and the right to the city in millennial Delhi', *Environment and Urbanization* 21:1, 127–42.

Bhowmik, Sharit (2005), 'Street vendors in Asia: a review', *Economic and Political Weekly* May 28–June 5.

Bicknell, Jane, David Dodman and David Satterthwaite (eds) (2009), *Adapting Cities to Climate Change: Understanding and Addressing the Development Challenges*, London: Earthscan Publications.

Bigsten, A. and Steve Kayizzi-Mugerwa (1992), 'Adoption and distress in the urban economy: a study of Kampala households', *World Development* 20:10, 1423–41.

Bigsten, Arne and Abebe Shimeles (2004), *Dynamics of Poverty in Ethiopia*, UNU-WIDER Research Paper, Helsinki: UNU World Institute for Development Economics Research (UNU/WIDER).

Bigsten, A., Bereket Kebede, Abebe Shimelis and Mekonnen Taddesse (2003), 'Growth and poverty reduction in Ethiopia: evidence from households panel surveys', *World Development* 31:1, 87–106.

Bijlmakers, L.A., Mary T. Bassett and David M. Sanders (1998), *Socio-Economic Stress, Health and Child Nutrition Status in Zimbabwe at a Time of Economic Structural Adjustment*, Research Report No. 105, Uppsala: Nordiska Afrikainstitutet.

Birdsall, Nancy and Juan Luis Londoño (1997), 'Asset inequality matters: an assessment of the World Bank's approach to poverty reduction', *The American Economic Review* 87:2, 32–7.

Blitzer, Silvia, Julio Davila, Jorge E. Hardoy and David Satterthwaite (1988), *Outside the Large Cities: Annotated Bibliography and Guide to the Literature on Small and Intermediate Urban Centres in the Third World*, London: International Institute for Environment and Development.

Blue, Ilona (1996), 'Urban inequalities in mental health: the case of Sao Paulo, Brazil', *Environment and Urbanization* 8:2, 91–100.

Blundo, Giorgio (2006), 'Dealing with the local state: the informal privatization of street-level bureaucracies in Senegal', *Development and Change* 37:4, 799–819.

Boadi, Owusu and Markku Kuitunen (2006), 'Factors affecting the choice of cooking fuel, cooking place and respiratory health in the Accra Metropolitan Area, Ghana', *Journal of Biosocial Science* 38:3, 403–12.

Bolnick, Joel (1993), 'The People's Dialogue on land and shelter: community-driven networking in South Africa's informal settlements', *Environment and Urbanization* 5:1, 91–110.

——(1996), 'uTshani Buyakhuluma (The grass speaks): People's Dialogue and the South African Homeless People's Federation, 1993–1996', *Environment and Urbanization* 8:2, 153–70.

Boonyabancha, Somsook (2003), *A Decade of Change: From the Urban Community Development Office (UCDO) to the Community Organizations Development Institute (CODI) in Thailand*, IIED Working Paper 12 on Poverty Reduction in Urban Areas, London: IIED.

——(2005), 'Baan Mankong: going to scale with 'slum' and squatter upgrading in Thailand', *Environment and Urbanization* 17:1, 21–46.

——(2009), 'Land for housing the poor by the poor: experiences from the Baan Mankong nationwide slum upgrading programme in Thailand', *Environment and Urbanization* 21:2, 309–30.

Boonyabancha, Somsook and Diana Mitlin (2012), 'Urban poverty reduction: learning by doing in Asia', *Environment and Urbanization* 24:2, 403–22.

Booysen, Frikkie, Ronelle Burger, Gideon Du Rand, Michael von Maltitz and Servaas Van der Berg (2007), *Trends in Poverty and Inequality in Seven African Countries*, Poverty and Economic Policy PMMA Working Paper, South Africa.

Bradley, D., C. Stephens, S. Cairncross and T. Harpham (1991), *A Review of Environmental Health Impacts in Developing Country Cities*, Urban Management Program Discussion Paper No. 6, Washington, DC: World Bank, United Nations Development Program and United Nations Centre for Human Settlements (HABITAT).

Bradlow, Ben, Joel Bolnick and Clifford Shearing (2011), 'Housing, institutions and money: the failures and the promise of human settlement policy and practice in South Africa', *Environment and Urbanization* 23:1, 267–76.

Brody, Jane E. (2009), 'Babies know: a little dirt is good for you', *The New York Times*, 26 January 2009. Available at: http://www.nytimes.com/2009/01/27/health/27brod.html (accessed 4 August 2012).

Brown, Alison (2006a), 'Setting the context: social, economic and political influences on the informal sector in Ghana, Lesotho, Nepal and Tanzania' in Alison Brown (ed.),

Contested Space: Street Trading, Public Space and Livelihoods in Developing Cities, Rugby: ITDG Publishing.

——(2006b), 'Street trading in four cities: a comparison' in Alison Brown (ed), *Contested Space: Street Trading, Public Space and Livelihoods in Developing Cities*, Rugby: ITDG Publishing, 169–83.

Brown, Alison and Michal Lyons (2010), 'Seen but not heard: urban voice and citizenship for street traders' in Ilda Lindell (ed.), *Africa's Informal Workers: Collective Agency, Alliances and Transnational Organizing in Urban Africa*, London: Zed Books, 33–45.

Bruce, Judith and Amy Joyce (eds) (2006), *The Girls Left Behind: The Failed Reach of Current Schooling, Child Health, Youth-Serving, and Livelihoods Programs for Girls Living in the Path of HIV*, synthesis paper, New York: Population Council.

Burra, Sundar, Sheela Patel and Tom Kerr (2003), 'Community-designed, built and managed toilet blocks in Indian cities', *Environment and Urbanization* 15:2, 11–32.

Cabannes, Yves (2004) 'Participatory budgeting: a significant contribution to participatory democracy', *Environment and Urbanization* 16:1, 27–46.

Cain, Allan, Mary Daly and Paul Robson (2002), *Basic Service Provision for the Urban Poor: The Experience of Development Workshop in Angola*, IIED Working Paper 8 on Poverty Reduction in Urban Areas, London: IIED.

Cairncross, Sandy (1990), 'Water supply and the urban poor' in Jorge E. Hardoy, Sandy Cairncross and David Satterthwaite (eds), *The Poor Die Young: Housing and Health in Third World Cities*, London: Earthscan Publications.

Cairncross, Sandy, Jorge E. Hardoy and David Satterthwaite (1990), 'The urban context' in Jorge E. Hardoy, Sandy Cairncross and David Satterthwaite (eds), *The Poor Die Young: Housing and Health in Third World Cities*, London: Earthscan Publications, 1–24.

Calderón, Julio (2004), 'The formalisation of property in Peru 2001–2002: the case of Lima', *Habitat International* 28, 289–300.

Cambodia, Kingdom of (2002), *National Poverty Reduction Strategy*, Phnom Penh: Council for Social Development.

Cameroon, Republic of (2002), *Living Conditions and Poverty Profile in Cameroon in 2001: Final Results*, Bureau of Statistics and National Accounts Ministry of Economy and Finance, Republic of Cameroon.

Campbell, Tim (2003), *The Quiet Revolution: Decentralization and the Rise of Political Participation in Latin American Cities*, Pittsburgh: University of Pittsburgh Press.

CARE/Bangladesh (1998), *Urban Livelihood Security Assessment in Bangladesh, Volume 1: Main Report*, edited by Phil Sutter and Chris Perine, Dhaka: CARE-Bangladesh.

Carruthers, R., M. Dick, and A. Saurkar (2005), *Affordability of Public Transport in Developing Countries*, Transport Paper 3, Washington, DC: World Bank.

Central Statistical Office, Zambia (1998), *Living Conditions in Zambia 1998: The Evolution of Poverty in Zambia 1990–1996*, Lusaka: Government of the Republic of Zambia.

Chad, Republic of (2003), *National Poverty Reduction Strategy Paper*, N'Djamena: PRSP Steering Committee, Ministry of Planning, Development and Cooperation.

Chakrabarti, Poulomi (2008), 'Inclusion or exclusion? Emerging effects of middle-class citizen participation on Delhi's urban poor', *IDS Bulletin* 38:6, 96–103.

Chambers, Robert (1995), 'Poverty and livelihoods; whose reality counts?', *Environment and Urbanization* 7:1, 173–204.

Champetier, Séverine and Mohamed Farid (2000), *Independent Water and Sanitation Providers in Africa: Nairobi, Kenya, Case Study 5*, Nairobi: Water and Sanitation Program – East and Southern Africa.

Champetier, Séverine and Bill Wandera (2000), *Independent Water and Sanitation Providers in Africa: Kampala, Uganda, Case Study 8*, Nairobi: Water and Sanitation Program – East and Southern Africa.

Champetier, Séverine, Adam Sykes and Bill Wandera (2000), *Independent Water and Sanitation Providers in Africa: Dar es Salaam, Tanzania, Case Study 10*, Nairobi: Water and Sanitation Program – East and Southern Africa.

Chandrasekhar, S. and Mark R. Montgomery (2010), *Broadening Poverty Definitions in India: Basic Needs in Urban Housing*, London: IIED Working Paper.

Chant, Sylvia (2013), 'Cities through a "gender lens": a golden "Urban Age" for women in the Global South?' *Environment and Urbanization* 25:1.

Chaplin, Susan E. (1999), 'Cities, sewers and poverty: India's politics of sanitation', *Environment and Urbanization* 11:1, 145–58.

——(2011), 'Indian cities, sanitation and the state: the politics of the failure to provide', *Environment and Urbanization* 23:1, 57–70.

Chatterjee, Ipsita (2011), 'Governance as "performed," governance as "inscribed": new urban politics in Ahmedabad', *Urban Studies* 48:12, 2571–90.

Chaturvedi, Bharati (2010), *Mainstreaming Waste Pickers and the Informal Recycling Sector in the Municipal Solid Waste*, research paper, New York: WIEGO.

Chen, Martha, Joann Vanek and James Heintz (2006), 'Informality, gender and poverty: a global picture', *Economic and Political Weekly* May 27, 2131–9.

Chen, Marty (2010), 'Informality, poverty and gender: evidence from the Global South' in Sylvia Chant (ed), *The International Handbook of Gender and Poverty: Concepts, Research, Policy*, Cheltenham: Edward Elgar, 463–71.

Chen, Shaohua and Martin Ravallion (2007), *Absolute Poverty Measures for the Developing World, 1981–2004*, Development Research Group, Washington, DC: World Bank.

——(2008), *The Developing World Is Poorer than We Thought, But No Less Successful in the Fight Against Poverty*, Policy Research Working Paper 4703, Washington, DC: World Bank.

Chenery, Hollis, Montek S. Ahluwalia, C.G.L. Bell, John H. Duloy and Richard Jolly (1974), *Redistribution with Growth*, Oxford: Oxford University Press.

Chibuye, Miniva (2011), *Interrogating Urban Poverty Lines: The Case of Zambia*, Human Settlements Working Paper Series: Poverty Reduction in Urban Areas, Working Paper 30, London: International Institute for Environment and Development.

Chitekwe, Beth and Diana Mitlin (2001), 'The urban poor under threat and in struggle: options for urban development in Zimbabwe, 1995–2000', *Environment and Urbanization* 13:2, 85–101.

Chitekwe-Biti, Beth (2011), *Dialogue on Shelter*, personal communication, 28 October 2011.

Chitekwe-Biti, Beth Patience Mudimu, George Masimba Nyama and Takudzwa Jera (2012), 'Developing an informal settlement upgrading protocol in Zimbabwe: the Epworth story', *Environment and Urbanization* 24:1, 131–48.

Christiaensen, Luc, Lionel Demery and Stefano Paternostro (2005), 'Reforms, remoteness and risk in Africa: Understanding inequality and poverty during the 1990s' in Ravi Kanbur and Anthony J. Venables (eds), *Spatial Inequality and Development*, Oxford: Oxford University Press, 209–34.

Citro, C. and R. Michael (1995), *Measuring Poverty: A New Approach*, National Research Council, Washington, DC: National Academy Press.

Clark, William (1981), 'Robert McNamara at the World Bank', *Foreign Affairs*, Fall, 167–84.

Cohen, Jennifer (2010), 'How the global economic crisis reaches marginalised workers: the case of street traders in Johannesburg, South Africa' *Gender & Development* 18:2, 277–89.

Cohen, Michael A. (1983), *Learning by Doing: World Bank Lending for Urban Development, 1972–82*, Washington, DC: World Bank.

COHRE (1994), 'The Centre on Housing Rights and Evictions (COHRE)', *Environment and Urbanization* 6:1, 147–57.

——(2006), *Forced Evictions: Violations of Human Rights*, Geneva: COHRE.

Colin, Jeremy and Joy Morgan (2000), *Provision of Water and Sanitation Services to Small Towns: Part B: Case Studies in Uganda and India*, WELL Studies in Water, Sanitation and Environmental Health Task 323, Loughborough, UK: WELL.

Conceição, Pedro and Pedro Ferreira (2000), *The Young Person's Guide to the Theil Index: Suggesting Intuitive Interpretations, and Exploring Analytical Applications*, UTIP Working Paper Number 14, University of Texas Inequality Project.

Congo, Democratic Republic of the (2006), *Poverty Reduction and Growth Strategy Paper*, June.

Conticini, Alessandro (2005), 'Urban livelihoods from children's perspectives: protecting and promoting assets on the streets of Dhaka', *Environment and Urbanization* 17:2, 69–82.

Copestake, James (2002), 'Inequality and the polarising impact of micro-credit: evidence from Zambia's Copperbelt', *Journal of International Development* 14:6, 743–55.

Corbridge, Stuart and Gareth A. Jones (2005), *The Continuing Debate about Urban Bias: The Thesis, Its Critics, Its Influence, and Implications for Poverty Reduction*, London: Department of Geography and Environment, London School of Economics and Political Science.

CORC (2005), *Profiles of Informal Settlements within the Johannesburg Metropole*, Cape Town: Community Organization Urban Resource Centre.

Cornia, Giovanni Andrea (1987a), 'Economic decline and human welfare in the first half of the 1980s' in Giovanni Andrea Cornia, Richard Jolly and Frances Stewart (eds), *Adjustment with a Human Face*, vol. 1, Oxford: Oxford University Press, 11–47.

——(1987b), 'Adjustment policies 1980–85: effects on child welfare' in Giovanni Andrea Cornia, Richard Jolly and Frances Stewart (eds), *Adjustment with a Human Face*, vol. 1, Oxford: Oxford University Press, 48–72.

Cornia, Giovanni, Richard Jolly and Frances Stewart (eds) (1987), *Adjustment with a Human Face*, vol. 1, Oxford: Oxford University Press.

Côte d'Ivoire, République de la (2000), *Profil et determinants de la pauvreté en Côte d'Ivoire en 1998*, Abidjan: Institut National de la Statistique.

Cowan, Bill (2008), *Alleviation of Poverty through the Provision of Local Energy Services: Identification and Demonstration of Selected Energy Best Practices for Low-Income Urban Communities in South Africa*, Cape Town: Energy Research Centre.

Crossa, Veronica (2009), 'Resisting the entrepreneurial city: street vendors' struggle in Mexico City's historic center', *International Journal of Urban and Regional Research* 33:1, 43–63.

Cuenya, Beatriz, Diego Armus, Maria Di Loreto and Susana Penalva (1990), 'Land invasions and grassroots organization: the Quilmes settlement in Greater Buenos Aires, Argentina', *Environment and Urbanization* 2:1, 61–73.

Cuenya, Beatriz, Hector Almada, Diego Armus, Julia Castells, Maria di Loreto and Susana Penalva (1990), 'Housing and health problems in Buenos Aires: the case of Barrio San Martin' in Sandy Cairncross, Jorge E. Hardoy and David Satterthwaite (eds), *The Poor Die Young: Housing and Health in Third World Cities*, London: Earthscan Publications.

Currie, Lauchlin (1967), *Obstacles to Development*, East Lansing: Michigan State University Press.

CUS, NIPORT and Measure Evaluation (2006), *Slums in Urban Bangladesh: Mapping and Census 2005*, Dhaka and Chapel Hill; CUS, NIPORT and Measure Evaluation.

Dasgupta, Nandini (1997), 'Problems and opportunities in providing appropriate assistance to green small recycling firms', *Environment and Urbanization* 9:2, 289–305.

Dasgupta, Partha and Martin Weale (1992), 'On measuring the quality of life', *World Development* 20:1, 119–31.

Dasgupta, S., M. Huq, M. Khaliquzzaman, K. Pandey and D. Wheeler (2006), 'Indoor air quality for poor families: new evidence from Bangladesh', *Indoor Air* 16:6, 426–44.

Datt, Gaurav and Dean Jolliffe (1999), *Determinants of Poverty in Egypt: 1997*, FCND Discussion Paper No 75, Washington, DC: IFPRI.

de la Rocha, Mercedes Gonzáles (2007), 'The construction of the myth of survival', *Development and Change* 38:1, 45–66.

De Swardt, Cobus, Thandi Puoane, Mickey Chopra and Andries du Toit (2005), 'Urban poverty in Cape Town', *Environment and Urbanization* 17:2, 101–11.

Deaton, Angus and Olivier Dupriez (2011), 'Purchasing power parity exchange rates for the global poor', in International Comparison Program, *Measuring the Size of the World Economy*, Washington, DC: ICP Book.

Deaton, Angus and Christina Paxson (1995), *Measuring Poverty among the Elderly*, NBER Working Paper 5296, Cambridge, MA: National Bureau of Economic Research.

Deaton, Angus and Alessandro Tarozzi (2000), *Prices and Poverty in India*, Research Program in Development Studies, Princeton, NJ: Princeton University.

Deaton, Angus and Salman Zaidi (2002), *Guidelines for Constructing Consumption Aggregates for Welfare Analysis*, LSMS Working Paper 135, Washington, DC: World Bank.

Desai, Meghnad (1991), 'Human development: concepts and measurement', *European Economic Review* 35, 350–7.

Devas, Nick and David Korboe (2000), 'City governance and poverty: the case of Kumasi', *Environment and Urbanization* 12:1, 123–35.

Dinye, Romanus D. (1995), 'A gender sensitive situation analysis of the urban poor, a case study in Kumasi, Ghana', *Trialog* 44, 34–7.

Dobson, Skye and Edith Samya (2012), 'Enumerations in five cities in Uganda', *Environment and Urbanization* 24:1.

Dodman, David (2009), 'Blaming cities for climate change? An analysis of urban greenhouse gas emissions inventories', *Environment and Urbanization* 21:1, 185–201.

Donnelly, Martin J., P.J. McCall, Christian Lengeler, Imelda Bates, Umberto D'Alessandro, Guy Barnish, Flemming Konradsen, Eveline Klinkenberg, Harold Townson, Jean-Francois Trape, Ian M. Hastings and Clifford Mutero (2005), 'Malaria and urbanization in sub-Saharan Africa', *Malaria Journal* 4:12.

du Toit, Andries (2005), *Chronic and Structural Poverty in South Africa: Challenges for Action and Research*, Chronic Poverty Research Centre Working Paper 56, Manchester: Chronic Poverty Research Centre, University of Manchester.

Dutta, Puja Vasudeva (2005) *Accounting for Wage Inequality in India*, PRSU Working Paper No. 29, Brighton: Poverty Research Unit at the University of Sussex.

Dutta, Shyam with Richard Batley (2000) *Urban Governance, Partnership and Poverty in Ahmedabad*, Urban Governance, Partnerships and Poverty Research Working Paper No. 16, Birmingham: University of Birmingham.

Dyson, T. (2003), 'HIV/AIDS and urbanization', *Population and Development Review* 29:3, 427–42.

Economic Commission for Latin America and the Caribbean (undated), *CEPALSTAT: Income Distribution.* Online. Available at: http://websie.eclac.cl/sisgen/Consulta Integrada.asp?idAplicacion=1&idTema=363&idioma=i (accessed March 2012).

Ekblad, Solvig (1993), 'Stressful environments and their effects on quality of life in Third World cities', *Environment and Urbanization* 5:2, 125–34.

Elbers, Chris, Peter Lanjouw, Johan Mistiaen, Berk Ozler and Kenneth R. Simler (2005), 'Are neighbours equal? Estimated local inequality in three developing countries' in Ravi Kanbur and Anthony J. Venables (eds), *Spatial Inequality and Development*, Oxford: Oxford University Press, 37–60.

Environment and Urbanization (1989), 'Beyond the stereotype of slums: how the poor find accommodation in Third World cities', editorial, 1:2, 2–15.

Escobar, Arturo (1995), *Encountering Development: The Making and Unmaking of the Third World*, Princeton Studies in Culture/Power/History. Princeton, New Jersey: Princeton University Press

ESMAP (2007), *Meeting the Energy Needs of the Urban Poor: Lessons from Electrification Practitioners*, ESMAP Technical Paper 118/07, Washington, DC: ESMAP.

ESMAP and UNDP (2003), *Household Fuel Use and Fuel Switching in Guatemala*, ESMAP Report 27274.

Etemadi, Felisa U. (2000), 'Civil society participation in city governance in Cebu City', *Environment and Urbanization* 12:1, 57–72.

Ethiopia, Federal Democratic Republic of and Ministry of Finance and Economic Development (2002), *Ethiopia: Sustainable Development and Poverty Reduction Programme.*

Fahmi, Wael Salah (2005), 'The impact of privatization of solid waste management on the Zabaleen garbage collectors of Cairo', *Environment and Urbanization* 17:2, 155–70.

Fajnzylber, Pablo, Daniel Lederma and Norman Loayza (2002) 'Inequality and violent crime', *Journal of Law and Economics* XLV (April), 1–40.

Fall, Abdoulaye, Sécou Sarr, Touria Dafrallah and Abdou Ndour (2008), 'Modern energy access in peri-urban areas of West Africa: the case of Dakar, Senegal', *Energy for Sustainable Development* 12:4, 22–37.

Fallon, Peter and Robert Lucas (2002), 'The impact of financial crises on labor markets, household incomes, and poverty: a review of the evidence' *The World Bank Research Observer* 17:1, 21–45.

Farouk, Braimah R. and Mensah Owusu (2012), 'If in doubt, count: the role of community-driven enumerations in blocking eviction in Old Fadama, Accra', *Environment and Urbanization* 24:1, 47–57.

Fergutz, Oscar, Sonia Dias and Diana Mitlin (2011), 'Developing urban waste management in Brazil with waste picker organizations', *Environment and Urbanization* 23:2, 597–608.

Fernandes, Leela (2004), 'The politics of forgetting: class politics, state power and the restructuring of urban space in India', *Urban Studies* 41:12, 2415–30.

Ferreira, Francisco and Ricardo Paes de Barros (1999) *The Slippery Slope: Explaining the Increase in Extreme Poverty in Urban Brazil 1976–96*, Policy Research Working Paper No. 2210, Washington, DC: World Bank.

Fotso, John-Christophe (2007), 'Urban–rural differentials in child malnutrition: trends and socioeconomic correlates in sub-Saharan Africa', *Health & Place* 13:1, 205–22.

Friedman, Jed (2005), 'How responsive is poverty to growth? A regional analysis of poverty, inequality and growth in Indonesia 1984–99' in Ravi Kanbur and Anthony J. Venables (eds), *Spatial Inequality and Development*, Oxford: Oxford University Press, 163–208.

Furedy, Christine (1994), 'Socio-environmental initiatives in solid waste management in Southern cities: developing international comparisons' in M. Huysman, B. Raman and A. Rosario (eds), *Proceedings of the Workshop on Linkages in Urban Solid Waste Management*, Bangalore: Karnataka State Council for Science and Technology.

Gaerlan, Kristina, Marion Cabrera, Patricia Samia and L. Santoalla (2010), 'Feminised recession: impact of the global financial crisis on women garment workers in the Philippines', *Gender & Development* 18:2, 229–40.

Gambia, Republic of (2002), *Strategy for Poverty Alleviation (SPAII)*, PRSP, Department of State for Finance and Economic Affairs.

Gangopadhyay, S., B. Ramaswami, and W. Wadhawa (2005), 'Reducing subsidies on household fuels in India: how will it affect the poor?' *Energy Policy* 33:18, 2326–36.

Gao, Q. (2006), *Social Benefits in Urban China: Determinants and Impact of Income Inequality in 1988 and 2002*, UNU/Wider Research Paper 2006/117, Helsinki: United Nations University – World Institute for Development Economics Research.

Garrett, James and Akhter Ahmed (2004), 'Incorporating crime in household surveys: a research note', *Environment and Urbanization* 16:2, 139–52.

Ghana, Republic of (2000), *Poverty Trends in Ghana in the 1990s*, Accra: Ghana Statistical Services.

GHK and IIED (2004), *China Urban Poverty Study*, prepared for the UK Department for International Development, Hong Kong: GHK.

Ghosh, A., S.S. Ahmad and Shipra Maitra (1994), *Basic Services for Urban Poor: A Study of Baroda, Bhilwara, Sambalpur and Siliguri*, Urban Studies Series No. 3, New Delhi: Institute of Social Sciences and Concept Publishing Company.

Gilbert, Alan (1997), 'Work and poverty during economic restructuring: the experience of Bogota, Colombia', *IDS Bulletin* 28:2, 24–34.

Glockner, Heike, Meki Mkanga and Timothy Ndezi (2004), 'Local empowerment through community mapping processes in Tanzania', *Environment and Urbanization* 16:1, 185–98.

Goldstein, G. (1990), 'Access to life-saving services in urban areas', in J.E. Hardoy, S. Cairncross and D. Satterthwaite (eds), *The Poor Die Young: Housing and Health in Third World Cities*, London: Earthscan, 213–27.

Good, Kenneth (1999), 'The state and extreme poverty in Botswana: the San and destitutes', *Journal of Modern African Studies* 37:2, 185–205.

Grewe, Christopher and Charles E. Becker (2001), *Characteristics of Poor Households in Indonesia*, Background Paper for the Panel on Urban Population Dynamics, Committee on Population, National Research Council/National Academy of Sciences.

GRNUHE (2010), *Improving Urban Health Equity through Action on the Social and Environmental Determinants of Health*, Global Research Network on Urban Health Equity, London: University College London and the Rockefeller Institute.

Grootaert, Christiaan (1996), *Analysing Poverty and Policy Reform: The Experience of Côte d'Ivoire*, Aldershot, UK: Avebury.

Gulyani, Sumila and Debabrata Talukdar (2008), 'Slum real estate: the low-quality high-price puzzle in Nairobi's slum rental market and its implications for theory and practice', *World Development* 36:10, 1916–37.

Gulyani S., D. Talukdar and D. Jack (2010), *Poverty, Living Conditions and Infrastructure Access: A Comparison of Slums in Dakar, Johannesburg, and Nairobi*, Policy Research Working Paper No. 5388, Washington, DC: World Bank.

Gupta, Kamla, Fred Arnold and H. Lhungdim (2009), *Health and Living Conditions in Eight Indian Cities: National Family Health Survey (NFHS-3), India, 2005–06*, Calverton, MD: International Institute for Population Sciences.

Haddad, Lawrence and Akhter U. Ahmed (2002), *Avoiding Chronic and Transitory Poverty: Evidence from Egypt 1997–9*, Food Consumption and Nutrition Division, International Food Policy Research Institute, Washington, DC: International Food Policy Research Institute.

Haddad, Lawrence, John Hoddinott and Harold Alderman (eds) (1997), *Intrahousehold Resource Allocation in Developing Countries: Methods, Models, and Policy*, Baltimore: Johns Hopkins University Press.

Hailu, Degol and Sergei Suarez Dillon Soares (2009), *What Explains the Decline in Brazil's Inequality?* International Policy Centre for Inclusive Growth, Brasilia: International Poverty Centre.

Hanchett, Suzanne, Shireen Akhter and Mohidul Hoque Khan, summarized by Stephen Mezulianik and Vicky Blagbrough (2003), 'Water, sanitation and hygiene in Bangladesh slums: a summary of WaterAid's Bangladesh Urban Programme Evaluation', *Environment and Urbanization* 15:2, 43–56.

Haque, Anika Nasra, Stelios Grafakos and Marijk Huijsman (2012), 'Participatory integrated assessment of flood protection measures for climate adaptation in Dhaka', *Environment and Urbanization* 24:1, 197–213.

Haque, R., D. Mondal, B.D. Kirkpatrick, S. Akther, B.M. Farr, R.B. Sack and W.A. Petri Jr (2003), 'Epidemiologic and clinical characteristics of acute diarrhoea with emphasis on *Entamoeba histolytica* infections in pre-school children in an urban slum of Dhaka, Bangladesh', *American Journal of Tropical Medicine and Hygiene* 69:4, 398–405.

Hardoy, Jorge E. and David Satterthwaite (1981), *Shelter: Need and Response: Housing, Land and Settlement Policies in Seventeen Third World Nations*, Chichester: John Wiley & Sons.

——(1984), 'Third World cities and the environment of poverty', *Geoforum* 15:3, 307–37.

——(1986a), 'A survey of the empirical material on the factors affecting the development of small and intermediate urban centres' in Jorge E. Hardoy and David Satterthwaite (eds), *Small and Intermediate Urban Centres: Their Role in Regional and National Development in the Third World*, London: Hodder and Stoughton.

——(1986b), 'Government policies and small and intermediate urban centres' in Jorge E. Hardoy and David Satterthwaite (eds), *Small and Intermediate Urban Centres: Their Role in Regional and National Development in the Third World*, London: Hodder and Stoughton.

——(1989), *Squatter Citizen: Life in the Urban Third World*, London: Earthscan Publications.

Hardoy, Jorge E., Sandy Cairncross and David Satterthwaite (eds) (1990), *The Poor Die Young: Housing and Health in Third World Cities*, London: Earthscan Publications.

Hardoy, Jorge E., Diana Mitlin and David Satterthwaite (1992), *Environmental Problems in Third World Cities*, London: Earthscan Publications.

——(2001), *Environmental Problems in an Urbanizing World: Finding Solutions for Cities in Africa, Asia and Latin America*, London: Earthscan Publications.

Hardoy, Jorgelina with Florencia Almansi (2011), *Assessing the Scale and Nature of Urban Poverty in Buenos Aires*, Human Settlements Working Paper 29, London: IIED.

Harpham, Trudy and Ilona Blue (eds) (1995), *Urbanization and Mental Health in Developing Countries*, Aldershot: Avebury.

Harris, Andrew (2008), 'From London to Mumbai and back again: gentrification and public policy in comparative perspective', *Urban Studies* 45:12, 2407–28.

Harriss-White, B. (2005), 'Destitution and the poverty of its politics: with special reference to south Asia', *World Development* 33:6, 881–92.

Hasan, Arif (1997), *Working with Government: The Story of the Orangi Pilot Project's Collaboration with State Agencies for Replicating its Low-Cost Sanitation Programme*, Karachi: City Press.

——(1999), *Understanding Karachi: Planning and Reform for the Future*, Karachi: City Press.

——(2002), 'The changing nature of the informal sector in Karachi as a result of global restructuring and liberalization', *Environment and Urbanization* 14:1, 69–78.

——(2006), 'Orangi Pilot Project: the expansion of work beyond Orangi and the mapping of informal settlements and infrastructure', *Environment and Urbanization* 18:2, 451–80.

——(2010), 'Migration, small towns and social transformations in Pakistan', *Environment and Urbanization* 22:1, 33–50.

Hasan, Arif and Mansoor Raza (2002), *Urban Change in Pakistan*, Urban Change Working Paper 6, London: IIED.

Heintz, James (2010), 'Women's employment, economic risk and poverty', in Sylvia Chant (ed), *The International Handbook of Gender and Poverty: Concepts, Research, Policy*, Cheltenham: Edward Elgar, 434–9.

Hentschel, J. and Peter Lanjouw (1996), *Constructing an Indicator for Consumption for the Analysis of Poverty*, LSMS Working Paper No. 124, Washington, DC: World Bank.

Herrera, J. and F. Roubaud (2005), 'Poverty dynamics in urban Peru and Madagascar: a comparative approach', *International Planning Studies Journal* 10:1, 21–48.

Herzer, Hilda, María Mercedes Di Virgilio, Máximo Lanzetta, María Carla Rodríguez and Adriana Redondo (2000), 'The formation of social organizations and their attempts to consolidate settlements undergoing transition in Buenos Aires, Argentina', *Environment and Urbanization* 12:1, 215–30.

Higgins, Benjamin (1968), *Economic Development: Problems, Principles, and Policies*, Revised Edition, New York: W.W. Norton and Co.

Honduras, Government of (2001), *Poverty Reduction Strategy Paper*.

Hooper, Michael and Leonard Ortolano (2012), 'Motivations for slum dweller social movement participation in urban Africa: a study of mobilization in Kurasini, Dar es Salaam', *Environment and Urbanization* 24:1, 99–114.

Hoornweg, Daniel, Lorraine Sugar and Claudia Lorena Trejos Gomez (2011), 'Cities and greenhouse gas emissions: moving forward', *Environment and Urbanization* 23:1, 207–27.

Horn, Zoe Elena (2009), *No Cushion to Fall Back On: The Global Economic Crisis and Informal Workers*, Inclusive Cities Study Report. Available at: http://www.inclusivecities.org/index.html

——(2011), *Coping with Crises: Lingering Recession, Rising Inflation and the Informal Workforce*, Inclusive Cities Study Report. Available at: http://www.inclusivecities.org/index.html

Houtzager, Peter P., Arnab Acharya and Adrián Gurza Lavalle (2007), *Associations and the Exercise of Citizenship in New Democracies: Evidence from São Paulo and Mexico City*, IDS Working Paper 285, Brighton: Institute for Development Studies.

Hulme, David and Maia Green (2005), 'From correlates and characteristics to causes: thinking about poverty from a chronic poverty perspective', *World Development* 33:6, 867–80.

Hunt, Caroline (1996), 'Child waste pickers in India: the occupation and its health risks', *Environment and Urbanization* 8:2, 111–8.

Huq, A.T., M. Zahurul and Borhan Uddin (1996), 'Transport and the urban poor' in Nazrul Islam (ed.), *The Urban Poor in Bangladesh*, Dhaka: Centre for Urban Studies.

Huq-Hussain, Shahnaz (1995) 'Fighting poverty: the economic adjustment of female migrants in Dhaka', *Environment and Urbanization* 7:2, 51–65.

Hurtado, Álvaro García (2006), *Development in Chile 1990–2005: Lessons from a Positive Experience*, UNU/Wider Research Paper No. 2006/13, Helsinki: UNU/Wider.

Huysman, Marijk (1994), 'The position of women-waste pickers in Bangalore' in Ida Baud and Hans Schenk (eds), *Solid Waste Management: Models, Assessment, Appraisals and Linkages in Bangalore*, New Delhi: Manohar, 24–5.

IFRC (2010), *World Disasters Report 2010: Focus on Urban Risk*, Geneva: International Federation of Red Cross and Red Crescent Societies.

ILO (1976), *Employment, Growth and Basic Needs: A One World Problem*, Geneva: International Labour Office.

——(2006), *Global Employment Trends for Youth*, Geneva: International Labour Office.

——(2011), *Statistical Update on Employment in the Informal Economy*, Geneva: ILO Department of Statistics.

International Monetary Fund (2008b), *Haiti: Poverty Reduction Strategy Paper*, IMF Country Report No. 08/115, Washington, DC: International Monetary Fund.

International Monetary Fund, IDA and Socialist Republic of Vietnam (2005), *Socialist Republic of Vietnam: Poverty Reduction Strategy Paper Annual Progress Report*, Report No. 33122, Washington, DC: International Monetary Fund, International Development Association and Socialist Republic of Vietnam.

Iskandar, Laila (2013) 'CID consulting and new models for poverty reduction', *Environment and Urbanization*.

Islam, Nazrul, Nurul Huda, Francis B. Narayan and Pradumna B. Rana (eds) (1997), *Addressing the Urban Poverty Agenda in Bangladesh: Critical Issues and the 1995 Survey Findings*, Dhaka: The University Press Limited.

IWA (undated), *IWA Water Wiki*. Online. Available at: http://www.iwawaterwiki.org/ (accessed 3 August 2012).

Iyenda, Guillaume (2005), 'Street enterprises, urban livelihoods and poverty in Kinshasa', *Environment and Urbanization* 17:2, 55–68.

Jabeen, Huraera, Adriana Allen and Cassidy Johnson (2010), 'Built-in resilience: learning from grassroots coping strategies to climate variability', *Environment and Urbanization* 22:2, 415–31.

Jenkins, Paul (2000), 'Urban management, urban poverty and urban governance: planning and land management in Maputo, Mozambique', *Environment and Urbanization* 12:1, 137–52.

Johansson, Thomas B., Nebojsa Nakicenovic, Anand Patwardhan and Luis Gomez-Echeverri (eds) (2012), *Global Energy Assessment: Toward a Sustainable Future*, Cambridge: Cambridge University Press.

Jonsson, Åsa and David Satterthwaite (2000), *Income-Based Poverty Lines*, paper prepared for the Panel on Urban Population Dynamics, Committee on Population, Washington, DC: National Research Council/National Academy of Sciences.

Joshi, Anuradha (2008), 'Producing social accountability? The impact of service delivery reforms', *IDS Bulletin* 38:6, 10–17.

Kabir, Md. Azmal, Ataur Rahman, Sarah Salway and Jane Pryer (2000) 'Sickness among the urban poor: a barrier to livelihood security', *Journal of International Development* 12:5, 707–22.

Kanbur, Ravi and Lyn Squire (2001), 'The evolution of thinking about poverty: exploring the interactions' in Gerald M. Meier and Joseph E. Stiglitz, *Frontiers of Development Economics; the Future in Perspective*, Oxford: Oxford University Press, 183–226.

Kanji, Nazneen (1995), 'Gender, poverty and economic adjustment in Harare, Zimbabwe', *Environment and Urbanization* 7:1, 37–55.

Kantor, Paula (2009), 'Women's exclusion and unfavorable inclusion in informal employment in Lucknow, India: barriers to voice and livelihood security', *World Development* 37:1, 194–207.

Kantor, Paula, Uma Rani and Jeemol Unni (2006), 'Decent work deficits in informal economy: case of Surat', *Economic and Political Weekly* 27 May, 2087–97.

Karanja, Irene (2010), 'An enumeration and mapping of informal settlements in Kisumu, Kenya, implemented by their inhabitants', *Environment and Urbanization* 22:1, 217–40.

Karekezi, S., J. Kimani and O. Onguru (2008), 'Energy access among the urban poor in Kenya', *Energy for Sustainable Development* 12:4, 38–48.

Katui-Katua, Munguti and Gordon McGranahan (2002), *Small Enterprises and Water Provision in Kibera, Nairobi: Public Private Partnerships and the Poor*, Loughborough, UK: Water, Engineering and Development Centre (WEDC).

Kebede, B., A. Bekele and E. Kedir (2002), 'Can the urban poor afford modern energy? The case of Ethiopia', *Energy Policy* 30, 1029–45.

Kedir, A. (2005), 'Understanding urban chronic poverty: crossing the qualitative and quantitative divide', *Environment and Urbanization* 17:2, 43–54

Kedir, Abbi M. and Andrew McKay (2005), 'Chronic poverty in urban Ethiopia: panel data evidence', *International Planning Studies* 10:1, 49–68.

Kennedy, G., G. Nantel, I.D. Brouwer and F.J. Kok (2006), 'Does living in an urban environment confer advantages for childhood nutritional status? Analysis of disparities in nutritional status by wealth and residence in Angola, Central African Republic and Senegal', *Public Health Nutrition* 9:2, 187–93.

Kenya, Government of (2000), *Poverty in Kenya*, Nairobi: Human Resources and Social Services Department and Central Bureau of Statistics, Ministry of Finance and Planning.

Khusro, A.M. (1999), *The Poverty of Nations*, Basingstoke: Macmillan.

Ki Kim, Ik (1995), 'Differentiation among the urban poor and the reproduction of poverty: the case of Nanjido', *Environment and Urbanization* 7:2, 183–94.

King, Anthony (1976), *Colonial Urban Development*, London: Routledge and Kegan Paul.

King, Rudith (2006), 'Fulcrum of the urban economy: governance and street livelihoods in Kumasi, Ghana' in Alison Brown (ed.), *Contested Space: Street Trading, Public Space and Livelihoods in Developing Cities*, Rugby, UK: ITDG Publishing, 99–118.

Kironde, J.M. Lusugga (1995), 'Access to land by the urban poor in Tanzania: some findings from Dar es Salaam', *Environment and Urbanization* 7:1, 77–95.

Kjellstrom, Tord and Susan Mercado (2008), 'Towards action on social determinants for health equity in urban settings', *Environment and Urbanization* 20:2, 551–74.

Klinkenberg, E., P.J. McCall, M.D. Wilson, A.O. Akoto, F.P. Amerasinghe, I. Bates, F.H. Verhoeff, G. Barnish and M.J. Donnelly (2006), 'Urban malaria and anaemia in children: a cross-sectional survey in two cities of Ghana', *Tropical Medicine and International Health* 11:5, 578–88.

Knight, John, Li Shi and Zhao Renwei (2004), *Divergent Means and Convergent Inequality of Incomes Among Provinces and Cities of Urban China*, UNI/Wider Research Paper No. 2004/52, Helsinki: UNU/Wider.

Kovats, R.S. and R. Akhtar (2008), 'Climate, climate change and human health in Asian cities', *Environment and Urbanization* 20:1, 165–76.

Kundu, Amitabh (2011), *Trends and Processes of Urbanisation in India*, Urbanization and Emerging Population Issues Working Paper 6, London: IIED and UNFPA.

Kuznets, Simon (ed) (1955), *Income and Wealth*, London: Bowes & Bowes.

Kwon, Soon-Won (1998), 'National profile of poverty' in UNDP, *Combating Poverty: The Korean Experience*, Seoul: United Nations Development Programme (UNDP).

Kyobutungi, Catherine, Abdhalah Kasiira Ziraba, Alex Ezeh and Yazoumé Yé (2008), 'The burden of disease profile of residents of Nairobi's slums: results from a Demographic Surveillance System', *Population Health Metrics* 6:1.

Lama-Rewal, Stéphanie Tawa (2011), 'Urban governance and health care provision in Delhi', *Environment and Urbanization* 23:2, 563–81.

Lamba, Davinder (1994), 'The forgotten half: environmental health in Nairobi's poverty areas', *Environment and Urbanization* 6:1, 164–73.

Lanjouw, Peter, Giovanna Prennushi and Salman Zaidi (1999), 'Poverty in Nepal today', in Giovanna Prennushi (ed.), *Nepal: Poverty at the Turn of the Twenty-First Century, Background Studies*, Report IDP 174, Washington, DC: World Bank, 1–28.

Lantz, Maria and Jonatan Habib Engqvist (eds) (2008), *Dharavi: Documenting Informalities*, Stockholm: The Royal University College of Fine Arts, Art and Architecture.

Latapí, Augustín Escobar and Mercedes González de la Rocha (1995), 'Crisis, restructuring and urban poverty in Mexico', *Environment and Urbanization* 7:1, 57–75.

Lee, Eddy (1981), 'Basic needs strategies: a frustrated response to development from below?' in Walter B. Stohr and D.R. Fraser Taylor (eds), *Development from Above or Below*, Chichester: John Wiley & Sons, 107–22.

Lee, Joung-Woo (1998), 'Urban poverty' in UNDP, *Combating Poverty: The Korean Experience*, Seoul: United Nations Development Programme (UNDP).

Lee-Smith, Diana (2010), 'Cities feeding people: an update on urban agriculture in equatorial Africa', *Environment and Urbanization* 22:2, 483–500.

Legros, Gwénaëlle, Ines Havet, Nigel Bruce and Sophie Bonjour (2009), *The Energy Access Situation in Developing Countries: A Review Focusing on the Least Developed Countries and Sub-Saharan Africa*, New York: World Health Organization and United Nations Development Programme.

Leite, Phillippe G., Terry McKinley and Rafeal Guerreiro Osorio (2006), *The Post-Apartheid Evolution of Earnings Inequality in South Africa*, Working Paper No. 32, Brasilia: International Poverty Centre.

Leonard, H. Jeffrey (1989), 'Environment and the poor: development strategies for a common agenda' in H. Jeffrey Leonard (ed.), *Environment and the Poor: Development Strategies for a Common Agenda*, Overseas Development Council, New Brunswick: Transaction Books.

Liberia, Republic of (2008), *Liberia Poverty Reduction Strategy*, Republic of Liberia.

Lipton, Michael (1977), *Why Poor People Stay Poor: Urban Bias in World Development*, London: Temple Smith.

Lister, Ruth (2004), *Poverty*, Cambridge: Polity Press.

Liu, Amy Y.C. (2010), 'Economic transition and the gender wage gap in Vietnam: 1992–2002' in Sylvia Chant (ed.), *The International Handbook of Gender and Poverty: Concepts, Research, Policy*, Cheltenham: Edward Elgar, 452–7.

Liu, Yuting and Fulong Wu (2006), 'Urban poverty neighbourhoods: typology and spatial concentration under China's market transition: a case study of Nanjing', *Geoforum* 37, 610–26.

Livengood, Avery and Keya Kunte (2012), 'Participatory settlement mapping by Mahila Milan', *Environment and Urbanization* 24:1, 77–97.

Llorca i Ibáñez, Enric (2011), 'Municipal government, territory and the social determinants of health', *Environment and Urbanization* 23:1, 113–17.

Losada, H., H. Martínez, J. Vieyra, R. Pealing, R. Zavala and J. Cortés (1998), 'Urban agriculture in the metropolitan zone of Mexico City: changes over time in urban, suburban and periurban areas', *Environment and Urbanization* 10:2, 37–54.

Mabala, Richard (2006), 'From HIV prevention to HIV protection: addressing the vulnerability of girls and young women in urban areas', *Environment and Urbanization* 18:2, 407–32.

McCarthy, James J., Osvaldo F. Canziani, Niel A. Leary, David J. Dokken and Kaskey S. White (2001), *Climate Change 2001: Impacts, Adaptation, and Vulnerability: Contribution of Working Group II to the Third Assessment Report of the Intergovernmental Panel on Climate Change*, Cambridge: Cambridge University Press.

McGranahan, Gordon (1991), *Environmental Problems and the Urban Household in Third World Countries*, Stockholm: Stockholm Environment Institute.

——(2007), *Urban Environments, Wealth and Health: Shifting Burdens and Possible Responses in Low and Middle-Income Nations*, Human Settlements Discussion Paper, London: IIED.

McGranahan, Gordon, Pedro Jacobi, Jacob Songsore, Charles Surjadi and Marianne Kjellén (2001), *The Citizens at Risk: From Urban Sanitation to Sustainable Cities*, London: Earthscan Publications.

McGranahan, Gordon, Deborah Balk and Bridget Anderson (2007), 'The rising tide: assessing the risks of climate change and human settlements in low-elevation coastal zones', *Environment and Urbanization* 19:1, 17–37.

MacGregor, H., N. Bucher, C. Durham, M. Falcao, J. Morrissey, I. Silverman, H. Smith and A. Taylor (2005), *Hazard Profile and Vulnerability Assessment for Informal Settlements: An Imizamo Yethu Case Study with Special Reference to the Experience of Children*, DiMP, Cape Town: University of Cape Town.

McHale, John and Magda Cordell McHale (1981), *Basic Human Needs: A Framework for Action*, New Brunswick: Transaction Books.

McIntosh, Arthur C. and Cesar E. Yñiguez (1997), *Second Water Utilities Data Book*, Manila: Asian Development Bank.

Maji na usafini? Njooni tujadiliane (2007), *Citizen's Report Card on Urban Water, Sanitation and Solid Waste Services in Kenya: Summary of Results from Nairobi, Kisumu and Mombasa*, Nairobi.

Makau, Jack, Skye Dobson and Edith Samia (2012), 'The five-city enumeration: the role of participatory enumerations in developing community capacity and partnerships with government in Uganda', *Environment and Urbanization* 24:1, 31–46.

Malawi, Government of (1994), *Survey of Household Expenditure and Small-Scale Economic Activities 1990/91*, National Statistics Office.

——(2000), *Profile of Poverty in Malawi, 1998*, Poverty Monitoring System, National Economic Council, Government of Malawi.

——(2002), *Malawi Poverty Reduction Strategy Paper*.

Malawi, Republic of (undated), *Malawi Growth and Development Strategy: From Poverty to Prosperity 2006–2011*, Republic of Malawi.

Manda, Mtafu A. Zeleza (2009), *Water and Sanitation Situation in Urban Malawi*, IIED Working Paper, London: IIED.

Manzanal, Mabel and Cesar Vapnarsky (1986), 'The development of the Upper Valley of Rio Negro and its periphery within the Comahue Region, Argentina' in Jorge E. Hardoy and David Satterthwaite (eds), *Small and Intermediate Urban Centres: Their Role in Regional and National Development in the Third World*, London: Hodder and Stoughton, 18–79.

Maoulidi, Moumié (2011), *Heath Needs Assessment for Kisumu, Kenya*, MCI Social Sector Working Paper Series No. 19/2011.

Martine, George and Gordon McGranahan (2010), *Brazil's Early Urban Transition: What Can It Teach Urbanizing Countries?* Urbanization and Emerging Population Issues Paper 7, London and New York: IIED and UNFPA.

Marx, Colin and Sarah Charlton (2003), *The Case of Durban, South Africa: Understanding Slums: Case Studies for the Global Report 2003*, London: Development Planning Unit, University College London.

Mason, Edward S. and Robert Asher (1973), *The World Bank Since Bretton Woods*, Washington, DC: The Brookings Institution.

Matthews, Zoe, Amos Channon, Sarah Neal, David Osrin, Nyovani Madise and William Stones (2010), 'Examining the "urban advantage" in maternal health care in developing countries', *Public Library of Science Medicine* 7:9, 1.

Mauritania, Islamic Republic of (2000), *Poverty Reduction Strategy Paper*.

Maxwell, Dan (1998), *The Political Economy of Urban Food Security in Sub-Saharan Africa*, FCND Discussion Papers, Washington, DC: International Food Policy Research Institute (IFPRI).

Maxwell, Daniel, Carol Levin, Margaret Armar-Klemesu, Marie Ruel, Saul Morris and Clement Ahiadeke (1998), *Urban Livelihoods and Food and Nutrition Security in Greater Accra, Ghana*, Washington, DC: International Food Policy Research Institute (IFPRI).

Maxwell, David, Carol Levin, Margaret Armar-Klemesu, Marie Ruel, Saul Morris and Clement Ahiadeke (2000), *Urban Livelihoods and Food and Nutrition Security in Greater Accra, Ghana*, Noguchi Memorial Institute for Medical Research and World Health Organization, Research Report No. 112, Washington, DC: International Food Policy Research Institute.

Mayank, S., R. Bahl, A. Rattan and N. Bhandari (2001), 'Prevalence and correlates of morbidity in pregnant women in an urban slum of New Delhi', *Asia Pacific Population Journal* 16:2, 29–45.

Meagher, Kate (2010), 'The empowerment trap: gender, poverty and the informal economy in sub-Saharan Africa' in Sylvia Chant (ed), *The International Handbook of Gender and Poverty: Concepts, Research, Policy*, Cheltenham: Edward Elgar, 472–7.

Mearns, Robin (2004), 'Sustaining livelihoods on Mongolia's pastoral commons: insights from a participatory assessment', *Development and Change* 35:1, 107–39.

Mejía, José Antonio and Rob Vos (1997), *Poverty in Latin America and the Caribbean: An Inventory 1980–95*, document prepared in the context of the programme for the Improvement of Surveys and the Measurement of Living Conditions in Latin America and the Caribbean, co-sponsored by the IDB, World Bank and CEPAL, Working Paper Series I-4.

Menegat, Rualdo (2002), 'Participatory democracy and sustainable development: integrated urban environmental management in Porto Alegre, Brazil', *Environment and Urbanization* 14:2, 181–206.

Menon, P., M.T. Ruel and S.S. Morris (2000), 'Socio-economic differentials in child stunting are consistently larger in urban than in rural areas', *Food and Nutrition Bulletin* 21, 282–9.

Mestl, H.E., K. Aunan, H.M. Seip, S. Wang, Y. Zhao, and D. Zhang (2007), 'Urban and rural exposure to indoor air pollution from domestic biomass and coal burning across China', *Science of the Total Environment* 377:1, 12–26.

Ministry of Planning and Finance, Government of Mozambique, Eduardo Mondlane University and the International Food Policy Research Institute (IFPRI) (1998), *Understanding Poverty and Well-Being in Mozambique: The First National Assessment (1996–97)*.

Minujin, Alberto (1995), 'Squeezed: the middle class in Latin America', *Environment and Urbanization* 7:2, 153–66.

——(1999), 'Monitoring rights and goals for children', paper presented at the Third Meeting of the Expert Group on Poverty Statistics (Rio Group), Lisbon, November.

Misra, Harikesh (1990), 'Housing and health problems in three squatter settlements in Allahabad, India' in Sandy Cairncross, Jorge E. Hardoy and David Satterthwaite (eds), *The Poor Die Young: Housing and Health in Third World Cities*, London: Earthscan Publications, London.

Mitlin, Diana (2000), 'Addressing urban poverty: increasing incomes, reducing costs, securing representation', *Development in Practice* 10:2, 204–16.

——(2001), 'Civil society and urban poverty: examining complexity', *Environment and Urbanization* 13:2, 151–73.

——(2004), *Understanding Urban Poverty: What the Poverty Reduction Strategy Papers Tell Us*, Poverty Reduction in Urban Areas Series Working Paper No. 13, London: International Institute for Environment and Development.

——(2008), 'With and beyond the state: co-production as a route to political influence, power and transformation for grassroots organizations', *Environment and Urbanization* 20:2, 339–60.

Mitlin, Diana and Anna Muller (2004), 'Windhoek, Namibia: towards progressive urban land policies in Southern Africa', *International Development Policy Review* 26:2, 167–86.

Mitlin, Diana and David Satterthwaite (2001), 'Urban poverty: some thoughts about its scale and nature and about responses to it' in Shahid Yusuf, Simon Evenett and Weiping Wu (eds), *Facets of Globalization: International and Local Dimensions of Development*, Washington, DC: World Bank, 193–220.

——(eds) (2004), *Empowering Squatter Citizen: Local Government, Civil Society and Urban Poverty Reduction*, London: Earthscan Publications.

Mitlin, Diana, David Satterthwaite and Sheridan Bartlett (2011), *Capital, Capacities and Collaboration: The Multiple Roles of Community Savings in Addressing Urban Poverty*, Human Settlements Working Paper No. 34, London: IIED.

Mitullah, Winnie V. (2010), 'Informal workers in Kenya and transnational organizing: networking and leveraging resources' in Ilda Lindell (ed), *Africa's Informal Workers: Collective Agency, Alliances and Transnational Organizing in Urban Africa*, London: Zed Books, 184–201.

Montgomery, Mark (2009), *Urban Poverty and Health in Developing Countries*, Population Reference Bureau 64:2, June.

Montgomery, Mark R., Richard Stren, Barney Cohen and Holly E. Reed (eds) (2003), *Cities Transformed: Demographic Change and Its Implications in the Developing World*, Washington, DC: National Academy Press.

Moser, Caroline O.N. (1993), *Urban Social Policy and Poverty Reduction*, TWURD Working Paper #10, Urban Development Division, Washington, DC: World Bank.

——(1995), 'Urban social policy and poverty reduction', *Environment and Urbanization* 7:1, 159–71.

——(1996), *Confronting Crisis: A Summary of Household Responses to Poverty and Vulnerability in Four Poor Urban Communities*, Environmentally Sustainable Development Studies and Monographs Series No. 7, Washington, DC: World Bank.

——(1997), *Household Responses to Poverty and Vulnerability, Volume 1: Confronting Crisis in Cisne Dos, Guayaquil, Ecuador*, Urban Management Programme Policy Paper No. 21, Washington, DC: World Bank.

——(1998), 'The asset vulnerability framework: reassessing urban poverty reduction strategies', *World Development* 26:1, 1–19.

——(2004), 'Urban violence and insecurity: an introductory roadmap', *Environment and Urbanization* 16:2, 3–15.

——(2006a), 'Assets, livelihoods and social policy', in C. Moser (ed), *Assets, Livelihoods and Social Policy*, Washington, DC: World Bank and Palgrave.

——(2006b), *Asset-Based Approaches to Poverty Reduction in a Globalized Context: An Introduction to Asset Accumulation Policy and Summary of Workshop Findings*, Global Economy and Development Working Paper, Washington, DC: Brookings Institution.

——(2007), 'Asset accumulation policy and poverty reduction' in Caroline Moser (ed), *Reducing Global Poverty: The Case for Asset Accumulation*, Washington, DC: Brookings Institution, 83–103.

——(2009), *Ordinary Families, Extraordinary Lives: Assets and Poverty Reduction in Guayaquil 1978–2004*, Washington, DC: Brookings Institution.

——(2011), 'Cancer note from the slums', *Environment and Urbanization* 23:1, 119–21.

Moser, Caroline O.N. and Andrew Felton (2007a), *The Construction of an Asset Index Measuring Asset Accumulation in Ecuador*, CPRC Working Paper 87, Manchester: Chronic Poverty Research Centre.

——(2007b), 'Intergenerational asset accumulation and poverty research in Guayaquil, Ecuador 1978–2004', in Caroline Moser (ed) *Reducing Global Poverty: The Case for Asset Accumulation*, Washington, DC: Brookings Institution, 15–50.

Moser, Caroline O.N. and Jeremy Holland (1997), *Household Responses to Poverty and Vulnerability, Volume 4: Confronting Crisis in Chawama, Lusaka, Zambia*, Urban Management Programme Policy Paper No. 24, Washington, DC: World Bank.

Moser, Caroline O.N. and Cathy McIlwaine (1997), *Household Responses to Poverty and Vulnerability, Volume 3: Confronting Crisis in Commonwealth, Metro Manila, the Philippines*, Urban Management Programme Policy Paper No. 23. Washington, DC: World Bank.

Moser, Caroline O.N., Alicia J. Herbert and Roza E. Makonnen (1993), *Urban Poverty in the Context of Structural Adjustment: Recent Evidence and Policy Responses*, TWU Discussion Paper DP #4, Urban Development Division, Washington, DC: World Bank.

Mosley, Paul, Jane Harrigan and John Toye (1991), *Aid and Power: The World Bank and Policy-Based Lending*, vol. 1, London: Routledge.

Mozambique, Republic of (2001), *Action Plan for the Reduction of Absolute Poverty (2001–2005)*, final version approved by the Council of Ministers.

Muller, Anna and Edith Mbanga (2012), 'Participatory enumerations at the national level in Namibia: the Community Land Information Program', *Environment and Urbanization* 24:1, 67–75.

Mupedziswa, Rodrick and Perpetua Gumbo (1998), *Structural Adjustment and Women Informal Sector Traders in Harare, Zimbabwe*, Nordic African Institute Research Report 106, Uppsala: Nordic African Institute.

Murphy, Denis and Ted Anana (1994), 'Evictions and fear of evictions in the Philippines', *Environment and Urbanization* 6:1, 40–9.

Myers, Garth A. (2003), *Verandahs of Power: Colonialism and Space in Urban Africa*, Syracuse: Syracuse University Press.

Myrdal, Gunnar (1968), *Asian Drama: An Inquiry into the Poverty of Nations*, London: Allan Lane/Penguin.

——(1970), *The Challenge of World Poverty*, London: Allan Lane/Penguin.

Nations, Marilyn K. and Cristina M.G. Monte (1996), '"I'm not a dog, no!" Cries of resistance against the cholera control campaigns', *Social Science and Medicine* 43:6, 1007–24.

Navarro, Lia (2001), 'Exploring the environmental and political dimensions of poverty: the cases of the cities of Mar del Plata and Necochea-Quequén', *Environment and Urbanization* 13:1, 185–99.

Ndezi, Tim (2009), 'The limit of community initiatives in addressing resettlement in Kurasini ward, Tanzania', *Environment and Urbanization* 21:1, 77–88.

Niger, République du (2002), *Poverty Reduction Strategy*, Niamey: Office of the Prime Minister, Permanent Secretariat of the PRSP.

Nnkya, Tumsifu (2006), 'An enabling framework? Governance and street trading in Dar es Salaam, Tanzania' in Alison Brown (ed.), *Contested Space: Street Trading, Public Space and Livelihoods in Developing Cities*, Rugby: ITDG Publishing, 79–98.

Nyamtema, Angelo S., David P. Urassa, Siriel Massawe, Augustine Massawe, D. Mtasiwa, G. Lindmark and J. van Roosmalen (2008), 'Dar es Salaam perinatal care study: needs assessment for quality of care', *East African Journal of Public Health* 5:1, 17–21.

Obrist, Briget (2004), 'Medicalization and morality in a weak state: health, hygiene and water in Dar es Salaam, Tanzania', *Anthropology and Medicine* 11:1, 43–57.

OECD (2003), *Improving Water Management: Recent OECD Experience*, Paris: Organisation for Economic Co-operation and Development.

Onakewhor, J.U., B.N. Olagbuji, A.B. Ande, M.C. Ezeanochie, O.E. Olokor and F.E. Okonofua (2011), 'HIV-AIDS related maternal mortality in Benin City, Nigeria', *Ghana Medical Journal* 46:2, 54–9.

OPP-RTI (2002), *Katchi Abadis of Karachi: Documentation of Sewerage, Water Supply Lines, Clinics, Schools and Thallas, Volume One: The First Hundred Katchi Abadis Surveyed*, Karachi: Orangi Pilot Project – Research and Training Institute.

Orangi Pilot Project (1995), 'Orangi Pilot Project', *Environment and Urbanization* 7:2, 227–36.

Pachauri, Shonali and Leiwen Jiang (2008), 'The household energy transition in India and China', *Energy Policy* 36, 4022–35.

Pakistan, Government of (2003), *Accelerating Economic Growth and Reducing Poverty: The Road Ahead: Poverty Reduction Strategy Paper*, Ministry of Finance, Government of Pakistan.

Pamoja Trust (2001), *Huruma Informal Settlements: Planning Survey Report*, Nairobi: Pamoja Trust.

Parry, Martin, Osvaldo Canziani, Jean Palutikof, Paul van der Linden and Clair Hanson (eds) (2007), *Climate Change 2007: Impacts, Adaptation and Vulnerability: Contribution of Working Group II to the Fourth Assessment Report of the Intergovernmental Panel on Climate Change*, New York: Cambridge University Press.

Patel, Sheela (1990), 'Street children, hotel boys and children of pavement dwellers and construction workers in Bombay: how they meet their daily needs', *Environment and Urbanization* 2:2, 9–26.

Patel, Sheela and Carrie Baptist (2012), 'Documenting by the undocumented', *Environment and Urbanization* 24:1, 3–12

Patel, Sheela and Celine d'Cruz (1993), 'The Mahila Milan crisis credit scheme: from a seed to a tree', *Environment and Urbanization* 5:1, 9–17.

Patel, Sheela and Diana Mitlin (2004), 'Grassroots-driven development: the alliance of SPARC, the National Slum Dwellers Federation and Mahila Milan', in Diana Mitlin and David Satterthwaite (eds), *Empowering Squatter Citizen: Local Government, Civil Society and Urban Poverty Reduction*, London: Earthscan Publications, 216–41.

Patel, Sheela, Celine D'Cruz and Sundar Burra (2002), 'Beyond evictions in a global city: people-managed resettlement in Mumbai', *Environment and Urbanization* 14:1, 159–72.

Paternostro, Stefano, Jean Razafindravonona and David Stifel (2001), *Changes in Poverty in Madagascar, 1993–1999*, Africa Region Working Paper Series 19, Washington, DC: World Bank.

Patton, G., C. Coffey, S. Sawyer, R. Viner, D. Haller, K. Bose, T. Vos, J. Ferguson and C. Mathers (2009), 'Global patterns of mortality in young people: a systematic analysis of population health data', *Lancet* 374:9693, 881–92.

Pauw, Kalie and Liberty Mncube (2007), *The Impact of Growth and Redistribution on Poverty and Inequality in South Africa*, Country Study No. 7, Brasilia: International Poverty Centre.

Peduzzi, P., B. Chatenoux, H. Dao, A. De Bono, H. Herold, J. Kossin, F. Mouton and O. Nordbeck (2012), 'Global trends in human exposure, vulnerability and risk from tropical cyclones', *Nature Climate Change*.

Pelling, Mark and Ben Wisner (eds) (2008), *Disaster Risk Reduction: Cases from Urban Africa*, London: Earthscan Publications.

Perlman, Janice (2004), 'Marginality: from myth to reality in the favelas of Rio de Janeiro' in Ananya Roy and Nezar Alsayyad (eds), *Urban Informality: Transnational Perspectives from the Middle East, Latin America and South Asia*, Lanham: Lexington Books, 105–46.

——(2007), *Globalization and the Urban Poor*, Wider Research Paper No. 2007/76, Helsinki: Wider.

——(2010), *Favela: Four Decades of Living on the Edge in Rio de Janeiro*, New York: Oxford University Press.

Perreault, Thomas (2006), 'From the Guerra Del Agua to the Guerra Del Gas: resource governance, neoliberalism and popular protest in Bolivia', *Antipode* 38:1, 150–72.

Pharoah, Robyn (2008), 'Fire risk in informal settlements in Cape Town, South Africa' in Mark Pelling and Ben Wisner (eds), *Disaster Risk Reduction: Cases from Urban Africa*, London: Earthscan Publications, 109–30.

Piachaud, David (1987), 'Problems in the definition and measurement of poverty', *Journal of Social Policy* 16:2, 147–64.

Pincus, John (1967), *Trade, Aid and Development: The Rich and the Poor Nations*, New York: McGraw-Hill.

Porio, Emma with the assistance of Christine S. Crisol, Nota F. Magno, David Cid and Evelyn N. Paul (2004), 'The Community Mortgage Program (CMP): an innovative social housing programme in the Philippines and its outcomes' in Diana Mitlin and David Satterthwaite (eds), *Empowering Squatter Citizen: Local Government, Civil Society and Urban Poverty Reduction*, London: Earthscan Publications, 54–80.

Potts, Deborah (2009), 'The slowing of sub-Saharan Africa's urbanization: evidence and implications for urban livelihoods', *Environment and Urbanization* 21:1, 253–9.

Potts, Deborah and C.C. Mutambirwa (1991), 'High-density housing in Harare: commodification and overcrowding', *Third World Planning Review* 13:1, 1–25.

Pow, Choon Piew (2007), 'Securing the "civilised" enclaves: gated communities and the moral geographies of exclusion in (post) socialist Shanghai', *Urban Studies* 44:8, 1539–58.

Pratt, Nicola (2006), 'Informal enterprise and street trading: a civil society and urban management perspective' in Alison Brown (ed), *Contested Space: Street Trading, Public Space and Livelihoods in Developing Cities*, Rugby: ITDG Publishing, 37–55.

Prennushi, Giovanna (1999), *Nepal: Poverty at the Turn of the Twenty-First Century: Main Report*, Report No. IDP 174, Washington, DC: World Bank.

Pryer, Jane (1993), 'The impact of adult ill-health on household income and nutrition in Khulna, Bangladesh', *Environment and Urbanization* 5:2, 3549.

Pryer, Jane A. (2003), *Poverty and Vulnerability in Dhaka Slums: The Urban Livelihood Study*, Aldershot: Ashgate.

Rahman, Perween (2008), *Water Supply in Karachi: Situation/Issues, Priority Issues and Solutions*, Karachi: Orangi Pilot Project – Research and Training Institute.

Rakodi, Carole (2006), 'Mombasa's missing link: marginalization or mismanagement?' in Deborah Fahy Bryceson and Deborah Potts (eds), *African Urban Economies: Viability, Vitality or Vitiation?* Basingstoke: Palgrave Macmillan, 131–50.

Rakodi, Carole and Penny Withers (1995), 'Housing aspirations and affordability in Harare and Gweru: a contribution to housing policy formation in Zimbabwe', *Cities* 12:3, 185–201.

Rakodi, Carole with Tony Lloyd-Jones (eds) (2002), *Urban Livelihoods: A People-Centred Approach to Reducing Poverty*, London: Earthscan Publications.

Rakodi, Carole, Rose Gatabaki-Kamau and Nick Devas (2000), 'Poverty and political conflict in Mombasa', *Environment and Urbanization* 12:1, 153–70.

Ravallion, Martin (1998), *Poverty Lines in Theory and Practice*, Living Standards Measurement Study Working Paper No. 133, Washington, DC: World Bank.

——(2011), *On Multidimensional Indices of Poverty*, Policy Research Working Paper 5580, Washington, DC: World Bank.

Ravallion, Martin and Benu Bidani (1994), 'How robust is a poverty profile?' *The World Bank Economic Review*, 8:1, 75–102.

Ravallion, Martin, Shaohua Chen and Prem Sangraula (2007), *New Evidence on the Urbanization of Global Poverty*, WPS4199, Washington, DC: World Bank.

Reardon, Sara (2011), 'A world of chronic diseases', *Science* 333, 558–9.

Reddy, Sanjay G. and Thomas W. Pogge (2003), *How Not to Count the Poor*, Version 4.5. Online. Available at: http://www.columbia.edu/~sr793/count.pdf (accessed 6 August 2012).

Richmond, Pattie (1997), 'From tenants to owners: experiences with a revolving fund for social housing', *Environment and Urbanization* 9:2, 119–39.

Rivera, Amaad, Jeannette Huezo, Christina Kasica and Dedrick Muhammad (2009), *State of the Dream 2009: The Silent Depression*, Boston: United for a Fair Economy.

Robert, Vincent, Kate Macintyre, Joseph Keating, Jean-Francois Trape, Jean-Bernard Duchemin, McWilson Warren and John C. Beier (2003), 'Malaria transmission in urban sub-Saharan Africa', *American Journal of Tropical Medicine and Hygiene* 68:2, 169–76.

Rodgers, Dennis (2010), 'Contingent democratisation? The rise and fall of participatory budgeting in Buenos Aires', *Journal of Latin American Studies* 42, 1–27.

Rodríguez, Alfredo and Ana Sugranyes (2007), 'The new housing problem in Latin America' in Fernando Carrion and Lisa Hanley (eds), *Urban Regeneration and Revitalization in the Americas: Towards a Stable State*, Washington, DC: Woodrow Wilson Center for International Scholars, 51–66.

Romeshun, Kulasabanathan and Geetha Mayadunne (2011), *Appropriateness of the Sri Lanka Poverty Line for Measuring Urban Poverty: The Case of Colombo*, Human Settlements Working Paper No. 36, London: IIED.

Rowntree, B. Seebohm (1902), *Poverty: A Study of Town Life*, 2nd edition, Chapter 5. Available at: http://www2.arts.gla.ac.uk/History/ESH/rowntree/chap5.html

Roy, A.N., Arputham Jockin and Ahmad Javed (2004), 'Community police stations in Mumbai's slums', *Environment and Urbanization* 16:2, 135–8.

Ruel, Marie T. and James L. Garrett (2004), 'Features of urban food and nutrition security and considerations for successful urban programming', *Journal of Agricultural and Development Economics*, 1:2, 242–71.

Sabry, Sarah (2009), *Poverty Lines in Greater Cairo: Under-Estimating and Misrepresenting Poverty*, Poverty Reduction in Urban Areas Series Working Paper 21, London: IIED.

——(2010), 'How poverty is underestimated in Greater Cairo, Egypt', *Environment and Urbanization* 22:2, 523–41.

Saghir, Jamal, Manuel Schiffler and Mathewos Woldu (2000), *Urban Water and Sanitation in the Middle East and North Africa Region: The Way Forward*, Middle East and North Africa Region Infrastructure Development Group, Washington, DC: World Bank.

Sahn, David E. and David C. Stifel (2003), 'Progress towards the Millennium Development Goals in Africa', *World Development* 31:1, 23–52.

Salon, D. and S. Gulyani (2010), 'Mobility, poverty, and gender: travel 'choices' of slum residents in Nairobi', *Transport Reviews* 30:5, 641–57.

Sandbrook, Richard (1982), *The Politics of Basic Needs: Urban Aspects of Assaulting Poverty in Africa*, London: Heinemann Educational.

Satterthwaite, David (1993), 'The impact on health of urban environments', *Environment and Urbanization* 5:2, 87–111.

——(1995), 'The underestimation of poverty and its health consequences', *Third World Planning Review* 17:4, iii–xii.

——(1997a), 'Urban poverty: reconsidering its scale and nature', *IDS Bulletin* 28:2, 9–23.

——(1997b), *The Scale and Nature of International Donor Assistance to Housing, Basic Services and Other Human Settlements-Related Projects*, Helsinki: Wider.

——(1998), *The Constraints on Aid and Development Assistance Agencies Giving a High Priority to Basic Needs*, PhD thesis, London: London School of Economics and Political Science.

——(2001), 'Reducing urban poverty: constraints on the effectiveness of aid agencies and development banks and some suggestions for change', *Environment and Urbanization* 13:1, 137–57.

——(2003), 'The links between poverty and the environment in urban areas of Africa, Asia, and Latin America', *Annals of the American Academy of Political and Social Science* 590, 73–92.

——(2004), *The Under-Estimation of Urban Poverty in Low and Middle-Income Nations*, IIED Working Paper 14 on Poverty Reduction in Urban Areas, London: IIED.

——(2005), 'Meeting the MDGs in urban areas: the forgotten role of local organizations', *Journal of International Affairs* 58:2, 87–112.

——(2006), *Outside the Large Cities: The Demographic Importance of Small Urban Centres and Large Villages in Africa, Asia and Latin America*, Human Settlements Discussion Paper, Urban Change-3, London: IIED.

——(2007a), *The Transition to a Predominantly Urban World and its Underpinnings*, Human Settlements Discussion Paper, London: IIED.

——(2007b), 'In pursuit of a healthy urban environment in low- and middle-income nations', in Peter J. Marcotullio and Gordon McGranahan (eds), *Scaling Urban Environmental Challenges: From Local to Global and Back*, London: Earthscan Publications, 69–105.

——(2009), 'What role for mayors in good city governance?' *Environment and Urbanization*, 21:1, 3–17.

——(2010), 'Urban myths and the mis-use of data that underpin them' in Jo Beall, Basudeb Guha-Khasnobis and Ravi Kanbur (eds), *Urbanization and Development: Multidisciplinary Perspectives*, Oxford: Oxford University Press, 83–99.

——(2011), 'How can urban centers adapt to climate change with ineffective or unrepresentative local governments?' *WIREs Climate Change* 2, 767–76.

Satterthwaite, David and Diana Mitlin (2013) *Reducing Urban Poverty in the Global South*, London: Routledge.

Satterthwaite, David and Alice Sverdlik (2012), 'Energy access and housing for low-income groups in urban areas' in Arnulf Grubler and David Fisk (eds), *Energizing Cities*, London: Earthscan Publications.

Satterthwaite, David and Cecilia Tacoli (2003), *The Urban Part of Rural Development: The Role of Small and Intermediate Urban Centres in Rural and Regional Development and Poverty Reduction*, Rural-Urban Interactions and Livelihood Strategies Working Paper 9, London: IIED.

Satterthwaite, David, Roger Hart, Caren Levy, Diana Mitlin, David Ross, Jac Smit and Carolyn Stephens (1996), *The Environment for Children*, London and New York: Earthscan and UNICEF.

Satterthwaite, David, Sheela Patel and Diana Mitlin (2011), *Engaging with the Urban Poor and Their Organizations for Poverty Reduction and Urban Governance*, New York: UNDP, Civil Society Division.

Schäfer, Dirk, Roland Werchota and Kirsten Dölle (2007), *MDG Monitoring for Urban Water Supply and Sanitation: Catching Up with Reality in Sub-Saharan Africa*, Eschborn: Deutsche Gesellschaft für Technische Zusammenarbeit (GTZ) GmbH.

Schenk, Hans (ed.) (2001), *Living in India's Slums: A Case Study of Bangalore*, New Delhi: IDPAD, Manohar.

Scheper-Hughes, Nancy (1992), *Death without Weeping: The Violence of Everyday Life in Brazil*, Berkeley: University of California Press.

Schlyter, Ann (1990), *Women Householders and Housing Strategies: The Case of Harare, Zimbabwe*, Stockholm: National Swedish Institute for Building Research.

——(2006), 'Esther's house: one woman's 'home economics' in Chitungwiza, Zimbabwe' in Deborah Fahy Bryceson and Deborah Potts (eds), *African Urban Economies: Viability, Vitality or Vitiation?* Basingstoke: Palgrave Macmillan, 254–77.

Schusterman, Ricardo and Ana Hardoy (1997), 'Reconstructing social capital in a poor urban settlement: the Integrated Improvement Programme, Barrio San Jorge', *Environment and Urbanization* 9:1, 91–119.

Schusterman, Ricardo, Florencia Almansi, Ana Hardoy, Cecilia Monti and Gastón Urquiza (2001), *Poverty Reduction in Action: Participatory Planning in San Fernando, Buenos Aires*, IIED Working Paper 6 on Poverty Reduction in Urban Areas, London: IIED.

Seager, Ashley (2006), 'Average income of richest 20% is 16 times that of the poorest', *The Guardian* 13 May 2006.

Semba, R.D., S. de Pee, K. Kraemer, K. Sun, A. Thorne-Lyman, R. Moench-Pfanner, M. Sari, N. Akhter and M.W. Bloem (2009), 'Purchase of drinking water is associated with increased child morbidity and mortality among urban slum-dwelling families in Indonesia', *International Journal of Hygiene and Environmental Health* 212:4, 387–97.

Sen, Amartya (1973), *On Economic Inequality* Oxford: Oxford University Press.

——(1992), *Inequality Re-examined*, Cambridge: Harvard University Press.

Senegal, Republic of (2002), *Poverty Reduction Strategy Paper: One People, One Goal, One Faith*, Dakar.

——(2006), *Poverty Reduction Strategy Paper: One People, One Goal, One Faith*, Dakar.

Shrestha, R.M., S. Kumar, S. Martin and A. Dhakal (2008), 'Modern energy use by the urban poor in Thailand: a study of slum households in two cities,' *Energy for Sustainable Development*, 12:4, 5–13.

Shrestha, Sudha (2006), 'The new urban economy: governance and street livelihoods in the Kathmandu Valley, Nepal' in Alison Brown (ed), *Contested Space: Street Trading, Public Space and Livelihoods in Developing Cities*, Rugby, UK: ITDG Publishing, 153–73.

Sikod, Fondo (2001), 'Constraints to managing urban poverty in Cameroon', *Environment and Urbanization* 13:1, 201–8.

Sinclair Knight Merz and Egis Consulting Australia in association with Brisbane City Enterprises and Feedback HSSI – STUP Consultants – Taru Leading Edge (2002), *Bangalore Water Supply and Environmental Sanitation Masterplan Project: Overview Report on Services to Urban Poor Stage 2*, AusAid, March.

Sinha, Saurabh and Michael Lipton with Joanna Church, Jennifer Leavy, Julie Litchfield, Loraine Ronchi, Rachael Straub and Shahin Yaqub (1999), *Damaging Fluctuations, Risks and Poverty: A Review*, Brighton: Poverty Research Unit at University of Sussex.

Smith, Kirk R. and Sameer Akbar (2003), 'Health-damaging air pollution: a matter of scale', in Gordon McGranahan and Frank Murray (eds), *Health and Air Pollution in Rapidly Developing Countries*, London: Earthscan Publications, 21–34.

Solinger, Dorothy J. (2006), 'The creation of an underclass in China and its implications', *Environment and Urbanization* 18:1, 177–94.

Solo, Tova María (2000), *Independent Water Entrepreneurs in Latin America: The Other Private Sector in Water Services*, draft, Washington, DC: World Bank.

——(2008), 'Financial exclusion in Latina America or the social costs of not banking the urban poor', *Environment and Urbanization* 20:1, 47–66.

Sommers, Mark (2010), 'Urban youth in Africa', *Environment and Urbanization* 22:2, 317–32.

Songsore, Jacob and Gordon McGranahan (1993), 'Environment, wealth and health: towards an analysis of intra-urban differentials within Greater Accra Metropolitan Area, Ghana', *Environment and Urbanization* 5:2, 10–24.

——(1998), 'The political economy of household environmental management: gender, environment and epidemiology in the Greater Accra Metropolitan Area', *World Development* 26:3, 395–412.

South African Institute of Race Relations (2009), 'From bare fields to the backyards of properties: the shifting pattern of informal dwelling erection', press release, 24 November 2008. Available at: http://www.sairr.org.za/press-office/archive/press_release_living_conditions_24_nov_2008.pdf (accessed 12 February 2009).

SPARC (1985), *'We the Invisible': A Census of Pavement Dwellers*, Bombay: SPARC.

SPARC and KRVIA (2010), *Reinterpreting, Re-imagining, Redeveloping Dharavi*, Mumbai: SPARC and Kamla Raheja Vidyanidhi Institute for Architecture and Environmental Studies.

Sri Lanka, Government of (2002), *Regaining Sri Lanka: Vision and Strategy for Accelerated Development.*

Stein, Alfredo (2001), *Participation and Sustainability in Social Projects: The Experience of the Local Development Programme (PRODEL) in Nicaragua*, IIED Working Paper 3 on Poverty Reduction in Urban Areas, London: IIED.

Stephens, C. (1996), 'Healthy cities or unhealthy islands: the health and social implications of urban inequality', *Environment and Urbanization* 8:2, 9–30.

Stephens, Carolyn, Rajesh Patnaik and Simon Lewin (1996), *This is My Beautiful Home: Risk Perceptions towards Flooding and Environment in Low Income Urban Communities: A Case Study in Indore, India*, London: London School of Hygiene and Tropical Medicine.

Stewart, Frances (1985), *Planning to Meet Basic Needs*, London: Macmillan Press.

——(2001), 'Horizontal inequalities: a neglected dimension of development', UNU Wider Annual Lectures 5, Helsinki: UNU/Wider.

Stohr, Walter B. and D.R.F. Taylor (1981), 'Introduction', in Walter B. Stohr and D.R. Fraser Taylor (eds), *Development from Above or Below*, Chichester: John Wiley & Sons, 1–12.

Streeten, Paul (1981), *First Things First: Meeting Basic Needs in Developing Countries*, Oxford: Oxford University Press.

Subbaraman, Ramnath, Jennifer O'Brien, Tejal Shitole, Shrutika Shitole, Kiran Sawant, David E. Bloom, Arjun Appadurai and Anita Patil-Deshmukh (2012), 'Off the map: the health and social implications of being an unrecognized slum', *Environment and Urbanization* 24:2, 643–64.

Sverdlik, Alice (2011), 'Ill-health and poverty: a literature review on health in informal settlements', *Environment and Urbanization*, 23:1, 123–56.

Swaminathan, Madhura (1995), 'Aspects of urban poverty in Bombay', *Environment and Urbanization* 7:1, 133–43.

Swaziland, Kingdom of (1998), *Welfare and Poverty in Swaziland, 1985–95*, Washington, DC: World Bank, AFT11.

Swyngedouw, Erik (2004), *Social Power and the Urbanization of Water: Flows of Power*, New York: Oxford University Press.

Szreter, Simon (2007), 'The right of registration; development, identity registration and social security: a historical perspective', *World Development* 35:1, 67–86.

Tabatabai, Hamid with Manal Fouad (1993), *The Incidence of Poverty in Developing Countries: An ILO Compendium of Data*, World Employment Programme Study, Geneva: International Labour Office.

Tacoli, Cecilia (1998), *Bridging the Divide: Rural–Urban Interactions and Livelihood Strategies*, Gatekeeper Series No. 77, IIED Sustainable Agriculture and Rural Livelihoods Programme, London: IIED.

——(2003), 'The links between urban and rural development', *Environment and Urbanization*, 15:1, 3–12.

——(ed) (2006), *The Earthscan Reader in Rural–Urban Linkages*, London: Earthscan Publications.

Tacoli, Cecilia and Richard Mabala (2010), 'Exploring mobility and migration in the context of rural-urban linkages: why gender and generation matter', *Environment and Urbanization* 22:2, 389–96.

Taneja, S. and S. Agarwal (2004), *Situational Analysis for Guiding USAID/EHP India's Technical Assistance Efforts in Indore, Madhya Pradesh, India*, Environmental Health Project Activity Report 133, Washington, DC.

Tanzania, United Republic of (2002a), *Tanzania: Poverty and Human Development Report (draft)*, Research and Analysis Working Group (R&AWG), Dar es Salaam: Bureau of Statistics.

——(2002b), *Household Budget Survey 2000/2001: Tanzania*, Dar es Salaam: National Bureau of Statistics.

Thieme, Tatiana (2010), 'Youth, waste and work in Mathare: whose business and whose politics?' *Environment and Urbanization* 22:2, 333–52.

Thomas, E.P., J.R. Seager, E. Viljoen, F. Potgieter, A. Rossouw, B. Tokota, G. McGranahan and M. Kjellen (1999), *Household Environment and Health in Port Elizabeth, South Africa*, Urban Environment Series Report No. 6, Stockholm Environment Institute in collaboration with South African Medical Research Council.

Thompson, John, Ina T. Porras, Elisabeth Wood, James K. Tumwine, Mark R. Mujwahuzi, Munguti Katui-Katua and Nick Johnstone (2000), 'Waiting at the tap: changes in urban water use in East Africa over three decades', *Environment and Urbanization* 12:2, 37–52.

Townsend, Peter (1993), *The International Analysis of Poverty*, Hemel Hempstead: Harvester Wheatsheaf.

Toye, John (1993), *Dilemmas of Development*, 2nd edition, Oxford: Blackwell.

Turner, John F.C. (1976), *Housing By People: Towards Autonomy in Building Environments*, London: Marion Boyars.

Uganda, Republic of (2004), *Poverty Eradication Action Plan (2004/5–2007/8)*, Kampala: Ministry of Finance, Planning and Economic Development.

——(2005), *Uganda Poverty Status Report: Progress in Implementing the Poverty Eradication Action Plan*, Kampala: Ministry of Finance, Planning and Economic Development.

ul Haq, Mahbub (1976), *The Poverty Curtain: Choices for the Third World*, New York: Columbia University Press.

UNCHS (1993), *Support Measures to Promote Rental Housing for Low-Income Groups*, United Nations Centre for Human Settlements, HS/294/93E, Nairobi.

——(1996), *An Urbanizing World: Global Report on Human Settlements, 1996*, Oxford: Oxford University Press.

UNCHS and World Bank (1993), *The Housing Indicators Programme III: Preliminary Findings*, Washington, DC: World Bank.

UNDP (1990), *Human Development Report 1990*, Oxford: Oxford University Press.

——(1993), *Human Development Report 1993*, Oxford: Oxford University Press.

——(1994), *Human Development Report 1994*, Oxford: Oxford University Press.

——(1998), *Combating Poverty: The Korean Experience*, Seoul: United Nations Development Programme.

UN-HABITAT (2003a), *Water and Sanitation in the World's Cities: Local Action for Global Goals*, London: Earthscan Publications.

——(2003b), *The Challenge of Slums: Global Report on Human Settlements 2003*, London: Earthscan Publications.

——(2006), *Meeting Development Goals in Small Urban Centres: Water and Sanitation in the World's Cities 2006*, London: Earthscan Publications.

——(2008), *State of the World's Cities 2008/9: Harmonious Cities*, London: Earthscan Publications.

——(2011), *Cairo: A City in Transition*, Nairobi: UN Human Settlements Programme.

UNICEF (2000), *Progotir Pathey: On the Road to Progress: Achieving the Goals for Children in Bangladesh*, Dhaka: Bangladesh Bureau of Statistics and UNICEF.

UNICEF and WHO (2000), *Global Water Supply and Sanitation Assessment, 2000 Report*, Geneva: World Health Organization, UNICEF and Water Supply and Sanitation Collaborative Council.

——(2012), *Progress on Drinking Water and Sanitation: 2012 Update*, Joint Monitoring Programme for Water Supply and Sanitation, New York and Geneva: UNICEF and WHO.

United Nations (1964), *Everyman's United Nations: A Basic History of the Organization 1945 to 1963*, New York: Office of Public Information, United Nations.

——(1971), 'Report of the 1969 meeting of exports on social policy and planning', *International Social Development Review*, 3.

——(2009), *Global Assessment Report on Disaster Risk Reduction: Risk and Poverty in a Changing Climate*, Geneva: United Nations.

——(2011a), *Revealing Risk, Redefining Development: The 2011 Global Assessment Report on Disaster Risk Reduction*, Geneva: United Nations International Strategy for Disaster Reduction.

——(2011b), *World Population Prospects: The 2010 Revision, Highlights and Advance Tables*, Department of Economic and Social Affairs, Population Division Working Paper No. ESA/P/WP.220, New York: United Nations.

——(2012), *World Urbanization Prospects: The 2011 Revision*, Department of Economic and Social Affairs, Population Division. Available at: http://esa.un.org/unpd/wup/index.htm

Urban Resource Centre (2001), 'Urban poverty and transport: a case study from Karachi' *Environment and Urbanization* 13:1, 223–34.

Urban Resource Centre (1994), 'The Urban Resource Centre, Karachi', *Environment and Urbanization* 6:1, 158–63.

USAID (2004), *Innovative Approaches to Slum Electrification*, Washington, DC. Available at: http://pdf.usaid.gov/pdf_docs/PNADB219.pdf

Valença, Márcio Moraes (2007), 'Poor politics – poor housing: policy under the Collor government in Brazil (1990–2)', *Environment and Urbanization* 19:2, 391–408.

Van de Poel, Ellen, Owen O'Donnell, and Eddy van Doorslaer (2007), 'Are urban children really healthier? Evidence from 47 developing countries', *Social Science and Medicine* 65:10, 1986–2003.

Van der Berg, Servaas (2005), *Fiscal Expenditure Incidence in South Africa, 1995 and 2000*, Stellenbosch: University of Stellenbosch.

Van der Berg, Servaas, Megan Louw and Ronelle Berger (2007), *Post-Apartheid South Africa: Poverty and Distribution Trends in an Era of Globalization*, UNU/Wider Research Paper No. 2007/57, Helsinki: United Nations University and World Institute for Development Economics Research.

Van der Berg, Servaas, Ronelle Burger, Rulof Burger, Megan Louw and Derek Yu (2005), *Trends in Poverty and Inequality Since the Political Transition*, Economic Working Papers 1/2005, Stellenbosch: University of Stellenbosch.

van Donk, Mirjam (2006), '"Positive" urban futures in sub-Saharan Africa: HIV/AIDS and the need for ABC (a broader conceptualization)', *Environment and Urbanization* 18:1, 155–76.

Velasquez, Luz Stella (1998), 'Agenda 21: a form of joint environmental management in Manizales, Colombia', *Environment and Urbanization* 10:2, 9–36.

Velez, Carlos E., Ricardo Paes de Barros and Francisco Ferreira (2004), 'Part 1: policy report', in Carlos E. Velez, Ricardo Paes de Barros and Francisco Ferreira (eds), *Inequality and Economic Development in Brazil*, Washington, DC: World Bank, 3–80.

Vietnam, Socialist Republic of (2002), *The Comprehensive Poverty Reduction and Growth Strategy*, Hanoi.

——(2006), *The Five Year Socio-Economic Development Plan 2006–2010*, National Assembly, Socialist Republic of Vietnam.

Viswanathan, B. and K.S.K. Kumar (2005), 'Cooking fuel use patterns in India: 1983–2000', *Energy Policy* 33:8, 1021–36.

Vlahov, David, Nicholas Freudenberg, Fernando Proietti, Danielle Ompad, Andrew Quinn, Vijay Nandi and Sandro Galea (2007), 'Urban as a determinant of health', *Journal of Urban Health* 84, Supplement 1, i16–i26.

Vlahov, David, Siddharth Raj Agarwal, Robert M. Buckley, Waleska Teixeira Caiaffa, Carlos F. Corvalan, Alex Chika Ezeh, Ruth Finkelstein, Sharon Friel, Trudy Harpham and Maharufa Hossain (2011), 'Roundtable on urban living environment research (RULER)', *Journal of Urban Health* 88:5, 793–857.

Ward, Barbara (1976), *The Home of Man*, New York: W.W. Norton.

Ward, Barbara and René Dubos (1972), *Only One Earth: The Care and Maintenance of a Small Planet*, London: Andre Deutsch.

WaterAid India (2009), *Burden of Inheritance: Can We Stop Manual Scavenging? Yes But First We Need to Accept It Exists*, New Delhi: WaterAid.

Water and Sanitation Program (2000), *Independent Water and Sanitation Providers in Africa: Beyond Facts and Figures*, WSP Africa Regional Office, Nairobi: World Bank.

Water and Sanitation Program – South Asia (2000), *Urban Environmental Sanitation Planning: Lessons from Bharatpur, Rajasthan, India*, field note, Delhi: Water and Sanitation Program – South Asia.

Weru, Jane (2004), 'Community federations and city upgrading: the work of Pamoja Trust and Muungano in Kenya', *Environment and Urbanization* 16: 1, 47–62.

Westhof, Dirk with Carel de Rooy, Siping Wang and Deqa Ibrahim Musa (2010), *Understanding Urban Inequalities in Bangladesh: A Prerequisite for Achieving Vision 2021*, Dhaka: UNICEF Bangladesh.

Whitfield, Peter (2006), *London: A Life in Maps*, London: The British Library.

WHO (1986), *Intersectoral Action for Health: The Role of Intersectoral Cooperation in National Strategies for Health for All, Background Document for the Technical Discussions, 39th World Health Assembly*, Geneva: World Health Organization.

——(1989), *Urbanization and Its Implications for Child Health: Potential for Action*, Geneva: World Health Organization.

——(1992), *Our Planet, Our Health*, report of the WHO Commission on Health and Environment, Geneva: World Health Organization.

——(1996), *Creating Healthy Cities in the 21st Century*, background paper prepared for the Dialogue on Health in Human Settlements for Habitat II, Geneva: World Health Organization.

——(1999), 'Creating healthy cities in the 21st Century' in David Satterthwaite (ed.), *The Earthscan Reader on Sustainable Cities*, London: Earthscan Publications, 137–72.

——(2006), 'Fuel for life: household energy and health'. Available at: http://www.who.int/indoorair/publications/fuelforlife/en/

——(2011a), 'The top 10 causes of death', fact sheet 310. Available at: http://www.who.int/mediacentre/factsheets/fs310/en/index.html (accessed 13 July 2012).

——(2011b), 'Road traffic injuries', fact sheet 358. Available at: http://www.who.int/mediacentre/factsheets/fs358/en/ (accessed 13 July 2012).

——(2011c), 'Indoor air pollution and health', fact sheet 292. Available at: http://www.who.int/mediacentre/factsheets/fs292/en/index.html (accessed 3 August 2012).

——(2011d), 'Air quality and health', fact sheet 313. Available at: http://www.who.int/mediacentre/factsheets/fs313/en/index.html (accessed 3 August 2012).

——(2011e), 'Tackling the global clean air challenge', news release. Available at: http://www.who.int/mediacentre/news/releases/2011/air_pollution_20110926/en/ (accessed 8 August 2012).

——(2012a), 'Tuberculosis', fact sheet 104. Available at: http://www.who.int/mediacentre/factsheets/fs104/en (accessed 12 July 2012).

——(2012b), 'Maternal mortality', fact sheet 348. Available at: http://www.who.int/mediacentre/factsheets/fs348/en/index.html (accessed 12 July 2012).

WHO and UNICEF (2011), *A Snapshot on Sanitation in South Asia with a Focus on Inequities: A Regional Perspective Based on Data from the WHO/UNICEF Joint Monitoring Programme for Water Support and Sanitation*, prepared for the WHO/UNICEF Fourth South Asia Conference on Sanitation (SACOSAN-4), 4–7 April 2011, Colombo, Sri Lanka.

Wilbanks, Tom, Patricia Romero-Lankao, Manzhu Bao, Frans Berkhout, Sandy Cairncross, Jean-Paul Ceron, Manmohan Kapshe, Robert Muir-Wood and Ricardo Zapata-Marti (2007), 'Industry, settlement and society', in M.L. Parry, O.F. Canziani, J.P. Palutikof, P.J. van der Linden and C.E. Hanson (eds), *Climate Change 2007: Impacts, Adaptation and Vulnerability*, Cambridge: Cambridge University Press, 357–90.

Wilkinson, Richard G. (2005), *The Impact of Inequality: How to Make Sick Societies Healthier*, Abingdon, UK: Routledge.

Winrock International (2005), *Enabling Urban Poor Livelihoods Policy Making: Understanding the Role of Energy Services: Brazil Country Report*. Available at: http://www.urbanenergy.utwente.nl/resources/reports/country_reports/rep_winrock.pdf

Wisner, Ben (1988), *Power and Need in Africa: Basic Human Needs and Development Policies*, London: Earthscan Publications.

Wodon, Quentin T. (2000), *Poverty and Policy in Latin America and the Caribbean*, World Bank Technical Paper No. 467, Washington, DC: World Bank.

Wood, Geof (2003), 'Staying secure, staying poor: the "Faustian bargain"', *World Development* 31:3, 455–71.

Wood, Robert E. (1986), *From Marshall Plan to Debt Crisis: Foreign Aid and Development Choices in the World Economy*, Berkeley: University of California Press.

Woodward, David (1992a), *Debt, Adjustment and Poverty in Developing Countries, Volume 1: National and International Dimensions of Debt and Adjustment in Developing Countries*, London: Pinter Publishers in association with Save the Children.

——(1992b), *Debt, Adjustment and Poverty in Developing Countries, Volume 2: The Impact of Debt and Adjustment at the Household Level in Developing Countries*, London: Pinter Publishers in association with Save the Children.

World Bank (1990), *World Development Report 1990: Poverty*, Oxford: Oxford University Press.

——(1991), *Urban Policy and Economic Development: An Agenda for the 1990s*, Washington, DC: World Bank.

——(1993), *World Development Report 1993: Investing in Health*, Oxford and New York: Oxford University Press.

——(1999), *Entering the 21st Century: World Development Report 1999/2000*, Oxford and New York: Oxford University Press.

——(2000), *World Development Report 2000/2001: Attacking Poverty*, Oxford and New York: Oxford University Press.

——(2012), *World Development Indicators*. Available at: http://data.worldbank.org/data-catalog/world-development-indicators

World Bank Bangladesh (2002) *Poverty in Bangladesh: Building on Progress*, Report No. 24299-BD, Poverty Reduction and Economic Management Sector Unit, South Asia Region, Washington, DC: World Bank.

——(2007), *To the MDGs and Beyond: Accountability and Institutional Innovation in Bangladesh*, Bangladesh Development Series No. 14, Dhaka: World Bank.

World Bank Bolivia (2002), *Bolivia Poverty Diagnostic 2000*, Report No. 20530-B0, Poverty Reduction and Economic Management Sector Unit, Latin America and the Caribbean Region.

World Bank Brazil (2007), *Measuring Poverty Using Household Consumption*, Report No. 36358-BR, Brazil Poverty Reduction and Economic Management Sector Unit, Washington, DC: World Bank.

World Bank Cambodia (2006), *Cambodia: Halving Poverty by 2015? Poverty Assessment 2006*, Report no. 35213, KH, East Asia and Pacific Region, Washington, DC: World Bank.

World Bank Central America (2002), *Urban Services Delivery and the Poor: The Case of Three Central American Cities*, Report No. 22590, Finance, Private Sector and Infrastructure Department, Central America Country Management Unit, Washington, DC: World Bank.

World Bank Costa Rica (2007), *Poverty Assessment: Recapturing Momentum for Poverty Reduction*; Report No. 35910-CR, Washington, DC: World Bank.

World Bank Dominican Republic (2006), *Poverty Assessment: Achieving More Pro-Poor Growth*, No. 32422-DO, Washington, DC: World Bank.

World Bank El Salvador (2005), *El Salvador Poverty Assessment: Strengthening Social Policy*, Report No. 29594-SV, Poverty Reduction and Economic Management and Human Development Sector Management Units, Latin America and the Caribbean Region, Washington, DC: World Bank.

World Bank Ethiopia (1999), *Ethiopia: Poverty and Policies for the New Millennium*, Report No 19804-ET, Country Department 6, Africa Region, Washington, DC: World Bank.

——(2005), *Ethiopia: Well-Being and Poverty in Ethiopia: The Role of Agriculture and Agency*, Report No. 29468-ET, Poverty Reduction and Economic Management 2 (AFTP2), Washington, DC: World Bank.

World Bank Guatemala (2003), *Guatemala Poverty Assessment*, Report No. 24221-GU, Poverty Reduction and Economic Management Unit, Human Development Sector Management Unit, Latin America and the Caribbean Region, Washington, DC: World Bank.

World Bank Honduras (2001), *Honduras Poverty Diagnostic 2000*, Poverty Reduction and Economic Management Sector Unit, Latin America and the Caribbean Region, Washington, DC: World Bank.

World Bank Kenya (1995), *Kenya Poverty Assessment*, Report No. 13152-KE, Washington, DC: World Bank.

——(2006), *Kenya Inside Informality: Poverty, Jobs, Housing and Services in Nairobi's Slums,* Report No. 36347-KE, Washington, DC: World Bank.

——(2009), *Kenya Poverty and Inequality Assessment: Executive Summary and Synthesis Report*, Report No. 44190- KE, Poverty Reduction and Economic Management Unit, Africa Region, Washington, DC: World Bank.

World Bank Malawi (2007), *Malawi Poverty and Vulnerability Assessment: Investing in Our Future*, Report No. 36546-MW, Poverty Reduction and Economic Management 1, Africa Region, Washington, DC: World Bank.

World Bank Mozambique (2008), *Mozambique Beating the Odds: Sustaining Inclusion in a Growing Economy (Volumes I and II)*, Report No. 40048-MZ, Africa Region, Poverty Reduction and Economic Management, Washington, DC: World Bank.

World Bank Namibia (2001), *Namibian Selected Development Impact of HIV/AIDS*, Macroeconomic Technical Group, Africa Region, Washington, DC: World Bank.

World Bank Nepal (2006), *Nepal Resilience Amidst Conflict: An Assessment of Poverty in Nepal, 1995–96 and 2003–04*, Report No. 34834-NP, Poverty Reduction and Economic Management Sector Unit, South Asia Region, Washington, DC: World Bank.

World Bank Nicaragua (2001), *Nicaragua Poverty Assessment: Challenges and Opportunities for Poverty Reduction, Volume I: Main Report*, Report No. 20488-NI, Poverty Reduction and Economic Management Sector Unit, Latin America and the Caribbean Region, Washington, DC: World Bank.

——(2008), *Nicaragua Poverty Assessment, Volume 1 (main report)*, Report No. 39736-NI, Central America Country Management Unit, Poverty Reduction and Economic Management Unit, Latin America and the Caribbean, Washington, DC: World Bank.

World Bank Pakistan (2002), *Pakistan Poverty Assessment: Poverty in Pakistan: Vulnerabilities, Social Gaps, and Rural Dynamics*, Report No. 24296-PAK, Poverty Reduction and Economic Management Sector Unit, South Asia Region, Washington, DC: World Bank.

World Bank Panama (1999), *Panama Poverty Report*, Report No. 18801 PAN Human Development Department, Latin American and Caribbean Region, Washington, DC: World Bank.

World Bank Philippines (2002), *Philippines Country Assistance Strategy*, Report No. 24042-PH, Philippines Country Management Unit, East Asia and Pacific Region, Washington, DC: World Bank.

World Bank Sri Lanka (2007), *Sri Lanka Poverty Assessment: Engendering Growth with Equity: Opportunities and Challenges*, Report No. 36568-LK, Poverty Reduction and

Economic Management Sector Unit, South Asia Region, Washington, DC: World Bank.

World Bank Togo (1996), *Togo: Overcoming the Crisis, Overcoming Poverty: A World Bank Poverty Assessment*, Report 13526-TO, Population and Human Resources Operations Division, West Central Africa Department, Washington, DC: World Bank.

World Bank Uganda (2006), *Uganda Poverty and Vulnerability Assessment*, Report No. 36996-UG, Poverty Reduction and Economic Management, Southern Africa, Washington, DC: World Bank.

World Bank Uruguay (2001), *Uruguay: Maintaining Social Equity in a Changing Economy*, Report No. 21262, Argentina, Chile, Paraguay and Uruguay Country Management Unit, PREM Sector Management Unit, Washington, DC: World Bank.

World Bank Vietnam (2003), *Vietnam Development Report 2004: Poverty*, Report No. 27130-VN, Poverty Reduction and Economic Management Unit, East Asia and Pacific Region, Washington, DC: World Bank.

World Bank Yemen (2002), *Yemen: Poverty Reduction Strategy Paper*, Report No. 24504-YEM, prepared by staffs of the International Development Association and the International Monetary Fund, Washington, DC: World Bank.

World Bank Zambia (2007), *Zambia Poverty and Vulnerability Assessment*, Report No. 32573-ZM, Human Development 1, Poverty Reduction and Economic Management 1, Africa Region, Washington, DC: World Bank.

World Energy Council (2006) *Alleviating Urban Energy Poverty in Latin America*, London. Available at http://www.worldenergy.org/documents/urbanenpov2006.pdf

Wratten, Ellen (1995), 'Conceptualizing urban poverty', *Environment and Urbanization* 7:1, 11–36.

Wu, Xiaogang and Donald J. Treiman (2004), 'The household registration system and social stratification in China 1955–1996', *Demography* 41:2, 363–84

Yapi-Diahou, Alphonse (1995), 'The informal housing sector of the metropolis of Abidjan, Ivory Coast', *Environment and Urbanization* 7:2, 11–29.

Yemen, Republic of (2002), *Poverty Reduction Strategy Paper, 2003–2005*.

Yifu Lin, Justin (2008), 'Shifting perceptions of poverty', *Finance and Development* 45:4.

Zambia, Republic of (2002a), *Zambia Poverty Reduction Strategy Paper 2004–6*, Lusaka: Ministry of Finance and National Planning.

——(2002b), *Zambia Poverty Reduction Strategy Paper 2002–2004*, Lusaka: Ministry of Finance and National Planning.

——(2006), *Fifth National Development Plan 2006–2010*, Lusaka: President of the Republic of Zambia.

Ziraba, Abdhalah Kasiira, Nyovani Madise, Samuel Mills, Catherine Kyobutungi and Alex Ezeh (2009), 'Maternal mortality in the informal settlements of Nairobi city: what do we know?' *Reproductive Health* 6. Available at: http://www.ncbi.nlm.nih.gov/pmc/articles/PMC2675520/

Index

References to tables are shown in bold, those for figures are in italics and text within boxes is indicated by the prefix 'b' before the page number.